The Linguistics of Speech

MW00777688

This insightful study proposes a unified theory of speech through which conflicting ideas about language might be understood. It is founded on a number of key points, such as the continuum of linguistic behavior, extensive variation in language features, the importance of regional and social proximity to shared linguistic production, and differential frequency as a key factor in linguistic production both in regional and social groups and in text corpora. The study shows how this new linguistics of speech does not reject rules in favor of language use, or reject language use in favor of rules; rather, it shows how rules can come from language as people use it. Written in a clear, engaging style and containing invaluably accessible introductions to complex theoretical concepts, this work will be of great interest to students and scholars of sociolinguistics, dialectology, and corpus linguistics.

WILLIAM A. KRETZSCHMAR, Jr. is Harry and Jane Willson Professor in Humanities at the University of Georgia.

The Linguistics of Speech

William A. Kretzschmar, Jr.

CAMBRIDGE
UNIVERSITY PRESS

CAMBRIDGE UNIVERSITY PRESS
Cambridge, New York, Melbourne, Madrid, Cape Town,
Singapore, São Paulo, Delhi, Mexico City

Cambridge University Press
The Edinburgh Building, Cambridge CB2 8RU, UK

Published in the United States of America by Cambridge University Press, New York

www.cambridge.org
Information on this title: www.cambridge.org/9780521715072

First published 2009
Reprinted 2010
First paperback edition 2012

A catalogue record for this publication is available from the British Library

ISBN 978-0-521-88703-8 Hardback
ISBN 978-0-521-71507-2 Paperback

Contents

Figures

Tables

Acknowledgments

I am grateful to my students over the years who have worked through these ideas with me, often as members of my language variation seminar. In particular, from among many excellent thinkers about language, I can mention Clai Rice, Matt Zimmerman, Allison Burkette, Susan Tamasi, and Joe Kuhl, as students who engaged seriously with this line of thought and, sometimes in collaborative articles and sometimes on their own, contributed to the development of the ideas presented here. I am also grateful to my colleagues, particularly Edgar Schneider, Chuck Meyer, and Lee Pederson (who collaborated with me on works and projects influential in the preparation of this book), as well as Salikoko Mufwene and John Nerbonne (whose views generally differ from my own), with whom I have carried on running conversations over many years about the ideas offered here. I must also thank Laura Wright, who has been most generous with her time and ideas for improvement of the work, and several anonymous readers engaged by Cambridge University Press whose comments have led to many real improvements in the text. Any mistakes in this book, of course, are my own problem, not theirs.

I cannot express enough my gratitude for her consistent support over many years to my wife Claudia, who has always had a keen interest in language as it is used in the real world. I am grateful to my son Russell, who continues to show me things that I did not know about language accommodation. And I am grateful to my son Brendan, himself a trained linguist, for the question to begin this book:

"What makes Ferdinand so sure?"

The road not taken

Two roads diverged in a yellow wood,
And sorry I could not travel both
And be one traveler, long I stood
And looked down one as far as I could
To where it bent in the undergrowth;

Then took the other, as just as fair,
And having perhaps the better claim,
Because it was grassy and wanted wear;
Though as for that the passing there
Had worn them really about the same,

And both that morning equally lay
In leaves no step had trodden black.
Oh, I kept the first for another day!
Yet knowing how way leads on to way,
I doubted if I should ever come back.

I shall be telling this with a sigh
Somewhere ages and ages hence:
Two roads diverged in a wood, and I –
I took the one less traveled by,
And that has made all the difference.

Robert Frost, from *Mountain Interval* (1916)

Introduction

Modern theories of linguistics rely upon the central assumption that "Language is a system." How could it be otherwise? How could we communicate with each other if there weren't rules for how we should talk and write, some sort of contract or agreement that we all share? Academic linguists are not the only ones to hold this view: in the schools, teachers of language arts prescribe for their students the rules of English (or other languages) so that they can get ahead in the world. The rules that linguists talk about are not always the same rules that language arts teachers talk about, but they both share the central assumption that there are indeed rules that help us to communicate with each other. Most people outside of universities and schools also hold the same assumption about rules. They believe that people around *here*, their neighbors, talk a certain way, and that other people from *there*, or at least not from *here*, talk a different way. American Southerners say *y'all*. Canadians say *oot* for *out*. British speakers say "the government are" when the Americans and Canadians say "the government is." That is how it is with language: the rules are a little different for people in different places or different social situations. The rules are certainly different for speakers of different languages, like Spanish and English, a lot different, so different in fact that we cannot understand each other. This fact seems to tell us that there must be rules, because speakers of different languages have such different rules that we cannot understand them. That said, even people who say that they speak our own language appear to have rules that are different enough that we just don't understand – to paraphrase the title of a famous book by Deborah Tannen (1990), which argues that men and women are like that. Still, where would be without rule systems? Men and women are different, sure, but after all, how different could they be in how they use the rules of their common language? We have the example of different languages, Spanish vs. English, or French vs. German, or any number of other different language rule systems that are not understandable to each other's speakers, to show us that without some sort of agreed-upon system we *really* would not be able to understand each other.

Yet the closer we look at how people try to understand each other, the more we find that the rules appear to be quite different from place to place, from situation to situation, and from person to person. We can, for instance, recognize each other's voices, even across the room or over the telephone. The rules for a language must permit a certain amount of individual variation for this to be so. We can often recognize different social groups that people might come from, just by how they talk. For instance, we can guess how far in school someone may have gotten by how they follow the kind of rules taught in language arts classes in school. We can recognize that somebody has experience with quilting, or darts, or American football, by how they talk about the subject, by their familiarity with the vocabulary of the activity and also by their familiarity with how people usually talk about it (like "It's 180!" as the announcers say in darts matches). We can guess where people we do not know might be from, just by their use of language, whether from another country or just from another county. The rules of a language must permit variation according to regional or social groups for us to be able to guess and often be right. And we do all of these things all at the same time, from personal to social to regional evaluation of the talk we hear from the people around us. We pay attention to the *differences* in people's language as well as to the regularities of rule systems.

Furthermore, we evaluate and act upon the differences we hear, all the time. We turn our heads in a crowded room when we hear a familiar voice. We decide not to trust the advice of somebody who does not use the right language, such as a salesman who wants to sell us a television but cannot use the right words to describe what's good or bad about the choices on offer. All else being equal, we have more trust in strangers who sound like we do and may come from our home place, our kind of people, as opposed to strangers who do not sound like us. Language variation thus also plays a role in the way that we communicate with each other, along with the rules. Indeed, sometimes hearing someone break the rules is what makes the most difference in our evaluation of how a con-versation is going, and so helps us to understand better how to react to it. We don't buy that new television from somebody who thinks that the "HD" in *HDTV* means 'huge-display' and not 'high-definition'!

Rule systems for languages and language variation within languages are at opposite poles of how we understand each other. Rule systems represent an ideal view, language in the abstract. Rule systems depend upon logical relation-ships between functional elements of language, whether those elements are features of pronunciation or lexicon or grammar. So, for example, the rules of English tell us that the word *lead* meaning 'a heavy metal' is different from the word *lead* meaning 'to guide,' even if they happen to be spelled the same, because their pronunciation is different. In terms of the pronunciation system of English, the /ɛ/ vowel (as in *bed*) is different from the /i/ vowel (as in *bee*), and we can use this systematic difference to tell words apart, and so to understand each other better. In the same way, we English speakers know that we are supposed to use pronouns like *I* or *they* when we make sentences where pronouns are the subject (*I go downtown* or *We go downtown* or *They go downtown*); Spanish speakers usually leave out the pronoun subjects ([*yo*] *Voy al centro* or [*nosotros*] *Vamos al centro* or [*ellas*] *Van al centro*). This kind of useful logic in system making relies on the assumption, in the famous words of Noam Chomsky, of an "ideal speaker-listener, in a completely homogenous speech-community" (1965: 3). That is, we assume that all of the speakers of a language are alike in order for us to develop the system of contrasting elements, and in so doing offer an explanation of how we understand each other. Of course we are not actually all alike in practice in the way that we use our language, but that fact does not stop us from *assuming for the moment* that we are alike, or thinking that *in some way deep down* we are all alike, so that we can try to understand the rule system that helps to explain how we can understand each other. Variation in language, on the other hand, is not merely a distraction from the underlying rules; it functions and has value in its own right, as we have seen. It makes language personal, and also allows us to distinguish characteristic use of language by different groups of people. Rules and variation are opposite poles, but that does not mean that we can get rid of one. They are two sides of the same coin, and we need to consider both sides.

Our clear perception both of rules and of variation in language makes life complicated, in that it allows for quite different ways of thinking about language. Academic ideas about language consider the two poles differently, and with different emphasis. Popular ideas about language also consider the two poles with different emphasis, and differently from the way that academics think of them. Moreover, since academics who need to think about language are also brought up with the popular ideas, the popular and the academic are not entirely separate in particular cases. Conflicting ideas about language can lead to conflict in the application of ideas about language. Popular and academic ideas often come to interact on matters of public policy, such as education, and such interactions are often not as successful as one might hope because of the contrast between the popular and academic points of view.

This book proposes a model of language, called "the linguistics of speech," that attempts to provide a framework under which conflicting ideas about language might be understood for what they are. The linguistics of speech does not reject rules in favor of variation, or reject variation in favor of rules, but instead finds a place for each one in how we might think about language. By way of preview, the argument of this book for the model of the linguistics of speech includes the following ideas:

- The foundations of the linguistics of speech, as distinguished from "the linguistics of linguistic structure" that characterizes many modern academic ideas about language, are: (1) the continuum of linguistic behavior; (2) extensive (really massive) variation in all features at all times; (3) the importance of regional/social proximity to "shared" linguistic production; and (4) differential frequency as a key factor in linguistic production both in regional/social groups and in collocations in text corpora (these points are all established with empirical study of surveys and corpora). Taken together, the basic elements of speech correspond to what has been called a "complex system" in sciences ranging from ecology and economics to physics. Order emerges from such systems by means of self-organization, but the order that arises from speech is not the same as what linguists study under the rubric of linguistic structure.

- In both texts and regional/social groups, the frequency distribution of features (variants per se or in proximate combinations, called collocations) occurs as the same curve: a "power law" or asymptotic hyperbolic curve (aka in this book, the "A-curve"). Speakers perceive what is "normal" or "different" for regional/social groups and for text types according to the A-curve: the most frequent variants are perceived as "normal," less frequent variants are perceived as "different," and since particular variants are more or less frequent among different groups of people or types of discourse, the variants come to mark identity of the groups or types by means of these perceptions. Particular variants also become more or less frequent in historical terms, which accounts for what we call "linguistic change," although of course any such "changes" are dependent on the populations or text types observed over time. In both synchronic and diachronic study the notion of "scale" (how big are the groups we observe, from local to regional/social to national) is necessary to manage our observations of frequency distributions.
- Finally, our perceptions of the whole range of "normal" variants (at any level of scale) create "observational artifacts." That is, the notion of the existence of any language or dialect is actually an "observational artifact" that comes from our perceptions of the available variants, at one point in time and for a particular group of speakers, as mediated by the A-curve. The notion "Standard," as distinct from "normal," represents institutional agreement about which variants to prefer, some less frequent than the "normal" variants for many groups of speakers, and this creates the appearance of parallel systems for "normal" and "Standard."
- The rule systems of North American academic linguistics, which we will come to call the "linguistics of linguistic structure," therefore, are related to the linguistics of speech in that language behavior, speech, is what creates the underlying distributional patterns (A-curves for all features) that yield the perceptual "observational artifacts," whether "normal" or "Standard," that we study as rule-bound systems of relationships in the linguistics of linguistic structure. Knowledge of how linguistic structure is related to language behavior, to speech, is no argument against interest in and study of structure, which will always be a useful way of looking at language. Such knowledge can help us to negotiate more effectively between different ideas in the marketplace of academic and popular notions of language.

This preview is not an argument in itself, but rather an invitation meant to help to guide readers through the course of the following chapters, in which each of its claims is developed and justified. Several central themes will emerge from this process. First, our study of language in the past has been constrained by our relative inability to store and manage evidence from speech, and modern technology (recording, computers) not only helps us to study language as we traditionally have, but it also changes the way that we can think about and model language. Second, given large bodies of stored evidence of speech, we cannot avoid quantitative methods and analysis of probabilities as a central fact about linguistic behavior. Third, our control and analysis of large bodies of speech evidence does reveal consistent principles for the organization of language behavior, at different scales of analysis, that can be assembled into an effective model for speech. The term "model" here is not the same as the traditional terms "grammar" or "language," because both of those terms assume an underlying system that makes language behavior into an object – avoidance of a priori objectification of language opens additional possibilities for how we can think about linguistic behavior. Finally, our control and analysis of speech evidence demonstrates that analysis of linguistic production alone is insufficient, and that we need also to incorporate analysis of linguistic perception in order to make an effective model of human language – and further, that linguistic perception is actually the key to the relationship between the linguistics of speech and other traditional approaches to the study of language. How we perceive language around us turns out, on the evidence of contemporary studies, to play an important role in our understanding of language itself, not just an incidental role in the evaluation of speech acts.

Unlike the point of view of some empirically oriented arguments, this book will not claim that its own approach is exclusive in order to attack competing rationalist, prescriptive, and cognitive approaches to language. An overarching theme of this book is that different approaches to language study can be well justified by the acceptance of different assumptions and priorities, and so the differing main approaches to linguistics do not really contradict each other so much as they represent different choices by their practitioners. In the market-place of ideas about language we do not now have and do not need a monopoly. We are all better off with an open market.

1 The contemporary marketplace of ideas about language

The first question that must arise for a book about "the linguistics of speech" is what we take "linguistics" to be. After we have an answer to that question, we can begin to be more specific about "the linguistics of speech." In the first chapter, we will consider contemporary ideas about language and linguistics, from both an academic and from a more popular point of view. We will see that the academic science of linguistics has not yet achieved the consensus about its basic principles that natural and physical scientists have attained for their areas of study. At the same time, the popular view of language (at least for English speakers in Britain and America) has indeed arrived at something like consensus. However, that popular view is quite different from what academic linguists think, which can lead to conflict when we need to make decisions about language and public policy, as in educational policy. This contemporary competition of ideas about language can be described as a marketplace, in which ideas about language are promoted and accepted, bought and sold. In order to understand "linguistics," and thus to prepare the way for a discussion of "the linguistics of speech," we need to try to understand what motivates the buyers and the sellers in the marketplace. For our purposes this will not mean a minute examination of academic theories or popular beliefs about language, but instead a sketch of the main differences between ideas so that we can observe the interaction of the ideas in a test case, the Ebonics controversy, in which the conflict of ideas becomes most clear.

The academic marketplace of ideas about language

Two different basic approaches to the creation of rule systems have been popular in modern American academic linguistics, and these approaches apply the assumption of a homogenous speech community in different ways. Under the first approach, *structuralism*, linguists gather information about a language from one or two or some small number of speakers, and attempt to describe the system of the language from what they say. It is not necessary to talk to more than a few speakers, perhaps just one, because the structuralist assumes that the speakers of a language are more or less alike in that they share a rule system. Such was the case at the beginning of American linguistics, when linguists like Leonard Bloomfield described the system of Native American languages on the basis of conversation with just a few speakers. The same was true of the Army Language Program, on which a great many American linguists collaborated during World War II in order to prepare dictionaries and grammars of the many languages of the world that English-speaking servicemen would encounter: Raven I. McDavid, Jr., otherwise best known for his work on American English, told me (p.c.) about writing the Army materials on Burmese on the basis of a single speaker seated in a chair by his desk in New Haven. In practice, structuralist descriptions of a language tend to get larger and more complex as linguists talk to more people and hear more and different details about the language. So, for example, *A Comprehensive Grammar of the English Language*, the famous "London School" grammar of English by Randolph Quirk, Sidney Greenbaum, Geoffry Leech, and Jan Svartvik (1985), requires 1779 large-format pages, nearly five pounds of book, to describe the grammar of English. Even so, ever since its publication linguists have been writing scholarly articles about facets of English that the book does not describe. The size of the *Comprehensive Grammar* pales beside the magnificent scale of the multi-volume *Oxford English Dictionary*, which does not even claim to list and define all the words of English (it leaves out proper names and chemical names, for instance). There is no complete description anywhere of every aspect of English grammar or of every word in the English vocabulary. No single person actually uses all of the grammar in the *Comprehensive*, or all of the words and senses in the *OED*, but that is not the point of a structuralist description of English. The assumption of an essentially homogenous speech community allows structuralists to create a description of the rule system of a language on the basis of a small number of speakers, and to enhance and improve the description as more evidence is collected, because the system of a language is independent of any particular individual speaker. To "share" the system does not mean that individuals have to embody or control every aspect of it, any more than individual bank customers own all the money in the banking system that they share with other customers. Individuals take part in the banking system with their own money, and we can get a fair idea of the system from one person's transactions; we can get to know more about the banking system per se as we look at more people's transactions. Structural linguistics improves its description of the system of a language as it integrates evidence from more speakers.

The other major modern American approach to linguistics is *generativism*. Generativists take the creation of rule systems, by means of the assumption of a homogenous speech community, to address our human capacity for speech. Generativist study of rule systems contributes to the description of a "universal" system upon which we draw in the formation of the rule system for our own particular language. Chomsky and generativism swept into American linguistics with the "linguistic shot heard 'round the world" (another comment from Raven McDavid (p.c.)), Chomsky's 1957 book *Syntactic Structures*. By that time American structuralism had entered a difficult period. The complexity of structuralist generalizations had to increase as more and more evidence for English and other languages piled up and required integration with existing structural descriptions of language systems. This often led to vigorous competition between linguists who offered different descriptions for the complex facts. Generativism, on the other hand, focused on the creation of the smallest possible rule systems that could "generate" the acceptable sentences of a language, according to grammaticality judgments of its speakers. Chomsky proposed an "evaluation metric" by which competing grammars could be justified, and explained that an evaluation metric is necessary if linguists seek to develop not simply a description of a particular language, but to extrapolate from particular languages towards a theory of natural language in general (1965: 41; for his early programmatic treatment of rules and grammars, see Chomsky 1961). Chomsky suggests that the central problem is deciding which generalizations are significant (1965: 41):

> We have a generalization when a set of rules about distinct items can be replaced by a single rule (or more generally, partially identical rules) about the whole set, or when it can be shown that a "natural class" of items undergoes a certain process or set of similar processes. Thus, choice of an evaluation measure constitutes a decision as to what are "similar processes" and "natural classes" – in short, what are significant generalizations.

Chomsky called generalizations that render the description of a system more complex "spurious generalizations" as opposed to significant ones, which of course reversed the structuralist process of evaluation that always led to greater complexity. The smaller rule system is by definition better in generativism, which in time drove generativist theory towards "minimalism" (as in Chomsky's 1995 *The Minimalist Program*). Structuralist descriptions started small and got bigger, while those of generativism started bigger and got smaller, all the while under the assumption that there must be a system of rules to help explain how the speakers of a language understand each other.[1]

Language variation, on the other hand, arises from language in use, from how people actually speak and write. The study of language in use for itself, not for the purpose of discovering any abstract rule system, does not assume the existence of a homogenous speech community – indeed it assumes that everybody and every group and every place, every situation, is different. The goal of

---

[1] Kretzschmar and Celis (1998) proposed that a better model of language would entertain "mid-level generalizations" as opposed to minimalist or global structural rules – the largest or smallest possible grammars are not the only possibilities. Structuralism and generativism are not the only choices in the marketplace, just the best known of many choices.

such study is not to reveal an underlying system that speakers share, but instead to characterize what speakers actually do with language. *Empirical linguistics* is one name for the study of language variation, although it is certainly true that both structuralism and generativism have an empirical component. Victoria Fromkin, late author of a best-selling textbook with a generativist approach (most recent edition, 2008), once complained to me (p.c.) about this use of "empirical linguistics" to describe such study of language variation, pointing out quite rightly that generativists must have some "empirical" contact with language in order to pursue their own approach. Structuralism, too, relies on empirical findings, at first from few speakers but eventually integrating evidence from many more, in order to pursue structural generalizations about a language. Nonetheless, the term *empirical linguistics* has emerged as a description for the kind of modern linguistics that begins with language in use and not with any assumption of rule systems. Geoffrey Sampson writes in a book actually called *Empirical Linguistics* that (2002: 1)

Language is people talking and writing. It is a concrete, tangible aspect of human behaviour. So, if we want to deepen our understanding of language, our best way forward is to apply the same empirical techniques which have deepened our understanding of other observable aspects of the universe during the four centuries since Galileo.

Yet Sampson finds that "[his research] suggests that one should not talk about different grammars for fiction or technical writing. Instead we need to think in terms of a single grammar, which generates a range of tree structures, some large and some small" (2002: 35). Sampson, though a British scholar, might best be categorized as one interested in the North American practice of Natural Language Processing (NLP), which features computational approaches to large corpora that focus on rule-based regularities, and whose object is the generation of tree banks of grammatical structures. Sampson creates an aggressively argued opposition between the "intuition" that he attributes to Chomsky and generativism, and the scientific method of hypothesis development and testing that he wants linguistics to share with the physical sciences. One might argue in reply that American structuralism was actually a good example of hypothesis development and testing, and that its practitioners nonetheless created the conditions under which Chomsky's approach could flourish by their apparent failure to find a way forward through the necessity for increasingly complex generalizations demanded by the weight of the evidence. Chomsky himself claims modern scientific procedure for generativism, and says that the preference for large collections of language data "is just a misunderstanding of the notion of empirical" (Andor 2004: 97–98). It does little good to argue about what "empirical" or "empiricism" might mean, when in fact both sides claim to be engaged in the scientific inquiry of hypothesis development and testing, even one with empirical contact with the language, just with a different means for evaluation of evidence (for more on this debate, see Kretzschmar 2006a). What is really different from structuralism and generativism about the study of language variation, of language as it is actually spoken by real people, comes not from paying empirical attention to what people say, but from the absence in language variation study (what will in this volume come to be called "the linguistics of speech") of any assumption of rule systems or of ideal speaker-listeners in completely homogenous speech communities.

Within North American linguistics, the area of sociolinguistics seems to be the most likely branch to concern itself with language variation. However, Labovian sociolinguistics is firmly associated with rule systems, in particular with "the vernacular." Shana Poplack offers a concise description (1993: 258):

The primary object of description of the [sociolinguist] is the speech of individuals qua members of a speech community, i.e. informants specifically chosen (through ethnographic or sociological methods) to represent the major axes of community structure ... A specific goal of this procedure is to gain access to the vernacular, the relatively homogeneous, spontaneous speech reserved for intimate or casual situations. This is taken to reflect the most systematic form of the language acquired by the speaker, prior to any subsequent efforts at (hyper-) correction or style-shifting (themselves imposed by the combined pressures of group membership and the social meaning within that group of the linguistic options available).

Poplack's terms are clearly associated with language as system. As she reports, sociolinguists take an interest in what people say not for their personal language behavior, but as individuals who may be chosen to represent collectivities (speech communities) that are assumed to exist. Sociolinguists are interested in "the most systematic form of the language," before it can be deflected by the messy details of human social organization. Labov is reported to have resisted the term "sociolinguistics" for his own work, preferring to think that he simply was doing "linguistics" (Trudgill 1984: 2–3). Labov's monumental volumes on *Principles of Linguistic Change* (1994, 2001) are defenses of the language-as-system approach to large collections of language evidence, historical evidence in the first volume, especially from New York, and contemporary evidence, especially from Philadelphia, in the second (see further Kretzschmar 1996b, 2005). Once more, as for Sampson, the empirical collection of speech evidence is not the same as analysis of language variation on its own merits, since it is perfectly possible, though controversial in contrast to those who provide isolated examples of usage, to collect bodies of speech evidence and to analyze the evidence in terms of rule systems.

While the structuralists and generativists pursued their approaches to linguistics in America, Firth, Halliday, Sinclair, and others were taking a quite different approach in Britain. While American linguists began with the idea of structured rule systems, British linguists began with conversation:

Conversation is much more of a roughly prescribed ritual than most people think. Once someone speaks to you, you are in a relatively determined context and you are not free just to say what you please. We are born individuals. But to satisfy our needs we have to become social persons ... [it is in] the study of conversation ... [that] we shall find the key to a better understanding of what language really is and how it works. (Firth 1935: 66, 70–71)

Language in use. In terms of modern linguistics, this British approach has been most influential in the development of discourse analysis and corpus linguistics, the areas in which linguists focus, respectively, on the interactivity of speech and on the collection for later analysis of large bodies of real speech (and writing) by real people. The focus of British linguistics has been meaning rather than structure. Indeed, British linguists like John Sinclair consider that the American focus on structure leads the linguist astray (1991: 108):

it is folly to decouple lexis and syntax, or either of those and semantics. The realization of meaning is far more explicit than is suggested by abstract grammars. The model of a highly generalized formal syntax, with slots into which fall neat lists of words, is suitable only in rare uses and specialized texts. By far the majority of text is made of the occurrence of common words in common patterns ... Most everyday words do not have an independent meaning, or meanings, but are components of a rich repertoire of multi-word patterns that make up text. This is totally obscured by the procedures of conventional grammar.

Sinclair thus shows this British tradition of linguistics to be more at odds with American structural or generative linguistics or "conventional grammar" (per-haps, *sotto voce*, even grammar as practiced by the London School in the work of Quirk and Greenbaum) than even Sampson's argument about scientific method would have it. If meaning comes from the repetition by speakers of common multi-word patterns, each of which means more than the sum of its constituent parts (the separate words), then speakers must understand each other more by habit than by rule. When asked the question "How could we commu-nicate with each other if there weren't rules for how we should talk and write?", British linguists of the so-called NeoFirthian tradition might answer, "Quite well, thank you." In the NeoFirthian tradition, the only way to get at how language works is by the observation of real language, the more the better. The intellectual gulf between either of the primary modern modes of American linguistics and the NeoFirthian tradition is so great that British linguists often report difficulty getting grant funding in Britain for projects that are too American (British linguists always have to collect corpora), while just the reverse is true in America where projects that sound too NeoFirthian may have a hard time winning acceptance (American linguists have difficulty being funded to build British-style corpora).

NeoFirthian ideas and methods have close relations with and definite differ-ences from the American approach in language variation study, what most

North Americans have accepted as the appropriate model for the study of language in actual communities, sociolinguistics. In the Labovian sociolinguistics tradition, evidence from speech is collected in order to be fit to parallel structures, as in Labov's description of ongoing American sound change as chain shifts (Labov 1981, 1991, 1994). The corollary assumption of "speech communities," speakers who share one of the parallel systems, leads to acceptance of the idea of "representative" speakers (i.e., selection of a speaker to interview who might best illustrate the shared system). On the other hand, as Stubbs concisely put it, the British tradition would have it that "Linguistics is concerned with the study of meaning: form and meaning are inseparable" (1996: 35). The American "form–function relations" even in sociolinguistics thus contrasts with the British form–meaning homology. Both sides, however, inspect evidence from language in use to make their claims. So, what do sociolinguistic interviews have to do with linguistic corpora? Aside from the obvious fact that a collection of interviews, when put together, turns into a linguistic corpus of material, to think of sociolinguistic interviews in corpus terms provides a different, non-structural way of looking at the interview evidence. Similarly, others of Stubbs' principles are very much in line with American sociolinguistics: "Linguistics is essentially a social science and an applied science" and "Language should be studied in actual, attested, authentic instances of use, not as intuitive, invented, isolated sentences" (1996: 25, 28). Stubbs cites Labov at several places in defense of these ideas, as against Chomskyan doctrine. We see that the British corpus linguistics tradition recapitulates the insistence of American sociolinguists on the social instantiation of language. The British approach just looks for collocational patterns and their meanings in the particular situations of use under study, while American sociolinguists prefer to see parallel systems in the different social groups. Both approaches find value in local settings for language, rather than just looking for global generalizations.

  Further, the British approach is actually closer to American sociolinguistics than to the American practice of NLP, of which we have seen Sampson as an example. NLP shares the assumption of rules and systems with the traditional American modes of linguistics (like the sociolinguists), and it is focused on global generalizations about the language (unlike the sociolinguists), both of which differ from the approach of NeoFirthian corpus builders. Bigger is better for corpora in NLP, because the chances of finding a new structure for the global system depend on great volume. However, since NLP is after evidence of the existence of new structures in the language as a whole, it does not matter so much where the words come from (e.g., all of the *Wall Street Journal*, or transcriptions from National Public Radio). In the British mode, on the other hand, everybody knows that the kind of text put into the corpus will constrain what can later be gotten out, and the value to get out is most often frequency evidence, not just the existence of features. NLP practitioners typically value quantity of data for their corpora as against particular sources, while sociolinguists and British corpus linguists insist on keeping track of the social circumstances of the speakers or writers who generated their data. The central question for NLP, as Manning and Schütze ask it, is what people usually do in their language, or "What are the common patterns that occur in language use?" (1999: 4). The question that NeoFirthian corpus linguists would ask is "What does this actual piece of language mean in this particular setting?" The latter question is compatible with the Labovian idea of parallel systems, and is even more like other recent modes of sociolinguistics such as community of practice studies. While NLP appears most often just to use aggregated data, corpus linguists usually compare the language in one text or set of texts against another one, and this sort of comparison, too, parallels what we commonly do for different sociolinguistic communities. There are of course some sociolinguists who do NLP, just as Sampson practices NLP in Britain, but in the end it is possible to make reasonable generalizations about language systems and language variation in America and Britain. American Labovian sociolinguistics, then, shares the notion of systems with the structuralists and generativists, but it approaches the NeoFirthians in its interest in local as opposed to wider global analysis of language. NeoFirthian analysis of language behavior is thus similar to but not quite the same as sociolinguistics. Similarly, both American NLP practitioners and British NeoFirthians build linguistic corpora, but they do so in different ways and to different ends.

There are of course other contemporary academic ideas about language – and academic linguists have been notably contentious in advocating them. The limited discussion here of generativism, structuralism, and the NeoFirthian approach just serves to show how differently the opposite poles of language variation and rule systems can be treated in the academic world. Other academic ideas about language can most often be related to these poles, the NeoFirthian focus on language in use vs. the American focus on rule systems, and for rule systems, the drive towards ever larger systems vs. the drive towards ever smaller systems. If it can be said that academic biologists or chemists or physicists have achieved consensus about basic principles of their sciences (and controversies do certainly still exist among specialists in these areas, even if they do not often attract notice from non-specialists), nobody should make that claim yet for academic linguists. The academic marketplace for ideas about language has not yet arrived at the level of agreement on basic principles that has been attained in the natural and physical sciences.

The popular marketplace for ideas about language: Writing and sounding *correct*

While the American linguists disagree with each other, and the British NeoFirthian linguists disagree with the Americans, popular opinion about language *has* reached a practical consensus in Britain and America. The schools, public and private, and the people of both countries have agreed that there is a right way to speak and write English, "correct grammar." At the same time, not very many people from either country have the self-confidence to say that they typically use "correct grammar" themselves. This property of "correctness" that people attribute to their language, whether or not they believe themselves to possess it as individual speakers, is different from anything that the structuralists or generativists or NeoFirthians might agree to. In America, professional linguists are often thought to be "too liberal" because they do not always support the model of "correctness," often cast as "Standard English," as it is taught in the schools (see Bailey 1991: 12–16). On the other hand, teachers of English in America, perhaps those in Britain as well, are all familiar with the same experience at social gatherings: when they are asked what they do for a living and say that they teach English, the conversation chills and people apologize for their lack of correctness. Sometimes they even cover their mouths with their hands and blurt out a muffled "I better watch what I say!" Richard Bailey cites an apt description of this kind of an encounter from an article by Leonard Bloomfield (1991: 2; the original article was published in 1944, which indicates the persistence through time of such situations):

The speaker who discourses about language sometimes adds that he himself has not a perfect command of his native language – the reasons differ with biographic details – but is aware of his weakness and tries to overcome it; he alludes patronizingly to other speakers who do not know enough to make a similar effort. In fact, it soon appears that the speaker possesses a fairly extensive stock of authoritative knowledge which enables him to condemn many forms that are used by other speakers ... If he knows that he is talking to a professional student of language, he first alleges ignorance and alludes modestly to the status of his own speech, but then advances the traditional lore in a fully authoritative tone.

In an encounter of this kind with a neighbor, I once asserted my authority as a person who helped to make language reference books like dictionaries, but she seemed to consider that irrelevant and carried on without pause in her account of what she considered to be notable and unfortunate breaches of correctness in our community.

When people (not only teachers of English, indeed not usually good English teachers) notice a public example of incorrectness, they can be eager to pounce on the malefactor. When my local newspaper published a picture of a high-school student wearing a T-shirt with a homemade slogan including the word "suspension" misspelled (with -*tion*), a flurry of editorial letters were sent to and printed by the paper, and the newspaper also published its own opinion on the editorial page:

the photograph contains a valuable lesson ... that having an argument or an opinion taken seriously requires the ability to clearly express that argument. The first thing that one wonders when seeing the T-shirt with the misspelling is whether the person wearing it has that ability. An educated mind is a disciplined mind, and a disciplined mind is one that pays attention to important details such as accurate spelling. (*Athens Banner-Herald*, February 6, 2006)

"Accurate spelling" is here equated with clear expression, mental discipline, and education itself. In America, the cultural phenomenon of the "spelling bee" elevates this aspect of correctness to the level of a community celebration. Winners of school spelling bees have their names posted on notice boards outside their schools; winners of district spelling bees are celebrated on the front page of their community newspapers; the national spelling bee is televised live. In American culture, such linguistic correctness (especially but not exclusively in spelling) has become a moral virtue, so that those who cannot or do not display it are just not, in the words of the newspaper, "taken seriously" as people who can have opinions. The medium has literally become the message for poor spellers and, by extension, for those who employ "non-standard" grammar.[2]

The association of literacy with both morality and government in America is of very long standing. Richard Bailey cites what could be taken as a credo for this belief from the Northwest Ordinance of 1787, which opened the American Midwest to settlement (Bailey 1996: 32): "Religion, morality and knowledge being necessary to good government and the happiness of mankind, schools and the means of education shall forever be encouraged." It is worthy of note that American elementary education in the nineteenth century relied on Noah Webster's *The American Spelling Book*, one of the most widely used textbooks of all time (Bailey used a nineteenth-century cover of an edition of Webster as an illustration, on the page facing the quotation above). Thomas Pyles describes Webster's explicit connection of his "easy, concise and systematic Method of Education, Designed for the Use of English Schools in America" with morality and government (1952: 97–98):

The spelling book which appeared in 1783 was the first of a series of three volumes somewhat pompously called *A Grammatical Institute of the English Language* ... In the Preface to the first volume Webster emphasized in a characteristically heavy-handed fashion the moral, religious, and patriotic value of the book and of those to come.

Pyles suggests that the book, during the time when it was republished as a small, separate volume over the next century, may have sold over a hundred million copies. The result for Americans is what Rosina Lippi-Green (1997) has called the "ideology" of Standard English. Lippi-Green's account shows that this popular ideology has been used to justify all sorts of discrimination and cultural bias (e.g., in employment, and in use of "non-standard" language for portrayals

---

[2] Irony is unavoidable here for the careful reader, who will have noticed the split infinitive "to clearly express" in the language of the newspaper editorial writer.

of marginal or threatening characters in Walt Disney children's movies). The ideology of Standard English has the benefit for those who use it, and of course the disadvantage for those who suffer from it, of allowing discrimination on linguistic grounds that would not be permitted on ethnic or cultural grounds (e.g., somebody who talks like *that* can't be a librarian, the point of one of Lippi-Green's case studies; see also Milroy and Milroy 1999: 2–3). In what must be seen as a terrible irony within the educational system, this popular notion of correctness in spelling, grammar, and other aspects of language tends to marginalize the views of academic linguists, as soon as the academics claim knowledge about language which does not support the popular ideology.

The tradition in Britain has a different pathway to essentially the same end. Mass public education was not required in Britain until the end of the nineteenth century, and the doctrine of correctness began not in the schools but in the (aristocratic) courts. As Bailey suggests (1991: 3),

Far from a nineteenth-century image, *standard* was applied to prestige varieties of a language as early as 1711, and then the term merely codified a notion already old. Before that, by the end of the sixteenth century, the phrase *King's English* had come into use to label normative forms if not actual royal usage.

This is a social preference; the best antonym for *standard* in this sense is probably *provincial*. Bailey points out that *the King's English* might not be the usage of the king himself (and cites modern complaints about the English of the royal family), yet the "idealized norm" of a standard equates the best speech with the best speakers. Samuel Johnson illustrated the entries in his 1755 *Dictionary*, the first generally acknowledged authoritative dictionary of English, with quotations from the "best" authors. In the twentieth century, the standard in Britain became known as "Received Pronunciation," or "RP," which H. C. Wyld had equated with "Good English, Well-bred English, Upper-class English" and named "Received Standard English" (or "RSE"; cited in Bailey 1991: 7). This form of language was not exclusively aristocratic, since it was said to be spoken by graduates of Oxford and Cambridge, many of whom were not of noble birth, although in the nineteenth and earlier twentieth centuries most of the students came from families of means. Dorothy Sayers has provided a popular example of the difference between aristocratic English and RP/RSE in her famous series of detective novels featuring amateur sleuth Lord Peter Wimsey, whose speech is represented as going back and forth between these two poles. In the well-known *Gaudy Night* (1935, set in Oxford; Americans usually put the stress on the *night*, not realizing that the title names an Oxford celebration and so in Britain the stress is on the *gaudy*), for example, the reader can tell by an abundance of apostrophes when Lord Peter is talking in his aristocratic role, as in phrases like "Was that obligin' observation addressed to me?" (Chapter 19). Lord Peter keeps his g's in other passages when enacting a "standard" role, for him often indicative of more serious talk. Sayers opposes both of these modes to the (literary) dialect of non-aristocratic characters, like the country Northern speakers in *Clouds of Witness* (1926), like "Howd toong! ... Doost want Ah should break ivery bwoan i' thi body?" (viz., 'Hold [your] tongue! Do you want me to break every bone in your body?'). Since the BBC adopted RP as its standard form of pronunciation for broadcasting, RP and RSE have also become known as BBC English.

When mass public education did become the law of the land in Britain, it taught RP and RSE. In the latter part of the twentieth century, educational white papers addressed the status of RP and RSE in the schools. For example, the 1988 Kingman Report advocated the teaching of the standard "dialect" in the schools without insistence on the RP style of pronunciation (see Honey 1989, Millar 1997, for evaluations of this recommendation). Still, the notion and doctrine of correctness is alive and well today in Britain. James and Lesley Milroy's 1999 book *Authority in Language* stands beside Lippi-Green's book in America to document the ideological role of correctness in Britain, including what they call "the complaint tradition" and "the moralistic tradition" which parallel similar strands of the American cultural pattern. While Standard English in Britain may have begun with aristocratic foundations from which American colonists wished to distance themselves, the popular notion of correctness has come to be shared across the Atlantic. The extent of this agreement is proven by the popularity on both sides of the Atlantic of the book *Eats, Shoots & Leaves: The Zero Tolerance Approach to Punctuation* (Truss 2004, paperback edition 2006), whose title comes from a joke that turns on the presence or absence of a comma: again ironically, this when British and many American writers would disagree about the proper punctuation of the title phrase![3]

Under the doctrine of correctness, rules are literally made to be broken, or perhaps it would be better to say that they are made because many, even most people break them. Rule systems made by American linguists describe, either with a large and complex or with a minimalist system, how the different pieces of a language fit together; it is the fit that makes the system. Rules under the doctrine of correctness come as a list of things not to say or write. Don't spell *suspension* with a *t*. Don't split infinitives. Don't say *ain't*. Don't drop your aitches so that *hair* sounds like *air* (this proscription of course more appropriate in Britain). Don't use more than one negative at a time, often phrased as "two negatives make a positive," which is nonetheless a proscription of multiple negation. And the list goes on. American school grammars, which continue to support the doctrine of correctness in the Webster tradition, do offer descriptions

---

[3] David Crystal has now responded with a book entitled *The Fight for English: How Language Pundits Ate, Shot, and Left* (2007).

of nouns and verbs as parts of speech, and offer some description of sentence formation and other grammatical points, but these descriptions typically do not incorporate the sense of comprehensive fit that characterizes the systems made by linguists. Instead, such "simplified" descriptions offer just enough information so that they can be used to justify more proscriptions. Don't use faulty agreement between the noun or pronoun subject and the verb. Don't connect two sentences with a comma (the dreaded "comma splice"), and don't just throw sentences together with no punctuation at all (the equally dreaded "run-on sentence"). Of course these proscriptions are just what many, even most people do normally say and write. The doctrine of correctness is most often called *prescriptive grammar*, because all of these negatives are thought to make a positive – Standard English in America, or RSE/RP in Britain. Perhaps in Britain they have actually resulted in a positive standard with RSE and RP, although even the BBC now permits its newsreaders to sound more like where they come from. But in America, Standard English consists of the avoidance of proscribed usages, and thus at best is only relatively enacted by even the most proper speaker. The unavoidable relativity of adherence to standards, on both sides of the Atlantic, supports the associated popular belief that English is in decline, that Standard English speakers in the past must have done better than we can do today (for "this love affair with the past" and "'antiquity' as a virtue of the English language," see Bailey 1991: 268–276).

The *right* language at home

People on both sides of the Atlantic have also long known that there were regional and social ways of using English that were *right*, in the sense of being both adequate and appropriate for their own regions and social groups. The point can be illustrated with an example from my own experience. A few years ago I was asked for an interview on a nationally syndicated show on a radio network, which turned out to be a revival of the idea of an old radio show. In "Where Are You From?" Professor Henry Lee Smith used to spend several minutes in conversation with his subjects and then told them exactly where in America they were from. I should have known better, but it was live radio and there was no graceful way out, so I agreed to play Henry Lee Smith and guess where people who called in might be from. In short, I was wrong about four out of five callers. After half an hour the switchboard was still full of people who wanted their speech publicly analyzed, but the host stopped the interview and I have not, I am glad to say, been invited back. A good part of the reason this exercise in "Stump the Professor" engaged the audience was that they wanted me to be able to guess correctly. That would have confirmed their belief that people's language helps them to belong where they live, that the callers were somehow OK if some expert on the radio told them that their speech fit the dialect of an area. It did not matter that they were asking the impossible of me because they in fact did not come from just one place, like the lady who was born in the Bronx and moved to Alabama. Neither did it matter to the callers that they all used a careful, formal, less-regional form of their speech because I was asking them leading questions in public on the radio. The callers expected, even on their best linguistic behavior, that their speech would mark them as being from a place. They believed that the expert could recognize their regional way of using English because it was just *right*, in the sense of being both adequate and appropriate and also distinctive, for their own region. This sort of regional or social speech might be called "normal," to distinguish it from "standard" (see further Kretzschmar 1992a).

The print media gives frequent confirmation of the popular view of the rightness of speech for a place or group. *The New York Times* developed an article (January 16, 2006) on the accent of Mayor Bloomberg on the occasion of his reelection, in which the reporter's feeling that the mayor's accent was less "Boston" (the mayor was born and raised in suburban Medford, MA) than it had been earlier was buttressed by testimony from many national figures in academic linguistics, including the present author. We academics were unanimous in our conclusion that the mayor had used fewer telltale signs of a "Boston" accent during his second inaugural address than he had in his first one. Why exactly this change might have occurred during his first term in office, when Bloomberg had been resident in New York for over thirty years before his first term began, is perhaps a more interesting question. Still, the reporter was attuned to the rightness of the sound of the mayor's accent, and correctly so according to the experts. I was recently consulted by an Atlanta magazine writer about the accent of actress Kyra Sedgwick, who has won an Emmy award for her role on TV as a detective from Atlanta who has moved to Los Angeles, and whose accent is part of her character. The writer, a lifelong Georgian, just did not think that the accent sounded right. Miss Sedgwick was born in New York City and is a graduate of the University of Southern California. It should be no surprise that her Southern accent does not sound genuine to a native of Atlanta – stage accents frequently annoy the natives of the places that such accents are supposed to represent. The press can also juxtapose the competing notions of correctness and of the rightness of local accents, as in an Associated Press article entitled "The fall of y'all" (November 24, 2005). While the article rounded up academic experts to talk about change in the Southern accent, the lead for the story featured a voice and diction instructor who is quoted as saying "Many come to see me because they want to sound less country … they say 'I don't want to lose my accent completely, but I want to be able to minimize it or modify it.'" The voice and diction students do not want to lose the voice that, in part, makes them who they are, but at the same time they acknowledge how the same voice can be a liability in the culture of correctness. The same can be said of the AP reporter, who was motivated to write a story on perceived change in the Southern accent but who needed to establish its relation to the doctrine of correctness before getting to the expert testimony.

Two different notions thus compete in popular ideas about language. The doctrine of correctness assigns a social value to the rules taught by the schools. Such rules are made because they are often broken in practice. School rules are not the same as academic rule systems, because school rules are lists of language do's and don't's, as opposed to the relational "fit" of rule systems from academic linguistics. However, language is also *right* in the popular view because it belongs to different groups of people, whether socially preferred groups or not.

The experts themselves engage the idea of the linkage of language and dialect with local culture. One of the earliest articles by William Labov (1963) showed that some residents of Martha's Vineyard, those who opposed cultural change on the island such as increasing tourism, preserved traditional features of local speech more than residents who supported change (Trudgill coined the term "covert prestige" for the preference by some speakers for non-standard local features (1972, 1974a)). Such studies develop an opposition between a standard system of a language and a different vernacular system of a language; the dynamics of the relationship between the systems, and especially of language change that arises from the dynamic, has become the primary object of study for American sociolinguistics. Indeed, the Linguistic Society of America maintains a standing committee on "Endangered Languages and Their Preservation," and the rubric has been extended to dialects as well (see the committee's page at the LSA website, www.lsadc.org). The committee seeks to document and preserve the structure of such languages and dialects. The committee also values the perceived connection between language and community. An example is the effort at the University of California, which holds extensive archives of Native American languages collected by its linguists, to offer classes to teach Native American communities the languages that they have already lost. The fact is that all languages and dialects are "endangered" at all times by constant linguistic change and cultural change, in the sense that no language or dialect can stay exactly the same as time passes, so some might say that the California effort to put the genie back into the bottle is a futile gesture. However, the idea of rightness of a language or dialect for its community of speakers has combined with American linguists' belief in rule systems to create a movement for celebration and conservation of such linguistic systems, even ones that the community no longer speaks or embodies.

American linguists' interest in the diversity of languages and dialects is not merely to support communities, however, but to support the dominant theory:

If the central concern of linguistics is essentially anthropological or psychological, i.e., to provide insight into the nature of "humanness" by investigating the structure of human language, then linguistics will without question benefit by supporting research on the documentation of dying or endangered languages. Taking the study of universal grammar and linguistic typology (the study of the restricted ways in which languages may differ from each other) as more concrete manifestations of this central concern, linguistic typology is obviously enriched by knowledge of linguistic diversity … Somewhat less obviously, the positing of language universals must necessarily be revised and thus become more accurate when the structure of divergent languages is made known. The loss to humankind of genetic diversity in the linguistic world is thus arguably greater than even the loss of genetic diversity in the biological world, given that the structure of human language represents a considerable testimony to human intellectual achievement. (committee page, www.lsadc.org)

The generativist view of endangered languages and dialects is that each one represents a separate system, and that each one is therefore valuable for the evidence it may provide about language universals. The analogy here between "genetic diversity" among language systems and genetic diversity in biology is more than mere metaphor, given the generativist interest in the human capacity for language which may itself have its basis in genetics. American linguists thus have multiple reasons to prefer and to preserve linguistic and dialectal diversity, structural and generative motivations as well as the popular notion, also pursued in academic anthropology and anthropological linguistics, of the rightness of identification of a community's language with its culture.

Academic linguists can readily agree with the popular idea of the *rightness* of a language or dialect for a particular group of people, because (unlike the doctrine of correctness) it can readily be integrated with structuralist or generativist ideas of language, as we have seen. Academic linguists can consider what is *right* about the characteristic language of a regional or social group of speakers to be part of a separate linguistic rule system (in the academic sense of the interconnection of its characteristic features) belonging to its speakers. In the popular view, what is *right* in this sense about the characteristic language of a regional or social group, what makes people who use it belong to their groups, is at the same time wrong according to the doctrine of correctness. What academic ideas of language are able to compartmentalize and keep separate, the popular idea of language must endure as an inherent contradiction between correctness and authenticity, the two popular assessments that coexist for the set of language features used by any person or group.

Ebonics: Correctness, rightness, and the marketplace of ideas about language in action

The interaction of popular notions of correctness and rightness, and also of academic interests, comes most to the fore in America on the issue of African American English, most spectacularly during the Ebonics affair of the late

1990s. The complexity of these interactions will make for a good example of what, if not so much in the public eye, is really also the case for other varieties of English.[4]

As eloquently described in Rickford and Rickford (2000), the two sides of the *right* language, correctness and authenticity, coexist in the African American community – but not easily. The Rickfords express the contrast between correctness, as in "Standard English," and the community vernacular as one that causes belittlement and denial. At the same time, the vernacular has "authenticity," its own rightness for the community. The contrast is not just imposed on the African American community from without, but is itself a property of the community's own view of its language. Their advice at the end of the book includes (p. 229)

Be conscious of our love-hate relationship with Spoken Soul. The next time a brother or sister starts speaking in deep vernacular during a city council meeting and you feel yourself stinging with embarrassment, try to remember the social conditioning and the historical circumstances behind that private shame. We don't promise that you'll overcome your shame, only that you may begin to understand it and, one hopes, reverse it. By the same token, the next time you find yourself submerged in and surrounded by Spoken Soul, acknowledge it silently. Adore it. Taste it as if for the first time. Try to imagine the same scene, the same ethos and ambience, without it.

The popular two notions fight it out with each other every day in public meetings and private thoughts.

Academic linguists' treatment of African American English effectively began with Raven and Virginia McDavid, in the first major academic defense of African American English in comparison with the English of the white population (1951). The McDavids defended the normal course of development of African American English, on the same grounds that any regional or social variety of English might emerge, and in the same way that survivals of European ancestral languages such as German or Swedish might be found in the English of, say, Milwaukee or Minnesota (as in fact they are). The McDavids clearly took a structuralist point of view, in which the system of English has been enlarged and enriched by the contributions of African Americans and other ethnic groups. They directly opposed the popular idea that African Americans violated the doctrine of correctness because of their race. They explicitly approved of the shared popular and academic idea that African American English could be *right* for its speakers, just as Wisconsin English could be *right* for its speakers.

[4] See Kretzschmar (2008a) for a more detailed account: this account is based on "Public and Academic Understandings about Language: The Intellectual History of Ebonics." In Edgar Schneider, ed., *English World Wide*. With the kind permission of John Benjamins Publishing Company, Amsterdam/Philadelphia, www.benjamins.com.

William Labov's defense of African American English two decades later in his famous essay "The Logic of Nonstandard English" (1972, but originally prepared in the late 1960s) specifically addressed conflicts between linguists and other academics, educational psychologists, as regards the education of black children. Critical examination of the assertions of educational psychologists became polemic later in the essay: "Like Bereiter and Engelmann, Jensen is handicapped by his ignorance of the most basic facts about human language and the people who speak it" (1972: 239). Labov clearly wrote from the viewpoint of somebody who had acquired "understanding of the nature of language" that surpassed the inadequate ideas of academic non-linguists whose ideas about language essentially recapitulated the views of the general public. Labov wanted to remove the debate about education of black children from the popular notion of correctness, because the doctrine of correctness might suggest that speakers of African American English were inadequate (or worse, as we have seen, immoral or unAmerican) because consistently "incorrect." Labov's own argument was still framed by the contrast between standard and non-standard English, but carefully differentiated from his characterization of typical attitudes of school teachers: "For many generations, American school teachers have devoted themselves to correcting a small number of nonstandard English rules to their standard equivalents, under the impression that they were teaching logic."[5] Labov objected to the idea that African American children have some sort of verbal or cultural deprivation or "deficit" in language or thought, and preferred the idea that African American English can be better described as having a different system of rules: "it differs from other dialects in regular and rule-governed ways" (1972: 238). The difference between systems had practical consequences, such as possible use of "the methods used in teaching English as a foreign language" (1972: 238). The key point here is that Labov's "standard English" (small s) was a rule system as academic linguists would have it, and not the ideological, list-of-errors "Standard English" (capital S) which embodies correctness and in which the public believes. African American English and "standard English" were both "coherent systems," which had "structural differences." His assertion of "substantive facts about language which are known to all linguists" sought to replace the popular notion of correctness with the idea of rule systems from academic American linguistics (for Labov, those of the generativist camp), which did not have associations with morality and government, or for some educational psychologists of the day, associations with mental ability. Just as for the McDavids, Labov showed that academic and popular ideas came into conflict, and his strategy was to try to substitute the academic idea for the popular one as

---

[5] (1972: 225). See Chapter 2 for discussion of the linkage between language study and logic beginning with Aristotle.

regards rules, while he supported the shared popular and academic idea of the rightness of a language or dialect for its speakers.

The views of academic linguists drew further apart from the popular notion of correctness because of the so-called creolist–Anglicist debate and the question of whether African American English was "diverging" from standard English. The creolist position emphasizes the difference between African American English and other Englishes by claiming that it has quite a different underlying rule system, as against the structuralist position (renamed Anglicism by the creolists) exemplified by the McDavids. The complex creolist–Anglicist debate always concerned academic linguists more than the public in any case, since the public view continued to be dominated by the doctrine of correctness. The judge in the famous Ann Arbor decision, C. W. Joiner, said as much in his formal opinion (*Martin Luther King Junior Elementary School Children et al., v. the Ann Arbor School District Board*; italics added):

The problem in this case revolves around the ability of the school system, King School in particular, to teach the reading of *standard English* to children who, it is alleged, speak "black English" as a matter of course at home and in their home community (the Green Road Housing Development). This case is not an effort on the part of the plaintiffs to require that they be taught "black English" or that their instruction throughout their schooling be in "black English" or that a dual language program be provided ... It is a straightforward effort to require the court to intervene on the children's behalf to require the defendant School District Board to take appropriate action to teach them to read in the *standard English* of the school, the commercial world, the arts, science, and professions.

The issue was teaching Standard English (big S, though the judge did not capitalize it in the opinion). The judge heard and approved of the opinions of academic linguists, including Geneva Smitherman and William Labov, and at several points refers to the "system" of "black English." Judge Joiner, however, described "black English," always presented in scare quotes which may be taken to indicate its non-standard status, in contrast to "the language used by society to carry on its business, to develop its science, arts and culture, and to carry on its professions and governmental functions." The judge thus actually applied common popular ideas of language, and explicitly rejected any "dual language program." Judge Joiner merely wanted teachers to stop being "insensitive" by rejecting the existence of "black English" as a home language (on grounds that it was merely incorrect Standard English). The Ann Arbor case was a success for academic linguists, in that they were able to convince the court of the value of the "difference" approach versus the "deficit" approach then used in the schools, but the case did not actually substitute the academic sense of language systems for popular notions of correctness and rightness.

In the ensuing decades, the academic debate between the creolists and the Anglicists could not help but be entangled in political questions, such as forced bussing for school integration, or the position taken by some leaders like

Malcolm X that the black community should reject integration with the white community that had exploited African Americans, because the creolist position highlighted separation between the languages and speakers, while the Anglicist position highlighted their integration. At this same time, Afrocentrism emerged as an academic movement that promotes the common experience of African Americans through their African heritage, and thus it can be used to justify the maintenance of separate cultural institutions, including schools. As regards language, Afrocentrism leads some to claim that there is a "genetic" connection between African languages and African American English, which takes the idea of separation even further by limiting even more the connection between European English and the language of African Americans. The Afrocentrist position contains an "explicit rejection of prevailing linguistic terminology" (Baugh 2000: 42); it discusses language essentially according to ideas from the popular marketplace, in particular the rightness of the language spoken by slave descendents. Afrocentrism may on occasion use terms derived from academic linguistics, but it really has nothing in common with academic linguistics.

The Oakland Ebonics controversy began with Afrocentrism. The Oakland school board, when they tried to formulate a plan to address the worsening compliance of the student population, of whom the majority were black, with the state of California's policy regarding Standard English Proficiency (SEP), took the Afrocentric position that, since their African American students were not speakers of English, they should not be deprived of the special resources given to other students who were not native English speakers. In the original version of the Ebonics resolution, the Oakland school board cited the Federal Bilingual Education Act and ordered "the best possible academic program for imparting instruction to African American students in their primary language for the combined purposes of maintaining the legitimacy and richness of such language [by whatever name], and to facilitate their acquisition and mastery of English language skills" (cited in Kretzschmar 1998a: 170–171). Dr Ernie Smith, who provided "the strongest linguistic influence" for the conference that generated the board's statement (Baugh 2000: 41), was a professor of medicine, not linguistics. He had written that (cited in Rickford and Rickford 2000: 170)

African Americans have, in fact, retained a West and Niger-Congo African thought process. It is this thought process that is dominant in the substratum phonology and morphosyntax of African American speech but stigmatized as being Black English. According to the Africanists the native language of African Americans is Ebonics – the linguistic continuation of Africa in black America … The Africanists posit that Ebonics is not genetically related to English. Therefore the term Ebonics is not a mere synonym for the more commonly used Black English … In fact, they argue that the term Black English is an oxymoron.

On the other hand, John Baugh, a former student of William Labov who was also involved in the conference, represented the view of academic linguistics (2005: 121):

> The vast majority of people in attendance at the Oakland SEP conference rejected my interpretation in favor of the Afrocological position espoused by Ernie Smith. Our disagreement was sufficiently cordial, but it was absolutely clear that Oakland's SEP administrators were not only unconvinced by my arguments, but they stated, on that occasion, that to accept my position would prevent them from making a case to the federal government to obtain bilingual education funding for their African American students ... I told Oakland's SEP administrators that their strategy would fly in the face of the linguistic evidence and inevitable political resistance.

Academic ideas of language offered by Baugh had no power for the others at the conference, who preferred the Afrocentric view that defined African Americans as non-native English speakers. Because the Afrocentrists were actually following popular ideas about language rather than academic ones, they went one step further than Labov to say, not that African American students should be taught *as if* they were speakers of another language, but that African American slave descendents *did* speak another language. While they remained on "cordial" terms, Baugh could not agree with the Afrocentrists on this point.

Nobody else did, either. As Baugh had predicted, violent controversy erupted among the public, both black and white, but not because of any academic ideas about language. The public shared popular ideas about language with the Afrocentrists, but ironically the doctrine of correctness was widely applied to Ebonics by the public on the understanding, explicitly rejected by the Oakland board, that Ebonics was merely "incorrect" English. As Walt Wolfram reported (1998: 111),

> Fuel was added to the fire of the Oakland Ebonics controversy when prominent public figures ranging from the president of the United States to educators and leaders in the African American community [such as Jesse Jackson and Bill Cosby] offered immediate and pronounced opinions that chastised the Oakland school board for its resolution recognizing Ebonics.
>
> One of the ironies of the public commentary on Ebonics was the seemingly ironic alliances of public figures who commented on the topic. Public commentary brought together leaders from the African American community known for their social activism and progressive sociopolitical views and those known for their conservative, reactionary political stances. On what other topic have a conservative icon such as the media commentator, Rush Limbaugh, and the social activist, Jesse Jackson, agreed on in their public condemnation?

Popular ideas about language caused African Americans like Jackson, on one hand, to complain about Ebonics because it seemed to be saying that African Americans were somehow not good enough to learn Standard English, and on the other hand complaints that Oakland was inappropriately trying to snatch federal bilingual education funding for people who were not immigrants and who did not grow up speaking a foreign language. These leaders in the African American community simply enacted the "love–hate relationship" with African American English reported in Rickford and Rickford (2000). The doctrine of correctness trumped the rightness of Ebonics for slave descendants.

Linguists immediately came to the defense of the Oakland school board, even though the original Oakland resolution was not motivated by academic ideas of language. One of the first reactions of linguists came from the Linguistic Society of America. As Baugh points out, the linguists' defense of the legitimacy of African American English in linguistic terms, as against raging criticism of the speech of many African Americans according to popular ideas, was carried out without realizing that the Oakland board had acted on Afrocentric ideas that did not actually go along with what linguists thought (Baugh 2000: 42). Subsequently, Baugh and John Rickford advised the Oakland board in a revision of the original Ebonics resolution that removed several contentious Afrocentric formulations in favor of those that could be defended by linguists (see texts indicating the changes in Baugh 2000: 43–47, Rickford and Rickford 2000: 166–169, and Kretzschmar 1998a: 172–174). These changes redirected the Afrocentric definitions of language towards the parallel systems view of Labov and other linguists, and more towards the terms of the Ann Arbor decision. Linguists could tread lightly around the issue of bilingual education, since they could approve in principle the idea of using the methods of bilingual education for African American speakers, without defining Ebonics as a language other than English. No North American linguist would object to recognition of the systematic differences between African American English and "standard English," or to the use of that knowledge to work towards state-mandated "Standard English" Proficiency – because the language of the Oakland resolution had been amended by linguists so that it no longer encoded the popular understanding of language, but the ideas of academic linguists.

The frustration for linguists was that still, even after the revision of the Oakland resolution that aligned it with academic ideas, nobody else was satisfied. Walt Wolfram reported that (1998: 110):

On numerous occasions during the recent Ebonics controversy, I was asked if I "believed in Ebonics," as if there were some article of religious belief attendant to the recognition of African American Vernacular English. In fact, one host on a radio talk show confronted my stance on the legitimacy of African American Vernacular English as a linguistic system with the comment, "You have to understand, professor, that I believe in a right and a wrong, a moral and an immoral, a correct and an incorrect, and Ebonics is simply incorrect English." Others have had similar experiences.

It was literally the case for Wolfram and other academic linguists that the popular belief in what was correct and *right* about language always trumped the academic idea of language systems. The fact that Wolfram took this as an affront to the honor of linguists and linguistics is shown by his comparison of the American Senate's use in hearings of a preacher and columnist as expert witnesses against two linguists, including Labov, to "two nonexperts arguing with two well-credentialed research physicists about the ramifications of a particular law of physics." As miraculous as the unanimity of usually contentious linguists in support of the legitimacy of African American English as a system, equally stunning (for Wolfram and other linguists, anyway) was the rejection by the American Senate and the public at large of such scientific views by respected academics. The lesson he wanted to offer from the Ebonics controversy, like Labov in 1972, was that "language professionals with an authentic understanding of the nature of language diversity have a responsibility and a challenge to educate other professionals, practitioners, and the general public about these issues" (1998: 118). In other words, he advises linguists to change the public mind by substitution of the ideas of academic linguists for the ones in which the public believes. For Wolfram and other linguists in the immediate situation of the Ebonics controversy, academic ideas about language were largely shut out; they simply could not compete with popular ideas, because the public just did not buy the terms and concepts that had meaning for linguists. Academic ideas became entangled in social movements and politics, either to be retasked for other purposes by Afrocentrists or simply rejected out of hand in favor of popular views. The revised Oakland resolution may have satisfied academic linguists, but it did not satisfy the public, whether in the decorum of the Senate or the rough humor of Internet postings (Scott 1998).

The great question for anyone interested in language, raised so clearly by the fallout from the Ebonics controversy, is just how we could have gotten ourselves into such a mess. How could academic ideas have become so disconnected from popular ideas? How could perfectly sensible people draw such different conclusions when presented with the same facts? In a society so firmly convinced of the value of science, what could cause such a rejection among the public of the science of language? What should we do when politics and social factors intrude on how we think about language? The Ebonics controversy demonstrates the ultimate failure of contemporary ideas from the academic marketplace to achieve much practical interaction with the popular understanding of language. The public is not buying what academic linguists have to sell. And it seems certain that we will continue to enact similar, if less spectacular failures of linguistic interaction and understanding every day, as long as the academic and popular marketplaces continue to stock a diverse inventory of radically conflicting ideas about language.

Such confidence by linguists in the ideas of the academic marketplace during the Ebonics affair, essentially comparable in view to the comments of Labov from 1972, was courageous and well-motivated – but no more realistic or practical at the turn of the century than it had been decades earlier. Is Labov's "understanding of the nature of language" or Wolfram's "authentic understanding of the nature of language diversity" to be taken as the generativist or the structuralist understanding? These American linguists are unlikely to be referring to any British NeoFirthian understanding, and so they leave at least one major academic idea out of account. More specifically with respect to African American English, should we be thinking of an Anglicist understanding or the creolist perspective? The academic marketplace of ideas about language, as it now stands, might better be characterized for its diversity of opinion than any shared understanding, and so any assertion of consensus or insistence on the truth of a single approach is unlikely on its face to be generally accepted. Another lesson of the Ebonics controversy, quite different from Wolfram's, might rather be that popular ideas about language cannot and should not be dismissed by linguists as mere "belief" in the name of linguistic science. We have seen that the Afrocentric view is apparently not within an "understanding of the nature of language," and neither is the doctrine of correctness in the popular marketplace. We have some idea of the motivation that drives advocates for Afrocentrism, and even if it does not conform to any understanding of academic linguists, still it must be reckoned with. The same is true of expressions in other circumstances of popular ideas about language, which have a long history with cultural roots. There is all the more reason to come to terms with the popular understanding when, unlike the situation among academic linguists, general consensus does appear to exist for the public, even while people maintain contradictory, mutually exclusive notions of language such as the conflict between correctness and rightness in the Ebonics controversy.

This book tries to build a model for language, call it "the linguistics of speech," which does not begin with academic linguistics where it is today. It starts with Saussure, and with the range of views about language available to him in about 1900. All of the points of view that he described then are still out there now, still competing for acceptance in either the popular marketplace or in the wider academic marketplace of the humanities and social sciences. The book will show that modern academic linguistics remains true to Saussure's choice for the "linguistics of linguistic structure." It will go on to develop the contemporary foundations for another possibility that Saussure also recognized, the "linguistics of speech." Finally, it will attempt to demonstrate the relationship between different approaches to linguistics, so that we can understand better how we could have gotten into such conflicts of ideas about language, and how we might reach a better accommodation of the ways in which different ideas of language can be valid and coexist with each other. That is, this book suggests how we might evaluate and decide between the choices available in the marketplace of ideas. This book is not about the one *right* idea of language, because there simply isn't just one. The book does not set forth yet another "authentic understanding" of language in which its readers are invited to believe. However, this book does argue that there are better ways to think about language than those resulting from our strange contemporary combination of overconfidence and self-contradiction in our academic and popular ideas about language. When the modern academic "understanding of the nature of language" embraced the idea of rule systems as its way to justify itself against other points of view, ironically it left itself open both to isolation from popular ideas leading to public rejection, and also to reapplication of its own principles to matters of correctness and rightness. The "linguistics of speech," on the other hand, will address, without subsuming either one, the two opposite poles of rule systems and natural variation in language.

2   Saussure

The confident belief of linguists such as William Labov and Walt Wolfram (cited in Chapter 1) that they share an "understanding of the nature of language" comes, according to Francis Dinneen, from foundational work in the field (1967: 18):

> the language of linguistics is set by linguists, and not all linguists share the same background and interests ... Despite the individual differences or interests, as well as different national traditions, all linguists share a basic understanding and agreement as the result of the influential work of scholars like de Saussure, Troubetzkoy, Martinet, and others among the European scholars, and Boas, Sapir, Bloomfield, Harris, Pike, Hockett, and Chomsky among the Americans.

This statement occurs at the beginning of a book still notable for its accounts of historical divisions in the history of ideas about language, such as etymology vs. prescriptive grammar vs. traditional grammar vs. linguistics, and its accounts of the varied contributions of half a dozen twentieth-century linguists, from Saussure to Bloomfield to Firth to Chomsky. As we have seen in Chapter 1, and as Dinneen's accounts themselves demonstrate, it may be difficult in practice to find the shared understanding between Bloomfieldian structuralism and Chomskyan generativism in America, and between either of those and the NeoFirthians in Britain. And yet Dinneen may have a point. He says of linguistics in the modern period, "which began with de Saussure," that "While there have been many developments that might appear to be revolutionary, there is more continuity of viewpoint and development than would appear on the surface" (1967: 404). C. F. Hockett cited four "revolutionary" figures in the history of modern linguistics, the first two of whom stimulated nineteenth-century comparative (Sir William Jones) and historical (Karl Verner) linguistics, while the last two (Saussure and Chomsky) dominated the last century (cited in Newmeyer 1996: 32). As R. H. Robins points out, Saussure was himself involved in the historical linguistics of the nineteenth century, and yet he was the "key figure in the change from nineteenth- to twentieth-century attitudes," i.e., "the rapid rise of descriptive linguistics, as opposed to historical linguistics" (1979: 199). Within the twentieth century, Frederick Newmeyer cites Saussure's "celebrated dichotomy between *langue* and *parole*" as the "roots" of Chomsky's *competence* and *performance*, while he also emphasizes Chomsky's development of the idea along the lines of "rule-governed creativity" (1996: 169–170). Saussure's ideas did mark a distinct change from the reliance on history of the nineteenth century. Whether one prefers to see continuity or revolutionary change in Chomsky's reformulation of *langue* and *parole* is the matter in some contention: one of the chapters in Newmeyer (1996) is entitled "Has there been a 'Chomskyan revolution' in linguistics?" If there is any shared understanding among contemporary linguists, Saussure's "celebrated dichotomy between *langue* and *parole*" must be its foundation.

This is not the place for a detailed exposition of Saussure's ideas of linguistics overall (for overviews in historical context, see Robins 1979: 199–201, Dinneen 1967: 192–212, Harris and Taylor 1989: 209–224; for his ideas, Harris 1987; for his influence, Harris 2002, Sanders 2004). The important task for this chapter is to discuss the decision that Saussure made about the direction that he wished linguistics to take. Saussure made a definite choice, which will repay our time to consider with some care. He wrote in reaction to the marketplace of ideas in his time and on the capacity for language study of his time. He chose to focus on linguistic structure as a result of that analysis of the available ideas and tools for study. As we shall see, structure was not his only choice, and the second task for this chapter is to describe what he had to say about the alternative he provided.

Saussure's *Course in General Linguistics* (first published in 1916, here described from the Harris translation, 1986) is perhaps the most famous book not written by its author. It was originally prepared by a group of his students from their own lecture notes. They received some assistance from Saussure's private papers, provided to them by Mme de Saussure, but these consisted of "only old jottings" which did not advance their work ((1916)1986: xvii). This publication history leaves room for doubt about what Saussure really thought. As Harris points out ((1916)1986: xii):

There is ample scope for doubt or scepticism on a variety of points. Indeed, it seems clear that in certain instances the editorial treatment of the original notes, far from clarifying what Saussure said, introduces an element of uncertainty as to the correct interpretation. Even the much quoted final sentence of the *Cours* [i.e., "From the excursions made above into regions bordering upon linguistics, there emerges a negative lesson, but one which is all the more interesting in that it supports the fundamental thesis of this course: *the only true object of study in linguistics is the language, considered in itself and for its own sake*" ((1916)1986: 230)] turns out to be an editorial pronouncement for which there is no specific textual authority in the manuscripts.

Still, as Harris also points out (p. xiii):

One comes back in the end to the fact that, whatever its imperfections, this publication was the authoritative text of Saussurian structuralism for a whole generation of scholars, and the instrument through which an entirely new approach to linguistic analysis was established. Thereby it acquires in its own right – "mistakes" and all – a place in the history of modern thought which cannot retrospectively be denied to it.

The book, then, even if not in the authentic voice of its author, greatly influenced linguistics in the twentieth century. That said, part of the attraction of the book comes from its origins: Saussure does seem to speak through it, as if in a series of course lectures. The *Course* does not try to present copious amounts of data in support of its points, but rather the sort of illustrations and examples that good teachers offer in the classroom. His arguments are attractively sketched as appropriate for a lecture, rather than provided with minutely reasoned proofs more appropriate to a written treatise. Along with his translation, Harris provides editorial notes on inconsistencies in terminology (surely for the purpose of validating the accuracy of the translation; see Harris (1987) for a more collected, cohesive commentary on these points), and these inconsistencies, too, indicate the nature of the work. What we can expect, then, from Saussure's *Course*, is more an assertion of direction than a rigorous demonstration of every nuance in a theoretical position. In what follows, then, I will sometimes provide some supplementary information to clarify a point, and in the main will attempt to discuss Saussure's circumstances and decisions at the same level of discourse in which he presented them.

Saussure's marketplace of ideas about language

Saussure introduced his course with "A Brief Survey of the History of Linguistics," in which he described three precursors in the history of linguistics, leading up to the NeoGrammarians and to his own work. The first was "grammar" ((1916) 1986: 1):

This discipline, first instituted by the Greeks and continued mainly by the French, is based on logic. It offers no scientific or objective approach to a language as such. Grammar aims solely at providing rules which distinguish between correct and incorrect forms. It is a prescriptive discipline, far removed from any concern with impartial observation, and its outlook is inevitably a narrow one.

This short paragraph requires a bit of unpacking. "Traditional grammar," as Saussure later calls it, is "concerned with the description of linguistic states," and not at all with any historical development in a language. It fails to be scientific because (p. 82):

Traditional grammar pays no attention to whole areas of linguistic structure, such as word formation. It is normative grammar, concerned with laying down rules instead of observing facts. It makes no attempt at syntheses. Often, it even fails to distinguish between the written word and the spoken word.

The implication here is that scientific observation is systematic and comprehensive, and traditional grammarians leave too much out of account in their attempt selectively to lay down rules. As Saussure later remarks (p. 6), "In each case due account must be taken not only of what is considered linguistically correct and 'elegant,' but of all forms of expression." The reference to "the French" in this passage must be to the Académie Française, which traditionally (since the seventeenth century) has attempted public regulation of the French language. The Académie Française has concerned itself not with spoken French throughout the country, but with what Saussure calls elsewhere the "literary language," which in France is descended from the French of Paris (although not identical with what one might hear in the streets of Paris, especially with the growth and increasing diversity of the population of the capital city). Thus what the Académie Française calls "French" comes not from observation of the facts of what French people do write, but instead prescribes what the French ought to write.

The reference to "the Greeks" and to "logic" is more complex. Language study in the West began with the Greeks (see Dinneen 1967: 70–124). Aristotle particularly stands out because he "dealt more consciously and extensively with language facts" (p. 79), but he did so in order to develop what we have come to know as "logic." His treatises called *Categories* and *On Interpretation* discuss kinds of words and how they can be assembled into propositions (sentences, with subjects and predicates); together with his *Prior Analytics*, which treats the syllogism, these works came to be known as the *Organon*, which Dinneen called "a cornerstone of education" (p. 84) in the Western tradition. Grammar and logic were linked for Aristotle (p. 87):

grammatical distinctions … are not explicitly grammatical as opposed to logical in Aristotle's works, since he did not know of this distinction. The purpose he had in mind was logical, but the definitions he gives of the forms he uses in his logic, as well as the examples he uses, justify our considering these distinctions as grammatical.

Moreover, this linkage continued in the Western educational tradition in the standard curriculum from late antiquity through the Renaissance. The educational plan of Boethius (b. 470 AD; Dinneen 1967: 127) proposed study first of the Trivium (grammar, rhetoric, and logic), to be followed by the Quadrivium (arithmetic, geometry, astronomy, music). Literally for a thousand years, educated Westerners studied Latin in the grammars of Donatus (fourth century AD) and Priscian (sixth century AD) so that they could proceed to the study of rhetoric and logic. Basic study of language remained linked to logic, and oftentimes elementary study of language and logic had to suffice when students never made it as far as the subjects of the Quadrivium (a conclusion we must reach when so vastly many more period documents concern the Trivium than the Quadrivium). It should come as no surprise, then, that grammar and logic have remained linked for many teachers in Western educational institutions. As Dinneen remarks (p. 71), "The terminology of traditional grammar, inherited from the Greeks, comprises the most widespread, best understood, and most generally applied grammatical distinctions in the world." We no longer teach language arts in elementary and secondary schools with Donatus and Priscian, but their example and their linkage with logic was carried over to the teaching of Western vernacular languages in the sixteenth, seventeenth, and eighteenth centuries. In France, this transition was accompanied by the creation of the Académie Française; in England and other countries in which an academy was not created, self-appointed arbiters of what was "correct" provided the necessary prescriptive rules (compare Labov's comments cited above that teachers correct grammar "under the impression that they were teaching logic" (1972: 225)). Thus, as Saussure said, traditional grammar, from its origins among the Greeks, came to be linked with logic and to be characterized by prescription. It remains the primary mode of language instruction in our elementary and secondary schools, and it has been accepted by the public as one of their central beliefs about language.

The second of Saussure's precursors was philology ((1916) 1986: 1):

Philology seeks primarily to establish, interpret and comment upon texts. This main preoccupation leads to a concern with literary history, customs, institutions, etc. In all these areas, philology applies its own method, which is that of criticism. Insofar as it touches upon linguistic questions, these arise principally in the comparison of texts of different periods, in establishing the language characteristic of each writer, and in deciphering and interpreting inscriptions couched in some archaic or problematic language ... But in this field philological criticism has one failing: it is too slavishly subservient to the written language, and so neglects the living language.

Saussure goes on to say that philology is mainly concerned with Greek and Roman antiquity, and in his day that was still largely the case as it was practiced in university Classics departments (or "Greats" at Oxford). The discipline of philology can trace its roots to the early Italian printers, who were trying to acquire and print the best texts of the Greek and Roman classics, greatly in demand during the Renaissance. Texts were preserved by highly inexact means through the Middle Ages, as scribes copied manuscripts by hand. Errors unavoidably crept in. Not all old texts were copied, or were not completely copied. For example, Varro's *De Lingua Latina*, an important classical source for linguists, survives in only six of its original twenty-five books (Dinneen 1967: 107). When texts were copied at different locations, separate manuscript traditions began, each tradition accumulating its own errors with each successive copy. Over long periods of time, the fact that the contemporary language of the scribe no longer matched the language of the author, or the imperfect learning by the scribe of the author's language, created additional problems for precise copies: scribes inadvertently or intentionally substituted their own linguistic forms for those of the text, and sometimes recast passages that they did not understand. Finally, the tribulations and displacements of life between the classical period and the invention of printing in Europe made the history, even the survival, of any manuscript or copy uncertain at best. What Saussure calls "criticism" consisted of the comparison and evaluation of discrete words or passages between different manuscripts, or of comparison and evaluation of the histories of the manuscripts. Conditions of transmission were thus important considerations, as were aspects of language change, for fifteenth- and sixteenth-century Venetian printers who were faced with a choice between multiple manuscripts, or with variant readings in passages in manuscripts. Perhaps riskiest of all for printers was a unique manuscript, whose errors thus could not be corrected by comparison with other witnesses, and which, while it might have unique value, might not even be a genuine work by the classical author to whom it was attributed. Early printers across Europe faced these problems, not only for the status of texts but also the status of their contents, as early printed editions of medieval Latin and vernacular works joined editions of the classics. The preface of William Caxton's edition of the *Morte Darthur*, for example, discusses his thinking about how to treat King Arthur as a historical figure (see Kretzschmar 1992c). Printers and their successors as text editors, sometimes private scholars but with the passage of time often faculty members in universities, developed elaborate methods for collation and evalua- tion of manuscript texts, and for evaluation of manuscript histories and potential authorship in the context of literary history, customs, and institutions. Over time the profit motive of the printers was replaced by a more academic search for the most reliable exemplar of a text in the manuscript tradition.

Today, textual editing is still a valuable pursuit in university departments, not only of Classics but of all modern languages. In a great monument to philology, John Manly and Edith Rickert, who had earlier served as wartime cryptogra- phers, published *The Text of the Canterbury Tales* (1940) in no fewer than eight large volumes, all of which were required to accommodate the extensive manu- script history of that work. The Early English Text Society, still in existence today, publishes editions of more obscure medieval writings. Studies of the printing variants of Dickens or Hardy novels illustrate philological work on more modern texts. However, as those modern-language departments grew during the twentieth century, especially following World War II, the study of literary history, customs, and institutions was liberated from its earlier focus on textual criticism, so that literary criticism has now taken pride of place from philology. "Style," for instance, is now generally considered first to be a literary property of an author's writing, and only secondarily to be a philological property that can help to identify a problematic text. "Criticism" thus means something different today than it did for Saussure, something even further removed from linguistics. It is something of an irony that criticism is frequently paired with traditional grammar in contemporary modern-language departments, whether for second-language or for native-language teaching. Modern-language faculty who are the inheritors of the mantle of philology have thus in many cases replaced serious attention to the actual language of manuscripts with a preoccupation with the normative grammar of what Saussure called the literary language. The consequence for many modern-language departments, like my own English Department, is no less than a three-way split in the way that its members deal with language: prescriptive grammar is taught in the First-Year Composition program and in a separate upper-division course, and it is monitored by the literary faculty in the writing that they assign; other faculty, typically medievalists, teach History of the English Language and still cover in their medieval literature courses what Saussure would have called "philology"; at the same time, a linguist on the English faculty teaches generative syntax. Such complexity only adds more layers to the competition between approaches that Saussure wanted to highlight.

Saussure's third precursor was the invention of the comparative method ((1916) 1986: 2):

The third period began when it was discovered that languages could be compared with one another. That discovery ushered in comparative philology, or "comparative grammar." In 1816, in a work entitled *The Sanskrit Conjugation System*, Franz Bopp studied the connexions between Sanskrit, Germanic, Greek, Latin, etc. … Although Bopp cannot be credited with having discovered the relationship between Sanskrit and various languages of Europe and Asia, he did see that connexions between related languages could furnish the data for an autonomous science. What was new was the elucidation of one language by reference to a related language, explaining the forms of one by appeal to the forms of the other.

The discovery of relationships between languages (credit Sir William Jones instead of Bopp, per Charles Hockett cited above), especially when the comparisons could be made systematically and comprehensively, took the first step towards modern linguistics as a science. Saussure goes on to say that the comparatists did not actually succeed in founding a scientific linguistics (p. 3), because they did not yet have a sufficient sense of the history of languages. Yet it is important to realize what "bizarre ways of thinking about language" (as Saussure put it, p. 4) their contemporaries could entertain. For example, Umberto Eco cites in *Serendipities: Language and Lunacy* (1998: 104), in a chapter called "The Linguistics of Joseph de Maistre" based on de Maistre's 1821 discussion of the nature of languages, a passage about Latin word formation:

From these three words, *CAro DAta VERmibus* they have formed the word *CA-DA-VER*, "meat abandoned to the worms." From two other words, *MAgis* and *voLO*, they have made *MALO* and *NOLO*, two splendid verbs that every language, Greek included, can envy Latin.

Such a passage is not "lunacy" but merely etymology, as it had been practiced for hundreds of years, for instance by the medieval encyclopedist Isidore of Seville, from whom Eco suggests that de Maistre borrowed this passage. De Maistre further suggests that French uses the same system of word formation (Eco 1998: 104–105):

The French have not totally ignored this system. For example, to give a name to those who were our ancestors, they formed the word *ANCETRE*, joining part of the word *ANCien* [old, ancient] with the verb *ETRE* [to be], just as they formed the term *BEFFROI* [alarm bell], joining *Bel* [beautiful] and *EFFROI* [fright].

Etymologies of a "fanciful" character are similarly to be found in Noah Webster's early-nineteenth-century American dictionary, his *American Dictionary of the English Language* (1828). Thomas Pyles has remarked that (1952: 116–117):

As an etymologist Webster was something less than adequate ... he chose to ignore (perhaps because of an inability to read German, one of those twenty-three languages he is reported to have "mastered") the really significant work which had been done in linguistics in his day, preferring the tower of Babel explanation of the origin of individual tongues to the scientific methods of the Indo-Europeanists ... subsequent editors have without comment excised by the basketful Webster's etymological "boners." ... his etymologies are frequently worse than worthless.

In the early-nineteenth-century marketplace of ideas about language, it would have been difficult to select the fruit from the chaff without a crystal ball (yes, mysticism was part of mix there, too, as indicated by other passages reported by Eco from de Maistre) to tell what direction linguistic science would take. Webster's name, after all, became so famous and is still so identified with dictionaries that nearly all American English trade dictionaries use it in their titles: who would have bet against *him*?

The culmination of Saussure's "brief history," no longer a precursor but his own contemporary linguistics, described the NeoGrammarians ((1916) 1986: 5):

The achievement of the NeoGrammarians was to place all the results of comparative philology in a historical sequence. The NeoGrammarians no longer looked upon a language as an organism developing of its own accord, but saw it as a product of the collective mind of a linguistic community. At the same time, there emerged a realisation of the errors and inadequacies of the concepts associated with philology and comparative grammar.

Saussure had studied in Leipzig as a fellow student with Brugman and Leskien, two prominent members of the NeoGrammarian movement, so he had cause to know the movement well. The NeoGrammarians added history to the comparative method, and made the study of language change the center of linguistics. It asserted a mechanical model of exceptionless sound change within a language community, and in so doing disposed of erratic reasoning, mysticism, and other such faults in favor of the systematic, comprehensive methods of science. Still, the NeoGrammarians merely set the stage for Saussure, because "it cannot be said that they shed light upon the fundamental problems of general linguistics" (p. 5). And they were not alone in the marketplace of ideas. Each of the "precursors" was still there, still active. Traditional grammar was present in the Académie Française, in the schools, and in the popular view. Philology was present in the universities, indeed enjoying an expansion as medieval manuscripts in the modern languages more and more came under study. Comparative philology had been incorporated as a component of the NeoGrammarian program, and before long comparisons between languages absent any historical component would re-emerge, for new purposes, as linguistic typology (cf. the statement cited in Chapter 1 of the LSA committee for Endangered Languages). Within this marketplace, however, Saussure recognized that linguistics per se had only emerged with the NeoGrammarians, and that other competing ideas about language and language study, while they might hold something of value for the linguist, were each too flawed, too incomplete to serve as a systematic and comprehensive science.

Once granted that linguistics could be scientific, Saussure also recognized that other "sciences" existed in close connection with it (p. 6):

Sometimes [other sciences] provide linguistics with data and sometimes linguistics provides them with data. The boundaries between linguistics and its neighboring sciences are not always clearly drawn. For example, linguistics must be carefully distinguished from ethnography and prehistory, both of them disciplines in which linguistic facts may be utilized as evidence. It must likewise be distinguished from anthropology, which studies mankind as a species; whereas language is a social phenomenon. But ought linguistics on that account be incorporated in sociology? What are the relations between linguistics and social psychology?

Saussure believed that the science of physiology was clearly distinct from linguistics, but some may be less sure of that today given the rise of experimental and acoustical phonetics. The problem, then, is not simply how to make linguistics into a science, but how to validate it in competition with other sciences whose means or ends overlap with those of linguistics. The stakes are high. Saussure asks "of what use is linguistics?", and answers that all academic fields that deal with texts need it, and that language is of such importance for culture in general that both individuals and societies require knowledge of it. He says (p. 7):

For the study of language to remain solely the business of a handful of specialists would be a quite unacceptable state of affairs. In practice, the study of language is in some degree or other the concern of everyone. But a paradoxical consequence of this general interest is that no other subject has fostered more absurd notions, more prejudices, more illusions, or more fantasies. From a psychological point of view, these errors are of interest in themselves. But it is the primary task of the linguist to denounce them, and to eradicate them as completely as possible.

These lines motivate the definition of linguistics as its own science in the market-place of competing ideas, and at the same time they cannot fail to remind the reader of the Ebonics affair in Chapter 1. Nearly a century after Saussure, a handful of specialists tried to make a stand against prejudices and what they believed to be absurd notions, to denounce them and to try to eradicate them. We know the result. What better reason could there be to examine once more the decisions that Saussure made in the context of his own marketplace of ideas, decisions which directed linguistics down the path that it has taken for the last century?

The aims of linguistics and linguistic structure

Saussure's "aims of linguistics" establish three goals:
(a) to describe all known languages and record their history. This involves tracing the history of language families and, as far as possible, reconstruct-ing the parent languages of each family;
(b) to determine the forces operating permanently and universally in all lan-guages, and to formulate general laws which account for all particular linguistic phenomena historically attested;
(c) to delimit and define linguistics itself.

The first aim encompasses the predominantly historical NeoGrammarian lin-guistics of his day. The second aim refers to the "fundamental problems of general linguistics" that the NeoGrammarians, according to Saussure, had not yet resolved. The third aim, and the one of most interest here, explicitly takes on the definition of linguistics. Saussure recognized how expansive the study of language might be, and decided from the beginning that for linguistics to be a science, it must be a science of its own with specific definable limits. The first two aims encode assumptions, propositions accepted as given that make it possible to create the limits. First, there are such things as "languages," which at all points must exist embedded in historical relationships with other lan-guages. Second, there are "forces" at work in all languages that can be described with "general laws." The existence of objects called "languages" is thus a premise, not a matter in dispute for Saussure's linguistics.[1] The existence of general laws that account for what happens in languages is also a premise and not a matter of dispute. The fact of languages and of such general laws might be debatable in another science, but not in the model that Saussure has created for his linguistics.[2] A scientific model, like the models commonly used in

---

[1] See Chapter 5 for Firth's characterization of Saussure's reification of language in relation to the social theory of Durkheim.

[2] It is unclear whether Saussure might have recognized the idea of a *model* as it is now applied in the sciences. This sense of the term, as in a mathematical model, arose in English at the turn of the twentieth century (s.v., *Oxford English Dictionary*), just as Saussure was in his prime. He does

economics or meteorology (those most familiar to most people today), simply adopts a subject for study (like the economy or the weather) and lays out the variables that the analyst considers relevant to the subject (like wages and prices, or temperatures and atmospheric pressures). Each variable will be subject to operational factors (wages and prices can "spiral"; differences in atmospheric pressure cause air movement, wind). Saussure's aims of linguistics lay out language as variables, for which the passage of time, history, will be one operational factor, and within which other operational factors, general laws, may be distinguished. In practice, models must be carefully adjusted, whether to define the variables themselves, or to weight variables for their relative impor-tance, or to add or subtract variables in the model. Given Saussure's premises, the assumption of the existence of languages and of general linguistic laws, we should expect that the delimitation and definition of his model of linguistics will adjust and weight the variables in his model, consistent with his premises.

Even from discussion just of the aims set forth by Saussure, we can see more clearly what motivates the division between the American structuralists and generativists on one hand, and the British NeoFirthians on the other, as described in Chapter 1. The structuralists and generativists accept languages and laws as premises, and the NeoFirthians do not make that commitment. This difference between the approaches makes for an essential incompatibility in their models for linguistics, no matter how many other terms or ideas they may share. Further, to the extent that Saussure's aims have come to be identified with the twentieth-century science of linguistics, some linguists may feel that NeoFirthian corpus linguistics is not linguistics at all – which is essentially what Chomsky expressed in the Andor (2004) interview cited in Chapter 1. And to the extent that the Saussurean model of linguistics is taken to represent science, in contrast to the unsystematic and incomprehensive modes of lan-guage study of its precursors, then NeoFirthian corpus linguistics might be considered by some linguists to be unscientific – which again is what Chomsky expressed in the Andor (2004) interview cited in Chapter 1. Chomsky is not wrong, provided that one accept the premises of the Saussurean model. But neither is Chomsky right, provided that one would be willing to dispute the premises, too, and not just the model made from them.

In fact, Saussure was careful, after establishing his aims, to work out the definition of "language" as an object of study. Linguistic phenomena can be considered from a number of viewpoints:

represent linguistic structure at one point with a formula (19): "1 + 1 + 1 + 1 ... = I (collective model)." His formula takes the generalized pattern of representation for modern scientific models, i.e. "$a + b + c + ... = R$," where a b c are variables and R is the result to be modeled. The notion of a scientific model is perfectly congenial to this discussion whether or not Saussure recognized the idea as we do today, because Saussure discusses what elements of language to include in linguistics, with what particular relations, just as we would do today in the creation of a model. I offer a formal model of this kind for speech in Chapter 8.

(a) oral articulation and auditory impressions of speech sounds
(b) the combination of speech sounds with an idea "to form another complex unit"
(c) the individual viewpoint vs. the social aspect of language
(d) the fact that "language at any given time involves an established system and an evolution. At any given time, it is an institution in the present and a product of the past … the connexion between the two is so close that it is hard to separate them … It is quite illusory to believe that where language is concerned the problem of origins is any different from the problem of permanent conditions. There is no way out of the circle." ((1916) 1986: 8–9)

Out of these considerations, "no one object of linguistic study emerges of its own accord." Thus the need for further decisions. The risk of trying to consider all of these aspects at once, according to Saussure, is to lose control of linguistics as a science, to "open the door" to competing sciences and to competing ideas about language study. The "muddle of disparate, unconnected things" that Saussure says would result from doing too much at once can again be usefully associated with the idea of a model. If each of these four aspects of language becomes a variable in a model, then the linguist is responsible for managing the relative weights and operational processes for each one. Such a model would require the linguist simultaneously to manage perceptual, cognitive, social, and historical information all at once, and all of these variables are admitted by Saussure to have relevance for language.

If linguistics were the only science in the marketplace, such a model might well have seemed more reasonable to him. However, linguistics in Saussure's day was the newcomer among the social and humanistic sciences and modes of study. Therefore, Saussure's approach was to control the variables in the model (p. 9):

One solution only, in our view, resolves these difficulties. *The linguist must take the study of linguistic structure as his primary concern, and relate all other manifestations of language to it.* Indeed, among so many dualities, linguistic structure seems to be the one thing that is independently definable and provides something our minds can satisfactorily grasp.

The resulting model weights the variable of linguistic structure as the most important, and subordinates other variables to it. Linguistic structure in Saussure's formulation exists outside of the individual speaker, as a "social product of our language faculty" and as "a body of necessary conventions adopted by society to enable members of society to use their language faculty" (pp. 9–10). The articulation and perception of speech sounds by individuals, merely personal associations of ideas with speech sounds, and all other aspects of the individual viewpoint must be subordinated to structure. The passage of time should not be ignored any more than the individual viewpoint, but history must give up the central position it had with the NeoGrammarians in order to be subordinated to structure in Saussure's model. Saussure's choice to weight linguistic structure so heavily in his model gave linguistics its own special place among the other sciences, and thus, in Saussure's view, allowed it to compete with the longer-established alternatives in the marketplace.

Saussure himself raises the question of whether his act to weight linguistic structure so heavily is actually a decision, or rather recognition of a "faculty endowed by nature" (p. 10). He first suggests that:

A language as a structured system ... is both a self-contained whole and a principle of classification. As soon as we give linguistic structure pride of place among the facts of language, we introduce a natural order into an aggregate which lends itself to no other classification.

The "natural order" is something that he has introduced, or imposed, "because language as such has no discernible unity." Lest this imposition of order be misunderstood, he replies in advance to an objection:

It might be objected to this principle of classification that our use of language depends on a faculty endowed by nature: whereas language systems are acquired and conventional, and so ought to be subordinated to – instead of being given priority over – our natural ability.

Saussure then provides three different arguments against ways in which language might be considered "natural" ('inborn,' or 'a property of species'), concluding (p. 11):

Finally, in support of giving linguistic structure pride of place in our study of language, there is this argument: that, whether natural or not, the faculty of articulating words is put to use only by means of the linguistic instrument created and provided by society. Therefore it is no absurdity to say that it is linguistic structure which gives language what unity it has.

In each of these statements Saussure makes clear that it is the linguist who gives linguistic structure "pride of place among the facts of language." The "natural order" for Saussure is the ordering of variables in a model, not the property of a "natural" language faculty. The preference for linguistic structure is not a given but instead a decision, a choice that both clarifies the relationship of language study to other modes of study and other sciences, and allows linguistics to be a science because it controls through subordination the other relevant variables in the model. Among all the possible choices for how to approach language study, Saussure's third aim of definition and delimitation was crucial.

Saussure summarized the benefits of his choice of linguistic structure under four arguments (pp. 14–15):
(a) "Amid the disparate mass of facts involved in language, it stands out as a well-defined entity."

(b) "A language system, as distinct from speech, is an object that may be studied independently ... A science which studies linguistic structure is not only able to dispense with other elements of language, but is possible only if those other elements are kept separate."
(c) "While language in general is heterogeneous, a language system is homogeneous in nature."
(d) "Linguistic structure is no less real than speech" [a repository of sound patterns, as opposed to the multitude of physical movements required for articulation in real speech as it occurs in real time].

Each of these benefits, all strong points, is portrayed as a contrast, as the result of a choice. The first point recognizes all of the facts involved with language, and promotes linguistic structure as "well-defined" instead of "disparate." The third point is reminiscent of Chomsky's "ideal speaker-listener, in a completely homogenous speech community" (1965: 3), while it also recognizes that "language in general" is inherently variable. The second point recognizes "speech" in contrast to "language system," and, as we have seen, does not so much dispose of elements of language related to speech as it isolates linguistic structure as a central fact to which the other elements are related. The last point also sets "speech" in contrast to linguistic structure, now to say that structure does not lack the reality of articulation. The choice of linguistic structure is not inevitable, not "natural" in the sense that it corresponds to an inborn faculty or property of species; it is the nucleus of an argument to create a science of linguistics, one based on a model with particular premises and with a definite arrangement of its variables.

The alternative to linguistic structure

The alternative to Saussure's decision to make a science of linguistics is to make a science of speech. Saussure entitles a chapter "Linguistics of Language Structure and Linguistics of Speech," in which he makes much more explicit the contrasts that he suggested in the summary of benefits for his heavy weighting for linguistic structure. He writes ((1916) 1986: 19):

The study of language thus comprises two parts. The essential part takes for its object the language itself, which is social in its essence and independent of the individual. This is a purely psychological study. The subsidiary part takes as its object of study the individual part of language, which means speech, including phonation. This is a psycho-physical study.

The two parts are "essential" and "subsidiary" by virtue of Saussure's model, but both parts are valid objects of language study. "Speech," according to Saussure, "is the sum total of what people say, and it comprises (a) individual combinations of words, depending on the will of the speakers, and (b) acts of phonation, which are also voluntary and are necessary for the execution of the speakers' combinations of words" (p. 19). To employ a term that later in the twentieth century Chomsky would come to oppose to linguistics, we can say that speech is kind of behavior, something that people do.[3] Their language behavior consists of the actual articulation, or phonation, of speech sounds and words, and also of the combination of words. Language behavior is a product of the will of individual speakers, a voluntary act. Speech therefore is "disparate," while linguistic structure constitutes a "well-defined entity," because at the very least speech requires consideration of phonation of words, combination of words, and the cognitive and psycho-social activity of speakers in the exercise of their volition. Accordingly, Saussure points out that "The activity of the speaker must be studied in a variety of disciplines" (p. 19) corresponding to each aspect of the speaker's behavior. The homogeneity of linguistic structure arises from seeing language as a "collective phenomenon," while "there is nothing collective about speech. Its manifestations are individual and ephemeral. It is no more than an aggregate of particular cases ... Language in its totality is unknowable, for it lacks homogeneity" (pp. 19–20). Finally, the reality of speech is epistemologically prior to the reality of linguistic structure (p. 19):

A language is necessary in order that speech should be intelligible and produce all its effects. But speech also is necessary in order that a language may be established. Historically, speech always takes precedence. How would we ever come to associate an idea with a verbal sound pattern, if we did not first of all grasp this association in an act of speech? Furthermore, it is by listening to others that we learn our native language. A language accumulates in our brain only as the result of countless experiences. Finally, it is speech which causes a language to evolve. The impressions received from listening to others modify our own linguistic habits.

Speech is not only indispensable for the establishment of linguistic structure, it also provides the mechanism for language acquisition and for language change. Saussure views speech, to the extent that it can be considered above the level of individual speakers, as a process in which experiences and impressions continuously modify both the speakers' linguistic habits and the collectivity of linguistic structure in which they participate.

Saussure concludes that (pp. 19–20):

For all these reasons, it would be impossible to consider language systems and speech from one and the same point of view ... That is the first parting of the ways that we come to when endeavoring to construct a theory of language. It is necessary to choose between two routes which cannot both be taken simultaneously. Each must be followed separately.

---

[3] "Language behavior" as discussed here and elsewhere in this volume is not the same thing as the stimulus–response model of the behaviorists, championed by B. F. Skinner and attacked by Chomsky (1959). Observation of what people say will take pride of place in this volume, but not any simple cause-and-effect, stimulus-and-response explanation for what people say.

It would be possible to keep the name *linguistics* for each of these two disciplines. We would then have a linguistics of speech. But it would be essential not to confuse the linguistics of speech with linguistics properly so called.

While Saussure did make his choice for the linguistics of linguistic structure, at the same time he not only admitted the possibility of an alternative linguistics of speech, he went a long way towards defining it. Indeed, recognition of the role of speech is inevitable: "Thus there is an interdependence between the language itself and speech. The former is at the same time the instrument and the product of the latter. But none of this compromises the absolute nature of the distinction between the two" (p. 19). *Langue* and *parole*, linguistic structure and speech, both present and objects of study, inextricably linked and absolutely to be distinguished. Saussure preferred the former, but he defended a science of *parole*, the linguistics of speech, as a valid path to follow, so long as we do not confuse it with the linguistics of linguistic structure.

Such a confusion is at the heart of the rejection of contemporary linguistics by the public. The popular view of language is above all about behavior: social evaluation of people's language, whether the language is Ebonics or a regional dialect or the spelling of a teenage T-shirt maker, means taking their language behavior as a sign of their mental (or moral or cultural) fitness. As the local newspaper said:

having an argument or an opinion taken seriously requires the ability to clearly express that argument. The first thing that one wonders when seeing the T-shirt with the misspelling is whether the person wearing it has that ability.

"Clear expression," of course, is here equated with the notion of correctness, rather than with the *right* language for the community. People also evaluate the rightness of community language, and take someone's language behavior as a sign of their status with respect to the community, as an insider or outsider, as someone in the know or somebody without a clue. Non-linguists are not generally interested in the relationships of elements within any language system, just in those details (as in school lists of grammatical faults) which allow the evaluation of language behavior. The Ebonics affair carries the same message: the actual language and education of the students in Oakland got lost in the social evaluation of the language behavior advocated by the Oakland board. Ebonics "jokes" were created by those who used purported characteristics of Ebonics to get at behavior, particularly to illustrate through language the contrasts thought to exist between the characteristic behavior of different groups. Assertion by linguists of their "understanding of the nature of language" simply does not address language behavior as the public sees it. Saussure tells us that "It is necessary to choose between two routes which cannot both be taken simultaneously," and perhaps it should be no cause for wonder that contemporary linguistics has had but little effect on a public, including an educational system still committed to prescriptive grammar, that consistently takes the other route in its constant attention to language behavior. The current problematic situation in which linguists and the public talk past each other, like ships in the night on their different routes, just proves that Saussure was right.

Foundations of the linguistics of speech

Saussure did not lecture about the linguistics of speech (as Harris points out in an editorial note, (1916) 1986: 141–142). He did, however, comment about matters concerning speech throughout his *Course*. Very early on as part of his definitional argument he wrote that, in order to get at the role of linguistic structure within language, "we must consider the individual act of speech and trace what takes place in the speech circuit" (p. 11). Saussure's sketch of the "speech circuit" is very concrete (p. 12):

Let us suppose that a given concept triggers in the brain a corresponding sound pattern. This is an entirely *psychological* phenomenon, followed in turn by a *physiological* process: the brain transmits to the organs of phonation an impulse corresponding to the pattern. Then sound waves are sent from *A*'s mouth to *B*'s ear: a purely *physical* process. Next, the circuit continues in *B* in the opposite order: from ear to brain, the physiological transmission of the sound pattern; in the brain, the psychological association of this pattern with the corresponding concept.

The sketch "makes no claim to be complete," and it may not correspond exactly to contemporary descriptions in neuroscience, but it does separate the physical component of speech from the physiological and psychological components, as we would today separate acoustical phonetics from neuroscience. In Saussure's formulation, each of these contemporary fields would be a part of the linguistics of speech, not of the linguistics of linguistic structure. Each one focuses on the "individual act" of speech and not on the social collectivity needed for the system of a language (p. 13):

the psychological part of the circuit is not involved in its entirety [any more than the physical side of the circuit]. The executive side of it plays no part, for execution is never carried out by the collectivity: it is always individual, and the individual is always master of it. This is what we shall designate as *speech*.

The system of language is established by "all the individuals linguistically linked" (p. 13):

if we could collect the totality of word patterns stored in all those individuals, we should have the social bond which constitutes their language. It is a fund accumulated by the members of the community through the practice of speech.

Part of the complexity of speech, then, comes from the integration of articulatory, perceptual, physiological, and cognitive factors by individuals.

Saussure located additional complexity for speech in the contrast between "internal" and "external" linguistics. Internal linguistics has to do with linguistic structure as a system. The conventional term "external linguistics" encompasses ethnology, political history, and institutions such as churches and schools. A literary language, Saussure says, "is inseparable from political history" (p. 22), and further:

The linguist must also examine the reciprocal relations between the language of books and the language of colloquial speech. Eventually, every literary language, as a product of culture, becomes cut off from the spoken word, which is a language's natural sphere of existence.

He cites "the influence of salons, of the court, and of academies" (p. 22) upon the literary language, perhaps a manner of expressing the effect of external factors like cultural institutions on any language that shows its connection to nineteenth-century France. Besides the standard literary language, Saussure particularly mentions areal factors (p. 22):

Finally, everything which relates to the geographical extension of languages and to their fragmentation into dialects concerns external linguistics. It is on this point, doubtless, that the distinction between external linguistics and internal linguistics appears most paradoxical. For every language in existence has its own geographical area. None the less, in fact geography has nothing to do with the internal structure of the language.

Geography has nothing to do with linguistic structure, but everything to do with speech. Speech must necessarily consider the different modes of external linguistics, whether intellectual or organizational aspects of human society such as anthropology, politics, and culture, or existential dimensions of human society like space (geography) and time (history). Saussure admits that "the study of external linguistic phenomena can teach linguists a great deal" (p. 22), but in the end these factors must be separate from linguistic structure, for "external linguistics can accumulate detail after detail, without ever being forced to conform to the constraints of a system." External linguistics adds another layer of complexity to speech, on top of the behavior of individuals within and according to the speech circuit. It addresses social aspects and dimensions of language which, while they are relevant, do not constrain the social collectivity that establishes a language system.

Saussure devoted an entire section of his *Course* to "Geographical Linguistics," now certainly less read than his discussion of linguistic structure because (along with a following section on "Questions of Retrospective Linguistics") it is one of two "excursions ... into regions bordering upon linguistics" (p. 230). These excursions, Saussure concluded in the final sentence of the *Course*, provide "a negative lesson, but one which is all the more interesting in that it supports the fundamental thesis of this course: *the only true object of study in linguistics is the language, considered in itself and for its own sake.*" And yet

Saussure did spend four chapters on the geographical aspect of external linguistics, and five more chapters on issues of retrospective linguistics (i.e., linguistic reconstruction, particularly involving language types and families). Linguistic structure can be studied only as the social collectivity that exists in one place and at one time. The role of the last two sections, which constitute commentary on aspects of speech, is to help to show the boundaries of language systems.

These two concluding sections on geography and retrospection are related because perception of the diversity between the speech of two different places leads to comparison of the languages, which may well turn out to have a historical, familial relationship. Saussure begins with the observation that (p. 189):

> The first thing that strikes one in studying languages is their diversity, the differences as between one country and another, or even one district and another. Whereas divergences over time often do not come to the notice of the observer, territorial differences leap immediately to the eye. Even savages grasp them, through contact with other tribes speaking other languages. It is even by means of such comparisons that a people becomes aware of its own language.

With regard to "savages," no doubt Saussure was here thinking of American tourists in Paris and Geneva ("race" or "ethnicity" for Saussure consisted of the difference between the Germanic peoples and the Celtic or Italic peoples, pp. 221–225; contemporary sensitivities to terms like *savage, race*, and *ethnicity* arose after the *Course*). The central fact of this diversity, of language variation, characterizes speech in the same way that system is taken to characterize linguistic structure; these are the two poles between which all ideas of language must be located. Saussure notes that "geographical diversity was the first observation ever made in linguistics, and determined the initial form taken by scientific research into linguistic matters, even by the Greeks" (p. 190). The linguistics of speech thus, somewhat ironically for the *Course*, predates the linguistics of linguistic structure. The perception of difference leads directly to comparison (p. 190):

> After recognizing that two languages differ, one is instinctively led to discover analogies between them. This is a natural tendency among language-users. Country people like to compare their own local speech with that of a neighbouring village. People who know several languages notice features they have in common ... Scientific observation of these analogies allows us to state in certain cases that two or more languages are related: that is to say, they have a common origin.

Increasing sophistication of comparison leads from geography to history. For Saussure's contemporary NeoGrammarian linguistics, such historical comparison was the primary focus (and subject of the preceding section in the *Course*). Comparison between unrelated languages may also be profitable, as it could lead to identification of "constant factors" (p. 191) which today we would call

universals. Even scientific observation, however, will not reveal absolute differences between related languages, because such differences are a matter of
degree: "Languages differing only slightly are called *dialects*: but this term is
not to be given a rigorously exact interpretation. As we shall see, between
dialects and languages there is a difference of quantity, not of nature" (p. 191).
Even in the same place, more than one language may be spoken and coexist,
usually because of external linguistic factors such as invasion or colonization or
the wandering of a people (pp. 192–193). The complexity of geographical
diversity may also often be increased by the origin or imposition of a literary
language, as "linguistic unity may disintegrate when a spoken language under-
goes the influence of a literary language" (pp. 193–195). Thus the diversity of
language is natural, and it immediately leads to comparisons that may implicate
linguistic history. As Saussure points out (p. 197):

One forgets the time factor, because it is less concrete than distance: but in fact it is time
on which linguistic differentiation depends. Geographical diversity has to be translated
into temporal diversity.

The diversity of language, however, is highly complex because social aspects of
external linguistics, like politics and culture, combine to distort the result of
interaction of the dimensions of time and space. The linguistics of speech must
deal with time and space as essential aspects of the real establishment and
distribution of linguistic features, and must also recognize external factors
related to human organizational and cultural behavior.

Saussure insists that geographical diversity is "the natural state of affairs"
(p. 194):[4]

We shall set aside everything that obscures a clear view of natural geographical diversity,
in order to consider the basic phenomenon unalloyed by any importation of foreign
languages or formation of a literary language. This schematic simplification may seem to
distort reality; but the natural state of affairs must first be studied in its own right.

In this section of the *Course*, Saussure is talking about external linguistics and
speech, not about linguistic structure, and so when he seeks "the basic phenomenon" for diverse dialects and languages, he is not talking about the social
collectivity that emerges from a speech community in the linguistics of linguistic structure. Many, even most people today accept a traditional definition that
"dialects," in the words of Nelson Francis (1983: 1), "are varieties of a language
used by groups smaller than the total community of speakers of the language."

---

[4] This section is based on Kretzschmar (1998b): "Analytical Procedure and Three Technical Types
of Dialect," in M. Montgomery and T. Nunnally, eds. *From the Gulf States and Beyond: The
Legacy of Lee Pederson and LAGS*, 1998, 167–85. With the kind permission of the University of
Alabama Press, Tuscaloosa.

That is, modern linguists attempt to apply the notion of a speech community from the linguistics of linguistic structure, and assert that a dialect represents the collectivity of a smaller group of speakers. To do so crosses over between Saussure's two distinct paths for linguistics. Perceptual and political factors contribute to such a belief in the reality of discrete dialects: exclusive groups of speakers kept separate from one another by geographical (e.g., rivers, mountains, oceans), social (e.g. age, sex, race), or political (e.g., national, ethnic) boundaries. Saussure admitted the attractions of this conception of dialect but had to disagree with it because of the evidence (p. 200):

The usual conception of dialects nowadays is quite different. They are envisaged as clearly defined linguistic types, determinate in all respects, and occupying areas on a map which are contiguous and distinct … But natural dialect changes give a quite different result. As soon as linguistics began to study each individual feature and establish its geographical distribution, the old notion had to be replaced by a new one: there are no natural dialects, but only natural dialect features. Or – which comes to the same thing – there are as many dialects as there are places.

The notion of natural dialects is thus in principle incompatible with the notion of a region. The linguist is faced with a choice. One possibility is to define a dialect by the totality of its features. In this case, one must concentrate on a single locality at a given point on the map. As soon as one moves from this locality, one will no longer be dealing with exactly the same set of dialect features. The other possibility is to define a dialect on the basis of just one feature. In this case, naturally, there will be an area, corresponding to the geographical extension of the feature selected. But it is hardly necessary to point out that this latter procedure is an artificial one, and the boundaries thus established correspond to no dialectal reality.

Saussure makes the point here that it is not so easy to find groups of speakers so naturally separate as we might wish them to be. Instead, he asserts, we must rely on procedure, the investigator's decision either to define a dialect by nominating a place, or to define a dialect according to the area of use of a linguistic feature.

Saussure's evidence for these remarks came from the linguistic atlases then being produced by Georg Wenker (Wenker and Wrede 1895) and Jules Gilliéron (1902–10). The field of dialectology was inaugurated by Wenker in response to the NeoGrammarian demand for systematic treatment of linguistic facts on the basis of the evidence. As Osthoff and Brugmann wrote:

Only that comparative linguist who forsakes the hypothesis-laden atmosphere of the workshop in which Indogermanic root-forms are forged, and comes out into the clear light of tangible present-day actuality in order to obtain from this source information which vague theory cannot ever afford him, can arrive at a correct presentation of the life and the transformations of linguistic forms. (1878; quoted in Robins 1979: 184–185)

Wenker was the first to conduct a dialect survey on the "tangible present-day actuality" of the German language, and thus scientifically and systematically to gather facts about dialects. Survey research thus began as the hallmark of dialectology because of NeoGrammarian positivism. And yet Wenker's expect-ations were not immediately rewarded. Walther Mitzka, the third director of the project initiated by Wenker, described the early results:

Im philologischen Streit um die Ausnahmslosigkeit der Lautgesetze sollten diese Zeugnisse der Mundarten rings um Düsseldorf den geographischen Beweis für die Anhänger dieser Lehre erbringen. Das Ergebnis führte zur gegenteiligen Meinung. 1885 berichtet er vor der Philologenversammlung in Gießen: "Ich lebte in der schönen und beruhigenden Überzeugung, diese Characteristika müßten ganz oder nahezu ganz zusammengehen. Jene Voraussetzung erwies sich bald genug als eine durchaus irrige, die Grenzen der vermeintlichen Characteristika liefen eigensinnig ihre eigenen Wege und kreutzen sich oft genug." (Mitzka 1943: 9)
[As regards the philological controversy about the exceptionlessness of sound laws, the evidence of dialect around Düsseldorf should have brought proof for the adherents of this teaching. The results supported the contrary view. [Wenker] reported in 1885 before the Giessen conference of philologists that, "I lived in the fair and calming conviction that these [linguistic] features must completely or nearly completely go together. That assumption turned out soon enough to be utterly mistaken: the boundaries of the contemplated features stubbornly took their own way and often crossed each other."]

The NeoGrammarians recovered soon enough from this shock, to find ways to accommodate contrary evidence from speech and preserve their notion of mechanical systems (see Kretzschmar 2002a, and Knoop, Putschke, and Wiegand 1982 on the Marburg School). Such NeoGrammarian arguments sup-port the view that many modern dialectologists and linguists still hold, as cited above from Nelson Francis. On the other hand, Gilliéron wrote, with particular application to French but clearly in opposition to the NeoGrammarians, that:

La réflexion et les faits s'accordent pour détruire cette fausse unité linguistique dénommé patois, cette conception d'une commune ou même d'un groupe qui serait resté le dépositaire fidèle d'un patrimonie latin … Force nous est donc de repousser le patois comme base d'opération scientifique. Aucune recherche de dialectologie ne partira de cette unité artificielle, impure and suspecte: et à l'étude du patois nous opposerons l'étude du *mot*. (emphasis original, Gilliéron and Mongin 1905: 27)
[Both reflection and the facts come together to destroy the false linguistic unity called "patois," this notion of a community or even of a group which remains the faithful recipient of an inheritance from Latin … Accordingly we must reject "patois" as the basis for any scientific study. No inquiry of dialectology will take for its starting point this artificial unity, impure and suspect; but against the study of "patois" we will set the study of the *word*.]

Gilliéron would reject even the notion of the "patois," a term which in French usually denoted the language of specific places instead of whole regions, in order to focus on etymology. Hans Goebl has written extensively (e.g., 1982, 1990, 2003) on the debate between these characteristically French and NeoGrammarian approaches, which he has labeled "typophobia" (for Gaston

Paris and Paul Meyer) and "typophilia" (for Graziadio Ascoli), respectively (see also Kretzschmar 1995, 2006b). Saussure, while he cites Wenker and Gilliéron, evidently does not align himself with either of these schools of thought, but instead uses their evidence to concentrate on the underlying dimension of geography as it affects particular features in the linguistics of speech.

Linguistic features in speech and structure

When Saussure talks about "features," he is referring to his earlier discussion of "concrete entities" and "linguistic value" ((1916) 1986: 101–120). "Linguistic features" can be anything that we can identify as an entity or unit having to do with what people say. Saussure offers two principles for such identification (pp. 101–102):

1. Any linguistic entity exists only in virtue of the association between signal and signification ... 2. A linguistic entity is not ultimately defined until it is *delimited*, i.e. separated from whatever there may be on either side of it in a sequence of sounds. It is these delimited entities or *units* which contrast with one another in the mechanism of language ... a language does not present itself to us as a set of signs already delimited, requiring us merely to study their meanings and organization. It is an indistinct mass, in which attention and habit alone enable us to distinguish particular elements. The unit has no special phonic character, and the only definition it can be given is the following: *a segment of sound which is, as distinct from what precedes and follows in the spoken sequence, the signal of a certain concept.*

Thus linguistic features are components that we choose to isolate (i.e., bits that we can identify as themselves) from the stream of speech. Concrete entities are thus not a given, not "natural," but derived by our choice in an act of identification. Concrete entities are generally located with respect to "words," but Saussure cautions that "what a word is taken to be does not correspond to our notion of a concrete unit" (p. 103). Since many words are complex (composed of smaller identifiable units) and many identifiable units are larger than words (compounds, phrases, collocations), Saussure concludes that "it is extremely difficult to unravel in a sequence of sounds the arrangement of units present, and to say which are the concrete elements the language is using" (p. 104).[5] A word, then, is no more than a unit of a language, say one that is conventionally identified as itself as in a dictionary, and we get into trouble as soon as we try to define "word" too closely. And yet Saussure concludes that "For the word, in spite of being so difficult to define, is a unit which compels recognition by the

---

[5] On just this ground Saussure argues against the use of the sentence as the central unit in linguistics:

With sentences ... it is diversity which is predominant. As soon as one looks for something to link them together in spite of this diversity, one finds that one has unintentionally come back to the word and its grammatical features, with all the attendant difficulties already familiar (p. 105).

mind. It has a central role in the linguistic mechanism" (p. 109). Linguistic features of speech, concrete entities, thus are commonly taken to be different words used for the same referent (synonyms), or alternative morphs or phones used as components of what we identify as the same word, or alternative arrangements of words in what we recognize to be sequences with equivalent meaning or organization. For Saussure, "identity" comes from such acts of recognition, as when we consider the word "messieurs" to be the same word even given variations in "delivery and intonation" by different speakers (p. 106). Thus perception is a necessary element of speech, because without it there could be no linguistic features.

Beyond the segmentation of the sequence of speech into units, commonly words, Saussure notes that traditional terminology for units of a language continues to have a strong influence (p. 108):

Linguistics is always working with concepts originally introduced by the grammarians. It is unclear whether or not these concepts really reflect constituent features of linguistic structure.

These are "realities," acts of classification that yield elements of linguistic structure described in the past and handed down by tradition. He does not reject classifications such as parts of speech just because they are traditional, products of precursor notions of language study. He does, however, suggest that "where languages are concerned, people have always been satisfied to work with poorly defined units" (p. 109). Saussure urges caution in the use of either traditional classifications or new "realities" (p. 108):

To avoid being misled, it is first of all important to realize that concrete linguistic entities do not just present themselves for inspection of their own accord. It is in seeking them out that one makes contact with linguistic reality. Taking this as our point of departure, we have to proceed to work out all the classifications linguistics needs to accommodate the facts it has to deal with. But to base these classifications on anything other than concrete entities – to say, for instance, that the parts of speech do reflect linguistic structure, simply because they are logically viable categories – is to forget that linguistic facts do not exist independently of sound-sequences divided into meaningful segments.

Classifications thus should derive from the facts, and they must meet the needs of the evidence and of the analysis to be made of it. Just as for the concrete entities on which they must be based, classifications are not given, not "natural," but are derived from our analytical choices.

Saussure accepts the necessity of concrete entities, as the segments are delimited from the sound-sequence by recognition of their identities, but he prefers the more abstract notion of linguistic value, the formal, structural counterpart of concrete entities (pp. 110–120). Linguistic value is the heart of the *Course*, the aspect of language that we can only describe through analysis of structure. The linguistics of linguistic structure consists of the description of linguistic values which are established in the collectivity of language in a community, as a result of the relational fit of each linguistic feature within the system of the language. Thus, in his example (p. 114), the French word *mouton* covers the same semantic space as both English *sheep* ('live animal') and English *mutton* ('meat from the animal'), and so the French word is the equivalent of neither English word. The French system has one element while the English system has two, and the linguistic values must therefore be different because of the relational fit of the elements. The same sort of difference in linguistic values obtains for elements in both paradigmatic and syntagmatic structures. Surely linguistic value will always justify an interest in linguistic structure as an appropriate mode of language study. In the linguistics of speech, on the other hand, we will take an equally valid interest in linguistic features as concrete entities or units that result from acts of recognition; the task of the linguist will then commonly be to study the linguistic behavior of different individuals, especially as they might be associated into groups, with respect to the same feature.

Aggregation of evidence from speech

To return to geography, Saussure continued his argument with discussion of isoglosses and what we have come to call bundles of isoglosses, lines on a map which indicate the limit of occurrence for some linguistic feature (see Kretzschmar 1992b). He prefers to call them "waves" (p. 201, in accordance with Schmidt's wave theory, on which see Dineen 1967: 281). He posited two points, A and B, separated by such a bundle:

When one looks at a linguistic map, one sometimes sees two or three of these waves almost coinciding or even merging over a certain distance. It is evident that the two points A and B separated by a zone of this kind will show a certain accumulation of contrasts and constitute two fairly distinct forms of speech. It may also happen that these convergences are not merely partial, but mark out the entire perimeter of two or more areas. When these convergences are numerous, one can use "dialects" as a roughly appropriate term. The convergences are explained by social, political, religious, etc. factors, which we are completely ignoring for present purposes. These convergences disguise but never entirely obscure the primary and natural phenomenon of differentiation into independent areas.

Saussure's remarks maintain a strong distinction between a "dialectal feature" and the notion of "natural dialect." The former is in practice the artifact of a dialect survey – Saussure mentions Wenker and Gilliéron specifically (p. 200) – one of those (word-level) linguistic features chosen for investigation in a survey. He denies that nature is so neat as to allow a dialect "area," but allows the "artificial" procedure of mapping separate linguistic features. When the investigator can find "numerous" linguistic features to delimit an area, that inventory of features constitutes a dialect, as a "roughly appropriate" designation; this kind of dialect is not the "natural dialect" that Saussure rejected, but instead an indication or measure of the natural differentiation that one may expect to find between any two localities or zones (cf. the comments of Gaston Paris, as quoted in Francis 1983: 2). Saussure does not, after all, refuse to acknowledge that localities have different speech habits, and admits "the primary and natural phenomenon of differentiation into independent areas"; he just refuses to say that speech differences between two localities constitute two "natural dialects" if, to pursue the implication of the argument, that assertion is taken to indicate self-consistent and mutually exclusive identities in real terms of two linguistic systems considered from the viewpoint of the linguistics of linguistic structure. He believes his view to be well-supported by non-concurrent distribution of dialect features, the result of historical forces.

It is important to note that the practical result of each of Saussure's choices for naming a dialect, either the conjunction of areas of occurrence for a number of dialect features, or specification of a locality which possesses a "totality" of speech forms, is a list of particular features. Saussure does not here recommend comprehensive description of the language of a locality; he wants a list of dialect features known to be used in the locality, exactly parallel to the list for an area that could be created from co-occurrence of dialect features. Either way, he presupposes a dialect survey or other method of collection that has searched for information about particular features, and a list that in itself constitutes the inventory of features shared to some extent by the speakers who live in the area specified. Such an artificially generated inventory would mirror the complete inventory and arrangement of linguistic features that would compose a natural dialect, if a natural dialect could exist – that is, if we were talking about the collectivity of a dialect that determined its linguistic structure. A natural dialect, as we might define one in the linguistics of linguistic structure, must in theory depend on a common inventory and system of features (or signs), but in practice, from the viewpoint of the linguistics of speech, in natural language that commonality never occurs because of linguistic continua created by historical processes. Since there are no natural dialects, then, the inventories of linguistic features that we collect constitute dialects because we so name them, and they are useful because they help us to conceive of "the primary and natural phenomenon of differentiation into independent areas."

Thus, in the linguistics of speech, the dialects that we can name, and any dialect boundaries that we assert, are arbitrary and conventional as opposed to natural. From the viewpoint of the linguistics of speech, so are languages and their boundaries ((1916) 1986: 202):

it is no more feasible to determine boundaries separating related languages than to determine dialect boundaries. The extent of the area involved makes no difference. Just as one cannot say where High German ends and Low German begins, so also it is impossible to establish a line of demarcation between German and Dutch, or between French and Italian. Taking points far enough apart, it is possible to say with certainty "French is spoken here; Italian is spoken there." But in the intervening regions, the distinction becomes blurred. The notion of smaller, compact intermediate zones acting as linguistic areas of transition (for example, Provençal as a half-way house between French and Italian) is not realistic either. In any case, it is impossible to imagine in any shape or form a precise linguistic boundary dividing an area covered throughout by evenly differentiated dialects. Language boundaries, just like dialect boundaries, get lost in these transitions. Just as dialects are only arbitrary subdivisions of the entire surface covered by a language, so the boundaries held to separate two languages can only be conventional ones.

Dialect boundaries, whether constituted selectively by a single isogloss or by assembling bundles of isoglosses, are not transitional – isoglosses are quite real and sharp, derived from data (see Kretzschmar 1992b) – but should rather be thought of as conventional because they indicate a merely conventional entity, a dialect, and not a division between unreal naturally occurring distinct varieties. To say that "boundaries … get lost in these transitions" is actually to say that there are no "natural" dividing lines between linguistic systems, that natural language and dialect, as we perceive them, are characterized by continual transitions. This finding is a central, foundational fact for the linguistics of speech, that language behavior is continuously variable across geographical and social space. The *linguistic continuum*, in association with the notions of *language variation* and *linguistic diversity*, serves to characterize the linguistics of speech in the same way that *linguistic structure* and *linguistic system* characterize the linguistics of linguistic structure. Differences in the inventory of dialect features at different locations make dialect for Saussure a term with only local reality by convention in the linguistics of speech, according to the two options he provides for creation of lists of dialect features.

Within the linguistics of speech, it will be important to identify two different procedural senses of the term *dialect*, corresponding to the two choices outlined by Saussure. For the first sense, call it *attributive dialect*, the linguist should predefine a locality or category of speakers and seek to describe the dialect features of that locality or category, as evidence about particular features is acquired by survey or other means. This is Saussure's first of two choices, with the object of defining a dialect through "the totality of its features." The second procedural sense of dialect, call it *blind dialect*, begins with the linguistic features that result from a survey designed to cover a large region or large group of people, as in the regional projects of the American Linguistic Atlas. Similarities in distributions of features may reveal unforeseen correspondences between features and areas, or between features and social groups, and thus suggest dialects. Saussure initially suggests that one may choose to define a dialect according to the limits of occurrence of a single linguistic feature, but later suggests that the areal limits of "numerous" features may overlap, and that such "convergences" might be used to designate a dialect. One and the same survey might be used for both purposes; the difference between attributive and blind dialects is a difference in procedure, subsequent to the collection of the data about particular features. Attributive procedure begins with the area or category and then matches dialect features to it; blind procedure begins with dialect features and matches areas or categories to them. Both kinds of dialect require a notion of sufficiency: what constitutes sufficient evidence and elaboration, in practice, to describe attributive dialects or, on the other hand, what number of correspondences constitutes enough shared dialectal features, with what degree of precision in areal or social identification, to define blind dialects. Saussure's initial procedural division, though not developed in its implications in the *Course*, suggests a procedural logic that can be widely applied.

A different linguistics

The logic and the premises of the linguistics of speech model thus go along with the serious study of language behavior in order to create a path for a different linguistics. Mere collection of written or spoken language does not, by itself, belong either to the linguistics of linguistic structure or to the linguistics of speech. Contact with real language is essential to both, but subject to a different logic of analysis and to different premises for the two different paths. The linguistics of linguistic structure cannot avoid contact with speech, but practitioners need not collect large quantities of speech in order to practice it. Further, if linguists interested in linguistic structure do decide to collect quantities of speech, their assumptions about *langue* will condition what they do with their collections. Practitioners of the linguistics of speech, on the other hand, need to collect large quantities of evidence in order to observe variability across time and space in the linguistic continuum.

We can observe the consequences of following these different pathways in the different attitudes that linguists have taken in the last century to collections of speech. One of the great figures of American dialectology, the founder of the Linguistic Atlas Project, Hans Kurath, accommodated the facts of language variation to his belief in the NeoGrammarian position on sound laws. In a passage entitled "How Systematic is Speech?", Kurath put the essential problem this way (Kurath and McDavid 1961: 2–3):

The task of presenting a complicated and fluid linguistic situation in readily intelligible simplified form exposes one to the risk of making the dialects look more regular and systematized than the observed facts warrant. One should, of course, uncover all the regularities; but one should not overlook recalcitrant data or play them down.

Kurath appears to recognize the linguistic continuum here, but then continues in a statement worth quoting in full (p. 3):

For, though language is essentially systematic, it is never wholly without irregularities and oddities, whatever their origin. This is a simple matter of observation and should surprise no one who is unwilling to forget that all natural languages are historical products developed in the give-and-take between individuals and social groups of a speech community and between speech communities. In this complicated historical process, so different from the creation, once and for all, of an artificial code, features taken from other social and regional dialects are not always adapted to the native system, and innovations in the native system may as yet not be established with consistency, so that elements of an older system survive as relics. To treat such tangible irregularities, current in all natural languages and dialects, as if they were built into the system is to misjudge linguistic realities for the sake of a working theory ... In our handling of the data we single out the inconsistencies and the vacillations in usage after the regularities have been established. Such deviations from the system are indicative of change in progress, of trends in usage. In fact, changes in systematization, which all living dialects undergo from time to time, are inconceivable without temporary disorganization.

Kurath's first commitment is to language as system. The old NeoGrammarian strategy of talking about dialect borrowing as an explanation for the unsystematic appearance of dialect facts appears here, along with arguments that address the messy facts of language that had earlier disturbed Wenker. That which is "regular" is by definition part of the system, and whatever else left over is peripheral. Kurath, the dialectologist, engages the premise of linguistic systems, and thus acts according to the linguistics of linguistic structure even though he was engaged in large-scale speech collection (see further Kretzschmar 2002a). The only early dialectologist not to do so, to work with evidence according to the linguistics of speech, was Gilliéron.

Similarly, in his landmark article promoting the notion of system in dialect study (1954), Uriel Weinreich, William Labov's mentor, pointed out that identical inventories of linguistic features may hide differences in paradigmatic or syntagmatic arrangement of features, and that differences in inventories have systematic consequences (compare Saussure's argument for linguistic value (1916)1986: 114–115). Weinreich's argument, essentially that vowel length is in free variation among one subgroup of his chosen speakers and is a distinctive feature among another subgroup, suggests that analysis of system can reveal the existence of different dialects in a population of speakers who have the same inventory of features. The key point here, as with Kurath, is Weinreich's primary commitment to language as system. If we accept his argument, then within the linguistics of linguistic structure we may well be able to distinguish dialects (call them "derived" dialects; see Kretzschmar 1998b) – but this matter does not arise in the linguistics of speech. Weinreich's derived dialects are an implication of linguistic value from linguistic structure, and are thus a possible outcome of studying collections of language evidence from the point of view of the linguistics of linguistic structure.

Disagreements about the status of "empirical" linguistics, such as the dispute between Sampson and Chomsky reported in Chapter 1, do not necessarily address the difference between the two pathways for linguistics. For instance, Samuel Keyser's review (1963) of Kurath and McDavid's (1961) *Pronunciation of English in the Atlantic States* attacked its phonemicization practices and used rule ordering in a generative subsystem to account for the diphthongs in Charleston, SC, New Bern, NC, and Winchester, VA. Some have taken the strongly negative review as an attack by a generativist upon empiricists. However, Keyser actually shared a primary commitment to language as system with Kurath and McDavid. However, Kurath and McDavid were looking for blind dialects across their entire survey region, while Keyser was working on what amounts to derived dialects like Weinreich's, where rules are applied within an inventory of features. Thus the conflict, as for Sampson and Chomsky in Chapter 1, comes down to a division in attitudes towards data collections, not a disagreement across the pathways of Saussure's two possibilities for linguistics. Traditional dialectologists like Kurath and McDavid did not practice the linguistics of speech as described in this volume, but instead attempted to accommodate aspects of language variation within a structuralist framework.[6] Keyser's review expressed a generative point of view as against a structural point of view, all within the linguistics of linguistic structure.

While Saussure concentrated on the areal boundaries in common use in his time, his characterization of all linguistic boundaries as "conventional" applies directly to the modern designation of social categories (by socio-economic status, education, age, gender, race, shared activity or practice, and other criteria), which are all arbitrary dividing lines between artificially created groupings, and so his ideas apply to social as well as to regional dialects. To drop constraints on linguistic consistency and exclusivity, as they emerge from study of linguistic systems under the linguistics of linguistic structure, immediately points towards the idea that individuals can participate simultaneously in several social groups. Individuals, then, should be able to wield linguistic characteristics associated with more than one group, and the linguistic repertoire of any individual might best be considered not as any single structure or system, but in relation to the linguistic behavior of the groups with which they are associated. Dialect is thus associated with groups of speakers as such groups may be defined by arbitrary and conventional dividing lines, especially as the linguistic features of a dialect can be shown to

---

[6] William Labov has followed them as perhaps the best traditional dialectologist of the next generation, and has incorporated more notions from generative linguistics.

contribute to group identity, and individual speakers "speak a dialect" only insofar as, and to the degree that, they adopt the linguistic behavior of a group. Current work on social networks and communities of practice (e.g., Milroy 1980; Eckert 2000; Childs 2005) consider networks and interactions in groups of only a few people, and can demonstrate linguistic effects even at this micro level, and so this contemporary work forces us to think even about very small groups rather than just about dialects as they are traditionally conceived for large groups. The association of abstract dialects with groups thus frees individual speakers from having to speak the same way all the time because they are "speakers of a dialect," an implication of the viewpoint of the linguistics of linguistic structure, and allows them instead to act as we know they really behave: to vary their linguistic behavior according to circumstance, as they are aligned with different groups (or wish to be so aligned, see Le Page and Tabouret-Keller 1985). At the same time that dialects are associated with groups, whether geographically or socially delimited, under the linguistics of speech the analyst will not describe the collectivity of the language of the group as a system or structure, but will instead describe the linguistic behavior of the group according to the presence or absence in it of particular linguistic features.

Sociolinguistics seems to be most like the linguistics of speech, but it has not been practiced in that way. In America, as we have seen in Chapter 1, Labovian sociolinguistics is firmly associated with the linguistics of linguistic structure, and more recent approaches to micro-level analysis and linguistic perception follow his lead. Eckert's groundbreaking study (2000) demonstrates the importance of language behavior by individuals in particular association with each other, and yet still attempts to relate the findings to superordinate linguistic systems like Labov's Northern Cities Shift. Preston's perceptual studies (e.g., 1989) similarly adopt the framework of linguistic structure. British sociolinguistics has not been dominated by the style/class formalism most common in America, and yet prominent studies such as those in Norwich (by Trudgill 1974a), Belfast (by the Milroys 1980), Tyneside (now pursued by Joan Beal and Karen Corrigan, www.ncl.ac.uk/necte), or Milton Keynes (by Kerswill 1996; Kerswill and Williams 2000) accept language structure as a major premise. The British mode of linguistics most aligned with the linguistics of speech is NeoFirthian corpus linguistics, not sociolinguistics (see, however, Kretzschmar, Anderson, Beal, Corrigan, Opas-Hänninen, and Plichta 2006, which approaches sociolinguistic datasets as corpora). Most recently, advanced computational work in sociolinguistics and dialectology by Nerbonne and Heeringa also begin with the model of linguistic structure (2001; Heeringa and Nerbonne 2001; see Kretzschmar 2006b for a general assessment of such computational approaches). Once more, the empirical collection of speech evidence is not the same as following the path of the linguistics of speech, since it is perfectly possible, though controversial, to collect bodies of speech evidence and to analyze it under the model of the linguistics of linguistic structure.

Principles of the linguistics of speech

While Saussure may not have lectured on the linguistics of speech per se, he did carefully distinguish it from the linguistics of linguistic structure, and he provided foundational statements about its scope, its object of study, and its basic materials. Saussure described linguistics in competition with other approaches in the marketplace of ideas about language study of his time (grammar, philology, comparative linguistics, and historical linguistics), and in competition with other, more established disciplines (physiology, psychology). The model for the linguistics of linguistic structure that he developed was not "natural," but the result of particular choices based on particular premises. He admitted that speech, language behavior, was a valid alternative choice as a focus for the study of language, and provided direction for the procedures necessary for working on the linguistics of speech.

The scientific model for the linguistics of speech does not accept languages and general laws as premises. Instead, it begins with the "speech circuit," which includes articulatory, perceptual, physiological, and cognitive "internal" aspects, with reference to "external" considerations like geography, ethnology, policies, and institutions. Language is thus naturally variable, naturally diverse. Its units of analysis are linguistic features, concrete entities that can be isolated from the stream of speech by recognition of "identities," as opposed to often-traditional classifications of structure that yield "linguistic values." The central assumption of the linguistics of speech is the existence of the *linguistic continuum*, the continuously variable behavior of individual speakers. Thus, the task of the linguist will commonly be to study the linguistic behavior of different individuals with respect to the same features. The two basic dimensions in which the linguistic behavior of individuals plays out are time and space. As opposed to general laws, the interactions of individual linguistic behavior over time and space are subject to a definite logic in analytical procedure. Study of empirical evidence alone does not characterize the linguistics of speech: early dialectologists (except for Gilliéron) and modern sociolinguists have been and are still generally committed to the linguistics of linguistic structure, along with generativists and practitioners of NLP. The linguistics of speech, then, remains a different path in the current marketplace of ideas about language.

While the linguistics of speech must deal with time and space as essential aspects of the real establishment and distribution of linguistic features, it must also recognize physical, cognitive, and perceptual factors in the production and reception of speech, along with external factors related to human organizational and cultural behavior. The special complexity of the speech model, then, comes from the integration of articulatory, perceptual, physiological, and cognitive factors by individuals, with inter-individual social and cultural factors. The linguistics of speech must embrace the resulting complexity because, unlike the linguistics of linguistic structure, it responds to a continuum of behavior instead of the creation of a static system.

The following chapters will develop the linguistics of speech under four heads: survey research, corpus linguistics, distributional facts about language behavior, and perception. Particular findings in each of these areas will show that speech is not chaotic or unmanageable, but rather offers regularities across the continuum that the linguist can use to address particular problems having to do with language.

3 Evidence from linguistic survey research: basic description

Saussure found much of the primary evidence for his limited description of the linguistics of speech in the work of the first dialect geographers, Wenker and Gilliéron. This chapter will address evidence from more recent linguistic survey research. We can now carry out systematic research on speech that Saussure could not, using recording devices and computers and modern methods of statistics. If we use such modern methods to analyze survey research on linguistic features, we find that we get consistent, regular results, not just the anarchy of erratic distributions. These findings will lead to formulation in more detail of principles of regional and social organization of language at different levels of scale, within an overall linguistic continuum.

A good part of Saussure's resistance to the linguistics of speech came from the circumstances of language study in his day. He did insist on the necessity of speech for the establishment of a language ((1916)1986: 19):

it is by listening to others that we learn our native language. A language accumulates in our brain only as the result of countless experiences. Finally, it is speech which causes a language to evolve. The impressions received from listening to others modify our own linguistic habits.

Human beings have the capacity to manage their experience of speech, both to acquire a language originally and to continue to adjust language habits in light of continuing impressions from experience. However, the academic study of language is not the same as enactment of our human capacity for language. Saussure's comments reveal his resistance to its complexity, as when he calls the facts of language, when not viewed as linguistic structure, a "muddle of disparate, unconnected things" (p. 9). As speakers we make sense of the muddle, but according to Saussure as linguists we have more trouble. Others of his comments tell us more about practical problems. For instance,

there is nothing collective about speech. Its manifestations are individual and ephemeral. It is no more than an aggregate of particular cases … Language in its totality is unknowable, for it lacks homogeneity (pp. 19–20).

Today, we have tools that can address what might be "collective" about speech. For one thing, we have the means to record speech, so that it is no longer simply ephemeral. In Saussure's day, writing was about the only means for a linguist to preserve speech evidence, and Saussure took a dim view of its accuracy for linguistic analysis: "writing obscures our view of the language. Writing is not a garment but a disguise" (p. 29). Edison's wax-cylinder recorder had recently been invented (1877),[1] but it was certainly not practical for a linguist to use one for field research. Acoustical phonetics began with mechanical devices that recorded speech signals on smoked drums, but progress in the field could only take off after widespread introduction of sound recording. The rapid advances in electronics that led to the oscilloscope, with which one might study the physics of the speech signal, were just ahead in the next few decades. Linguists were quick to use technology as it became available. For example, as early as the 1930s and 1940s field workers from the American Linguistic Atlas Project experimented with recorders (an early Atlas Dictaphone has been donated to the Library of Congress). They also recorded speakers in the field with equipment that preserved speech on aluminum platters (now also preserved in the Library of Congress) – the batteries for the equipment filled a car trunk, and their mass may have contributed to the death of Guy Lowman, the principal Atlas field worker of his time, in a car crash in 1941. Reel-to-reel audio tape-recording was introduced from Germany after World War II, and effective portable tape recorders appeared from Grundig and Sony in the early 1950s. These tools allowed linguists not only to preserve speech recorded in the field, but to listen to the same speech segments over and over again for the purposes of analysis. The introduction of computer tools has only made the possibilities for such analysis more extensive, more and more adequate to the complexities of speech.

The data upon which much of this and the following chapter will be based comes from the survey conducted for the Linguistic Atlas of the Middle and South Atlantic States (LAMSAS). The Linguistic Atlas Project overall is the largest single project covering regional and social differences in spoken American English. Regional surveys extend from New England to California; some field work was conducted as early as the 1930s, with records on paper, and some field work continues today, with recorded interviews on tape and digital media. Along with the *Linguistic Atlas of New England* (LANE; Kurath 1939–43; see also the project handbook, Kurath 1939), the Linguistic Atlas of the Middle and South Atlantic States treats the primary settlement areas of the original colonies (see www.lap.uga.edu). LAMSAS consists of interviews, transcribed in fine phonetic notation, with 1162 selected, native informants

---

[1] For general information, whether about historical events like the invention of Edison's wax-cylinder recorder, or descriptions of widely accepted scientific terms like "Bayesian statistics" below, I refer the reader to our web-friend Wikipedia (www.wikipedia.org). It is not exactly authoritative, but it is admirable as a voluntarily contributed, generally reliable information source. Information and opinion for which personal credit is due is, of course, cited here according to scholarly practice.

from 483 communities, typically counties, within the region. Interviews were conducted with a questionnaire of 104 pages averaging seven items per page (an "item" is an aspect of language which has variant means of expression, such as different words for the same thing, or different pronunciations for a vowel or consonant in the same word), designed to reveal regional and social differences in everyday vocabulary and pronunciation, with some attention to grammar in verb forms and function words. Ideally, field workers were supposed to find at least one older, less educated speaker (Kurath's Type I), and one middle-aged and moderately educated speaker (Kurath's Type II) in each location studied, typically the counties of each state in the survey region; a "cultivated" speaker, usually with higher education (Kurath's Type III), was to be located in about 20% of the locations. Field work was largely complete by 1949. LAMSAS records the English spoken along the Atlantic Coast at mid-century, among people of various social positions and degrees of education, and so provides a benchmark for the English language in its varied shapes for a particular region at a particular time, with special reference to the development of the language in the preceding century. The significance of LAMSAS is thus historical. LAMSAS, along with LANE, is also the key to making best use of all the other regional Atlas projects, which describe the English spoken in secondary and tertiary American settlement areas (see www.lap.uga.edu). The LAMSAS *Handbook* describes in detail the methods, speakers, and communities of the project (Kretzschmar, McDavid, Lerud, and Johnson 1993).

Findings from the LAMSAS survey: Boundaries and plots

Saussure described the usual way of thinking about language and geography "as clearly defined linguistic types, determinate in all respects, and occupying areas on a map which are contiguous and distinct" ((1916)1986: 200). Such a view emerges from the NeoGrammarians and from the linguistics of linguistic structure, and it is still the most common way of thinking about language and the land today, as dialects. For example, Hans Kurath interpreted the evidence from LAMSAS in order to make his famous map of American dialects in his (1949) *Word Geography of the Eastern United States* (see Figure 3.1).

  Since Kurath was interested in drawing the boundaries between the "linguistic types" that he believed to exist (as an inheritor of the NeoGrammarian view, and an advocate of the linguistics of linguistic structure), he reviewed LAMSAS evidence to find variants of linguistic features, particular words or short phrases, or particular pronunciations of words, that occurred in about the same place (see Kretzschmar 1996a). Kurath described his method in *Studies in Area Linguistics* as selecting those items from the survey which show "fairly clear-cut dissemination patterns" (1972: 24). He then generalized the boundaries for individual variants: "one finds that in some parts of the area [isoglosses]

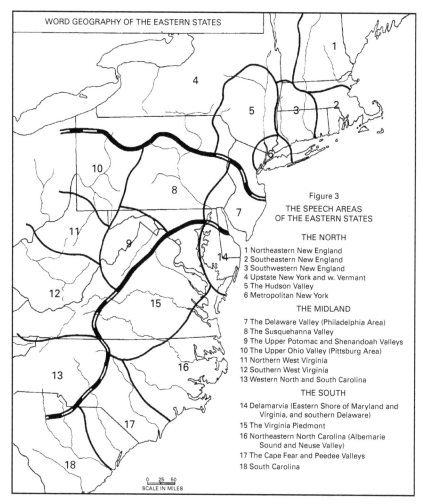

Figure 3
THE SPEECH AREAS
OF THE EASTERN STATES

THE NORTH

1 Northeastern New England
2 Southeastern New England
3 Southwestern New England
4 Upstate New York and w. Vermant
5 The Hudson Valley
6 Metropolitan New York

THE MIDLAND

7 The Delaware Valley (Philadelphia Area)
8 The Susquehanna Valley
9 The Upper Potomac and Shenandoah Valleys
10 The Upper Ohio Valley (Pittsburg Area)
11 Northern West Virginia
12 Southern West Virginia
13 Western North and South Carolina

THE SOUTH

14 Delamarvia (Eastern Shore of Maryland and
   Virginia, and southern Delaware)
15 The Virginia Piedmont
16 Northeastern North Carolina (Albemarie
   Sound and Neuse Valley)
17 The Cape Fear and Peedee Valleys
18 South Carolina

WORD GEOGRAPHY OF THE EASTERN STATES

0 25 50
SCALE IN MILES

Figure 3.1 Kurath's dialect map (1949: Figure 3)
(Source: *A Word Geography of the Eastern United States*, by Hans Kurath.
With the kind permission of the University of Michigan Press, Ann Arbor)

run in bundles of various sizes – close-knit or spaced. These bundles show the
location of major and minor dialect boundaries and thus indicate the dialectal
structure of the total area" (1972: 24). This is a deductive process, in that Kurath
knew that he wanted to subdivide the survey region, and he only needed to find
diagnostic isoglosses to match his perceptions, guided by his wide experience
(see also Chapter 7 in this volume). In recent years Labov has published a quite

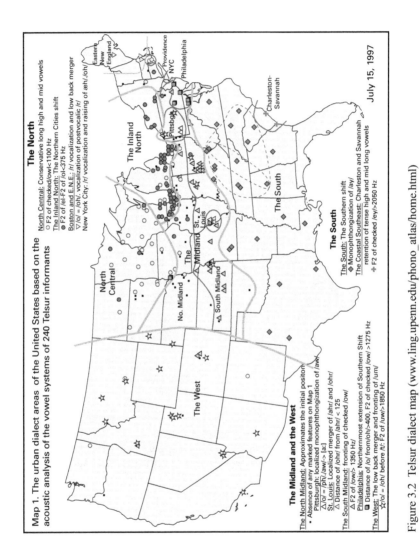

Figure 3.2 Telsur dialect map (www.ling.upenn.edu/phono_atlas/home.html) (Source: Telsur website. With the kind permission of William Labov)

similar national map based on Telsur data (Figure 3.2; a national survey whose major publication is now Labov, Boberg, and Ash 2006). This map features boundary lines that separate the country into regions corresponding to three major chain shifts in the vowel system, certainly an idea only viable within the linguistics of linguistic structure.

In the linguistics of speech, however, we begin with language behavior, what individual people say. Our basic question, then, no longer asks about "linguistic types," but instead asks "who says what where?" Kurath did publish maps of who said what where in his *Word Geography*, as part of the process of finding diagnostic isoglosses. The following figure shows three diagnostic isoglosses on which Kurath based the boundary of the Northern dialect area (Figure 3.3). Each of these three lines is in turn based on a plot for an individual linguistic variant. Kurath's map for lexical variants of *dragonfly* shows six of the different terms in use for the insect (Figure 3.4). His isogloss for *darning needle* supposedly generalizes the southern limit of occurrence for the term, but in fact a close look at the plot shows that the term occurs in Philadelphia, in West Virginia, and in scattered other places south of the isogloss. Kurath did have reason to draw a line where he did, a change in the frequency of use of the term (used more often north of the line, less often south of it), and yet a line is perhaps not the best tool to describe where the term *darning needle* occurred in the survey. These maps illustrate how Kurath's need to draw lines and divide areas, according to the linguistics of linguistic structure, determined how he interpreted the evidence.

The same process of analysis has occurred in England. The basic pattern of Northern, East and West Midlands, Southwestern, and Kentish dialects was established by the early English political and settlement history of Britain (largely maintained today in governmental administrative regions). Moore, Meech, and Whitehall (1935) and Moore and Marckwardt (1951: 24–31, 110–140) describe the early history, and supply diagnostic isoglosses from Middle English to support their status as dialect areas. Figure 3.5 shows a bundle of isoglosses that can be taken to mark the modern boundary between the North and the Midlands, in nearly the same location that Moore, Meech, and Whitehall, and later Moore and Marckwardt, had shown a bundle of Middle English isoglosses.

Each isogloss of Figure 3.5, from a popular textbook, suggests that one pronunciation is current north of the line, and another pronunciation is current south of the line in complementary distribution. In fact, just as for Kurath, the evidence is actually mixed and the lines make a generalization about the evidence when they mark the difference. For example, if we compare line a of Figure 3.5 to the relevant map based on the Survey of English Dialects (SED) (Figure 3.6), we find that the mid-twentieth-century situation for realization of the vowel in *cow* in England is actually quite complex. While Orton, Sanderson, and Widdowson did use isoglosses to display the status of the vowel, they drew many more lines than just one; they also indicated the presence of alternative

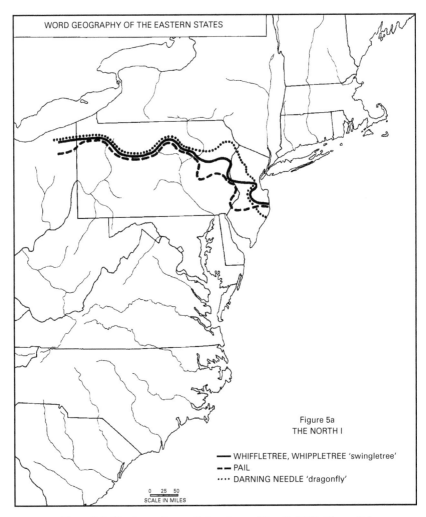

WORD GEOGRAPHY OF THE EASTERN STATES

Figure 5a
THE NORTH I

—— WHIFFLETREE, WHIPPLETREE 'swingletree'
– – PAIL
•••• DARNING NEEDLE 'dragonfly'

0   25   50
SCALE IN MILES

Figure 3.3 Northern diagnostic isoglosses (Kurath 1949: Figure 5a)
(Source: *A Word Geography of the Eastern United States*, by Hans Kurath.
With the kind permission of the University of Michigan Press, Ann Arbor)

pronunciations within each region by the use of symbols plotted on the map.
Figure 3.5 is not incorrect or inexact; it just makes a generalization from the
evidence without exactly saying so. A prominent current researcher on the SED,
Clive Upton, is more critical: "the idea of a 'dialect area' is, in reality, a fiction"
(2006: 311). Upton prefers to talk about "features, and their distributions and
implications, without attempting that definition of dialect types which can only
be safely done using a small number of items" (2006: 311). The most recent

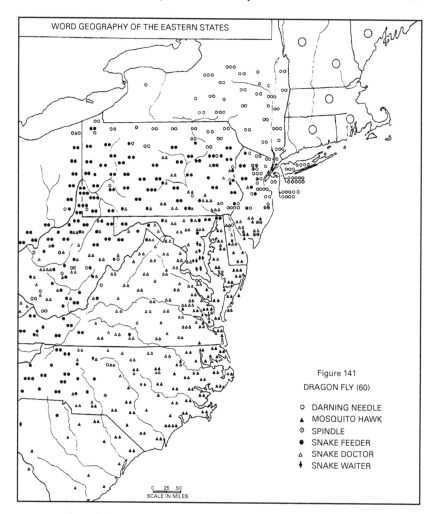

Figure 3.4 Kurath's map of *dragonfly* variants (1949: Figure 141)
(Source: *A Word Geography of the Eastern United States*, by Hans Kurath.
With the kind permission of the University of Michigan Press, Ann Arbor)

volume to chart SED data, Upton and Widdowson (2006), does not offer any
maps with isogloss bundles for dialect areas, but also dispenses with symbols
for alternative pronunciations. This method still indicates numerous variants
with isoglosses, as in Figure 3.7 for the vowel in *find* (compare line g from
Figure 3.5, for *blind*), but it changes the quality of generalization being made,
from dialect area in Figure 3.5 to something like "feature area" for Figure 3.7, in

a [ku:] (cow)
  [kaʊ]

b [giɔs] (goose)
  [gʊɪs][guːs]

c [lɪɔf] (loaf)
  [lʊəf][lɔʊf]

d [iɪt][iət] (eat)
  [eɪt]

e [gɪʊnd] (ground)
  [gɹaʊnd]

f [kʊəl] (coal)
  [kɒɪl][kɔʊl]

g [blɪnd] (blind)
  [blaɪnd]

h [ɹaŋ] (wrong)
  [ɹɒŋ]

Figure 3.5 Northern isoglosses from Graddol, Leith, and Swann (1996: 271)
(Source: *English: History, Diversity, and Change*, by David Graddol, Dick
Leith, and Joan Swann. With the kind permission of Cengage Learning
Services Limited, on behalf of Taylor and Francis Books, Andover, Hants)

which features are shown in complementary distribution.[2] The creation of
dialect boundaries in England clearly derives from the assumption that there

---

[2] Upton does refer to "fudged lects" in which speakers used mixed sets of variants. In this he carries
over the term from Chambers and Trudgill 1998 – but Chambers and Trudgill, like Upton, do so in
the context of the linguistics of linguistic structure. The assertion of fudged lects is an attempt to
solve the evident problem of mixed use of variants within local dialects.

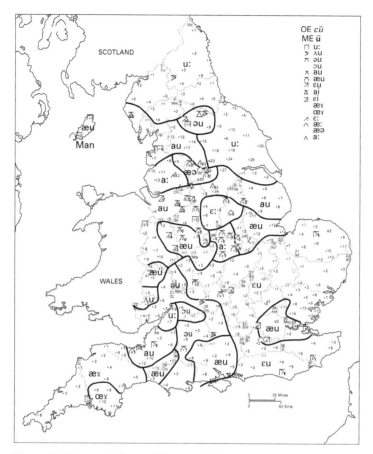

Figure 3.6 Pronunciations of the vowel in *cow* (Orton, Sanderson, and Widdowson 1978: Ph154)
(Source: *The Linguistic Atlas of England*, by Harold Orton, Stewart Sanderson, and John Widdowson. With the kind permission of Cengage Learning Services Limited, on behalf of Taylor and Francis Books, Andover, Hants)

will be "linguistic types," the indication of a whole dialect region with a bundle of isoglosses. More recently, those charting data from the SED have preferred to use a single isogloss to show the area in which one variant of a linguistic feature may be found, which still makes a generalization, but one not as broad. All of these practices are in accordance with the linguistics of linguistic structure, because they make generalizations about the structure of the evidence with respect to geography. Just as Kurath did, Orton, Sanderson, and Widdowson (and in other places, Upton, too) do indicate isolated occurrences of variants that differ from the usage described by isoglosses but, just as for Kurath, they have

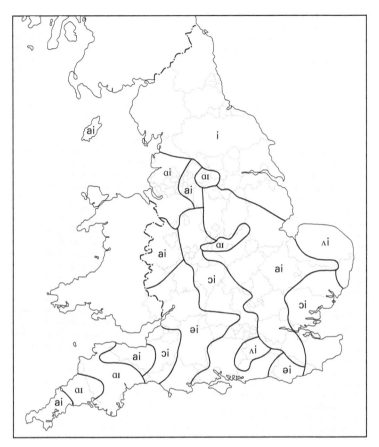

Figure 3.7 Pronunciations of the vowel in *find* (Upton and Widdowson 2006: Map 9)
(Source: *An Atlas of English Dialects*, Clive Upton and John Widdowson. With the kind permission of Cengage Learning Services Limited, on behalf of Taylor and Francis Books, Andover, Hants)

done so under the general model of the linguistics of linguistic structure because they are willing to accept the generalizations made by isoglosses.

A map more appropriate to the linguistics of speech shows just a single word at a time, the better to see who said what where (Figure 3.8). Plotting multiple variants for a linguistic feature on a single map, as Kurath did and as Orton, Sanderson, and Widdowson did, usually aims to find complementary distribution of the variants across the survey area, separate areas where different variants occur, and so matches better with the linguistics of linguistic structure. Plotting a single variant on a map highlights its particular areal distribution,

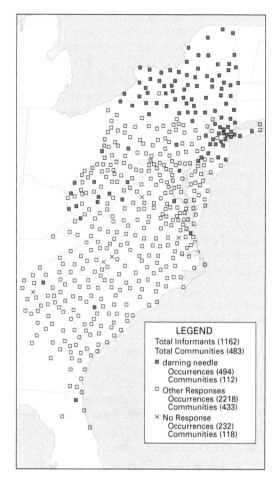

Figure 3.8 *darning needle* variant for *dragonfly*
(generated from www.lap.uga.edu)

instead of forcing the user of the map to pick out occurrences here and there
among the other variants. Figure 3.8 happens not to represent individual speakers directly but instead shows whether or not the word occurred in the survey at
each of the 483 LAMSAS communities. A dark square box appears if at least
one speaker said *darning needle*, an open square box appears if *darning needle*
was not elicited but other responses were collected at that location, and a small x
appears if no responses were collected in the community for this question.
These alternatives exhaust the logical possibilities for any location: presence,
absence, or no evidence about the feature. Other Atlas maps just show dark and

open boxes, which shows the presence of a word at a location, and merges together the other two logical possibilities. For most maps, those with just a few places where the question was not asked, this change makes little difference in the visualization; users can always check the data listings to find out if, as happens in a few cases, a question was not asked in larger areas. The choice to plot by community instead of by individual speaker was made because maps of the size to be read on a computer screen, especially those in use in the early 1990s, would look too cluttered with 1162 points instead of 483. It may be that there is mixed usage among the people at any location, and in the same way individual speakers can and do use more than one of the variant terms for *dragonfly*. We cannot expect that, for any individual or location, only a single variant will be in use; instead, we need to consider the possibility for multiple possible responses (see Kretzschmar and Schneider 1996). Therefore, with respect to a single variant of a linguistic feature, we need to know for individuals and locations alike whether the word is present or absent, given the evidence. It is immediately clear from Figure 3.8 that, while *darning needle* does mostly occur in the north, it is not the only term for *dragonfly* that occurred there at the time of the survey, and that *darning needle* does occur outside of the north. These facts are more difficult to ascertain from Kurath's map of multiple variants, not to mention the maps created with isoglosses.

Computers make it possible to visualize more data. Kurath's *Word Geography* included data on only a portion of the questions in LAMSAS, and each of its 160-odd maps required as much as six or eight hours to prepare by hand, with draftsman's tools and shadings. Draft maps were prepared by hand with colored pencils, and required a similar amount of labor. Thus, to ask any question about the distribution of any feature demanded the same six or eight hours of labor, and so the number of questions that could be asked had a practical limit. The time problem would be that much worse for maps of single variants, which would take nearly the same six or eight hours per variant, much more time overall than plotting several variants on a single map. Now, however, computerization of a large portion of the LAMSAS data has allowed for quick and easy map-making, beginning in the early 1990s. Even at that time, generation of maps by desktop computers took only 90 seconds, at least a 250-fold improvement over the time required for hand charting. More recently, maps like Figure 3.8 of *darning needle* can be generated from LAMSAS evidence online practically instantaneously (www.lap.uga.edu), which effectively removes any constraint on the number of maps that any analyst might make. In consequence, the possibility for efficient comprehensive mapping of data also allows for consideration of the LAMSAS evidence according to the linguistics of speech, in that it is now possible to make maps for every different variant elicited in the survey.

The maps for several of Kurath's main variants for *dragonfly* illustrate how the logic of presence or absence of variants for a linguistic feature, in the

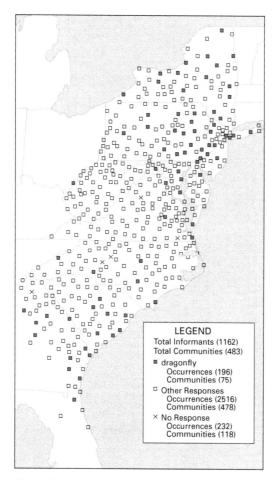

Figure 3.9 *dragonfly* variant for *dragonfly*
(generated from www.lap.uga.edu)

linguistics of speech, differs from the boundary perspective in the linguistics
of linguistic structure. The variant that many would accept as the "standard"
form, *dragonfly* (Figure 3.9), has scattered occurrences over the entire survey
region. Two related variants, *mosquito hawk* (Figure 3.10) and *skeeter hawk*
(Figure 3.11), are mainly but not exclusively found in Kurath's Southern
area. Two other related variants, *snake feeder* (Figure 3.12) and *snake doctor*
(Figure 3.13), are mainly but not exclusively found in what Kurath called the
Midland area. It is no wonder that the variants for *dragonfly* are one of the
favorite items for American traditional dialectologists, because most of them

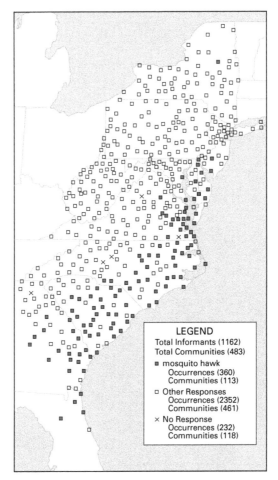

LEGEND
Total Informants (1162)
Total Communities (483)
■ mosquito hawk
    Occurrences (360)
    Communities (113)
□ Other Responses
    Occurrences (2352)
    Communities (461)
× No Response
    Occurrences (232)
    Communities (118)

Figure 3.10 *mosquito hawk* variant for *dragonfly*
(generated from www.lap.uga.edu)

do generally lend themselves to the drawing of lines. And yet plots made from the point of view of the linguistics of speech show that linguistic variants even for this favorite item, to paraphrase Wenker, stubbornly refuse to stay within boundaries, and that in consequence they combine in every area in different proportions. Perhaps most in conflict with the linguistics of linguistic structure is the finding that the word *dragonfly* has such a broad and scattered distribution: if that is the word that most people are supposed to agree upon, one must wonder why it was not found more regularly, and also wonder how it could have come to be considered as the "standard" term (Chapters 6 and 7 will address these questions).

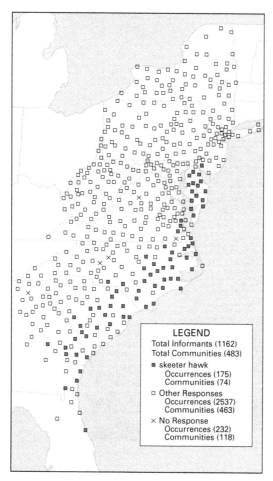

Figure 3.11 *skeeter hawk* variant for *dragonfly*
(generated from www.lap.uga.edu)

If we consider words that are not favorites of traditional dialectologists, scattered distributions like the one for the word *dragonfly* quickly begin to look familiar.

Three common words for the room in the house where you entertain a guest are *front room, parlor,* and *living room* (Figures 3.14, 3.15, 3.16), of which the last might now be considered "standard." At the time of the LAMSAS survey, the word *parlor* was elicited a bit more often than *living room*. Each of these words, however, occurred all across the survey region, and it would be difficult to draw any line that could serve as a boundary.

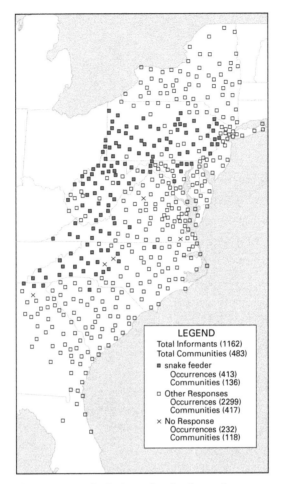

Figure 3.12 *snake feeder* variant for *dragonfly*
(generated from www.lap.uga.edu)

The same finding appears for matters of pronunciation, as in two variant pronunciations of the word *fog* (Figures 3.17, 3.18[3]). Pronunciations with [ɔ] and with [ɑ] (using the simplified phonetics available on the Atlas website; see below for how these segments may actually be modified by shift signs or be diphthongal in their full, detailed transcriptions) have roughly the same number of speakers who use them, all across the LAMSAS survey region. Some areas certainly have more of one pronunciation than the other, but the variants coexist.

[3] Owing to a small glitch in the online system, some diagrams, as here, show 484 communities, rather than 483.

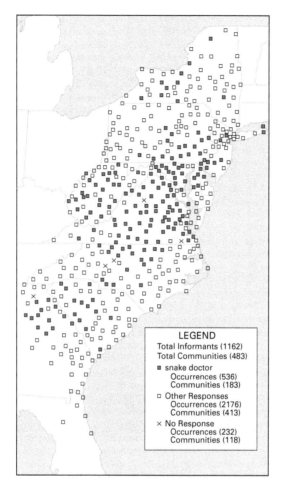

Figure 3.13 *snake doctor* variant for *dragonfly*
(generated from www.lap.uga.edu)

Features of pronunciation are not essentially different from lexical features in
this way; both kinds of concrete entities, in Saussure's terms, are distributed as
he suggested without natural boundaries.

The bottom line for plots of who says what where is that, the more maps that
the analyst can make (thousands upon thousands of maps can be made quickly
on the Atlas website), the more it appears that variants for linguistic features just
do not restrict themselves to neat areas. Some features do have distributions that
might encourage analysts interested in the linguistics of linguistic structure to
draw boundaries, but most of these features are at best characterized by changes
in local frequency of their variants, not by absolute limits of occurrence. For the

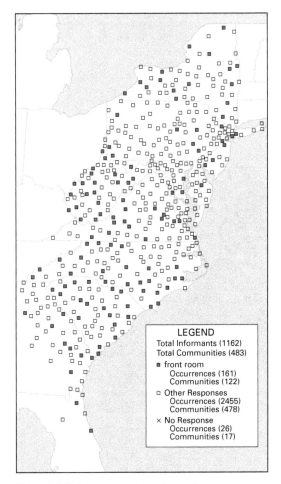

Figure 3.14 *front room* variant for *parlor*
(generated from www.lap.uga.edu)

linguistics of speech, we will need a model that can cope with such widespread distributions in the linguistic continuum.

Findings from the LAMSAS survey: Lists and counts

Simple plotting of who says what where provides for effective areal visualization of single variants of linguistic features. While the maps of single variants provide visual information, their legends offer counts of occurrences, both for the community locations shown and for individual speakers. We can see from

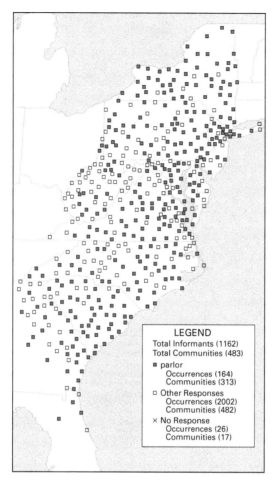

Figure 3.15 *parlor* variant for *parlor*
(generated from www.lap.uga.edu)

Kurath's maps that changes in the relative frequency of feature variants in different areas may be interpreted as boundaries in the linguistics of linguistic structure. For the linguistics of speech, we can see from the single-variant maps that boundaries may not be the best way to describe feature distributions, and instead we need to be able to cope with linguistic continua. Good systematic counting directly addresses the relative frequency of feature variants, and allows the analyst to cope with the continuous variability of linguistic features across an area, as in maps, or across the social landscape for characteristics of speakers other than their location.

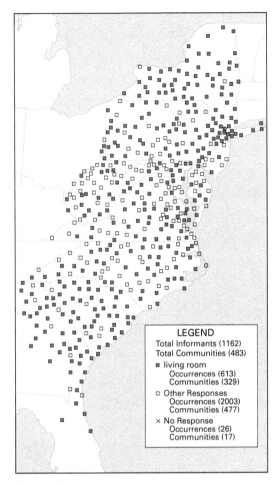

Figure 3.16 *living room* variant for *parlor*
(generated from www.lap.uga.edu)

Good counting consists of two operations, first sorting a linguistic feature into different variant "types," and then counting the "tokens." As Saussure pointed out, the division of the speech signal into "concrete entities," whether phonetic segments or words or phrases or sentences, is essentially arbitrary, not natural: "concrete linguistic entities do not just present themselves for inspection of their own accord" ((1916)1986: 108). In order to extract concrete entities we must be able to recognize "identities," sets of entities which are in some sense the same. Saussure preferred to use words as units, as an element basic to language no matter how difficult it may be to define them in practice, but he

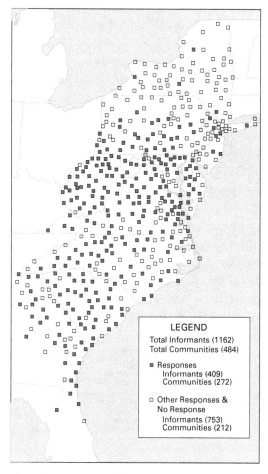

Figure 3.17 Pronunciations of *fog* containing [ɔ]
(generated from www.lap.uga.edu)

accepted that linguists must delimit entities of different kinds for different
purposes. Once having defined a linguistic feature, a more familiar name for
what Saussure called an "identity," whether a set composed of phonetic segments or of words, in the linguistics of speech we must immediately recognize
that each feature has variant forms. Just as Saussure wrote, the concrete entities
that we consider to be the same as parts of the linguistic feature will not all be
alike, whether somewhat different pronunciations of what we recognize as the
same segment or different words or phrases for the same meaning. For example,
once having defined *dragonfly* as 'a long-bodied predatory insect with two pairs

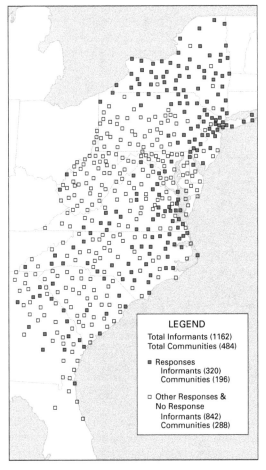

Figure 3.18 Pronunciations of *fog* containing [ɑ]
(generated from www.lap.uga.edu)

of wings,' we immediately recognize that there are other words or short phrases that designate the same insect. Similarly we recognize, once having decided that *fog* is a different word from *fig* on the basis of its vowel, that people pronounce that vowel somewhat differently while still saying *fog*. In each of these cases, we must ask how many different words there are that are used for *dragonfly*, and how many pronunciations there are for the vowel of *fog*. Each different word for the predatory insect is a "type," including the word *dragonfly* itself; so, too, each different pronunciation of the vowel of *fog* could be a type. The idea of a type is thus similar to Saussure's idea of an identity: within the set of entities that belong to a linguistic feature, the variants may themselves be classified into types on the basis of recognition of sameness of some kind. We might, for example, recognize that some pronunciations of *fog* might belong to a type including realizations with [ɔ], and that other pronunciations might belong to a type including realizations with [ɑ]. Just as for the delimitation of linguistic features, identification of variant types is an essentially arbitrary decision. There is no natural principle that would lead us to count *mosquito hawk* and *skeeter hawk* in the same type among variant realizations for the feature *dragonfly* (if we did so, it would be because we judged *mosquito* and *skeeter* to be the same thing); similarly, there is no natural principle that would lead us to count *snake doctor* and *snake feeder* in different types among variant realizations for the feature *dragonfly* (if we did so, it would be because we judged *doctor* and *feeder* to be different things, even if both happen to be modified by *snake*). What matters is that the linguist define each type carefully, according to the needs of the situation, so that it is clear which realizations should count as examples of one type and not another. There is no limit to the number of variant types that may be in use for any linguistic feature, whether a word or a pronunciation. The number of types defined for a linguistic feature is often a matter of convenience; one can, for instance, focus on one or a few types and define an "other" type to encompass all of the realizations that do occur but are not the same as the one or a few types of interest (a "binomial" count, see Kretzschmar and Schneider 1996: 38–48). The set of types defined, however, must comprehensively include all of the realizations in the evidence, so that none of the data has to be left out.

Once the set of types has been identified for any given linguistic feature, it is possible to count how many "tokens" there are for the types, i.e., how many occurrences of each type there may be in the data. Systematic counting means identifying all of the occurrences of a type. This often means finding all of the possible locations where a feature of interest might occur in order to decide whether it did or did not, and if it did, which type it was. Counts can be carried out in any number of ways. Counts per person (how many times an individual speaker uses each type for a linguistic feature) yield a relative frequency by type for an individual speaker; this is the usual practice in sociolinguistic studies. Counts per category (how many times the members of some group of people as defined by area or any social variable use each type for a linguistic feature) yield a relative frequency by type for the category; this is the usual practice in LAMSAS or other survey research. The binary decision, whether a realization is the same or different from another realization, parallels the binary decision whether a person uses a variant or does not use it, or whether a variant was elicited from a location or not. Thus the logic of the linguistics of speech comes down to the decision, given some particular realization of a linguistic feature, whether it is the same or different in terms of its type, and whether it is present or absent in terms of its use. The most basic unit of analysis for the linguistics of speech is not the person (whose speech will have mixed use of different variant types for any feature), not the community (whose speech will also have mixed use of different variant types for any feature), and not even the individual word (in the sense, as Gilliéron is reputed to have said, "chaque mot a son histoire," 'each word has its own history'). The most basic unit of analysis for the linguistics of speech is each separate token of a linguistic feature, each example of a Saussurean concrete entity from the stream of speech, as we recognize the token as belonging to one of the possible variant types that we have delimited for a linguistic feature, after we have recognized the feature itself for its identity.

The tally of types and tokens for the LAMSAS *cloudburst* item 'a brief heavy rain' will illustrate the process (see Table 3.1). There are no fewer than 220 different types of responses for this item, if each of the entries of the tally is granted the status of a type. Each of the entries corresponds to what the LAMSAS field worker wrote down phonetically as what a speaker said. Some entries may seem odd, but in the judgment of the field worker each is the authentic response of a speaker for this item. Some responses, like *cloud* and *sky*, are authentic but hard to understand as responses for the item. Others are not the nominal word or phrase that was expected, such as *in floods*, *it poured in torrents*, and *it's steady*. These responses illustrate the difficulty of delimiting types and features in the wide and continuous variability of language. Two other entries represent the lack of a response from a speaker. "NR" means that a speaker offered no response when the item was raised, and "NA" means that the speaker was not asked about the item. These represent different logical possibilities: "NR" is a genuine kind of response because the speaker's response to the item was to say nothing, while "NA" must count as missing data because the speaker had no opportunity to provide a response. In any large survey or other means of data collection, there are bound to be some irregularities (like a field worker forgetting to raise a few items out of hundreds of items) in the otherwise systematic execution of a plan. These blemishes in practice just add to the natural difficulty of trying to deal with language variation, and provision must be made for all such realities.

Among the 220 different kinds of entries, there are some entries that we might reasonably combine into a single type (see Table 3.2). There are separate entries for "a good rain" and for "good rain," and it would seem odd to count these as separate types just because a field worker recorded the article with one and not the other. Similarly, there are separate entries for "heavy rain" and "heavy rains," where the plural <s> on one entry does not seem to justify making two types. On the other hand, there are fifteen different entries that contain the word "shower"; one of them is the simplex form "shower" and another the plural "showers," but in thirteen other entries the word is modified in some way ("a devil of a," "awful," "big," and so on). For some purposes, it might be a

Table 3.1 *LAMSAS tally for* cloudburst *'a brief heavy rain'*

1	a devil of a shower	1	flash floods	1	heavy flood of rain
1	a good rain	1	flash shower	2	heavy pourdown
1	a pour	1	flash storm	168	heavy rain
1	a very heavy rain	84	flood	1	heavy rainfall
1	a washing rain	1	flood down	3	heavy rains
2	a-pouring down	9	flood of rain	4	heavy rainstorm
1	ant mire	1	flood rain	47	heavy shower
1	awful hard rain	1	flop down	1	heavy storm
1	awful heavy rain	2	fresh	1	heavy weather
7	awful rain	14	freshet	1	heavy weather that
1	awful rainstorm	1	freshets		make up
2	awful shower	6	frog strangler	1	hell of a downpour
1	big fall of water	1	go over kind	3	hell of a rain
1	big fresh		of quick	1	in floods
1	big hard washing	1	godsend	1	it poured in torrents
	rains	1	good big heavy rain	1	it's steady
3	big heavy rain	8	good rain	1	knot floater
1	big lot of rain	1	good seeding	1	large rain
1	big pour of rain	2	good shower	5	lighterd knot floater
83	big rain	4	ground soaker	1	lighterd knot floaters
1	big rainfall	1	gully buster	1	lighterd knot lifter
1	big rains	1	gully digger	2	lighterd knot mover
5	big shower	1	gully mover	1	lighterd knot soaker
1	big storm	1	gully rinser	2	lightwood knot
1	blows heavy	1	gully wash		floater
1	bottle washers	109	gully washer	1	liquid sunshine
1	bottom drop out	1	gully washer and	1	log mover
1	bottom fell out the		trash mover	1	long rain
	cloud	10	gully washers	1	lot of rain
1	chunk mover	1	gush	1	main coast storm
1	clay soaker	1	gushing rain	2	mighty hard rain
1	cloud	1	hard falling down	1	mighty lot of rain
343	cloudburst		rain	1	milldam buster
1	cloudbursters	1	hard mild rain	62	NA
2	cloudbursts	145	hard rain	1	near flood
21	deluge	1	hard rains	1	nice rain
2	deluge of rain	1	hard rainstorm	45	NR
1	ditch maker	57	hard shower	1	old time rain
1	dog mire	2	hard storm	1	potato bed soaker
7	downfall	1	hardest rain	1	pour
331	downpour	1	hasty	1	pour out
3	downpour of rain	1	heap of rain	61	pourdown
1	downpours	1	heavy dash of rain	2	pourdown of rain
3	downspout	6	heavy downpour	7	pourdown rain
1	drencher	2	heavy downpour	2	poured
1	dropdown		of rain	1	poured down
1	drowned	1	heavy fall of water	1	poured rain

Table 3.1 (*cont.*)

1	pouring	1	regular pouring	1	toad frog drownder
2	pouring down		down rain	1	toad frog strangler
14	pouring down rain	1	right smart rain	3	toad strangler
15	pouring rain	1	root soaker	7	torrent
1	pourout	1	sand sifter	2	torrential rain
1	pours	1	set rain	2	torrents
5	powerful rain	1	severe rain	1	trash floater
1	powerful shower	1	sharp shower	3	trash lifter
1	pretty big rain	18	shower	1	trash lifters
1	pretty good rain	1	shower of rain	32	trash mover
1	pretty heavy rain	2	showers	4	trash movers
1	quick rain	1	sight of rain	2	trash piler
3	quite a shower	1	sky	1	trash pilers
5	rain	1	soak	1	tremendous rain
1	rain pourdown	3	soaker	1	tub soaker
2	rained	1	soakers	1	very hard rain
1	rained cats and	1	soaking rain	3	very heavy rain
	dogs	25	squall	1	very heavy
1	rained in torrents	1	squash up		shower
2	rainfall	1	storm	5	washing rain
1	raining	1	storm rain	7	washout
2	raining bullfrog	1	stormed	6	washup
1	raining bullfrogs	1	stump lifter	8	water spout
3	raining cats and dogs	1	stump lifters	2	waterfall
2	raining hard	1	teemed right down	1	watergall burst
1	raining pitchfork	1	temperance flood	8	wet spell
9	rainstorm		rain	1	wet weather
7	rainy spell	1	temperance rain		shower
1	real heavy rain	1	terrible big rain	1	wouldn't that soak
1	regular deluge	6	terrible rain		you
1	regular flood	1	terrific rain		young flood

good idea to define as a single type all of the different entries that contained the word "shower," but for other purposes it would be best to keep them separate. If we remove just the superficial morphological differences like articles and plurals while retaining phrasal entries, and if we create an "other" category for entries that are not the nominal forms we expected or have some other difficulty of interpretation, we can compose a new, shorter list – of only 171 types. Even if we decide to grant the status of type only to the different noun heads of the nominals, there are 49 different noun heads among the *cloudburst* entries ("shower," "mire," "rain," "rainstorm," "fall," and so on). Good management of types certainly clarifies what we study for our own purposes, but it does not get rid of the wide range of variation.

Table 3.2 *List of types for* cloudburst *'a brief heavy rain'*

1	a devil of a shower	4	ground soaker	1	long rain
1	ant mire	1	gully buster	1	lot of rain
1	awful hard rain	1	gully digger	1	main coast storm
1	awful heavy rain	1	gully mover	2	mighty hard rain
7	awful rain	2	gully rinser	1	mighty lot of rain
1	awful rainstorm	1	gully wash	1	milldam buster
2	awful shower	119	gully washer (. s)	1	near flood
1	big fall of water	1	gully washer and	1	nice rain
1	big hard washing rains		trash mover	45	NR
3	big heavy rain	1	gush	1	old time rain
1	big lot of rain	1	gushing rain	1	potato bed soaker
1	big pour of rain	1	hard falling down rain	2	pour (a .)
84	big rain (. s)	1	hard mild rain	1	pour out
1	big rainfall	146	hard rain (. s)	61	pourdown
5	big shower	1	hard rainstorm	2	pourdown of rain
1	big storm	57	hard shower	7	pourdown rain
1	bottle washers	2	hard storm	1	poured rain
1	chunk mover	1	hardest rain	1	pouring
1	clay soaker	1	heap of rain	2	pouring down
345	cloudburst (. s)	1	heavy dash of rain	14	pouring down rain
1	cloudbursters	6	heavy downpour	15	pouring rain
21	deluge	2	heavy downpour of	1	pourout
2	deluge of rain		rain	5	powerful rain
1	ditch maker	1	heavy fall of water	1	powerful shower
1	dog mire	1	heavy flood of rain	1	pretty big rain
7	downfall	2	heavy pourdown	1	pretty good rain
332	downpour (. s)	168	heavy rain	1	pretty heavy rain
3	downpour of rain	1	heavy rainfall	1	quick rain
3	downspout	3	heavy rains	5	rain
1	drencher	4	heavy rainstorm	1	rain pourdown
1	dropdown	47	heavy shower	2	rainfall
1	flash floods	1	heavy storm	1	raining
1	flash shower	1	heavy weather	9	rainstorm
1	flash storm	1	heavy weather that	1	real heavy rain
84	flood		make up	1	regular deluge
1	flood down	1	hell of a downpour	1	regular flood
9	flood of rain	3	hell of a rain	1	regular pouring
1	flood rain	1	knot floater		down rain
1	flop down	1	large rain	1	right smart rain
2	fresh	6	lighterd knot floater	1	root soaker
15	freshet (. s)		(. s)	1	sand sifter
6	frog strangler	1	lighterd knot lifter	1	set rain
1	godsend	2	lighterd knot mover	1	severe rain
1	good big heavy rain	1	lighterd knot soaker	1	sharp shower
9	good rain (a .)	2	lightwood knot floater	20	shower (. s)
1	good seeding	1	liquid sunshine	1	shower of rain
2	good shower	1	log mover	1	sight of rain

Table 3.2 (*cont.*)

1	soak	6	terrible rain	1	tub soaker
4	soaker (. s)	1	terrific rain	1	very hard rain
1	soaking rain	1	toad frog drownder	4	very heavy rain (a .)
25	squall	1	toad frog strangler	1	very heavy shower
1	squash up	3	toad strangler	6	washing rain (a .)
1	storm	9	torrent (. s)	7	washout
1	storm rain	2	torrential rain	6	washup
2	stump lifter (. s)	1	trash floater	8	water spout
1	temperance flood	4	trash lifter (. s)	2	waterfall
	rain	36	trash mover (. s)	1	watergall burst
1	temperance rain	3	trash piler (. s)	1	wet weather shower
1	terrible big rain	1	tremendous rain	1	young flood

Other (2 a-pouring down,1 big fresh, 1 blows heavy, 1 bottom drop out, 1 bottom fell out the cloud, 1 cloud, 1 drowned, 1 go over kind of quick, 1 hasty, 1 in floods, 1 it poured in torrents, 1 it's steady, 2 poured, 1 poured down, 1 pours, 3 quite a shower, 2 rained, 1 rained cats and dogs, 1 rained in torrents, 2 raining bullfrog, 1 raining bullfrogs, 3 raining cats and dogs, 2 raining hard, 1 raining pitchfork, 7 rainy spell, 1 sky, 1 stormed, 1 teemed right down, 8 wet spell, 1 wouldn't that soak you): 52
Missing data: 62 NA

A wide range of variant types is not just a property of the lexicon. If we consider the vowel of *fog*, we also see a long list of entries in a tally (see Table 3.3). These entries are arranged into the different qualities of the vowel nucleus (vowel 1a) and the qualities of the vowel glide (vowel 1b). The entries for the vowel nucleus are divided first into a set organized in order of vowel height. The next set indicates the vowels subject to lengthening [raised dot], extra lengthening [colon], or shortening [breve]; these entries represent the same tokens as the first set, so the entry for [o · 2] means that two of the four pronunciations with [o] in the first set were lengthened. The third set for vowel 1a represents other qualitative differences in the vowels, [underscore] for lip spreading (unrounding) and [strikethrough] for a more centralized realization; these entries should be read like those of the second set, so that the entry for [o̲ 1] means that one of the pronunciations with [o] in the first set was spread/ unrounded. The entries for vowel 1a are separated into sets in this way to enable a better view of three different dimensions of the vowel, relative height, relative length, and other modifications in quality of articulation. The entries for vowel 1b are represented in a single set that illustrates how these dimensions work together, plus the additional quality of weak realization, indicated by curly braces { }.

Within the height dimension, there are no fewer than fifteen different variant types represented by the field workers, each with the best available intensive training in impressionistic phonetics and long experience. The field workers

Table 3.3 *LAMSAS tally of vowel characteristics of* fog

vowel 1a (nucleus)		ɑ·	42	ɒ<	4
height		ɒ:	2	{ɒ}	1
o	4	ã	3	{ɒˏ}	7
oᵛ	3	*other*		{ɐˏ}	1
ɐˆ	1	o̩	1	o	19
ɔˆ	29	ɒ̩	22	oˏ	2
ɔ	132	ɐ	21	oᵛ<	1
ɔᵛ	177	ɔ̩	1	oᵛ	2
a:	2	ə	14	oˏ<	1
a	14	ɡ̩	2	{oˏ}	4
ɑˆ	115	ɕ	10	{o̩}	1
ɑ	214	**vowel 1b (glide)**		ɔ	53
ɑˆ	66	ø	513	ɔᵛ	26
ɑ	75	U	2	ɔˏ	17
ɒˆ	224	{U}	3	ə	2
ɒ	66	{Uˇ}	1	ɔ<	1
ɒᵛ	1	{ʌˆˇ}	1	{ɔˏ}	16
length		{ɣ}	1	{ɔ}	32
a·	14	ə	3	{ɔᵛ}	17
a:	2	{ə}	343	{ɔ<}	2
o·	2	{ə>}	3	{ɔˏ<}	1
ɑ·	202	{ɚˇ}	4	{ɔˇ}	1
ɒ·	173	{ə}	20	{ɔˏ}	4
ɒ:	9	{ɕ}	4	{ə}	4
ɔ·	211	ɒ	1	{əᵛ}	3
ɔ:	33	ɒˏ<	2		

were clearly able to use all of the resources of their phonetic transcription system.[4] The nucleus of the vowel of *fog* can be realized by fully a quarter of the range of sixty different degrees of height offered by the transcription system. The number of possible variant types is much larger when different dimensions of variation are considered together: there are thirty-six different variant types for vowel 1b, even though nearly half of the tokens of *fog* have no glide at all.

---

[4] The phonetic transcription system used by Atlas field workers derives from the International Phonetic Alphabet (IPA), which was the best available tool for recording pronunciation when the survey started. The inventory of vowel symbols offered a total of twenty different degrees of height with the base symbols, sixty levels with diacritical marks (i.e., each base symbol may be indicated with a raising diacritic, be unmodified, or be indicated with a lowering diacritic). Here are the twenty in order by relative height, with rounding, which is not considered in this system to affect height, indicated by parentheses:

i (y), ɨ (ʉ), ɯ (u), ɪ (Y), ᵻ(ᵾ), ʏ (U), e (ø), ə,
o, ɘ, ɚ, ɛ (ɵ), ɜ (ɞ), ʌ, ɐ, æ, ɔ, a, ɑ, ɑ (ɒ)

Table 3.4 *Atlanta Survey African American*
F1/F2 mean frequencies for [i]

F1	F2
A01Mw	262, 2112
A02Mw	319, 2311
A03Mb	263, 2163
A04Mb	300, 2192
A05Mb	349, 2442
A01Fb	402, 2904
A02Fb	380, 2779
A03Fw	464, 2592
A04Fw	409, 2931
A05Fw	459, 3146

Even this large number of variant types is constrained by the possibilities of the transcription system. When vowels are measured acoustically, the formants are identified on the continuously variable scale of frequency in hertz. In the F1/F2 means for [i] for African Americans interviewed in the Atlanta Survey (a recent pilot study of Atlanta speech, described in Kretzschmar and Lanehart 2005), no two of the speakers have the same frequency measurement for either F1 (which roughly corresponds to vowel height) or for F2 (which roughly corresponds to the front/back dimension for vowels), much less for the two values combined (see Table 3.4). Moreover, F1/F2 are not the only formants in acoustical phonetic analysis that play a role in our impressions of the variability of the speech signal, and other aspects of speech sounds such as duration also make audible differences. When the resources of the system used to record and measure speech sounds are greater, we are better able to observe the continuous variability of the speech signal.

The evidence of pronunciation therefore requires even greater attention to the creation of types than lexical evidence. It would be a mistake to think either that every possible difference deserves to be a type in an analysis (perhaps pronunciations indicated with different symbols in transcription should be grouped and counted as one type), or that these symbols represent the only possible way to delimit the continuum of vowel realizations into types (perhaps some levels should be split into more than one type, such as when some height levels have different symbols for rounded and unrounded vowels). Acoustical phonetic evidence is not constrained by a limited inventory of symbols, but it is no less in need of type delimitation. The common practice in sociophonetics is to draw an ellipse around the tokens on an acoustical F1/F2 plot that correspond to a vowel in a word or word class, in order to consider the relationship between vowels. This method clearly relates to the linguistics of linguistic structure, because the ellipses fit the data to the structure preferred by the analyst, to the set of vowels considered to exist before any inspection of the data. Indeed, such ellipses are often applied in the same way that isoglosses have been, in that some tokens from the word or word class under study are allowed to remain outside of the ellipse as "isolated examples." A different method which does not permit the leeway of drawing ellipses is to devise a grid for an F1/F2 plot so that tokens can be said to vary by the "steps" of the grid (as in Kretzschmar, Lanehart, Barry, Osiapem, and Kim 2004); this method arbitrarily measures types at intervals of 50 Hz for F1 and 200 Hz for F2, which offers a systematic and comprehensive means of delimiting the continuous variation in sound frequency. Whether we accept the divisions that we inherit from the IPA (as Saussure remarked that we often accept older terms), or whether we create new divisions into types, the variability of pronunciation is certainly no less than variability in the lexicon, and just as much in need of good sorting and counting practices.

Once we have good lists and counts, we can observe a curious property that they all possess. If we count the frequency of occurrence of each realization for a survey question (whether lexical or phonetic), we find that there will be few realizations that occur very frequently, and a great many realizations that occur only infrequently. In fact, the most common frequency observed in all of our lexical data sets is the single occurrence. Figure 3.19 shows a graph of the *cloudburst* data ordered by frequency of responses. There are five response types with more than 100 tokens: *cloudburst* (343), *downpour* (331), *heavy rain* (168), *hard rain* (145), and *gully washer* (109). But there are 141 response types with only a single occurrence, and 57 other response types with fewer than 10 tokens. This frequency distribution yields the sharp curve of the graph. Figure 3.20 charts the data from Table 3.2, after all the types with superficial differences have been removed and an "other" category has been created to include all responses that are not nominals, and clearly the same curve remains. Figure 3.21 shows the chart by response frequency for the height of the vowels of *fog*, from Table 3.3. The curve here appears to be shallower, but that comes from the constraints on possible types from the limited IPA symbol set.

Lest anyone think that this is a distributional oddity of *cloudburst* and *fog*, the same distributional pattern appears over and over again in our lexical and phonetic analyses. In the original data set for the *thunderstorm* item, there are 44 different response types that occur twice or more, and 63 response types that occur only once (see Figure 3.22). If we adjust the list for plurals and possibly inappropriate response types, as for *cloudburst*, the reduced data set for *thunderstorm* still has 27 response types that occur twice or more, and 46 response types that occur only once. The relevant numbers for *mantel* 'shelf over a fireplace' are 23 types that occur more than once versus 27 that occur just once in the

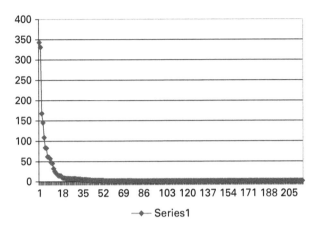

Figure 3.19 *cloudburst* data (Table 3.1) charted by frequency of response

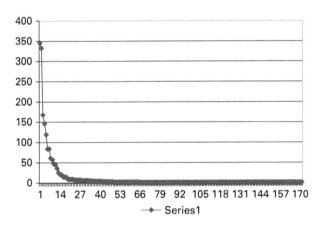

Figure 3.20 Adjusted *cloudburst* data (Table 3.2) charted by frequency of response

original data set (Figure 3.23), and 18 more than once and 16 just once in the reduced data set. The large number of single occurrences does not go away in the set of responses without pluralizations and possibly inappropriate responses. The basic distribution persists, just with the "tail" of the curve shortened somewhat; this is true in our Atlas experience no matter how severely we lemmatize and otherwise restrict the response types. Because of the more restricted number of possible realizations from the impressionistic transcriptions in the phonetic data sets, we do not always see that the single response

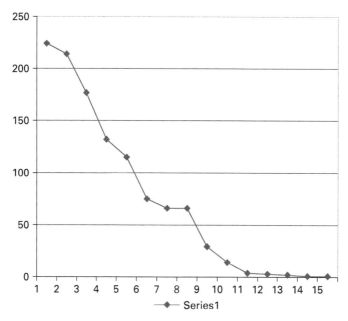

Figure 3.21 *fog*, plot of vowel 1a height (Table 3.3)

is the most commonly observed frequency, but we do see the same curve that describes the small number of frequently occurring realizations and the larger number of infrequently occurring realizations (Figures 3.24, 3.25, and 3.26, each with a plot of vowel 1a height). Only the stressed vowel has been charted for these cases, but similar charts could be plotted for the other segments in these and other words in the data, including glides, unstressed vowels, and even some consonants (IPA options for variation in consonants are even more restricted than for vowels). Each of these curves from the phonetic data is also shallower than the curves from the lexical data, because of the constraint upon possible transcription types. However, the pronunciation data always follows the same basic distributional pattern as the lexical data.

Thus, to sum up, not only are there massive amounts of lexical and phonetic variation in the data (much of it in places that many linguists might have thought to be invariant), but the variation always shows the same basic pattern of distribution. Each of these cases has a frequency distribution of realizations which, when charted, generates the same kind of curve, an asymptotic curve with a high limit at the Y-axis and a low limit along the X-axis. Henceforth I will refer to this distribution as the "A-curve" (for asymptotic hyperbolic curve). The A-curve, then, is a general property of the distribution of feature variants in

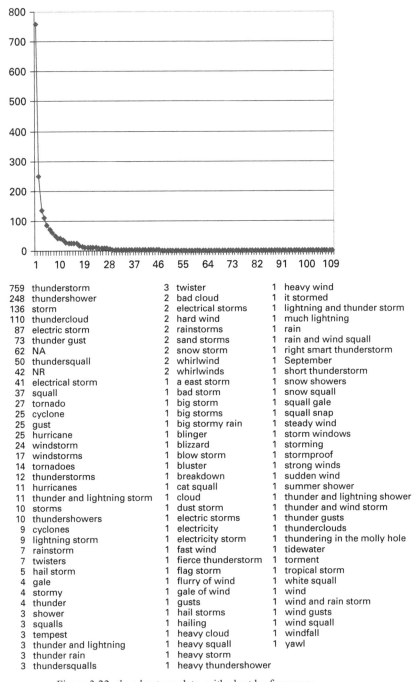

759	thunderstorm	3	twister	1	heavy wind
248	thundershower	2	bad cloud	1	it stormed
136	storm	2	electrical storms	1	lightning and thunder storm
110	thundercloud	2	hard wind	1	much lightning
87	electric storm	2	rainstorms	1	rain
73	thunder gust	2	sand storms	1	rain and wind squall
62	NA	2	snow storm	1	right smart thunderstorm
50	thundersquall	2	whirlwind	1	September
42	NR	2	whirlwinds	1	short thunderstorm
41	electrical storm	1	a east storm	1	snow showers
37	squall	1	bad storm	1	snow squall
27	tornado	1	big storm	1	squall gale
25	cyclone	1	big storms	1	squall snap
25	gust	1	big stormy rain	1	steady wind
25	hurricane	1	blinger	1	storm windows
24	windstorm	1	blizzard	1	storming
17	windstorms	1	blow storm	1	stormproof
14	tornadoes	1	bluster	1	strong winds
12	thunderstorms	1	breakdown	1	sudden wind
11	hurricanes	1	cat squall	1	summer shower
11	thunder and lightning storm	1	cloud	1	thunder and lightning shower
10	storms	1	dust storm	1	thunder and wind storm
10	thundershowers	1	electric storms	1	thunder gusts
9	cyclones	1	electricity	1	thunderclouds
9	lightning storm	1	electricity storm	1	thundering in the molly hole
7	rainstorm	1	fast wind	1	tidewater
7	twisters	1	fierce thunderstorm	1	torment
5	hail storm	1	flag storm	1	tropical storm
4	gale	1	flurry of wind	1	white squall
4	stormy	1	gale of wind	1	wind
4	thunder	1	gusts	1	wind and rain storm
3	shower	1	hail storms	1	wind gusts
3	squalls	1	hailing	1	wind squall
3	tempest	1	heavy cloud	1	windfall
3	thunder and lightning	1	heavy squall	1	yawl
3	thunder rain	1	heavy storm		
3	thundersqualls	1	heavy thundershower		

Figure 3.22 *thunderstorm* data, with chart by frequency

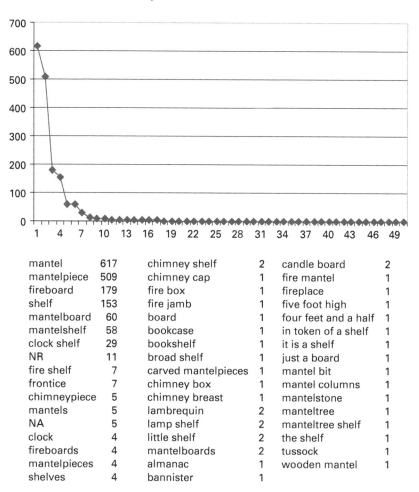

mantel	617	chimney shelf	2	candle board	2
mantelpiece	509	chimney cap	1	fire mantel	1
fireboard	179	fire box	1	fireplace	1
shelf	153	fire jamb	1	five foot high	1
mantelboard	60	board	1	four feet and a half	1
mantelshelf	58	bookcase	1	in token of a shelf	1
clock shelf	29	bookshelf	1	it is a shelf	1
NR	11	broad shelf	1	just a board	1
fire shelf	7	carved mantelpieces	1	mantel bit	1
frontice	7	chimney box	1	mantel columns	1
chimneypiece	5	chimney breast	1	mantelstone	1
mantels	5	lambrequin	2	manteltree	1
NA	5	lamp shelf	2	manteltree shelf	1
clock	4	little shelf	2	the shelf	1
fireboards	4	mantelboards	2	tussock	1
mantelpieces	4	almanac	1	wooden mantel	1
shelves	4	bannister	1		

Figure 3.23 *mantel* data, with chart by frequency

speech. For the moment, the A-curve distribution pattern of response types may appear just to be a curious property of speech – but the pattern will turn out to be of great importance for a general model of speech (Chapter 6).

In the linguistics of linguistic structure, the variability of speech is sharply constrained by idealization, by the need to work with system and structure. That is, indeed, one of the reasons that Saussure chose the linguistics of linguistic structure, the better to be able to manage what he saw as the intractability of language variation. Now we have the means to record and to manipulate massive quantities of speech, not the totality of speech in a community but quantities on a scale that begins to reflect it. What was intractable for Saussure

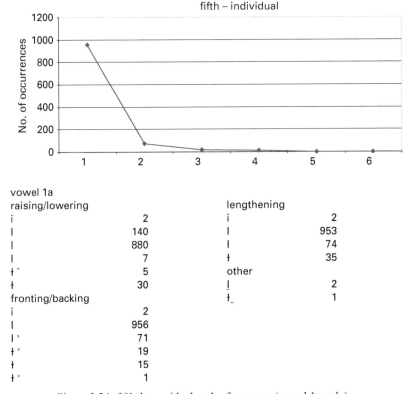

vowel 1a

raising/lowering		lengthening	
i	2	i	2
I	140	I	953
I	880	I	74
I	7	ɨ	35
ɨˆ	5	other	
ɨ	30	ɪ̞	2
fronting/backing		ɨ̞	1
i	2		
I	956		
Iʾ	71		
ɨˑ	19		
ɨ	15		
ɨʾ	1		

Figure 3.24 *fifth* data, with chart by frequency (vowel 1a only)

has become conceivable for us today. The tremendous variability of speech has become something to embrace and to study. In the linguistics of speech, the central question is "who says what where?" It is one of the key findings for the linguistics of speech of large-scale surveys like LAMSAS, that language is ever so much more variable than any individual could predict from personal experience. As individuals we manage to make sense out of the variation that we experience personally in order to acquire language. As linguists, in order to make sense of language variation beyond the experience of individual speakers, we require reasonable means first to identify linguistic features from the stream of speech, and then to delimit variant types with which a given feature can be realized. In this chapter, we have seen that lines and boundaries fail to capture the facts of variation as well as we might like them to, both in their selection of what to plot and in how the lines are applied. We have also seen that the great range of variability in both the lexicon and pronunciation can be managed, but

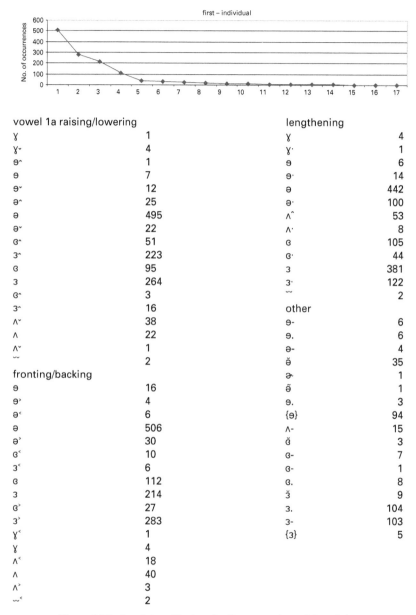

vowel 1a raising/lowering

ɣ	1
ɣˇ	4
ə̂	1
ə	7
əˇ	12
ə̂	25
ə	495
əˇ	22
ɞ̂	51
ɜ̂	223
ɞ	95
ɜ	264
ɞ̂	3
ɜ̂	16
ʌˇ	38
ʌ	22
ʌˇ	1
̮̮	2

fronting/backing

ə	16
ə'	4
ə<	6
ə	506
ə'	30
ɞ<	10
ɜ<	6
ɞ	112
ɜ	214
ɞ'	27
ɜ'	283
ɣ<	1
ɣ	4
ʌ<	18
ʌ	40
ʌ'	3
̮̮<	2

lengthening

ɣ	4
ɣ·	1
ə	6
ə·	14
ə	442
ə·	100
ʌ̂	53
ʌ·	8
ɞ	105
ɞ·	44
ɜ	381
ɜ·	122
̮̮	2

other

ə-	6
ə.	6
ə-	4
ə̆	35
ɚ	1
ə̄	1
ə.	3
{ə}	94
ʌ-	15
ʌ̆	3
ɞ-	7
ɞ-	1
ɞ.	8
ɜ̆	9
ɜ.	104
ɜ-	103
{ɜ}	5

Figure 3.25 *first* data, with chart by frequency (vowel 1a only)

Vowel 1a only (nucleus of diphthong); other segments deleted

vowel 1a raising/lowering

ə	12
ə˘	20
ɜ˘	1
e˘	42
ɐ	161
ɐ˘	79
a^	183
a	410
a˘	1
ɑ^	83
ɑ	93

fronting/backing

a‹	1
a	264
a›	329
ə‹	3
ə	27
ə›	2
ɜ	1
ɐ‹	37
ɐ	224
ɐ›	21
ɑ‹	82
ɑ	79
ɑ›	15

lengthening

a	396
a·	197
a:	1
ɐ	273
ɐ·	9
ə	32
ɜ	1
ɑ	117
ɑ·	59

other

a-	1
ă	10
ā	5
ĕ	8
ɐ̆	1
ɑ̃	2

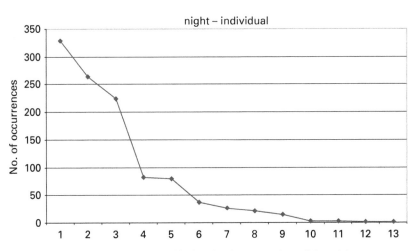

Figure 3.26 *night* data, with chart by frequency (vowel 1a only)

never eliminated, by good sorting. In both maps and lists, traditional tools like lines and the IPA should not determine the results of our analyses, although they may well inform what we decide to do. Finally, we have seen that good counting and good sorting itself produces a regular, reliable result, the A-curve distributional pattern when variants are charted by their frequencies. In the next chapter, we will count the tokens for each type in order to gain some idea of frequency effects that, as suggested by the discussion of plots and boundaries, play a role in how variants are distributed across areas and social categories.

4   Statistical evidence from linguistic
     survey research

Yet another modern development also addresses, though in a different way, Saussure's complaint that "language in its totality is unknowable" – modern methods of sampling and inferential statistics. Probability theory in mathematics, as it is used in inferential statistics, was certainly available to Saussure, but modern applications of the mathematical principles of probability to inferential statistics mostly occurred after his time. Thomas Bayes, for instance, after whom "Bayesian statistics" and "Bayesian probability" and "Bayesian inference" are named (these notions reflect input probabilities, or perceived probabilities, in the drawing of statistical inferences), lived in the eighteenth century, which is also the time that the notion "statistics" originated in connection with census data. Yet it is unlikely that Bayes himself would recognize the concepts to which his name has been attached, which are currently important in domains such as search engine performance and email spam control. Applications of statistics in manufacturing and science, and the great refinement of its potential, only occurred during the twentieth century. William Sealy Gosset, who used the pseudonym "Student" and originated the "Student's *t*-test," worked for the Guinness brewery at just about the time that Saussure was teaching the *Course*. Gosset developed his small-sample test as an industrial tool, for use in quality control in the brewery and to maximize barley yields on its associated farms. Perhaps the best gauge of the recent impact of statistics in science is the well-known resistance of the tobacco companies in the 1960s to statistical analyses of the occurrence of cancer among the smoking and non-smoking population. The use of statistics for epidemiology and public health was so new at that time that tobacco executives were able to argue that mere statistics could not show that cigarettes caused cancer – the greater acceptance of statistical inferences today makes us consider such arguments to be duplicitous (and big tobacco no longer makes them).

Kretzschmar and Schneider (1996: Chapter 2) provides a brief introduction to inferential statistics for linguists, and several other books attempt the same task at greater length (e.g., Davis 1990; Woods, Fletcher and Hughes 1986; Oakes 1998). Here, it will be enough just to characterize how the inferences are made. Descriptive statistics are raw numbers, counts of tokens and the percentages derived from the counts. When we compare counts for two (or more) different categories, we usually see more and less, not all or none. So, for example, we see that more LAMSAS speakers in northern locations used the word *darning needle*, and that further south the word appeared to be used less. Inferential statistics tell us when to take note of differences between counts; they tell us when such a difference in frequency should be considered to be "significant." Such an inference is possible because, as it turns out, variation in many aspects of real life is more predictable than we might have thought: all else being equal, repeated measures often have a "normal distribution" (the bell curve, a central feature of "Gaussian" statistics known to statisticians as the Empirical Rule). Moreover, all else being equal, results of repeated experiments also have a "normal distribution" (known to statisticians as the Central Limit Theorem). The key point in inferential statistics is that the nature of the "normal distribution" is such that, for repeated measures or repeated experiments, we can calculate how different any given result may be from the mean value of the measures or experiments, a value called the "standard deviation." This value depends on the "variance" of all the results (how different they all are from the mean result). Again as it turns out, in a normal distribution 68% of results will be within one standard deviation, 95% within two standard deviations, and 99.7% within three standard deviations. The normal distribution and its standard deviation are properties of the natural world, like magnetism, or like the propagation of sound waves, and we can use them to help us evaluate results of our experiments, just as we can use the physics of magnetism and of sound waves to help us make speech recordings. For any experiment, we can decide on a degree of difference that we should care about, a threshold level for "significance," based on how far away any individual result may be from the mean. That is, if any result does not achieve this threshold, we cannot say that it is really different (a state that statisticians call the "null hypothesis"); however, if any result does achieve the threshold level, we are entitled to ask what caused this result to be different from the others. The usual threshold for significance in the social sciences is expressed as $p < .05$. That is, in order to consider any result to be "significant," we want it to be at least two standard deviations from the mean, in that 5% of results that occur outside of the 95% of results that we know will occur within two standard deviations. Sometimes analysts will apply different threshold levels of significance, such as $p < .01$ or $p < .001$ (about three standard deviations from the mean), for particular purposes; the analyst always gets to select the threshold for significance appropriate to the analysis. Any result can be more or less probable (the p), but is either significant or not (where p is higher or lower than the chosen threshold for significance). Thus the inference: when we formulate a statistical experiment in the appropriate way, we can use the Empirical Rule and Central Limit Theorem, which describe a property of the natural world, to help us evaluate differences in frequency at the level of significance that we require for our analysis. Statistical significance is not magic, and neither does it actually explain anything; properly carried out, it just tells us when to take note of a result from our experiment.

There are many different choices for inferential statistics. Sometimes it makes sense to compare the mean values of two groups or samples, such as with Gosset's "Student's *t*-test." On other occasions, it is better to use a Chi Square test, which considers the expected and actual values in a contingency table, to assess whether at least one actual value in the table is significantly different from what is expected. Multivariate analysis can take multiple variables into account all at the same time. Each of these test statistics has its own particular conditions under which it may be used. So-called "parametric" tests are sensitive to the Gaussian normal distribution; other tests are called "nonparametric," and are not sensitive to that. Some tests are called "robust" because they allow for use under a wide variety of conditions. All tests, however, will give their users an answer whether their conditions are satisfied or not, and so it is up to the user to make sure that the data to be analyzed does meet the conditions – or risk being misled by the statistical results. The key thing is the choice of the right test statistic to match the research question and conditions of the experiment.

The development of effective survey research is even more recent than manufacturing and scientific applications of inferential statistics. Informal polling of some members to predict the behavior of a larger population has a long history, and an equally long history of mixed results. Modern random sampling procedures, especially in support of election polling, developed rapidly after George Gallup incorrectly predicted the victory of Dewey instead of Truman in the 1948 American presidential election. While political polling is subject to manipulation, so that sponsors of polls can report or be told what they want to hear (it matters greatly how the questions are asked), the procedures for conducting opinion polls improved markedly in the last decades of the twentieth century. The accuracy of election polls today is so great that American exit poll results are not supposed to be broadcast before the polls are closed in later time zones, for fear that the poll results will keep people from voting if they believe that the election has already been decided (a Bayesian notion!). The sampling is "random," not in the common sense of 'accidental,' but because every member of the population being surveyed has an equal chance of being selected for the survey. Earlier mixed results of surveys stemmed from non-random selection of people from the population surveyed. So, for example, if an election poll only sampled subscribers to the *Wall Street Journal* (people with a demonstrated interest in business affairs), the result would likely be biased and might not represent the opinions of the entire voting population. Similarly, if an election poll only talked to several members of the Kretzschmar family, the result would likely be biased and might not represent the opinions of the entire voting population, even though various Kretzschmars have different political opinions and the family as a whole might be considered "typical" or "representative" of American families. Potential bias is not always easy to predict, so the selection of "typical" or "representative" respondents may well have unforeseen consequences. The great improvement in election polling has come in large part from improvements in randomization of sampling, so that surveys can avoid potential bias.

The combination of random sampling and inferential statistics allows analysts to make effective estimates of the behavior of entire populations on the basis of a greatly restricted sample. That is, the application of probability theory in survey research allows analysts to measure how just a few members of some population behave, whether lightbulbs in a manufacturing process or people in an election, and to estimate how the entire population of lightbulbs or people will behave. It is not necessary to test every lightbulb in order to make a good estimate of how many bulbs are faulty. Thus, linguists need no longer consider that the "totality of language," all of the language behavior of all the members of a population of speakers, is "unknowable," at least for particular linguistic features, because we have effective means to estimate the behavior of the whole population of speakers on the basis of some smaller group of them whose speech we have actually recorded and measured. We need not talk to every speaker in a population, which would be impossible for most populations of speakers that linguists are interested in describing, in order to make a good estimate of how they will realize some linguistic feature. Rather, we need only follow the procedures of modern survey research in order to reap the benefits of statistical estimation of the language behavior of the population. Conversely, in the linguistics of speech, we cannot consider that we would get a good estimate of the language behavior of a population of speakers from the evidence of just one or a few speakers without following such sampling procedures. Practitioners of the linguistics of linguistic structure can and typically do rely on evidence from typical speakers, as we have seen, because their model *assumes* the relative homogeneity of *langue* in a speech community. For the linguistics of speech, a good estimate of the language behavior of a population of speakers is the goal of research, not an assumption.

By way of illustration, contemporary procedures for random sampling were used recently in a survey of the speech of Atlanta (Kretzschmar and Lanehart 2005). Atlanta has a big metropolitan area, and our team's resources would not allow us to survey all of it.[1] Therefore we elected to survey just Fulton County and DeKalb County, the two most populous counties of the Atlanta metropolitan area, with a total population of approximately 1.5 million people according to the 2000 census (www.census.gov), divided approximately evenly between

---

[1] We relied on funding from a grant from the National Science Foundation, NSF SBR-0233448, "SGER: Atlanta Speech Sample."

African Americans and Non African Americans. We considered the two counties as one geographical unit for analysis, and drew the sample without attempting to balance Fulton against DeKalb. We created parallel samples based on three binary variables: race (African American vs. Non African American), sex (female vs. male), and occupational type (blue collar vs. white collar). Because of housing patterns in Atlanta, we ended up with the African American speakers all in the southern part of the survey area, and the Non African Americans in the northern part. Our resources did not permit any additional quota categories, or finer gradations within categories. All of the subjects had to have English as their primary language, had to be adults (age eighteen or older), and, while ideally lifelong residents, must have lived in the area for at least half of their lives including early childhood. We thus explicitly considered as many of the messy facts of human demographic and social organization as our resources would allow, just the kind of complexity that Saussure preferred not to address. Our requirements for primary language, minimum age, and long-term residence restrictions leave out some of the residents of Atlanta (non-English speakers, children, transient residents, and as we shall see, people who do not have or who do not answer their landline telephones) to establish a target population. While we might in a general way describe our survey as treating the speech of Atlanta, we should not forget that "Atlanta" is merely a convenient designation for the particular people who had a chance to be surveyed in our target population (English-speaking adults who had lived there over the long term). We applied very specific means to decide who was eligible for our survey, and these in turn also must describe the population to whom the results of the survey would apply. Our quotas, then, balanced several social variables within the target population.

We then followed current standard methods for randomized field research to draw our sample from our target population. This meant buying a random telephone list for the two counties, and then making calls from the list. Two field workers used a standard phone script to qualify potential speakers for the Non African American and for the African American parallel samples, respectively. They arranged for a personal interview at the speakers' homes for those admitted to the sample. Early in the calling it was not difficult to qualify speakers and get them to agree to interviews. Later, when our quotas were mostly full, it was very hard indeed. We would say, however, that our use of randomized speaker selection did not place an undue burden on the survey; it generally worked well, and it was certainly not impossible to carry out. The benefit of the trouble we did take is that it permitted the use of inferential statistics in analysis of the evidence collected. We could feel justified that our results did represent the language behavior of our target population in Atlanta. Some contemporary sociolinguists argue, to the contrary, that it is too difficult and not worthwhile to use random samples, or that it is not necessary to use random samples no matter the difficulty, to collect evidence of language behavior (e.g., Chambers 2003). Such views actually derive from a point of view like Saussure's: if members of a community share a *langue*, why would a linguist go to any extra trouble to sample a population that by definition serves as a collectivity? That might be a defensible position for the linguistics of linguistic structure, but of course in this chapter we are interested in the linguistics of speech, and so the assumption of a shared *langue* does not apply here. Randomized sampling may not perfectly represent the entire population of an area – some people are left out on purpose – but it does support valid estimates of the language behavior for the members of the target population from which the sample is drawn. That is just what the linguistics of speech requires, in order to get at the "totality" of language behavior for the area or group under study.

As survey research, the LAMSAS project was planned and created before reliable contemporary methods were developed. Kurath and his associates assumed that careful selection of communities and speakers, as "representative" of the speech of their areas, would improve the quality of the survey. The notion of "representative speakers" has meaning from the viewpoint of the linguistics of linguistic structure, under the assumption that there is a linguistic structure for which some speakers or places might be more "representative" than others. In the linguistics of speech, however, since we do not assume the existence of *langue*, we must abandon the notion of representative speakers and fall back on what we understand about populations. We must treat each speaker as merely an individual user of language, and we must rely on randomized sampling in order to get some idea of the totality of speech in any regional or other group of speakers we study. As for LAMSAS, to throw out the historical evidence of 1162 speakers just because survey research standards have changed would be silly; rather, we can try to establish the relationship between the LAMSAS evidence as it was collected and the evidence that a modern random sample could offer.

As it turns out, what Kurath and his field workers actually did is not so different from survey research as it is done today, and we can quantify its accuracy.[2] First of all, as in our recent Atlanta Survey, not every member of the population of the region surveyed was eligible to be interviewed. Kurath wanted adult natives of their region, which leaves out transient residents and younger speakers. Kurath also did not systematically survey African Americans. He did collect evidence from forty-one black speakers in the South, sixty-two if we count the twenty-one Gullah speakers interviewed with the Atlas questionnaire by Lorenzo Turner but not included in the LAMSAS

---

[2] The following section is based on Kretzschmar, McDavid, Lerud, and Johnson 1993: 16–19.

tally, more African American speech than was systematically collected by anybody else during the period – but even so African Americans were not included on the same terms as white adult speakers. We can therefore describe Kurath's plan as a quota sample of a target population, in which there was a systematic and regular plan for sampling by county according to Kurath's speaker types.

While Kurath could have no notion of random sampling at his time, he did create a systematic and regular plan for how field workers were supposed to locate speakers in each community: recommendation of appropriate speakers for the survey by librarians, local history groups, newspapermen, or other representatives of local institutions. We need to consider whether Kurath's method of working from local contacts introduced any particular bias. While Kurath's method may have introduced some bias, it would be difficult to say that it biased his results in any particular direction (not, for example, as sampling only *Wall Street Journal* subscribers might bias an election survey towards a particular point of view). In order to protect against accidentally introducing destructive bias, researchers cannot select people on the basis of their speech characteristics, so that the selection criteria were the same as the characteristics that the researcher wanted to measure. There is no evidence that this occurred in the Atlas. Speakers were sometimes rejected when they could not produce speech normally because of physical defects (say, owing to missing teeth), or were unable to complete the interview (say, owing to mental status), but speakers were not included or rejected for how they spoke.

The only aspect of Kurath's plan that really did not give each member of his target population an equal chance of being selected for an interview was the use of counties as the unit of geographical coverage without equal attention to how many people lived there. Kurath tried to create even areal coverage, at the expense of sampling with respect to population density. The county plan meant that proportionately fewer people were interviewed in urban areas, although in fact additional speakers were often interviewed in urban places beyond what the plan called for as a minimum. According to the 1940 census, at that time over 60% of the population lived in urban places (defined by the 1940 census as conurbations of over 2500 people!). The even areal coverage of LAMSAS resulted in three-quarters of its speakers having rural residence. Thus urban members of the target population had a somewhat lower chance of being selected, and in consequence the survey somewhat favored rural speakers. The county plan also resulted in differences in the proportion of speakers sampled from each state in comparison to population. The sampling scale, the number of speakers selected in comparison to the total target population, varies from 1:51,595 in New Jersey, a densely populated state, to about 1:10,000 for several less-populated states (and 1:5188 for South Carolina, the home state of Raven McDavid, who conducted by far the majority of the Southern interviews). Such a plan would not be acceptable today as the basis for random sampling, though some linguists still follow survey plans that do not account for demographics. The Telsur (later *Atlas of North American English*) plan followed by Labov, Boberg, and Ash (2006), for instance, specified that two speakers were supposed to be selected from each Metropolitan Statistical Area (MSA) nationwide; even though some supplemental speakers were added later in some MSAs, this plan does not try to account systematically for population differences or for differences in area. In Kurath's survey we do have even coverage by area, if not population, and if we are aware of the potential bias introduced by the Atlas county plan, we can try to watch out for, and try to avoid being misled by, results that may come more from the plan than from the evidence itself.

Comparison of the LAMSAS speakers interviewed against the proportions of different people by sex or education as they appear in the 1940 census figures also shows some variation from state to state, no doubt caused by the way in which the survey plan was applied by the field workers. In practice men are overrepresented (70% men vs. 30% women), although women are somewhat overrepresented in urban areas (54% vs. 46%). Kurath's plan explicitly tried to select speakers from different educational levels, and the LAMSAS sample turned out to be remarkably similar to the distribution of speakers by education. Overall, the LAMSAS sample does appear to be generally faithful to its target population, with the greatest sampling bias occurring by population density and by sex. Even though Kurath and his field workers could not yet be aware of random sampling, the LAMSAS sample, though definitely skewed, is not that far from a modern quota sample. There are large enough numbers of speakers selected from each of the quota categories in order to be able to perform statistical testing (as we shall see below, statistics take such issues in the data into account), always with the proviso that the sampling was not carried out according to modern standards; no class of speakers, among those eligible to be interviewed, was so badly unrepresented that we have to reject the evidence completely. LAMSAS cannot fairly be accused of having *only* selected "NORMs" ('Non-mobile Old Rural Males') as its speakers, as sociolinguists have sometimes asserted, and which was in fact the case in the Survey of English Dialects in England (Orton *et al.* 1962–71). For LAMSAS, as for all linguistic surveys, we need to be aware that sampling human populations necessarily involves more problems with randomness than statisticians see, for example, in manufacturing applications.

Given the general resemblance of the LAMSAS sample to a quota sample, we should ask whether variation in the execution of the plan created links between categories of interest, like only having women speakers from urban places, and thus created problems that would get in the way of effective statistical analysis. In order for inferential statistics to work, each case must be measured under the

Table 4.1 *Pooled within-groups correlation matrix for LAMSAS variables*

	SEX	AGE	FW	EDUC	COMMTYP	RACE	NTOS	WTOE
SEX	1.000							
AGE	.040	1.000						
FW	−.087	.097	1.000					
EDU	−.082	−.342	.072	1.000				
COMMTYP	−.504	−.016	.215	.242	1.000			
RACE	.046	−.081	−.214	.147	−.074	1.000		
NTOS	−.192	.021	.385	.011	.183	−.157	1.000	
WTOE	−.037	.011	−.154	−.087	.068	−.064	.054	1.000

same conditions, and each variable must be handled separately from each other variable, so that in statistical terms each is "independent." While the LAMSAS sampling plan does have some characteristics that challenge whether the cases and variables are entirely independent (for example, having more interviews with women in urban areas; see Kretzschmar and Schneider 1996: 38–51), that can be hard to avoid in all cases when sampling human populations, and it is possible to test whether any correlations between variables are so damaging as to get in the way of statistical processing. Kretzschmar and Schneider (1996: 48) prepared a correlation matrix for LAMSAS that shows eight categories of interest: sex, age, field worker, education, community type (urban vs. rural residence), race, North to South (the north/south dimension of a regional analysis), and West to East (the west/east dimension of a regional analysis). Table 4.1 gives Pearson correlation coefficients, which show the degree of interrelation between each category on a scale between 0 and 1.0.

Disregarding the + and − signs, which indicate positive and inverse correlations, the three greatest relationships are between community type and sex (.504), the NtoS dimension and field worker (.385), and education and age (.342). The three highest coefficients do match what we know about the execution of the LAMSAS sample. In LAMSAS more women were chosen from urban areas, Raven McDavid did indeed do the lion's share of the Deep South field work, and the survey design did weight selection practices towards at least one old, uneducated speaker in each community. None of these coefficients, however, approaches the limit of ± .70 at which it is advisable to change the test categories (Hedderson 1987: 136), and therefore the test suggests that the categories are indeed independent and appropriate for statistical testing. We should use extra care in our analyses with respect to the correlations noted, but we can feel justified to carry out analyses.

If we accept the LAMSAS sampling frame for what it is and compare what Kurath accomplished in the survey to modern opinion polling, we find that it is not so different in its results. Instead of asking for a preference between two political candidates, the question for the linguistic survey would be "given LAMSAS evidence, what is the proportion of people from the target population who use a given linguistic feature, as opposed to those not using that feature?" Given the generally accepted confidence interval (level of significance) for opinion polling and other statistical results in the social sciences (95%, or $p < .05$), and given the facts of the LAMSAS sample, we can apply a standard statistical formula to determine the standard error of the prediction made by the LAMSAS sample about the use of any linguistic feature among the target population at the time of the survey: $\pm$ 3%. This means that the prediction of the LAMSAS sample has a 95% likelihood of being within 3% of the actual usage among the target population of the feature under study – just the standard error often reported by contemporary political pollsters.

   The combination of modern survey research methods and inferential statistics provide a way to look at the "totality" of language in a way that even the largest collections of raw data cannot. No matter how large a survey or corpus, there must be some way to assess how the collection might be related to the language behavior of the entire population under study. That said, the size of a sample is important, because the quality of the estimate that we can make for a population depends in part on the size of the sample: very small samples cannot be used to make estimates as good as those made with larger samples. Statisticians use standard formulas to determine how large a sample should be in order to make good estimates, and there are diminishing returns for increasing the sample size beyond a certain threshold. So, in the linguistics of speech, we need to follow the Goldilocks principle: we should not listen to just one or a few people (because the idea of representative speakers belongs to the linguistics of linguistic structure), and we need not listen to every speaker in a population that we want to study; we need our sample to be "just right," enough people to make a good estimate according to the laws of probability and statistics.

Findings from the LAMSAS survey: Density estimation (DE)

In the previous chapter there were important differences between maps made according to the linguistics of linguistic structure and those made according to the linguistics of speech. Visualization of the evidence with lines and plots relied on implicit assumptions about the frequency of responses. Maps made with statistics, with the density estimation (DE) procedure, begin to account effectively for the frequency issue, while the difference in linguistic approach remains. It is possible to draw an isogloss by statistical means with DE (first accomplished in Light and Kretzschmar 1996), but it is also possible to improve our understanding of the linguistics of speech with it. DE makes use of the discriminant analysis statistic (commonly found in statistical software pack-ages). In our linguistic application, for any target feature there will be a set of points (the 1162 locations where informants lived) which can be divided into two classes, those where a particular variant response was elicited and those at which it was not. DE estimates the probability that any given coordinate location will belong to either of the classes, given the known values of the points in the survey. We can use DE to make plots that show the density of occurrence of a target feature, show the probability that the feature variant might occur in any part of the survey region, and estimate comprehensively where a variant might be expected to occur in the survey region.

Figures 4.1 and 4.2 juxtapose a plot of the raw responses for the *cloudburst* variant with a DE plot for the *cloudburst* variant. Whereas the boxes of the raw data map symbolically plot a dark or open box for each of 483 locations, the

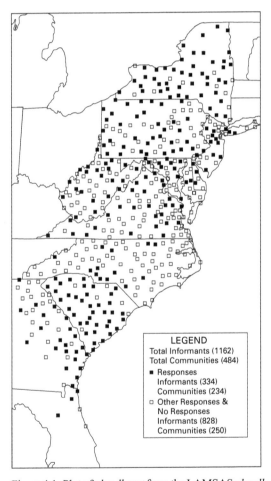

LEGEND
Total Informants (1162)
Total Communities (484)
■ Responses
Informants (334)
Communities (234)
□ Other Responses &
No Responses
Informants (828)
Communities (250)

Figure 4.1 Plot of *cloudburst* from the LAMSAS *cloudburst* item, 'heavy rain'

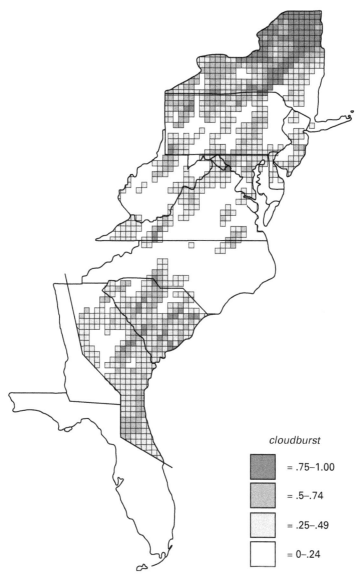

Figure 4.2 DE plot of *cloudburst* from the LAMSAS *cloudburst* item, 'heavy rain'

squares of the DE plot represent a grid for the entire area. The application of a regular grid to a region is part of what, in technical geography, is called "point pattern analysis." Point pattern analysis makes use of identical sampling areas, called "quadrats," which may contain different numbers of data points, in our case the speakers of a survey. The quadrats of the grid applied to the LAMSAS region are square or rectangular areas, one for every 0.2 degree of longitude and latitude.[3] The LAMSAS survey region contains about 3000 quadrats, for its 1162 speakers, so some quadrats have no speakers in them while others may have more than one. The DE statistic makes an independent estimate of the likelihood that a feature variant will be found in each of the quadrats of the grid. The plot shows estimates of the probability of occurrence of target linguistic features comprehensively throughout the LAMSAS survey region (in four levels, from white for little probability to the darkest shading for highest probability), at a resolution of areas of roughly 150 square miles per quadrat.

The data plot of Figure 4.1 improves upon maps with multiple variants or drawn with just isoglosses, because it clearly shows where the *cloudburst* variant was elicited and where it was not. It is still difficult, however, to generalize how the variant occurs across the area; how likely is it that *cloudburst* might be elicited at those places where it was not actually found? The DE plot in Figure 4.2 answers this question explicitly. Since there was no data from western Georgia or from western and southern Florida, no prediction is valid for those areas (a line has been drawn on Figure 4.2 to highlight that edge of the survey region); within the survey region, however, the map, based on its underlying statistic, now takes the guesswork out of eyeballing the data plot. The estimates are revealing: while they show some areas of high probability and some areas of low probability, there are many shades of grey. The map has a blotchy or patchy appearance, rather than neat areas of occurrence.

This result deepens our understanding of the distribution of a single variant feature. Saussure said that "naturally, there will be an area, corresponding to the geographical extension of [a single linguistic] feature" ((1916)1986: 200). True enough, but the DE plots tell us that inside of the geographical extension of the distribution of the variant, there will be differences in frequency, changes in the likelihood that the variant will be found from place to place. We can call this the "coherence" of the distribution of a feature variant, whether it is found with a relatively uniform frequency across its areal extension, or whether it is more or less common from place to place. Saussure may have been thinking that a feature variant would be found at all locations within its areal extension, and in some cases that does happen. Figure 4.3 illustrates the DE plot for *blinds*, which has a dense, regular, coherent distribution within what Kurath called the Midland dialect area (besides some likelihood of occurrence in some localities outside of that distribution); this variant provided principal diagnostic isoglosses for both

---

[3] While the grid holds the 0.2 degrees equal, the relationship of longitude to miles changes with distance from equator, so that the quadrats are not exactly equal in square miles. 0.2 degrees of latitude is always about fourteen miles, while 0.2 degrees of longitude ranges from about twelve miles in Georgia to about ten miles in New York State.

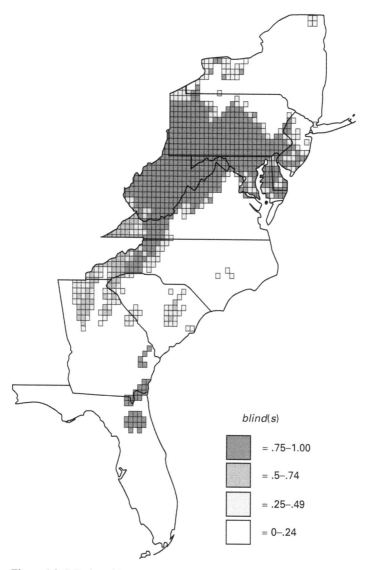

Figure 4.3 DE plot of *blinds* from the LAMSAS *blinds* item, 'roller window coverings'

the northern and southern boundaries of the Midland region. And yet even the dialectologists' old favorite variants for drawing isoglosses most often fail to show a coherent frequency within their areas of occurrence. In Figure 4.4, the *lightwood* variant for 'kindling,' which Kurath used as a principal diagnostic

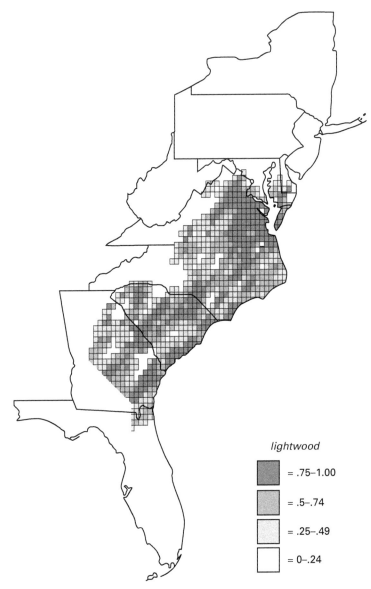

lightwood

■ = .75–1.00

▨ = .5–.74

□ = .25–.49

□ = 0–.24

Figure 4.4 DE plot of *lightwood* from the LAMSAS *kindling* item

isogloss for his Southern dialect region, has its densest likelihood of occurrence in eastern Virginia, while in the rest of the region it alternates between higher likelihood at the coast, less likelihood a ways inland, then more likely again at the "fall line" (where rivers have waterfalls, at the break between the coastal plain and the uplands), and finally again generally less likely and spottier in the piedmont, heading towards the mountains where it is very unlikely to occur at all. The coherence of the distribution of a feature variant, then, its variability between localities within a region, is something for which the linguistics of speech needs to account. Not only will the relative frequency of a feature variant change between different areas, it will be variable within the geographical extension of the variant. We would have no very good way to understand this property unless we use statistics to help us to estimate the probability of eliciting a variant across the survey area.

Feature variants other than lexical differences can also be mapped with DE. Figure 4.5 shows the probability that LAMSAS speakers would pronounce the

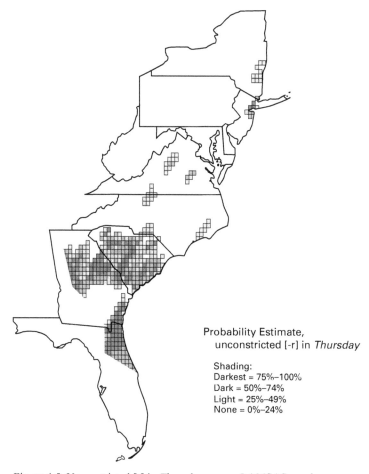

Probability Estimate,
unconstricted [-r] in *Thursday*

Shading:
Darkest = 75%–100%
Dark = 50%–74%
Light = 25%–49%
None = 0%–24%

Figure 4.5 Unconstricted [r] in *Thursday* among LAMSAS speakers

word *Thursday* without "constriction," i.e., without any indication of the [r] sound (Kretzschmar and Johnson 1993). The loss of [r] after vowels but not between vowels, as in *Thursday*, is usually taken to be a hallmark of Plantation Southern pronunciation, and yet the DE plot shows that the loss of [r] in this word is likely only in the lower half of Kurath's Southern dialect region (where *lightwood* was elicited), with only patchy areas in eastern Virginia and North Carolina. The plot does show that loss of [r] in *Thursday* is likely in a small area around New York City (less likely a bit north up the Hudson), the other location in the LAMSAS survey area where loss of [r] is usually taken to characterize the speech of the area.

DE by itself does not account for the observation of the coherence of the distribution of features variants; it matters *how* DE is applied. There are two basic means for calculation in DE, the kernel method and the nearest-neighbors method, and the two yield different ways of looking at the evidence. The kernel method calculates the radius of circles set around each of the speaker locations (the LAMSAS speaker locations are illustrated in Figure 4.6; circles may overlap). Then, for a particular feature variant, the density of occurrence within the circles is calculated. The separate densities are assembled in order to derive a map that shows changes in the density across the entire region. Figure 4.7 shows the result of this calculation for *pail*. The appearance of two dark core areas for *pail*, with other areas of lesser density, in a "bullseye" pattern is an artifact of the kernel method, which contains a "smoothing" function to generalize the densities from all 1162 circles into a coherent pattern. "Coherence" here comes from the statistic, because the smoothing function itself creates the bullseye pattern. This method clearly corresponds to the linguistics of linguistic structure, because it embodies the assumption that patterns will have clear boundaries and generalizes the different density figures within areas in order to highlight clear regions. Indeed, if the plot is restricted to showing only two levels of probability, say "over 50%" vs. "under 50%," the plot looks quite like a map prepared with isoglosses (Figure 4.8). The dark northern area corresponds to where Kurath drew an isogloss for *pail* as a principal diagnostic isogloss for his northern dialect region. Kurath did not draw an isogloss for *pail* in the south, where the variant coexists with *bucket* and *piggin*.

The nearest-neighbors method is the other means of calculation in DE. Figure 4.9 shows the same data for *pail*, this time processed with the nearest-neighbors method, here using the five nearest neighbors. The method calculates a value for the coordinate based on how many of the five nearest neighboring informants said *pail*. Gone are the bullseye patterns that come from the smoothing function of the kernel method, replaced by the spottier, more local distributions natural to regional variation. For *pail*, we can see that the smoothing function of the kernel method generalized the probability estimates in the southern part of the region to remove the blotchy, patchy, incoherent appearance

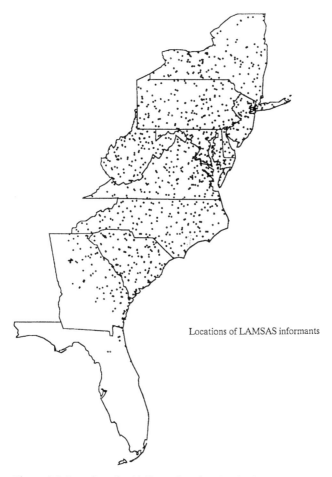

Locations of LAMSAS informants

Figure 4.6 Locations for 1162 speakers in LAMSAS

produced by the nearest-neighbors method. However, the smoothing function of the kernel method also took the dense, regular appearance of the northern occurrences of *pail* from the nearest neighbors display, and made it, too, into the bullseye pattern centered near New York City shown in Figure 4.7. If the kernel method yields the same picture whether the underlying distribution is coherent or not, this is certainly not what the model for the linguistics of speech requires, in which the same regular pattern of coherence is not assumed for every feature variant. Instead, coherence is to be observed for what it is, given what the speakers said for any feature variant.

Both of these DE methods make highly successful estimates. For the *pail* variant, the kernel method has an error rate of 23%. That is, the kernel method

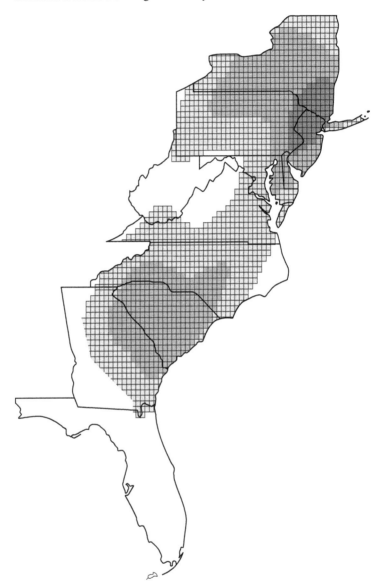

Figure 4.7 Kernel method DE plot for *pail* from the LAMSAS *pail/bucket* item (four probability levels)

misclassified 23% of the data points known from the survey, given that an estimate of 50% or higher probability should match a location where *pail* was actually elicited (and vice versa). That is, the kernel method produces maps that correctly represent whether or not *pail* was elicited from speakers at about

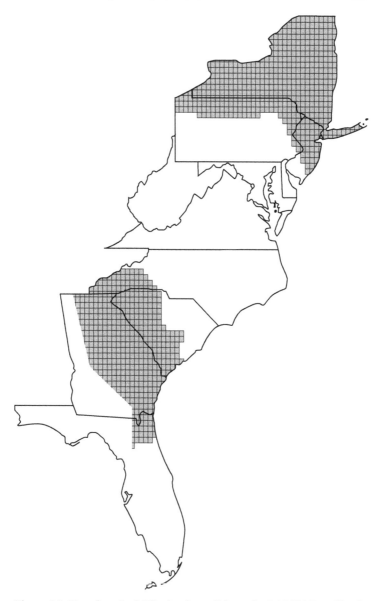

Figure 4.8 Kernel method DE plot for *pail* from the LAMSAS *pail/bucket* item (two probability levels)

three-quarters of the LAMSAS locations. The nearest-neighbors method is even more successful, as one might expect when the smoothing function is not there to generalize distributions: the error rate for *pail* is 17%. The error rates for other variants for the *pail* feature, like *bucket* and *piggin*, are even better, though

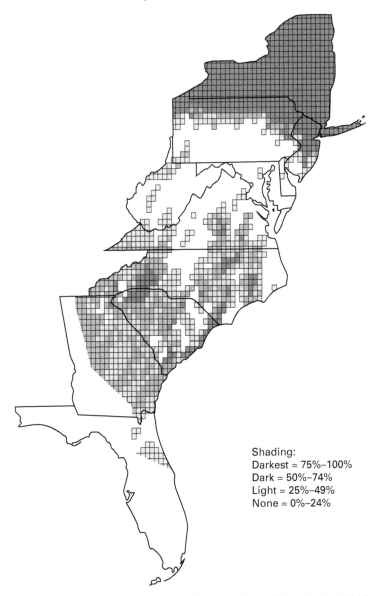

Shading:
Darkest = 75%–100%
Dark = 50%–74%
Light = 25%–49%
None = 0%–24%

Figure 4.9 Nearest-neighbors method DE plot for *pail* from the LAMSAS *pail/bucket* item

always the error rate is lower for nearest neighbors than for the kernel method. The smoothing function costs some accuracy, but it is not unreasonable to apply it if the analyst is committed to the linguistics of linguistic structure. On the other hand, the nearest-neighbors maps allow the analyst to see the evidence not only more accurately but differently, in a way more in keeping with the linguistics of speech. They allow us to observe the coherence of distributions, rather than just to assume it.

Findings from the LAMSAS survey: Spatial autocorrelation

Technical geography offers linguistic geography, for the linguistics of speech, a particular logic that can be used to analyze geographical patterns (see Lee and Kretzschmar 1993). The basic property for distributions of data points across an area is whether a geographical pattern under study exhibits the property of "Complete Spatial Randomness" (CSR). As in survey sampling, "random" does not mean 'accidental' but rather 'without a particular pattern.' If the distribution of data points does not conform to CSR, it may be possible, by means of a test statistic, to specify whether the pattern is more regular than a random pattern (like the white squares of a chess board) or more clustered than a random pattern (like the locations of the white pieces at or near the beginning of a chess game, all on one side of the board). As for LAMSAS, its wide network of many speakers, each of whom either did or did not offer a particular feature variant, provides just the sort of black/white, binary, point-pattern data for which the statistics of technical geography were designed. To establish areas for comparison, technical geographers often apply a polygon technique that completely divides the region under study into unequal areas corresponding to the data points, rather than applying a grid of equal quadrats to the survey region as in the previous description of DE.[4] As for the linguistics of speech, the problem of the coherence of areal distribution of feature variants is a very good match for point-pattern analysis, which can help us to assess the arrangement of locations where a variant was elicited, whether they are distributed according to CSR (the null hypothesis), or they tend to show a regular or clustered pattern in the study area.

When we use the methods of technical geography to compare neighboring speakers, we can learn more about the coherence of a distribution. Spatial

---

[4] Each of these polygons, called Thiessen polygons, is created by drawing a line halfway between the data location at the center of the polygon and each neighboring data location; in this way the study area is completely divided, but the area corresponding to any data point is determined by how densely or sparsely the data points are spread out in any part of the region under study. Unlike the quadrat grid, there is always one data point per polygon. One advantage of Thiessen polygons, as a replacement for the political boundary of each existing LAMSAS community, is that they are space exhaustive (some counties were combined and some went unsampled in the LAMSAS survey, so that there were occasional gaps in the survey). Another advantage is that Thiessen polygons have well-defined borders and established sets of neighboring polygons, unlike irregular county borders and uncertainty about the definition of what constitutes a neighboring county, say cases where counties meet only at a corner point as compared to counties that share a long border. Using the precise knowledge of neighboring areas from the Thiessen polygons, it is possible to use a process called Delaunay triangulation to chart all of the neighbor relations in an area.

autocorrelation is the set of statistics used for this purpose, more specifically the join-count statistics appropriate to binary data like whether a speaker used a particular variant or not. In the terminology of join-count statistics, a location where a variant was observed would be called "black" and an area where it was not observed would be called "white." We can then observe the status of each of the neighbor relations in the survey region, called "joins," and count how many joins occurred between a "black" and a "white" location, as opposed to joins between similarly marked areas ("black" vs. "black" or "white" vs. "white"). The test statistic compares the actual join count against the count expected from the overall probability of occurrence of the feature variant. The statistic accommodates two different kinds of data. "Free sampling" does not assume that the "black" areas are necessarily the only areas where the target feature variant might be found, so that we must understand the observed overall probability as an estimate. Since we can never know whether a speaker did in fact use a variant but just did not say so to the field worker, free sampling matches the reality of LAMSAS sampling.[5] The z score of the test statistic is what statisticians call a "two-tailed" test, in that the observed value can be either significantly higher or significantly lower than the mean. For our LAMSAS situation, each "tail" corresponds to one of the possible deviations from CSR, whether a distribution is more regular than random, or whether it is more clustered than random. Given the standard LAMSAS confidence level of $p < .01$,[6] negative z scores of 2.58 or more ($-3, -4, -5 \ldots$) indicate significantly more clustering of responses than CSR; positive z scores of 2.58 or more ($+3, +4, +5 \ldots$) indicate a significantly more regular pattern of responses than CSR.

Figure 4.10 shows a typical map produced with the join-count statistic. Speaker locations look like an asterix or little star if the joins do not connect with another location, but the map appears as an interconnected network of locations in areas where neighboring locations do use the variant, as in parts of Pennsylvania and West Virginia. For *gully* the z score for free sampling is -4.83, which indicates that the places where *gully* was elicited in the survey are significantly clustered. The result of the test statistic confirms what we see on the map. Thus, we may say that the coherence of the *gully* variant is characterized by clustering, as opposed to CSR or to occurrences at regular, evenly spaced intervals.

---

[5] The alternative, "non-free sampling," is appropriate when all of the data is certain, for instance in a study of counties which voted Republican (or Conservative) in the last election. The free sampling procedure is less likely than non-free sampling to render a significant test result because of the estimated values in the calculation.

[6] Since the LAMSAS sample is relatively large, small differences in distributions may be significant at the usual $p < .05$ level for significance in the social sciences. We have preferred a more exacting level before we claim significance, viz. we require a 1 in 100 probability as opposed to 1 in 20 probability that our result could have occurred by chance.

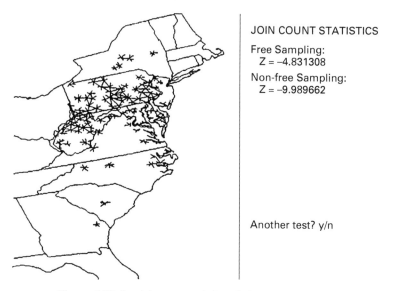

JOIN COUNT STATISTICS

Free Sampling:
  Z = –4.831308
Non-free Sampling:
  Z = –9.989662

Another test? y/n

Figure 4.10 Spatial autocorrelation (join-count) map for *gully* from the LAMSAS item for 'washed out place in a field'

When we consider not just a single feature variant but many different variants, we find that *gully* is not unusual. For the eleven lexical features available for testing (at the time of the experiment conducted for Lee and Kretzschmar 1993), there were sixty different variants that occurred in at least 5% of the speaker locations (at least 24 places) but no more than 90% of the speaker locations (no more than 435 places). There were many, many more variants for these features than just these, but the test statistic, again an application of discriminant analysis (as for DE), is sensitive to skewed distributions.[7] For the linguistics of speech the design of the statistic limits how we can study the distributions of variants as they actually occur (see Chapter 6). However, the test statistic works well as long as we consider with it just the distributions of variants for which it is well suited. Table 4.2 shows the results of join-count analysis for each of the variants eligible for testing, including the number of locations where it was found and the associated free-sampling z score. The left column of Table 4.2 shows the forty-one variants that occurred at least 72 times and no more than 411 times, in at least

---

[7] That is, if a variant occurs in too few places or in too many places out of the total number, the statistic either ignores the variant or considers that it occurs everywhere, respectively. Such behavior of the statistic is not a flaw but just a characteristic of its mathematical formula; in many applications, users might well prefer not to consider observations that just did not occur very often, or to consider as categorical ones that occurred just about all the time.

Table 4.2 *Results of join-count analysis for 11 LAMSAS lexical features (60 variants)*

Variants (=/equals) (c/contains)	Pres/Abs in 483 locs.	Z score > |2.33| p < .01	Additional Variants, occurring between 24 and 72 times, or between 412 and 435 times		
andirons (8.3)					
andiron c	302/181	−6.519	dogs =	50/433	−1.087
dog iron c	154/329	−6.821	fire iron c	49/434	−0.583
firedog c	182/301	−12.961			
handiron c	85/398	−3.437			
backlog (8.5)					
backlog c	400/83	−0.978	stick =	35/448	−0.007
chunk c	89/394	−2.012	back stick =	69/414	−3.228
log =	173/310	−3.483			
clear up [weather] (5.4)					
breaking c	74/409	−1.976	fairing off =	67/416	−3.882
clearing =	114/369	−2.416			
clearing off =	219/264	−5.439			
clearing up =	291/192	−2.089			
dresser (9.2)					
chest c	148/335	−1.647	bureau c	427/56	−1.094
dresser c	186/297	−6.671			
heavy rain (6.1)					
big rain =	74/409	−2.008	heavy shower =	38/445	−1.479
cloudburst c	223/260	−4.247	hard shower =	51/432	−0.003
downpour c	227/256	−1.079	pourdown c	59/424	−0.671
flood c	82/401	−2.662			
gully+ c	76/407	−2.079			
hard rain =	118/365	−0.969			
heavy rain =	133/350	−2.273			
half past [the hour] (4.4)					
half after c	82/401	−1.938	half past c	435/48	−0.242
mantel (8.4)					
fireboard c	97/386	−7.057	mantel shelf =	38/445	−0.301
mantel =	345/138	−2.669	mantelboard c	42/441	−0.909
mantelpiece c	243/240	−11.318			
shelf =	94/389	−2.582			
quarter of [the hour] (4.5)					
quarter of c	219/264	−9.355			
quarter till c	213/270	−17.161			
quarter to c	247/236	−13.111			

Table 4.2 (*cont.*)

Variants (=/equals) (c/contains)	Pres/Abs in 483 locs.	Z score > |2.33| p < .01	Additional Variants, occurring between 24 and 72 times, or between 412 and 435 times		
shades [for window] (9.4)					
blinds =	164/319	− 5.671	window curtain c	70/413	− 1.004
curtains =	196/287	− 6.798			
shades =	275/208	− 8.151			
window blind c	104/379	− 5.199			
window shade c	177/306	− 3.466			
sofa (9.1)					
bench c	81/402	− 3.684	davenport c	28/455	− 0.924
couch c	77/406	− 1.879	settee c	65/418	− 3.297
lounge c	157/326	− 2.337	sofa =	426/57	− 1.223
thunderstorm (6.2)					
electric storm c	76/407	− 2.583	electrical storm c	31/452	− 0.703
storm =	76/407	− 5.892	thundersqual c	35/448	− 3.544
thundercloud c	76/407	− 5.136	thunder gust c	48/435	− 2.759
thundershower c	176/307	− 6.260			
thunderstorm c	393/90	− 1.107			

15% of locations and no more than 85% of locations. The right column shows additional variants that occurred just outside of this range; between 24 and 72 times at the low end, and between 412 and 435 times at the high end. The first thing to notice about these variants is that every single z score has a negative sign: every single variant on this list is on the clustering side of CSR, and none are on the regularly spaced side. Not all of the results show statistically significant clustering (a z score beyond −2.33, at the LAMSAS confidence level of $p < .01$), but all of the results tend in just one of the two possible directions from CSR. The results from the left column, those that are the best fit for the test statistic, in fact show statistically significant clustering no less than 68% of the time (28 of 41 variants). Of the variants in the next 5% of locations beyond the best fit range (those that occurred in 48 to 72 locations, and 412 to 435 locations, in the right column), 40% show statistically significant clustering (4 of 10 variants). The remaining variants in the right column, which occurred between 24 and 47 times, show statistically significant clustering only 11% of the time (1 of 9 variants). We can thus observe the effects of the sensitivity of the test statistic to very frequent and to very infrequent variants. The main trend, however, is clear: the variants are not regularly spaced but instead the distributions always tend towards clustering, very often significantly so.

This finding has very strong implications for the linguistics of speech. If there is lexical variation, it is highly likely to be spatially correlated. In other words, the geographical proximity of speakers is an important factor in the areal distribution of feature variants. Perhaps one ought not be surprised, since join-count analysis tests only whether data points correlate in space (i.e., whether similar answers tend to be located next to each other), and we might well suspect that people who live near each other would tend to produce the same feature variant in answer to a question. Still, the mathematical treatment of the issue allows us to make a general statement about American English at the time of the interviews (and by analogy about other times and other languages) about which we before had no real evidence, only assumptions or suspicions. While linguistic feature variants do have an area in which they are found (a geographical extension, in some cases one for which a limit of occurrence might reasonably be indicated by a line), DE shows us that we should be concerned about the quality of coherence of the distribution within that area; in turn, spatial autocorrelation shows us that coherence of distributions is very likely to be characterized by clustering. Indeed, the findings of join-count analysis help to explain the spotty or patchy appearance that we usually observe in DE plots. Together, DE and spatial autocorrelation suggest the importance of localities in the linguistics of speech as organizational points for language, not necessarily the regions, larger or smaller, that are usually described as dialect areas according to the linguistics of linguistic structure. Gilliéron's complaint about "the false linguistic unity called 'patois'" (Chapter 2) may certainly be true, in the sense that we should not assume that every speaker in a locality will use the same variant for a feature, much less all of the same variants for all of their features, and yet the French idea of "patois" does have merit for geographical distributions of any given variant. Spatial autocorrelation clearly shows that people talking together in localities at least tend to know and to use the same variant for a feature more often than speakers who live far apart. For the linguistics of speech, proximity matters.

Findings from the LAMSAS survey: Social categories

While the LAMSAS survey effectively and comprehensively covered the geography of its region, it was also designed from the beginning to take account of the social characteristics of its speakers. Hans Kurath made it possible to conduct analyses with sociolinguistic variables before anybody else had acted on an idea of sociolinguistic variables. As he explained in the New England *Handbook*, "After the period of preliminary field work it was decided that three types of informants should be represented in the New England Atlas, and the field workers were given directions accordingly" (1939 (1973): 41). As mentioned in Chapter 3, Kurath had his field workers categorize informants according to one of three "Type" classifications, which were based on speakers' age and education, and an assessment of their social connections (for further details, see Kretzschmar, McDavid, Lerud, and Johnson 1993). Type I speakers are old, uneducated, and relatively uncon-nected socially; Type II, younger, better educated, and connected with the local social life (churches, clubs); Type III, the most educated and most involved in local social life. What Kurath did with his Type classifications was to create a model for American speech, a comprehensive classification system of what he called "folk," "common," and "cultivated" speech. As Kurath explained (1972: 164),

Until rather recently the techniques of area linguistics have been brought to bear almost exclusively on folk speech. All of the European atlases have, in principle, restricted their selective sampling to this social level of usage. Nevertheless, the sociocultural interpre-tation of the geographic patterning of variants in folk speech has inevitably led to the recognition of prestige dialects, whether geographical or social, as a potent force of diffusion within the several subareas as well as from area to area ... Only systematic sampling of middle class and upper class speech will provide the evidence for dealing with diffusion realistically.

To put Kurath's position in terms of variables, he is saying that in earlier studies geography was the only variable in play because European atlases always collected evidence from the same sociocultural type of speaker, folk speakers. Moreover, in Gilliéron's French Atlas (1902–10), and even still in Orton's SED (1962–71), only men were selected as folk speakers (later often called "NORMs," Non-mobile Old Rural Men, by sociolinguists); in these surveys, more than one individual contributed to a single local interview because they were all assumed to possess the local dialect. In contrast, Kurath supposed that "dialects" were not just geographical properties but were affected also by the social fabric and by the psychological factor of "prestige." He thus specified that interviews in a locality were to be collected from individuals with different social characteristics, not from just anybody. Kurath's choice of variables (age, education, social connections) reflected what he thought were the most impor-tant social factors in speech, along with his primary interest in geography. In this 1972 comment, he wrote of social "class" differences in speech, following the terminology of sociolinguistics introduced by Labov. In the 1930s, however, his use of the terms "folk," "common," and "cultivated" clearly began with the traditional notion of folk speech and added two more Types. These did not correspond directly to class, in the sense of economic level or SES (socio economic status) as developed by later sociolinguists, but instead to the facts of American educational attainment and its social consequences. Kurath did not invent Labovian sociolinguistics, appropriately named after its primary expo-nent, but he did introduce a model more complex than earlier European atlas models and, while he remained committed to the linguistics of linguistic structure (as later also Labov), he did explicitly recognize the importance of social variables for analysis of language variation.

Kurath created a deliberate arrangement of relevant variables (i.e., a model) which can be tested against the reality of the empirical evidence that he caused to be collected. Today, LAMSAS can be used for more than Kurath could have imagined. While Kurath's field workers were guided in selection of speakers first by geography and next by the Type classifications, they also regularly recorded enough information about speakers to support correlations of quite a number of social characteristics with what the speakers said. Brief LAMSAS speaker biographies (all published in Kretzschmar *et al.* 1993: Chapter 10) contain information about the sex, race, and occupation of speakers. They also talk about the speakers' parents and grandparents, and about their religious preferences. LAMSAS and other American Atlases also describe the communities in which speakers were interviewed, including population statistics and indication of local history, industry, and development. Thus, it is quite possible to consider the different variables included in Kurath's model separately, and to consider variables beyond those that he used for speaker selection. The LAMSAS survey, therefore, provides an opportunity for new analysts to compose different models, in line with the need of the linguistics of speech, to take into account all of the messy social and cultural facts that Saussure wanted to exclude from the linguistics of linguistic structure.

Table 4.3 shows an array of some of the characteristics maintained for LAMSAS speakers. The entries of the first column of the table correspond to the speaker locations illustrated in Figure 4.11; while not represented explicitly in Table 4.3, each speaker's location has been "geocoded" (i.e., provided with longitude and latitude coordinates) so that speakers can be represented accurately on maps. The next two columns indicate the field worker who conducted the interview and the year in which it was conducted. While these facts are not social variables, they can affect analyses and so might well be included as variables in a model of speech that uses LAMSAS evidence. There are differences in practices (assessed in detail in Kretzschmar *et al.* 1993: Chapter 6) between the two main LAMSAS field workers, Guy Lowman and Raven McDavid, and interviews were carried out over a considerable span of time. The Type classification is listed. Age (at the time of the interview) and education are then listed separately. Among Type I Maryland speakers, supposed to be old and uneducated in the model, the age variable ranges from 38 years to 95 years of age, and education varies from level 0 (no education) to level 4 (high school). Clearly the field workers exercised judgment in their assignment of Type classifications, and did not apply a rigid template. Thus reliance on the Type model (through use of the Type variable as listed in Table 4.3) may yield good results, based on the judgment of the field workers, and yet separate consideration of age and education may be well justified in the context of another model. The

Table 4.3 *LAMSAS speaker characteristics, Maryland (from www.lap.uga.edu)*

Speaker#	Fieldwrkr	Date	Type	Sex	Age	Educ	Occup	Race	ComType	County
MD1A	L	1939	I	F	95	3	K	W	R	Cecil Co.
MD1B	L	1939	II	M	58	6	F	W	R	Cecil Co.
MD2A	L	1939	I	M	82	1	F	W	R	Kent Co.
MD2B	L	1939	I	M	48	2	F	W	R	Kent Co.
MD3A	L	1939	I	M	73	2	L	W	R	Queen Annes Co.
MD3B	L	1939	II	M	43	4	F	W	R	Queen Annes Co.
MD4A	L	1939	I	F	85	3	K	W	R	Caroline Co.
MD4B	L	1939	II	M	80	4	F	W	R	Caroline Co.
MD4C	L	1934	II	M	53	3	F	W	R	Caroline Co.
MD5A	L	1939	I	M	69	1	O	W	R	Talbot Co.
MD5B	L	1939	II	M	48	4	F	W	R	Talbot Co.
MD6A	L	1939	I	F	79	2	K	W	R	Dorchester Co.
MD6B	L	1939	II	M	58	4	F	W	R	Dorchester Co.
MD7A	L	1939	I	M	73	1	F	W	R	Wicomico Co.
MD7B	L	1939	I	M	44	3	F	W	R	Wicomico Co.
MD7C!	L	1939	III	M	55	6	C	W	U	Wicomico Co.
MD8A	L	1939	I	M	70	0	F	W	R	Worcester Co.
MD8B	L	1939	II	M	51	3	F	W	R	Worcester Co.
MD9N	L	1934	I	F	70	1	H	B	R	Somerset Co.
MD9A	L	1939	II	F	68	3	K	W	R	Somerset Co.
MD9B	L	1939	II	M	42	2	F	W	R	Somerset Co.
MD10A	L	1939	I	M	82	3	F	W	R	Harford Co.
MD10B	L	1939	II	M	41	3	F	W	R	Harford Co.
MD11	L	1939	I	M	77	1	F	W	R	Baltimore Co.
MD12A	L	1939	I	F	87	2	K	W	R	Baltimore Co.
MD12B	L	1939	I	M	52	1	F	W	R	Baltimore Co.
MD13A	L	1939	I	F	70	4	H	W	U	Baltimore Co.
MD13B	L	1939	I	M	45		C	W	U	Baltimore Co.
MD13C	L	1939	II	M	55	5	R	W	U	Baltimore Co.
MD13D!	L	1939	III	F	70	4	K	W	U	Baltimore Co.
MD13E!	L	1934	III	F	76	4	K	W	U	Baltimore Co.
MD13F!	L	1939	III	F	50	4	K	W	U	Baltimore Co.
MD13G	L	1939	I	F		1	K	W	U	Baltimore Co.
MD14	L	1939	II	M	52	2	F	W	R	Carroll Co.
MD15A	L	1939	I	M	71	2	W	W	R	Howard Co.
MD15B	L	1939	II	M	42		F	W	R	Howard Co.
MD16	L	1934	I	F	60		F	W	R	Frederick Co.
MD17A	L	1939	II	M	77	2	M	W	U	Frederick Co.
MD17B	L	1939	II	M	39	3	F	W	R	Frederick Co.
MD18A	L	1939	I	M	65	0	F	W	R	Montgomery Co.
MD18B	L	1939	II	M	49	4	F	W	R	Montgomery Co.
MD19A	L	1939	I	M	78	1	F	W	R	Prince Georges Co.

Table 4.3 (*cont.*)

Speaker#	Fieldwrkr	Date	Type	Sex	Age	Educ	Occup	Race	ComType	County
MD19B	L	1939	I	M	38	4	F	W	R	Prince Georges Co.
MD20A	L	1934	I	M	68	1	L	W	R	Anne Arundel Co.
MD20B	L	1939	II	M	46		F	W	R	Anne Arundel Co.
MD20C!	L	1939	III	M	33	5	R	W	U	Annapolis
MD21A	L	1939	I	M	85	1	F	W	R	Calvert Co.
MD21B	L	1939	I	M	48		F	W	R	Calvert Co.
MD22N	L	1939	I	M	92	0	F	B	R	St. Marys Co.
MD22M	L	1939	I	M	83	0	W	B	R	St. Marys Co.
MD22A	L	1934	I	M	76	0	F	W	R	St. Marys Co.
MD22B	L	1939	II	M	54	3	F	W	R	St. Marys Co.
MD22C!	L	1939	III	F	65	5	K	W	R	St. Marys Co.
MD23A	L	1939	I	M	79	3	F	W	R	Charles Co.
MD23B	L	1939	I	M	70	0	F	W	R	Charles Co.
MD23C	L	1939	II	M	39	4	F	W	R	Charles Co.
MD24	L	1939	I	M	82	1	F	W	R	Charles Co.
MD25	L	1939	II	M	48	3	F	W	R	Washington Co.
MD26A	L	1939	I	F	70	3	K	W	R	Washington Co.
MD26B	L	1939	II	M	80	2	M	W	U	Washington Co.
MD27A	L	1939	I	M	76	1	F	W	R	Garrett Co.
MD27B	L	1939	II	M	39	3	F	W	R	Garrett Co.

Maryland speakers worked at no fewer than nine different occupations, though most were farmers (F) or "kept house" (K; see www.lap.uga.edu for the full list of codes). Finally, Maryland speakers came from two races, black and white, and from both urban and rural kinds of communities (again, see www.lap.uga.edu for discussion of these variables). Information about speakers' religion and families, and additional information about speakers' communities could have been included in Table 4.3, but was not.

Given an array of characteristics relevant to each speaker, the question arises of how to make a model from the separate parts. Which variables should be included, and how should they be weighted within the model? Kurath and the sociolinguists made their models from the top down, on the basis of their commitment to the linguistics of linguistic structure. They assumed that there was a speech community, whether defined primarily on the basis of geography (Kurath) or on the basis of social class (the sociolinguists), and then they tested empirical evidence that they collected against their models. From the point of view of the linguistics of speech, however, without a commitment to a speech community that shares a linguistic structure, models should be constructed from

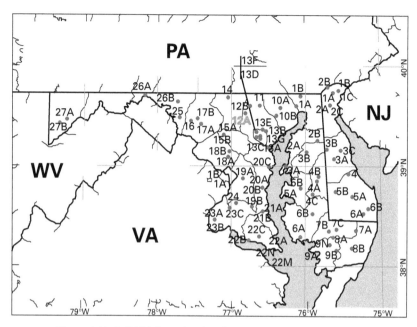

Figure 4.11 LAMSAS speaker locations, Maryland (www.lap.uga.edu)

the bottom up, on the basis of how different variables correspond to the behavior of linguistic feature variants.

Kretzschmar and Schneider (1996: Chapter 5) considered in some detail the behavior of the linguistic variants of the LAMSAS *clearing up* and *cowpen* items with respect to an array of eight different variables, geography plus the social variables of Type, age, education, sex, race, occupation, and kind of community. Table 4.4 shows the number of LAMSAS speakers who can be classified into each cell (i.e., each subclassification) for each of the social variables. "Community Type" in this table is divided into three subcategories, Farm, Rural, and Urban, while the other variables have the same subcategories as currently maintained for LAMSAS. In their analysis, Kretzschmar and Schneider applied the common Chi Square test to the subcategories of each social variable in turn, for a large number of variants of the *clearing up* and *cowpen* items.[8] This statistic compares the number of occurrences for a

---

[8] Kretzschmar and Schneider also used the Kruskal–Wallis statistic, an alternative to the Chi Square test which permits that a subcategory can have no speakers who used the variant under study. Results of the Chi Square statistic are also subject to the Cochran restriction, that each subcategory must have an expected total of at least 5. Both of these situations are common in analysis of linguistic survey data.

Table 4.4 *Number of LAMSAS speakers classified into social variables*

Type:	I	II	III		sex:	F	M		
	582	439	138			360	802		
age:	− 39	40 −	50 −		60 −	70 −	80 +		
	50	169	189		189	347	212		
race:	B	W	comm.type:		F	R	U		
	41	1121			618	265	276		
educ:	–	0	1		2	3	4	5	6
	57	90	177		217	249	212	95	65
occup:	–	C	F		G	H	K	D	
	24	30	567		2	12	278	27	
	M	O	P		R	S	U	W	
	96	19	47		29	17	1	13	

particular variant in each subcategory to the number that might have been expected there, and yields a score that indicates the probability of whether at least one of the subcategories is different from what was expected. A relatively low score, one that does not correspond to a p value beyond the chosen level for significance, indicates that the analyst cannot rule out the null hypothesis that the observed number of occurrences is not different from the expected number. A score that exceeds the p value for the chosen threshold for significance (here $p < .01$) indicates that at least one of the subcategories is significantly different from what was expected, and therefore we are entitled to ask how the variable was correlated with the evidence collected (say, for the variable "age," whether older or younger speakers used the variant disproportionately often).

Table 4.5 shows the division of the LAMSAS speakers into a grid of eighteen geographical quadrats, six in the North/South dimension by three in the East/West dimension.[9] In order to assess the geography variable, Kretzschmar and Schneider used a Chi Square statistic for the eighteen quadrats taken together, which would indicate whether the geography variable could be considered significant overall. They also compared the number of speakers who used a particular variant in each pair of adjoining quadrats with a "Student's t-test," in order to try to ascertain significant differences between the quadrats taken one at a time. In such a long series of thirty-five simultaneous t-tests (a "multiple comparison"), the p value for significance should be lower than usual: $p < .0025$

---

[9] The proportions of the grid match the aspect ratio of the LAMSAS survey region. Each quadrat has approximately the same number of speakers, and which speakers belonged to which quadrat was established by "best fit," given the need to make eighteen quadrats, each of which should have about 65 speakers in it.

Table 4.5 *Number of LAMSAS speakers classified
into geographical quadrats*

A1	A2	A3
64	64	65
B1	B2	B3
64	64	66
C1	C2	C3
65	62	63
D1	D2	D3
66	63	65
E1	E2	E3
65	65	66
F1	F2	F3
65	66	64

Table 4.6 *Variable results for* clearing *from the LAMSAS* clearing up
item

(*) = significant result. Total users: 152 (13%)
Geography: (*) one significant quadrat boundary

Type:	I	II	III		sex:	F	M		
(*)	42	65	45		(*)	71	81		
%	7	15	33		%	18	10		
age:	−39	40	50		60	70	80+		
(*)	4	24	45		39	23	17		
%	8	14	24		21	7	8		
race:	B	W	comm.type:		F	R	U		
	1	151	(*)		58	28	66		
%	2	13	%		9	11	24		
educ:	–	0	1		2	3	4	5	6
(*)	7	4	4		18	38	40	21	20
%	12	4	2		8	15	19	22	31
occup:	–	C	F		G	H	K	D	
(*)	3	5	53		0	1	53	0	
%	13	10	9		0	8	19	0	
	M	O	P		R	S	U	W	
	14	1	14		6	0	0	2	
%	15	5	30		21	0	0	16	

was the threshold for significance calculated to correspond in the multiple
comparison to the usual LAMSAS threshold of $p < .01$.

The results of the evaluation of the *clearing up* and *cowpen* variants were
highly enlightening for the linguistics of speech. Table 4.6 shows the results for

the *clearing* variant of the *clearing up* item. No fewer than seven of the eight variables showed a significant correspondence to the evidence collected. The geography variable had only one significant quadrat boundary (between A2 and A3), but inspection of the quadrat values shows that they are higher in the North. This result once more shows that it is difficult to draw isoglosses (here, to draw lines between significantly different quadrats), but that clustering is an important characteristic of linguistic distributions. The *clearing* variant was used more by Type III speakers, women, speakers in the middle age range, urban speakers, more highly educated speakers, and by speakers in several occupational categories. The *clearing* variant is thus not what German dialectologists would call a *Kennwort*, a word by which one can recognize a speaker as coming from a particular place or group because of a categorical difference between language behavior in different places or groups. Speakers from nearly all of the subcategories of all the variables did use it, more or less. A significant difference in the statistical tests from what was expected suggests that there is something about the social circumstances of being a Type III speaker, or a woman, or in the middle age range, or an urban or more highly educated speaker, that has an affect on what *clearing up* variant such speakers use. Statistics applied to social categories thus suggest, not the categorical differences assumed for the linguistics of linguistic structure, but the social equivalent of geographical clustering.

Several more tables show the same relative results. Table 4.7 shows results for another variant, *clearing off*. In this case, five of the eight variables turned out to be significant. The significant quadrat boundaries occurred in the middle of the LAMSAS region; the *clearing off* variant was more common among Type I speakers, whites, non-urbanites, and the less educated. Again, speakers from nearly all of the subcategories of all the variables did use the variant, more or less. Table 4.8 shows results for the *clearing up* variant. In this case, only the geography, age, and education variables were significant. Table 4.9 shows results from variants that have *fair* as the head of the phrase.[10] Here, only geography and education are significant variables. Table 4.10 similarly shows results from variants that contain the head *break*. The variant turned out to be significantly associated with three variables, geography, sex, and occupation. Table 4.11 shows results from combining tokens in a different way, all those phrasal tokens that contain the word *off*. Verbal particles like *off* are often not considered to be very important in language use since they are optional, sometimes said to be in "free variation" or to be erratic in the way that speakers apply them. However, it turns out that no fewer than five of the eight variables have a

---

[10] *Fairing off, fair up,* and so on. Relatively infrequent response types are more difficult to test with Gaussian "normal" statistics, and so combining tokens that have a common element of interest makes sense. As argued earlier, the creation of categories for analysis is arbitrary and up to the analyst, but such decisions should be made deliberately so that they are defensible.

Table 4.7 *Variable results for* clearing off *from the LAMSAS* clearing up *item*

(*) = significant result. Total users: 291 (25%)
Geography: (*) five significant quadrat boundaries

Type:	I	II	III	sex:	F	M			
(*)	172	100	19		94	197			
%	30	23	14	%	26	25			
age:	− 39	40	50	60	70	80+			
	9	36	48	48	103	47			
%	18	21	25	25	30	22			
race:	B	W	comm.type:	F	R	U			
(*)	1	290	(*)	170	81	40			
%	2	26	%	28	31	14			
educ:	–	0	1	2	3	4	5	6	
(*)	12	36	61	49	63	46	14	10	
%	21	40	34	23	25	22	15	15	
occup:	–	C	F	G	H	K	D		
	7	3	162	0	3	74	7		
%	29	10	29	0	25	27	26		
	M	O	P	R	S	U	W		
	14	1	9	3	3	0	5		
%	15	5	19	10	18	0	38		

Table 4.8 *Variable results for* clearing up *from the LAMSAS* clearing up *item*

(*) = significant result. Total users: 426 (37%)
Geography: (*) four significant quadrat boundaries

Type:	I	II	III	sex:	F	M			
	195	178	53		119	307			
%	34	41	38	%	33	38			
age:	− 39	40	50	60	70	80+			
(*)	31	91	71	50	121	62			
%	62	54	38	26	35	29			
race:	B	W	comm.type:	F	R	U			
	7	419		252	82	92			
%	17	37	%	48	31	33			
educ:	–	0	1	2	3	4	5	6	
(*)	8	24	52	76	119	87	39	21	
%	14	27	29	35	48	41	41	32	

Table 4.8 (*cont.*)

occup:	–	C	F		G	H	K	D
	6	7	235		2	3	97	14
%	25	23	41		100	25	35	52
	M	O	P		R	S	U	W
	26	6	13		13	2	0	2
%	27	32	28		45	12	0	15

Table 4.9 *Variable results for tokens containing* fair *from the LAMSAS* clearing up *item*

(*) = significant result. Total users: 206 (18%)
Geography: (*) six significant quadrat boundaries

Type:	I	II	III		sex:	F	M			
	111	73	22			73	133			
%	19	17	16		%	20	17			
age:	– 39	40	50		60	70	80+			
	5	29	30		40	63	39			
%	10	17	16		21	18	18			
race:	B	W	comm.type:		F	R	U			
	9	197			114	47	45			
%	22	16	%		18	18	16			
educ:	–	0	1		2	3	4	5	6	
(*)	10	17	54		42	28	22	17	16	
%	18	19	31		19	11	10	18	25	
occup:	–	C	F		G	H	K	D		
	2	2	96		0	4	55	1		
%	8	7	17		0	33	20	4		
	M	O	P		R	S	U	W		
	23	3	10		5	4	0	1		
%	24	16	21		17	24	0	8		

significant association with the particle *off* in the LAMSAS evidence for *clearing up* – definitely not a case of free or erratic variation in this population. Finally, Table 4.12 shows the results when speakers chose not to employ any particle – a linguistic variant distribution for the "zero" case. This aspect of language behavior was significant for no fewer than seven of the eight variables. It would be possible to multiply the number of tables presented here from the *clearing up* item, but all of them show the same kind of results, that speakers from many categories use a variant at different relative frequencies, and that very often multiple variables have significant associations with a single variant. Overall, of the eleven variants tested in Kretzschmar and Schneider (1996) for the

Table 4.10 *Variable results for tokens containing* break *from the* LAMSAS *clearing up* item

(*) = significant result. Total users: 99 (9%)
Geography: (*) three significant quadrant boundaries

Type:	I	II	III		sex:	F	M			
	49	35	15		(*)	17	82			
%	8	8	11		%	5	10			
age:	−39	40	50		60	70	80+			
	3	3	15		23	34	21			
%	6	2	8		12	10	10			
race:	B	W	comm.type:		F	R	U			
	3	96			59	17	23			
%	7	9	%		10	6	8			
educ:	–	0	1		2	3	4	5	6	
	2	6	22		25	12	12	11	9	
%	4	7	12		12	5	6	12	14	
occup:	–	C	F		G	H	K	D		
(*)	0	3	49		0	2	13	2		
%	0	10	9		0	17	5	7		
	M	O	P		R	S	U	W		
	21	2	3		1	3	0	0		
%	22	11	6		3	18	0	0		

Table 4.11 *Variable results for tokens containing* off *from the* LAMSAS *clearing up* item

(*) = significant result. Total users: 449 (39%)
Geography: (*) five significant quadrant boundaries

Type:	I	II	III		sex:	F	M		
(*)	247	165	37		sex:	142	307		
%	42	38	27		%	40	38		
age:	−39	40	50		60	70	80+		
	15	53	65		78	156	82		
%	30	31	34		41	45	39		
race:	B	W	comm.type:		F	R	U		
(*)	7	442	(*)		257	118	74		
%	17	39	%		42	45	27		
educ:	–	0	1		2	3	4	5	6
(*)	21	45	100		84	85	62	32	20
%	37	50	56		39	34	29	34	31

Table 4.11 (*cont.*)

occup:	–	C	F		G	H	K	D
	9	7	233		0	5	109	9
%	38	23	41		0	42	39	33
	M	O	P		R	S	U	W
	37	3	16		7	8	0	6
%	39	16	34		24	47	0	46

Table 4.12 *Variable results for tokens containing* no verbal particle *("zero" particle) from the LAMSAS* clearing up *item*

(*) = significant result. Total users: 196 (17%)
Geography: (*) one significant quadrat boundary

Type:	I	II	III		sex:	F	M			
(*)	55	85	56		(*)	87	109			
%	9	19	41		%	24	14			
age:	– 39	40	50		60	70	80+			
(*)	6	25	53		48	37	27			
%	12	15	28		25	11	13			
race:	B	W	comm.type:		F	R	U			
	6	190	(*)		71	39	86			
%	15	17	%		11	15	31			
educ:	–	0	1		2	3	4	5	6	
(*)	8	6	9		29	42	45	31	26	
%	14	7	5		13	17	21	33	40	
occup:	–	C	F		G	H	K	D		
(*)	3	6	63		0	3	66	1		
%	13	20	11		0	25	24	4		
	M	O	P		R	S	U	W		
	25	3	15		7	2	0	2		
%	26	16	32		24	12	0	15		

clearing up item, ten had at least one statistically significant geographical or social correlate; for the seven variants of the *cowpen* item, six had at least one significantly correlated variable.

Once more, these findings have strong implications for the linguistics of speech. The statistics tell us that the social aspect of language is every bit as complex as Saussure expected it to be. No model that fails to account both for geography and for a range of social variables is likely to offer much of a description or prediction of what the speakers actually have to say. The LAMSAS evidence presented here suggests that *Kennwörter* will be the exception rather than the rule. Feature variants will not be significantly associated with just a single region or with a single social category, and neither are they very likely to be absent from an area or social group. Instead, for any set of areas or groups, no matter how they are characterized, feature variants will occur in wide use, just at different levels of frequency. This finding expresses another side of the notion of the linguistic continuum, that feature variants occur in continuous variation from place to place, but also from social group to social group. Moreover, the use of statistics tells us that the frequency levels of variants in some areas or groups will be significantly higher than in other areas or groups, so that particular variants will indeed still have significant associations with particular areas or particular social groups, even while their distributions participate in the linguistic continuum. Finally, and perhaps of greatest importance for the linguistics of speech, particular feature variants can and do have significant associations with subcategories of more than one variable at once – indeed, they often have significant associations with sub-categories of multiple geographical and social variables at the same time. Since we know from Table 4.1 that the regional and social variables for LAMSAS speakers are not excessively cross-correlated (i.e., that significance in one category is unlikely also to cause significance in another category, because of the cross-correlation between categories), we can predict for the linguistics of speech that one and the same feature variant can help to characterize the speech of many different groups of speakers.

Before accepting these findings as valid for the linguistics of speech, on the basis of the feature variants of just two items, we should attempt to determine how general they might be. In a paired sample study of thirty Southern LAMSAS communities where interviews were conducted in the 1930s with her own interviews in 1990 with speakers of similar characteristics, Ellen Johnson has calculated the percentage of variation that can be found by stat-istical testing to be significantly associated with different regional and social characteristics (Table 4.13). We see that the number of words found to be significantly associated with any variable in Johnson's study was quite low for the LAMSAS data, and is somewhat lower still in the modern replication. Johnson found a lower proportion of variants to be significantly correlated with external factors in her study of a subset of the LAMSAS area, than Kretzschmar and Schneider found for their two feature variants across the entire LAMSAS survey region. The lower figures most likely come from Johnson's much lower sample size (32 communities, vs. 483 for LAMSAS overall), and they raise the interesting question of the salience of correlates in local terms vs. their salience in large-area terms (see Chapter 7). Johnson's data is all from within the South, in which the previously distinctive Plantation variety is becoming less common after its cultural basis of large-scale agriculture was largely eliminated by the boll weevil, the dust bowl, and subsequent depopulation. Change in association of words with urban or rural residence and with education level seem more

Table 4.13 *Percentage of feature variants found significant for regional and social variables (adapted from Johnson 1996)*

	1930s	1990
Region	6.4%	1.5%
Urban/Rural	4.5%	2.9%
Sex	1.4%	1.7%
Age	2.1%	2.7%
Race	2.7%	2.9%
Education	4.1%	2.9%
TOTAL	21.2%	14.6%

likely to hold for American English in general than the change in proportion of significant variants for Johnson's region category. The most striking feature of Table 4.13, however, is how few of the observed variants can actually be significantly associated with any regional or social characteristic. Only one in five of the variants could be so mapped in the 1930s, and only one variant in seven from the 1990 survey, even though there was a larger (not smaller, as one might think) inventory of variants in the 1990 field work than in the 1930s. The primary reason that the proportion of significant feature variants is low is that the total number of variants is high, and many variants occur so infrequently that they cannot be tested statistically (see Chapter 6). That is, it is not that most variant types fail to be associated with social or geographical variables, but they just do not occur often enough to be measured in this way. Kretzschmar and Schneider, for instance, ran eleven tests on variants of the *clearing up* item, when there were actually a total of 115 different response types for the item. Some of the tests included several response types (23 response types contained *fair*, 29 response types contained *break/broke*), but even after such grouping there remains a large number of untestable response types. It is also true that Kretzschmar and Schneider and later Johnson did not pick as many social variables to test as they might have. Hamilton-Brehm (2003) and Antieau (2006), for instance, have found significant associations with the geographical origin of parents and grandparents in their studies of the Western States. Wikle and Bailey (1993) reported a number of non-traditional associations, such as whether or not an Oklahoma speaker drives a pickup truck or wears cowboy boots. We must face the strong probability that not all lexical variation is structurally functional or motivated, an idea assumed by many linguists. Still, Johnson has documented the scale of variation in her study (more about this in Chapter 6), and the fact that variation is increasing and not decreasing over time. The relatively small proportion of feature variants significantly associated with a regional or social variable is another important finding, but one that must be understood in the context of how statistical tests are carried out. Johnson's work validates the findings in Kretzschmar and Schneider (1996) as part of a general pattern of language variation.

For the linguistics of speech, statistical results make a great difference. Saussure demonstrated a keen intuitive sense of language as it is used, in his sketch of the linguistics of speech, when he opposed the common idea of languages in well-bounded areas and when he cited the complications of social factors as a reason to prefer the linguistics of linguistic structure. Because we now have computers and statistics to help us, we can demonstrate the validity of the idea of linguistic continuum for both geography and social variables, and we can begin to make sense of social complexity as it helps to shape the distribution of feature variants through a target population. We can visualize clearly how, from the viewpoint of the linguistics of speech, the geographical distribution of feature variants resists analysis with isoglosses and boundary lines. We know that the coherence of distributions of linguistic feature variants, involving geographical proximity and clustering, must be considered as an important characteristic in a model for the linguistics of speech. When social variables are added to geography for the model, we know that feature variants are not categorically associated with social variables any more than they are with well-bounded geographical regions. And yet, parallel with our experience with geography, neither are feature variants evenly spread over the social landscape. The variants have more or less frequency in different social subcategories, just as they have greater or lesser frequency in different areas; moreover, they can be significantly associated with multiple social subcategories, just as they can be associated with multiple areas across the survey region. As a variable, geography works in much the same way with linguistic variants as social variables do. Any effective model for language variation in the linguistics of speech will include both geography and social variables. The idea of coherence serves as an important correlate to the central principle of the linguistic continuum.

That said, we are not yet ready to jump in and make a model. Statistics cannot do that for us, and neither can computers. We require further insight about distributions of feature variants before we can assemble what we know so far into a well-reasoned model. Our results so far are still too indeterminate to say how one variable might relate to another. It is also worth pointing out that none of these findings invalidate the point of view of the linguistics of linguistic structure. The findings do, however, begin to address how, in the words of Chapter 1, we could have gotten ourselves into such a mess over ideas about language. Given the complexity of any model of the linguistics of speech, it begins to seem perfectly reasonable that sensible people could draw such different conclusions when presented with the same facts.

5   Evidence from corpus linguistics

The use of computers, through their storage capacity rather than through their processing ability, begins to address Saussure's statement that "language in its totality is unknowable." At the beginning of the computer age, processing dominated computer applications because memory was quite limited, whether in RAM or on longer-term media like tape or disk. Now, however, mass storage is much more available, so that it is possible to create tremendous corpora of language data, whether as sound files or as text files. At this writing, the use of networked storage arrays allows linguists to build linguistic corpora reaching many terabytes in size, whereas the largest storage device available to the Linguistic Atlas Project when it began to be computerized in the early 1980s was ten megabytes – growth by a factor of a million times over a quarter century. One million words of running text, as in the 1961-vintage Brown Corpus of American English and in the parallel LOB Corpus of British English, and in each of their later replications in the Freiburg-Brown (Frown) Corpus and Freiburg-LOB (FLOB) Corpus of the 1990s (all available in ICAME 1999), occupies about six or seven megabytes, massive storage in the 1960s, most of a computer's hard drive in the mid-1980s, now easily manageable on even the smallest of storage devices. Dictionaries demand the use of large corpora, in which as many different words of the language as possible may be found. At this writing, the size of the "Bank of English," an early and continuing effort to monitor the English language by incremental collection of speech and writing each year, is now over 500 million words. HarperCollins Publishers maintains the Bank of English as a part of its "Collins Word Web" (s.v., www.collins.co.uk):

The purpose of Collins Dictionaries is simple: to take as sharp and as true a picture of language as possible. In order to stay at the forefront of language developments we have an extensive reading, listening and viewing programme, taking in broadcasts, websites and publications from around the globe – from the *British Medical Journal* to *The Sun*, from *Channel Africa* to *CBC News*. These are fed into our monitoring system, an unparalleled 2.5 billion-word analytical database: the Collins Word Web. Every month the Collins Word Web grows by 35 million words, making it the largest resource of its type.

Many other dictionary publishers also maintain very large corpus collections.

146

We can try to obtain some idea of how the size of such a collection compares to the "totality" of language as used in a community. Mehl, Vazire, Ramirez-Esparza, Slatcher, and Pennebaker (2007) is the first study to have "systematically recorded natural conversations of large groups of people for extended periods of time" (p. 82). They found that both men and women spoke about 16,000 words a day during an average waking period of 17 hours. If we assume that conversations are roughly symmetrical, then people speak and hear about 32,000 words a day in interactive conversation. For recent Atlas conversational interviews, we have recorded about 8,000 words in an hour of steady talk. These two numbers together suggest that active conversation may be occurring, in rough terms, in about a quarter of a person's waking hours. At other times, people may be the passive recipients of language, say from reading or from listening to the radio or from watching television, or they may be "silent," in the sense of not experiencing language. Taking all this together, we can consider, then, in the roughest of terms, that a person may encounter (say, hear, see) at most about 100,000 words of their language in an average day. We can calculate the following totals for a person's experience of words:

One day: 100,000 words
One year: 36,500,000 words
A lifetime of eighty years: 2,920,000,000 words

Thus, in the roughest and roundest of terms, we can estimate that one person experiences about three billion words in a lifetime – approximately the number of words contained in the Collins Word Web, which grows each month by about the number of words that one person might experience in a year. "The largest resource of its type" compares in scale today to the life experience of language by a single person, or, to think of it in another way, to one year's experience of language by eighty different people, adding one more person to that group each month. Thus, even the great size of contemporary corpus collections pales besides the "totality" of actual use of language in speech and in writing by all of the people in a "collectivity," and yet the scale of such collections, and the ability of computers to process them, does provide a much better sense of the range and use of language than anything available at the time of Saussure. What we can learn from corpus developments will be treated in this chapter in relation to the linguistics of speech. The term "corpus," in the sense required here, refers to electronic collections of naturally occurring text, whether of written or spoken language.[1]

---

[1] There are many other kinds of collections of evidence from speech. There are surveys of the kind described in the previous chapters, in which linguists interview speakers, whether with a form of directed elicitation such as a questionnaire or through free conversation. There are ethnographic studies in which linguists participate in communities and record interactions. There are laboratory or panel studies in which linguists control as many linguistic variables as possible the better to manipulate aspects of language of interest to them. Many of these studies originally recorded their

Firthian linguistics

J. R. Firth was the figure who inaugurated a way of thinking about language that should make us want to preserve corpora of real speech by real people. In the first decades of the twentieth century, at the same time that Gilliéron championed etymology and the centrality of the word in his French survey research, in Britain the focus came down on the problem of meaning and the situational contexts of language use. In 1923, C. K. Ogden and I. A. Richards published *The Meaning of Meaning*, which expanded upon the semiotics of Saussure through their influential "semiotic triangle," and which made the study of meaning the centerpiece of both British literary criticism and linguistics. The book also contained a supplementary essay by Bronislaw Malinowski, who treated the problem of meaning in language from the point of view of an anthropologist who studied "primitive" culture. As Dinneen paraphrases Malinowski:

> We have stated the meaning of an utterance when we have put it into its context of situation and we see what it does. Therefore, MEANING = USE. (emphasis in the original; Dinneen 1967: 301)

Meaning cannot, in this view, come solely from linguistic structure, but instead is dependent upon the particular situation of use of any utterance. In linguistic anthropology, this idea has been notably developed by, among others, Whorf, Gumperz, Hymes, and most recently Silverstein and Agha (see Duranti 1997, 2001, 2004, for discussion and exemplary essays by these authors; see also Agha 2007). In the decades following Ogden and Richards, Firth developed the implications for British linguistics of this focus on meaning in language use in situational context (for a brief, useful account of Firth's ideas, see Dinneen 1967: 299–325).

---

data on paper, whether as fine phonetic transcriptions or rough field notes, and many studies over the last half century recorded data on audio tape. Many of these remain on paper or on tape, but great efforts are in progress to convert the data to digital storage, since in many cases the paper and tape media are beyond their useful life and subject to degradation and loss. Even early computer records must be converted to more modern storage formats before they can no longer be accessed by more recent computers and software. One hour of tape-recorded speech will occupy up to about one gigabyte of computer storage, depending upon the file type and compression. A high-quality image of one page of a field record makes a file of about half a megabyte, again depending on capture specifications, so that one entire Linguistic Atlas field record of a hundred pages or so would require fifty megabytes of storage. Thousands of Linguistic Atlas interviews on paper and tape thus will require many terabytes of storage, a massive project even today, though becoming more manageable every year as computer storage possibilities improve. Digital conversion of our stock of linguistic evidence, and not just from the Atlas project, is a big job worth doing so that we can preserve and augment collections that can tell us about speech on a large scale. And once preserved, at least some of these records could be prepared as electronic corpora in the sense described in this chapter, those which preserve unedited, unmanipulated speech by research subjects (see Kretzschmar, Anderson, Beal, Corrigan, Opas-Hänninen, and Plichta 2006).

Firth clearly distinguished his own theory from Saussure (see especially Firth 1957: 179–181). Perhaps surprisingly for many contemporary linguists, Firth asserted that (1957: 179):

De Saussure's general linguistics is closely linked with the sociology of Durkheim. His theoretical approach may fairly be described as Durkheimian structuralism ... De Saussure, thinking in Durkheimian terms, regarded social facts as *sui generis* and external to and on a different plane from individual phenomena ... The group constrains the individual, and the group culture determines a great deal of his humanity.

He further describes Saussure's *langue* as "structural formalism," completely abstracted from language in use (1957: 180):

Such a language in the Saussurean sense is a system of signs placed in categories. It is a system of differential values, not of concrete and positive terms. Actual people do not talk such "a language." However systematically you may talk, you do not talk systematics. According to strict Saussurean doctrine, therefore, there are *no sentences* in a language considered as a system. Sentences are used by *sujets parlants* in *parole*. Strictly speaking, in "a language" there are no real words either, but only examples of phonological and morphological categories.

As a summary statement, he says that (1957: 181):

true Saussureans, like true Durkheimians, regard the structures formulated by linguistics or sociology as *in rebus*. The structure is existent and is treated as a thing. As Durkheim said, such social facts must be regarded "comme des choses." This is structural realism, or social realism.

In contrast, Firth says that "in this country such theory has not taken root in professional linguistics," and then makes a clear statement of his own position worth quoting in extenso (1957: 181):

For my own part and for a number of my colleagues, I venture to think linguistics is a group of related techniques for the handling of language events. We regard our group of disciplines as designed for systematic empirical analysis and as autonomous in the sense that they do not necessarily have a point of departure in another science or discipline such as psychology, sociology, or in a school of metaphysics.

In the most general terms we study language as part of the social process, and what we may call the systematics of phonetics and phonology, of grammatical categories or of semantics, are ordered schematic constructs, frames of reference, a sort of scaffolding for the handling of events. The study of the social process and of single human beings is simultaneous and of equal validity, and for both, structural hypotheses are proved by their own social functioning in the scientific process of dealing with events. Our schematic constructs must be judged with reference to their combined tool power in our dealings with linguistic events in the social process. Such constructs have no ontological status and we do not project them as having being or existence. They are neither immanent nor transcendent, but just language turned back on itself. By means of linguistics we hope to state facts systematically, and especially to make *statements of meaning*.

Language events, language in use, lead not to real structures but instead to meaning.

Several key ideas distinguish Firth's contribution to the linguistic market-place. First and foremost he emphasized that, if we are to be able to deal with meaning, we must be able to get back to the source, to the situation of use in which the example of language that we are trying to interpret originally occurred. We must, therefore, record and consider authentic uses of language, as opposed to hypothetical or edited examples of language. For instance, the movement in contemporary lexicography led by John Sinclair to use only real example sentences to illustrate the meanings of words, as opposed to made-up or edited sentences, comes directly from this Firthian principle to preserve the "renewal of connection" for statements that we wish to make about utterances. By extension, Firth also applied the idea of contextual situation to uses of language below the level of text or sentence, such as phonetics or the lexicon. Speech sounds do what they do (or "function," according to the more recent NeoFirthian functionalists like Halliday) both because of situations of their use and potential contrasts with other sounds. For example, phonetic environments of use (like initial or final position, or constraints on co-occurrence of one speech sound with another speech sound) constitute situational contexts. For the lexicon, words are not considered to have essential meaning, as they are usually presented to have in dictionaries, but instead often or usually occur in the context of other words. In colloca-tions, words occur near (but not necessarily next to) other words, and the meaning of a word in any actual situation of its use is conditioned by whether or not its frequent collocates are present. So, we think well of *showers* in *April* or in the *spring* because they bring forth new growth, but we do not think so well of *showers* in November or January; we may even avoid the word *showers* for the latter months because of its association with April, and prefer just to use the word *rain*. This emphasis on contextual situation leads directly to a lesser commitment to fixed units of analysis than North American linguists typically have. The North American idea of a fixed structure of speech sounds in phonemic systems establishes a basic inventory of sounds, which then receive modification, as allophones, in specific phonetic envi-ronments. The Firthian view would not recognize any a priori basic set of sounds and would instead place value on description of the wider range of allophones in their contextual settings. At other levels of analysis, Firth preferred not just to accept single words as units but admitted the possibility of collocations, and did not grant the sentence the preeminent position it is usually accorded in North America. The best units of analysis for Firth are those that emerge from particular contextual situations, not just those inherited from traditional historical or grammatical accounts. Finally, as Dinneen suggests (1967: 319):

it can be seen that the objection to the establishment of phonemes as "basic units" of language merely on the criterion of minimal lexical contrasts can be expressed by calling the American structuralist approach "monosystemic," whereas Firth's approach is designed to be "polysystemic."

Firth did not consider language merely to be idiosyncratic, but instead preferred to think about recurrent situations of language in use, whether phonetic environments or conversations, so that language is used "in a relatively determined context [where] you are not free just to say what you please" (Firth 1935: 66, 70–71; cited in Stubbs 1996: 41). Firth did not accept that language had a single system or structure that controlled its every use, but instead preferred to think that a language must have many possible systems for different contextual situations. These systems, however, are not important in themselves *in rebus*, but are merely "scaffolding" for assertions about meaning, important just as the means to another end.

Corpus linguistics

Corpus linguistics has become one of the two prominent contemporary expressions of Firth's ideas, now known as the NeoFirthian approach because of how Firth's viewpoint has been extended and adapted as technological advances have become available.[2] Using electronic corpora, it has become possible to study collocations in ways that, while conceivable, were too difficult in practice to accomplish very well before computer assistance. It has also become possible to study recurrent situations of use in text, "text types," more systematically and comprehensively than ever before. Electronic corpora offer advantages for all four of the key ideas that distinguish the Firthian approach. First, it is possible to preserve electronically both sound and text from authentic examples of language in use, so that there is a better chance now than ever before of being able to refer back to the original situation of use in order to confirm the interpretations we have derived. It is possible to examine the contextual situation of language use at all levels, and to move freely between different levels of analysis, from pronunciation to lexicon to morphology to syntax and back again. In the course of such an analysis, it is possible freely to change the units of analysis, whether these consist of words or collocations or grammatical

---

[2] The other prominent approach is called systemic functional linguistics (SFL), or systemic functional grammar for treatments of grammatical relations, and its primary exponent has been M. A. K. Halliday (e.g., 1985; Halliday and Matthiessen 2004). A current SFL text which also offers commentary on the historical development of SFL is Bloor and Bloor (2004). SFL is not engaged in this volume, in favor of treatment of corpus linguistics as a better companion for the linguistics of speech. Halliday (1991), however, is a notable article that describes the contribution of corpus studies to probabilistic grammar. For comparison of traditional grammars to corpus-based grammars, see also Aarts (1991).

labels. Finally, it is possible to describe and calculate multiple potential systems in the Firthian sense, specific arrays of units and their frequencies that correspond to different recurring situations of use. For each of these possibilities, the use of computer technology, both storage and processing, leads to a much greater ability to inspect large quantities of language evidence, so that analysts are no longer restricted to talking about what is *possible* within a language on the basis of a few observations, and instead arguments can be made much more convincingly about what is *usual* or *normal* in any number of situations of use.

Michael Stubbs has illustrated the difference that inspection of corpus evidence can make to arguments about possibility versus arguments about what is actually normal or usual in language (Stubbs 2001: 13–19). His first illustration shows that, while the word *surgery* has four different dictionary meanings in British English (briefly, 'medical procedure,' 'branch of medicine,' 'doctor's office,' 'doctor's hours') and thus might be considered to be ambiguous, the ambiguity disappears in actual situations of use. Corpus evidence shows that, in practice, the word *surgery* co-occurs with other words that restrict the meaning in situ, e.g., *undergo surgery, progress in surgery has made heart transplants possible, rushed to the surgery,* and *she was taking evening surgery.* As Stubbs says, "it is not the words that tell you the meaning of the phrase, but the phrase which tells you the meaning of the words" (Stubbs 2001: 14). Stubbs based his analysis on a 200-million-word corpus composed mainly of British English. If we extend Stubbs' argument about the meaning of *surgery* to American English, we find that only the first two of these meanings for *surgery* exist in the US. The 1961-vintage Brown Corpus and the Frown Corpus of the early 1990s (about two million words combined, from written American English) have twenty-five tokens of the word *surgery*, always in the company of words like *knee, heart,* and *underwent* that specify which meaning was to be realized in the situation. Thus the potential ambiguity of *surgery* from its possible dictionary senses is different in Britain and America, but in both places, in practice, the ambiguity disappears in situations of use.

Stubbs illustrated the same principle from the word *bank*, which he divided into two "basic" dictionary meanings, 'money-bank' and 'ground-bank' (which includes extended senses like *bank of fog*). Of the 82 occurrences of the word in the 1961-vintage LOB Corpus, plus 28 more of *banks*, he says that "in the vast majority of cases" other words near the target word indicated which sense was realized, whether in fixed phrases like *bank account*, or in proper names, or in collocating words that specified senses from fishing such as *cod, fish,* and *haddock* (Stubbs 2001: 15). Independent inspection for American English finds 83 tokens of *bank* from the Brown Corpus, and 124 more from the Frown Corpus, and in every case the meaning of the word was made clear by collocates of different kinds. There were no cases in these American corpora, however, of collocates from the semantic field for fishing. Undoubtedly it is

Table 5.1 *Frequency of top collocates (data from Stubbs 2001: 81–83)*

Co-occurrence of top collocate	% of node words
20+%	4%
10%–20%	20%
5%–10%	40%
2%–5%	30%+

possible for Americans to talk about fishing banks like the Grand Banks or Icelandic Banks, but it is not as usual for them to do so as it is in British culture to refer to fishing banks. The point of the illustration is the same: even if the situations of use are somewhat different from place to place and from culture to culture, what appears to be a problem – which meaning is realized for polysemic words – is very frequently solved in actual situations of use by the presence of disambiguating collocates.

Collocates are also subject to frequency analysis, parallel to the use of frequency to understand geographical and social variables. Stubbs has offered some figures for illustrations of collocation based on his 200-million-word corpus (Stubbs 2001: 81–97). Stubbs calculated how often a particular word form or type (called a "node" word) co-occurred with its top collocate, excluding function words as either node words or collocates.

The figures in Table 5.1 for co-occurrence of top collocates do not include percentages below 2%, and figures for node words do not add up to 100% owing to Stubbs' discursive mode of presentation of his data. The point, however, is clear: the word that most frequently collocates with a particular node word does so at an extremely high proportion of the time. Stubbs calculates the expected rate of collocation as follows (2001: 73–74):

Suppose the absolute frequencies of node and top collocate in the 200-million-word corpus are each 2,000 ... The chance of both node and collocate occurring together at some random point is the product of their individual probabilities of occurrence ($1 / 100,000 \times 1 / 100,000$): one in 10,000 million. Across the whole corpus, they could be expected to co-occur 0.02 times (= 200 million $\times 1 / 10,000$ million). This assumes adjacent co-occurrence. If we calculate co-occurrence in a span of 4 : 4 [i.e., within four words on either side of the node word] then they could be expected to occur 0.16 times (= 8×0.02) ... If node and collocate co-occur in only 1 per cent of cases, this rate of co-occurrence is ... 125 times more frequent than expected by chance.

Even at 2%, the lowest rate reported from Stubbs in Table 5.1, this means that the top collocate occurred near the node word 250 times more often than the rate expected by chance. In Stubbs' experiment, well over 90% of node words have a top collocate with a rate of co-occurrence at least this high. Thus it is clear from frequency analysis that words are not deployed randomly in speech, or evenly spaced, but instead they normally occur in clusters (to use the key term from the previous chapter) in proximate association with other words as collocates.

Moreover, the evidence presented by Stubbs shows unexpectedly high rates of co-occurrence for collocates besides the top collocate. In his most extended example of what he calls a "lexical profile," Stubbs provided the frequencies of a node word, *undergo*, and its top twenty collocates from the same 200-million-word corpus.

We see in Table 5.2 that not just the top collocate, but *all twenty* of the most frequent collocates co-occur with *undergo* at a rate at least 125 times what might be expected by chance. While Stubbs does not provide enough information from his experiment to suggest that *undergo* is typical of other words in this regard, he does provide compelling evidence about other nodes to show that multiple collocates co-occur at extremely high rates with a great many content words. It is, therefore, a normal feature of language in use that any given word,

Table 5.2 undergo *with its top twenty collocates (adapted from Stubbs 2001: 89)*

Undergo Collocate	1205 Frequency	Percent co-occurrence
surgery	108	9%
tests	67	6%
treatment	62	5%
change	53	4%
training	43	4%
test	41	3%
medical	40	3%
before	37	3%
changes	35	3%
operation	34	3%
women	31	3%
forced	26	2%
further	25	2%
testing	25	2%
major	24	2%
examination	23	2%
extensive	21	2%
heart	20	2%
required	19	2%
transformation	17	1%

when considered as a node word, is likely to have multiple collocates with unexpectedly high rates of co-occurrence.[3]

Table 5.2 includes 751 cases of collocation of *undergo* with a frequent collocate. This must mean that a large number of the total of 1205 occurrences of *undergo* were *not* accompanied by one of the top collocates, at least 454/1205 (38%). Many of the 751 cases of collocation overlap, when more than one of the frequent collocates occurs in the same sentence (see Stubbs 2001: 93–94), and so a better estimate might be that over half of the occurrences of *undergo* were not accompanied by one of the twenty top collocates. Twenty tokens of *undergo* can be found in the combined Brown–Frown set (two million words, compared to Stubbs' 200-million-word corpus), enough to illustrate the relationship of occurrences with and without top collocates (Table 5.3).

Four of the examples (1, 2, 7, 10) include one of the top collocates (assuming for the moment that the top collocates for the Brown–Frown set are the same as they were in Stubbs' general corpus, which did contain 35 million words of American English). Seven others include words that are similar in meaning to a top collocate (3, 5, and 11 denoting change; 8 and 12 denoting compulsion; 4 denoting a medical process; and 9 denoting a marked gender). Of the remaining nine examples, six contain scientific descriptions (6, 15, 16, 17, 18, 19). The evidence thus suggests that *undergo* may be commonly used in science writing, not just in medical contexts, and perhaps more specifically in American science writing since the Brown–Frown corpus contains all American samples.[4] These examples, then, suggest that even when the node word is not accompanied by a top collocate, its meaning is most often constrained by its co-occurrence with words that, though not top collocates themselves, are like the top collocates. The top collocates belong to the semantic sets of words that help to determine the meaning of the node word, as described above for *surgery* and *bank*. The existence of top collocates, then, is just the tip of the iceberg – those patterns of co-occurrence that can easily be collected and shown to be especially frequent – when in fact the constraints on meaning of a node word are actually being enacted by a great many other words. Frequent collocates are not merely fixed phrases, but tend to be part of the company words keep (to paraphrase Firth). Frequency analysis reinforces the observation that "you are

---

[3] This discussion has considered content words, as opposed to function words like prepositions and articles. Function words, too, enter into collocational patterns and occur at different frequencies in different places and times (see below for examples), but in the literature, as in Stubbs 2001, they are not often analyzed as the node in a pattern.

[4] Three Brown–Frown tokens of *undergo* are from the same science article (16, 17, 18), which might be thought to skew any conclusion drawn about science writing. This is a frequent problem in work with smaller corpora. Still, five other tokens of *undergo* in this set come from different pieces of science writing.

Table 5.3 *Twenty tokens of* undergo *from the Brown and Frown corpora (edited to remove coding and partial words)*

1   for the San Francisco 49ers of the National Football League, will *undergo* a knee operation tomorrow at Franklin Hospital here. Waters

2   off the train right now. First of all, the recruits will have to *undergo* arduous schooling. It will be a 16-hour training day. Then off

3   promises; but, as a second-look safeguard, each new project must *undergo* a Board of Estimate public hearing before construction

4   the orgiastic release that jazz can give them, they *undergo* psychoanalysis or flirt with mysticism or turn to prostitutes

5   vertebrate tropocollagen. This unusual collagen also was shown to *undergo* a reversible thermal phase transformation.

6   to the mechanochemically active proteins of muscle, has been shown to *undergo* a contraction which is highly sensitive both to temperature

7   At this moment, all he could think of was what he'd been forced to *undergo*. "Did you hear them? Do you know what they think of me?"

8   light, "you and I can't understand the many hardships they have to *undergo*". "Why is that?" She apparently wasn't satisfied with

9   situations. It's not the kind of thing you'd want your daughter to *undergo*." Still, a recent city licensing hearing for

10   compensation consultants." While companies are required to *undergo* an annual audit, he noted, not all companies hire consultants

11   of the growing pains communities in our country experience as they *undergo* the transition from big towns to small cities.

12   After Auschwitz, Luther's paradoxical two-kingdom ethic must *undergo* a fundamental revision. What is at stake here is more than

13   against more than those who are fairer. Darker-skinned people *undergo* more streets because they feel powerless over their condition

14   jazz musician Rahsaan Roland Kirk told an audience they might *undergo* when he simultaneously played the melodies of 'Sentimental

15   it describes a mixture of different species which can *undergo* phase separation at sufficiently low temperatures. In the

16   while those with nunch4 also *undergo* dissociative proton transfer (DPT) to form

17   cluster ion is the smallest sized 1:n cluster to *undergo* intracluster ion-molecule chemistry. The appearance of

18   ions with internal energies above the fragmentation threshold would *undergo* fragmentation, while the remaining, lower energy cluster ions

19   protein, will allow the yeast cell to respond to catecholamines and *undergo* the mating response (King *et al.* 1991). The obvious

20   that bone that, they play upon my brittle spine like a musician. We *undergo* the same tortures, myself and the Jew, but it is a small price

not free just to say what you please," and leads to the conclusion that language behavior relies on proximity in the distribution of words in texts.

From the NeoFirthian point of view, observation of the co-occurrence of words in texts will prompt discussion of what we should consider to be units of analysis in the study of language. As we have seen, the meaning of single words is strongly constrained by frequent co-occurrence with other words, but not just in fixed phrases (sometimes called idioms). In John Sinclair's words, "Complete freedom of choice, then, for a single word is rare. So is complete determination" (2004: 29). In a chapter entitled "The Search for Units of Meaning" (originally published as an article in 1996) Sinclair described four categories of co-occurrence relationships that bear on meaning: collocation, colligation, semantic preference, and semantic prosody. He hoped that they "will assume a central rather than a peripheral role in language description" (2004: 39). For example, in discussion of *naked eye* (also discussed in Stubbs 2001: 108–110), Sinclair notes that the word that occurs two words to the left of *naked eye* (N–2) is most often a preposition, a case of colligation, co-occurrence of a grammatical choice (2004: 31–32). He describes N–3 as a case of semantic preference (2004: 32):

Whatever the word class, whatever the collocation, almost all of the instances with a preposition at N-2 have a word or phrase to do with visibility either at N-3 or nearby. This new criterion is another stage removed from the actual words in the text, just as colligation is one step more abstract than collocation. But it captures more of the patterning than the others.

Finally, Sinclair describes his corpus uses of *naked eye* as a case of semantic prosody as "one further element in the structure of a lexical item" (2004: 33):

We postulate a *semantic prosody* of 'difficulty,' which is evident in over 85 per cent of the instances. It may be shown by a word such as *small, faint, weak, difficult* with *see* ... or by a negative with 'visibility' or *invisible* itself, or it may just be hinted at by a modal verb such as *can* or *could*.

Such co-occurrence need not be based on single lexical nodes, but instead may be based on grammatical patterns such as "*the ... of*" (Sinclair 2004: 39; Renouf and Sinclair 1991). Sinclair's interest here is "the structure of a lexical item," which may become an element in the (Neo)Firthian polysystemic account of language.[5]

If we stand back for a moment from any notion of system or structure that might be applied to corpus evidence, whether of "the lexical item" for Sinclair or in the larger polysystemic sense of the Firthian approach, we can consider the evident significance of proximity in word choices, both in statistical terms and for construction of meaning, as a property in itself. These illustrations all show an effect for language in use that parallels an effect of distributional coherence that we have observed from survey research. Proximity matters in the linguistics

[5] Besides Stubbs' and Sinclair's work, on the subject of collocations it is worth noting Cowie (1998), a collection of articles on theory and more practical applications, and Hoey (2005), which offers a new comprehensive theoretical approach.

of speech. For geographical and social proximity it is the speakers who are near each other and we can observe, through differential frequency of occurrence of linguistic feature variants, that speakers' choices of variants are associated in complex ways with geographical and social variables. Within naturally occurring speech in corpora, it is the words that are near each other. The proximity of the words affects textual coherence (or cohesion; see Widdowson 1978, and Halliday and Hasan 1976, 1989, for potential differences and relationships between these terms), in the sense that their association in the particular situation of use constrains the possibilities for meaning to create a particular meaning. The distribution of words in texts, then, is no more random or evenly spaced than the distribution of feature variants across geographical or social space.

In order to describe the linguistics of speech, we should distinguish between the importance of proximity as a property from the evidence of survey research, and proximity as a property from the evidence of corpus analysis. Language at the level of words in texts must be considered as one dimension in the model, and language at the level of word distributions in geographical and social space must be another dimension. Proximity matters at each level. And the levels interact with one another. That is, if particular words are used more or less frequently by speakers from different geographical locations or different social circumstances (as we know they are), then it must be the case that those words are more or less available to be employed in collocations (and colligations, and semantic preferences, and semantic prosodies) in the texts of language in use at different geographical locations or in different social circumstances. That effect has appeared already in the discussion above of the words *surgery* and *bank* and *undergo*, in that British and American speakers have different possibilities, owing to their geographical locations, to be factored into the construction of meanings for the words in their frequent collocational patterns. Neither corpus evidence by itself, nor survey evidence by itself, can account for the language behavior that we can observe and collect.

Text types

The evidence from corpus linguistics suggests that language behavior also varies by text types.[6] Text types are recognizable situations of use for speech, whether written or spoken. Some are large in scale, like "writing" considered as

---

[6] The term "text type" will be preferred here to the term "genre," which is also in common use by corpus linguists but which bears possibly confounding senses carried over from literary theory and discourse analysis. H. R. Jauss, for example, has written extensively about the importance of literary genres in his development of reception theory (1977, 1979, 1982). John Swales has contributed significantly to genre studies in discourse analysis (1990, which addresses genre in other fields, and 2004).

a text type, as opposed to "spoken language" as a text type. Others are small, such as "letter," and even the smaller types can be further delimited, as in the sequence "letter," "business letter," "job application letter," and even "job application letter for which the applicant does not have all of the qualifications." Each text type can be recognized because it has characteristics that allow it to be distinguished for itself, as for example in the matrices of characteristics developed by Paltridge for academic theses and dissertations (2002).[7] Kennedy (1998: 180–203) offers a concise account of the development of different approaches to text types in corpus analyses. Important early findings distinguished spoken from written texts, as in analysis of the written LOB Corpus and the spoken London-Lund Corpus for British English (also available in ICAME 1999). Both individual word frequencies and collocational patterns differed greatly between speech and writing, considered as types of text. The early Brown and LOB corpora were constructed from written samples of text types, now in the sense of situations of use in writing rather than the large distinction between speech and writing. These collections were designed to represent everything written in English at a particular time, in America and Britain respectively, and for this purpose text types were thought of as different kinds of writing. Two major groupings were created, informative prose and imaginative prose. Within informative prose, samples were taken from newspapers in the categories of reportage, editorial writing, and reviews, from both dailies and weeklies. Samples, some from books and some from periodicals, were also taken from the areas of religion, skills and hobbies, popular lore, belles lettres, learned writing, and a miscellaneous category consisting of government, institutional, and corporate documents. Samples of imaginative prose were extracted from general fiction, mysteries, science fiction, adventure writing and westerns, romance, and humor writing, again both from books and from shorter pieces. This array of written text types represents many kinds of writing that readers would recognize as different, but certainly is not a complete set. Stubbs, for example, has described the language of lonely-hearts ads (2001: 17–19), and newspapers frequently also contain recipes, features on travel and other subjects, humor, and other ads besides the personal ones, none of which were included in the Brown/LOB sampling plans. The notion "text type" is thus a flexible way to categorize situations of use of language into larger or smaller contrasting groups; there is no "natural" (to use Saussure's term) set of text types that exhausts the possible categorizations, any more than there are "natural" boundaries between dialects that exhaust some region of geographical space. Still, as Kennedy reported from numerous analyses over the years, relative frequencies of particular words, collocational patterns, and grammatical

---

[7] Cf. the matrix of characteristics prepared by Jauss for literary application, following from the formalist analysis of André Jolles (1930/1972).

features have all been found to be quite different in the different text types that were included in the early national corpora, and in other later corpora as well.

Douglas Biber has preferred not to focus just on text types as traditionally described, either as speech vs. writing or as popularly accepted types of writing like novels vs. government documents vs. newspaper sports reportage. Instead, he has created lists of linguistic features (largely grammatical features), and used the statistics of multidimensional analysis to create five sets of features which tend to share relative frequencies (Biber 1988, 1989; Biber, Conrad, and Reppen 1998). Biber prefers to locate texts with respect to these feature groups, expressed as continua in which particular texts can be rated as being more or less associated with one or the other end of the continuum: involved vs. informational, narrative vs. non-narrative, elaborated vs. situation-dependent, relative overtness of argumentation, and impersonal vs. personal. In so doing, Biber is able to show both that traditional popularly accepted text types tend to occur at different places on each of the different continua, and that subcategories of the accepted text types may differ greatly among themselves on the different continua. For example, Biber is able to show that, while early corpora grouped academic writing together as one category and collected samples from different academic disciplines, history research articles differ greatly from ecology research articles on the five continua in his own more detailed analysis, and that even different sections of articles from the same discipline, such as intro-ductions and discussion sections, also differed on the continua (Biber, Conrad, and Reppen 1998: 158–169). Thus, Biber's analysis does not reify sharp boun-daries for accepted text types. Still, he shows that language use appears to be constrained within different "registers" (his term for the set of features associated with some text type or group of texts), and that it is possible to measure differ-ences in language use for groups of texts that may not be members of accepted text types, and even for sections within a single group of texts. As Biber, Conrad, and Reppen conclude (1998: 234):

one of the most consistent findings in corpus-based studies concerns the importance of register variation … linguistic features from all levels – including lexical collocations, word frequencies, nominalizations, dependent clauses, and a full range of co-occurring features – have patterned differences across registers. Therefore, characterizations of "general English" are usually not characterizations of any variety at all, but rather a middle ground that describes no actual text or register.

Biber and colleagues would thus find broad generalizations about a language to be dubious because they are insufficiently situation-dependent, in contrast to lower-level generalizations about text types. Generalizations at this level, too, may be dubious because popular recognition of text types is no guarantee that texts included within the accepted type will share the frequency of use for various linguistic features. Nonetheless, variation in language use by text types, or in Biber's terms by register, consistently emerges as an important finding, in line with the Firthian principle about language behavior in recurring situations of use.

For the linguistics of speech, text types in the dimension of words in text are the counterpart to geographical and social variables in the dimension of word distributions in space among speakers. The notion "text type" describes a relatively recurrent situation of use (to use the Firthian term), along a continuum of possible types. There are no sharp boundaries for text types, any more than there are sharp boundaries between geographical or social categories. In every case the distinctions we draw between texts are arbitrary, so that for naturally occurring discourse, text types amount to what Saussure would have called "concrete entities" for units extracted from the stream of speech. As even Firth admitted, situations of use recur only "in a relatively determined context," which suggests that every actual situation of use may be a little different – and thus his corresponding insistence on "renewal of connection" with the actual situation, with actual language in use. The categories that we accept for different kinds of texts (as for different categories for geography or in society) are strongly influenced by traditionally accepted notions, in Saussure's terms "realities." Even popularly accepted distinctions can come into question, as the one between speech and writing has recently come in for discussion of whether electronic modes of communication like email or text messaging are more like speech or more like writing.[8] We can expect, then, that particular words or collocations may be associated in significant ways with multiple text classifications, just as words collected in surveys may be significantly associated with more than one place or social category. "Job application letters," for example, may be more or less "involved" or "informational" in Biber's terms, more like "reports" or more an exposition of personal qualities or situation. The words and collocations used in any such text will tend to differ as the particular "job application letter" reflects the different possibilities for its text type along the continuum of possible "letters" and other forms within the horizon of expectation of the author (for its composition) and of its receivers (for its interpretation).

Further, we can see that the two different procedural senses of the term *dialect* developed for survey research in Chapter 2 can also apply to corpus evidence. The first procedural sense, called *attributive dialect*, described predefinition of a locality or category of speakers and sought to describe the linguistic features of that locality or category. This is the same as establishing a reference corpus of texts considered to belong to the same text type (a corpus composed just of

[8] Compare the general acceptance of a binary distinction between the sexes, usefully questioned in social terms by Penelope Eckert in an early major article (1990), and more extensively in Eckert and McConnell-Ginet (2003).

academic history articles, say, or just of novels) and then describing the word and collocational frequencies of that corpus. The second procedural sense of dialect, called *blind dialect*, began with the linguistic features that result from a broad sample, as in a regional survey, and sought similarities in distributions of features corresponding to different areas or social groups. This is the same as establishing a broad general or balanced corpus, like Brown or LOB or later Stubbs' 200-million-word corpus, in which correspondences may be sought between the relative frequencies of words or collocations in different text types, as well as in the general corpus overall. "Register variation," as Biber calls it, can be seen to be the counterpart for corpus analysis of "dialect variation" from traditional dialect surveys, whether attributive or blind depending on the particular analysis. Kennedy's survey of the corpus literature reports attributive results from analysis of groups of texts considered a priori to be part of the same text type, while Biber's approach using his five feature sets derived from multidimensional analysis begins with the logic of a blind analysis. The same analytical procedure can be applied both to the dimension of words in texts and to the dimension of words in geographical and social space. Again, these two dimensions can interact: we can introduce geographical or social variables for consideration alongside text types, say when we compare the language of a balanced corpus of American English with one of British English, or the language of a reference corpus of American novels to the language of a corpus of British novels.

Sampling text

Just as for the dimension of word distributions in space, sampling and rigorous statistical processing can be applied to analysis of words in the dimension of text.[9] An important methodological question for corpus linguists, in parallel with the work of survey researchers, is to ask whether the texts included in corpora have been selected in a manner that reflects the speech or writing of the population of texts to be examined. For the dimension of words in space, it is the speakers who must be sampled; in the dimension of words in texts, it is the texts that must be sampled. In the linguistics of speech the dimensions interact, and so the analyst must consider sampling for both speakers and texts. No corpus has been constructed in a way that makes it representative of American, British, or any other type of English, at the most general level, in the sense that such representation can only come from random sampling. In fact, it would be nearly impossible to create a corpus that represents, for instance, American English, because it is not possible even to imagine, must less to sample randomly, all of

---

[9] This section is based on Kretzschmar, Meyer, and Ingegneri (1999), and Kretzschmar and Meyer (1997).

the speech and writing and other English in use in America at any one time. A careful examination of the Brown Corpus, for instance, reveals that it hardly represents the breadth of edited written American English: the writing of only native speakers of American English was included, as selected from collections of edited writing at the New York Public Library (newspapers), the Providence Athenaeum (a private library, detective and romantic fiction), a large second-hand magazine store in New York City (ephemeral and popular periodical material), and the Brown University Library (everything else; see Francis and Kucera 1999). Other corpora have employed other non-probability sampling techniques. The American component of the International Corpus of English attempted to collect speech and writing from a balanced group of constituencies (e.g., equal numbers of males and females), but ultimately what was finally included in the corpus was a consequence of whose speech or writing could be readily obtained (for instance, most of its fiction consists of unpublished samples from the Internet which did not require royalty payments). While these collections are not random, they are useful to the extent that they reflect the language behavior of some specific population of interest. Selection of elements from that population, particular texts in this case, can be accomplished using a sampling frame, a systematic and regular method to pick texts from the population. If all of the published books in the US in a given year are of interest as the target population, for example, the analyst might use published lists such as *Publisher's Weekly* to select works for inclusion. No list will be all-inclusive, however, so linguists must in the end rely on the principle of avoiding destructive bias (Woods, Fletcher, and Hughes 1986: 55–56):

a sensible way to proceed is to accept the results of each study, in the first place, as though any sampling had been carried out in a theoretically "correct" fashion … Judge the results as though they were based on random samples and then look at the possibility that they may have been distorted by the way the sample was, in fact, obtained. However, this imposes on researchers the inescapable duty of describing carefully how their experimental material – including subjects – was actually obtained.

After the analyst accepts the necessity for sampling instead of the assumption of a homogeneous *langue*, the goal should be to specify the grounds on which the sample is taken, and to avoid destructive bias whenever possible. As Biber (1993: 256) observes, those who created the Brown and LOB corpora did not have a "pilot corpus to guide their designs" or a fully developed sampling methodology for creating their corpora. Still, as shown above for the Brown corpus, the designers did have a systematic sampling frame, and we can use the corpus in statistical processing so long as we align our analyses with the way in which the corpus was constructed. For corpus studies, as was the case for survey research, the most important thing is to make only claims that are appropriate to the qualities of the sample. The field need not be deprived of the use of statistical

Table 5.4 *Frequency of coordinators in a corpus of speech and writing*

Coordinator	Speech N (% in speech)	Writing N (% in writing)
and	400 (60%)	609 (75%)
but	154 (23%)	53 (7%)
or	97 (15%)	82 (10%)
other	3 (1%)	31 (4%)
none	11 (2%)	35 (4%)
Total	665 (100%)	810 (100%)

Table 5.5 *Univariate statistics for coordination corpus across 20 selections*

Variable	N	Mean	Std Dev	Minimum	Maximum
AND	20	50.4500	18.1063	22.0000	92.0000
OR	20	8.9500	4.2361	3.0000	18.0000
BUT	20	10.3500	10.4794	0.0000	38.0000
OTHER	20	1.7000	2.0800	0.0000	7.0000
NONE	20	2.2500	4.3027	0.0000	20.0000

methods, so long as generalizations made from corpus evidence are limited to what sampling procedures allow, and so long as the audience for the generalizations is willing to grant the latitude that Woods, Fletcher, and Hughes recommend.

As a brief example, the figures in Table 5.4 display the results of a study of coordination based on ten 2,000-word selections of speech and ten 2,000-word selections of writing taken from the British and American components of the International Corpus of English (see Meyer 1996 for details). The selections were chosen specifically to offer a contrast between speech and writing, on the one hand, and British versus American usage on the other, following a quota for balanced representation of British and American speech and writing to satisfy the condition that selections be chosen according to a systematic sampling frame. Essentially, this data set consists of two parallel corpora, one for British English and one for American English, with each corpus subdivided into a spoken and written component.

Table 5.5 shows the minimum and maximum values for the five coordinators across the twenty selections, with their associated means and standard deviations. We see from the minimum and maximum values that the selections are highly variable in the number of coordinators, and in the number of each kind of coordinator, that they contain. The mean scores and standard deviations tell the

Table 5.6 *Correlation matrix for coordination corpus*

	CNTRY	MDM	SMPL	AND	OR	BUT	OTHER	NONE
CNTRY	1.0000	0.0000	0.0000	0.3598	−0.0121	0.0734	0.0493	0.2027
MDM	0.0000	1.0000	0.0000	0.5921	−0.1816	−0.4944	0.6906	0.2981
SMPL	0.0000	0.0000	1.0000	0.1462	−0.1798	0.4119	0.1046	−0.1855
AND	0.3598	0.5921	0.1462	1.0000	−0.1280	−0.1462	0.1379	0.3923
OR	−0.0121	−0.1816	−0.1798	−0.1280	1.0000	0.1652	−0.1213	−0.1177
BUT	0.0734	−0.4944	0.4119	−0.1462	0.1652	1.0000	−0.2002	−0.0102
OTHER	0.0493	0.6906	0.1046	0.1379	−0.1213	1.0000	−0.2002	−0.0102
NONE	0.2027	0.2981	−0.1855	0.3923	−0.1177	−0.0102	0.4028	1.0000

same story, since "standard deviation" is a measure of how different from the mean, or average, across the twenty selections the separate counts are likely to be. This kind of distribution again parallels the findings from survey research in the previous chapters, in that the variability of the data appears to be much greater than might be supposed from a structural viewpoint. When a data distribution like this occurs, it is all the more desirable to use inferential statistics because it is difficult to assess the results just by observation: the highly variable data may well give different impressions to different people, any of them potentially misleading, and the aggregate scores conceal as much as they reveal about the total picture.

Table 5.6 is a correlation matrix, a measure of how much the different variables are interrelated. The more a number on the table approaches a value of 1.0, the more relationship there is between different variables. We are interested primarily in relationships between our independent variables – the geographical variable "country" (US or Britain), and the textual variable "medium" (speech or writing) – and our dependent linguistic variables, the counts of the coordinators. However, we are also interested to see whether any of the linguistic variables are correlated, i.e., whether *and* tends to vary right along with another coordinator, perhaps the more *and*s the more *or*s as well, or the more *and*s the fewer *but*s. The highest numbers among the correlations are all between medium (MDM) and a linguistic variable: "other" .6906, *and* .5921, and *but* − .4944.[10] The negative value for *but* suggests an inverse correlation, which just means that fewer *but*s than expected occurred in one of the media. The correlation matrix suggests that it would be profitable to take a further look at each of these coordinators to find out what might be going on. As it turns out

---

[10] The correlation at .4119 between *but* and SMPL is another example of a problem from using small corpora, as above in the science examples taken from the Brown–Frown set for *undergo*; again, as above, this correlation does not materially affect the discussion.

for this tiny corpus of 40,000 words, the only statistically significant differences are for *and* and medium (i.e., *and* is used more in writing than in speech), and for "other" and medium (i.e., coordinators other than *and*, *but*, and *or*, such as *yet*, are used more in writing than in speech). In a comparison of larger corpora, *and* turns out to occur at statistically significantly different rates in the British LOB corpus versus the American Brown corpus, which was a trend suggested by the numbers from the tiny ICE corpus sample but not a statistically significant result. Sampling and statistical processing even on a small scale can tell us something about language in texts, and we can learn more from larger corpora. Smaller corpora normally reveal trends for only the most frequent features such as function words, here coordinators. Even function words, however, are subject to significantly different frequencies of use in different text types and in different geographical and social circumstances.[11]

Sampling documents

The fact that textual sampling actually works in practice as it should in theory can be shown through an experiment in which a team at the University of Georgia created a reference corpus composed of documents from the tobacco industry for the purpose of linguistic analysis.[12] The extant set of tobacco documents (TDs) comprises millions of documents, ranging in length from just a few words to hundreds of pages. We wanted to determine what types of documents exist in the set of TDs, and the extent of those documents, both the quantity of different kinds of documents and how long they tended to be. To establish clear boundaries for the study, we based our sample on the seven industry organizations and documents found in the National Association of Attorneys General (NAAG), Master Settlement Agreement, 1999 Digital Snapshot.[13] We also included the roughly 33,000 documents of the so-called Bliley Collections, the tobacco documents delivered to Chairman Bliley of the House Committee on Commerce. Thus, the population of TDs to be sampled contained approximately 3.4 million documents. There is no reason to suspect that the contents of this set of TDs, a large subset of the total, are materially

[11] Because of their high rates of occurrence, function words are frequently the words used in authorship attribution studies, which typically are conducted on the basis of small collections of texts. See Oakes (1998: 199–257) for a convenient survey of "literary detective work" and related studies.

[12] This section is based on Kretzschmar, Darwin, Brown, Rubin, and Biber (2004). The research was conducted with funding from a grant from the National Cancer Institute. To view the data from this project, including applications for selective viewing, see www.tobaccodocs.uga.edu.

[13] See http://caag.state.ca.us/tobacco/resources/msasumm.htm. The set includes the documents of The Tobacco Institute, The Center for Tobacco Research, Lorillard, R. J. Reynolds, Philip Morris, Brown & Williamson, and The American Tobacco Company prior to July 1999. See www.energycommercehouse.gov for the Bliley set.

Table 5.7 *Distribution of documents by classification categories (adapted from Kretzschmar, Darwin, Brown, Rubin, and Biber 2004: 37)*

	19xx	Bliley	1950	1960	1970	1980	1990	Totals
Total Docs.	10	10	10	22	66	132	99	349
S. Internal	8	9	8	20	55	108	93	301
A. Internal	8	9	6	20	53	109	88	293
Named Rec.	0	7	3	13	27	62	33	145
Public Health	9	10	10	22	61	126	96	334
Form	2	0	0	2	8	18	19	49
Image	0	0	2	1	1	0	0	4
English	10	9	10	22	63	130	99	343
Editing	3	1	0	2	3	3	5	17
Marginalia	4	9	5	12	34	73	39	176
Short	3	2	2	4	20	37	33	101

different from the entire TD set found in the complete depository in Minnesota except that the overall collection now contains documents from after 1999.[14] From our subset, we drew an initial "core" sample at the rate of 1:10000, 349 documents, according to a fixed random sampling frame by decades, with additional categories for all of the earlier decades combined, for undated documents, and for the Bliley set, a procedure which gave every document in the collection an approximately equal chance of selection, given selection of a minimum of ten documents per category.

Once collected, the documents were classified by three primary criteria of interest – Source (industry internal vs. industry external), Audience (industry internal vs. industry external), and Addressee (named individual(s) vs. unnamed individuals) – and six secondary criteria: whether a document consisted of a form (like an invoice), whether it consisted of an image with fewer than 50 words of text, whether it was primarily written in English, whether it showed evidence of editing, whether it contained marginalia, and whether the document was short (i.e., consisted of fewer than fifty words of running text excluding replicated or standardized prose). This classification did not employ traditional text types like "report" or "letter," but instead considered variables that made a difference for the overall goal of the grant, study of rhetorical manipulation of texts by the tobacco industry. Table 5.7 shows the result.

As expected, we found that the documents were not evenly distributed among our primary classification categories. Most of the documents in our sample

---

[14] See www.uga.edu/tobaccodocs/examples.html for examples of documents. At this writing the Legacy Tobacco Documents site (http://legacy.library.ucsf.edu) offers nearly 42 million pages from over 7.5 million tobacco documents.

consisted of industry-internal documents with industry-internal audiences, less than half with named recipients. Almost all of our documents were in English. We did not find many forms or images, but many of the documents were short. Only a small number of documents showed evidence of editing, but about half had marginalia of some kind. Only a very small fraction of the documents in the sample did not have an industry-internal source and an industry-internal audience. In other words, people in the tobacco industry spent a great deal more time talking to themselves than they did to outsiders. These tendencies were generally consistent across all seven of our groups of documents, so that there did not appear to be any great deviation over time for these criteria, or between the Bliley Collections and the 1999 NAAG Digital Snapshot.

We then created a much larger "reference" sample, based upon our findings from the "core" sample. Because the experiment was funded to examine linguistic characteristics of possible rhetorical manipulation in the TDs, we decided to include in the "reference" sample only documents which had an industry-internal source written in English, and decided to exclude short documents, which offered less scope for eventual discourse analysis. Only 57.87% of the documents in the "core" sample (202 out of 349) would have met these criteria. So, to create the "reference" sample, we gathered four additional sets of 202 documents in exact correspondence to the proportions of documents in the "core" sample that met our criteria, according to the same fixed, randomized selection method. The proof that textual sampling does actually create reproducible results comes from our replication of the "core" sample: the replication showed the same proportion of documents, 57.96% (808 out of 1394), a difference of less than one tenth of one percent from the selection rate of the core sample. For the 808 documents collected (four sets of 202) for the "reference" sample, we expected to reject 588 documents during the selection process; the actual number was 586. The point here is that textual sampling is neither unmanageable nor erratic in practice, given clear decisions about the population to be sampled and the criteria for selection.

Such sampling is also highly effective. Word frequency lists from the "reference" sample were compared with the lists from the Brown Corpus. The top fifty content words (i.e., not single letters, not titles like *Mr*, not mechanical writing terms like *page* or *cc*) that were statistically significantly more frequent in the "reference" sample than in the Brown Corpus were classified into four groups relevant to the tobacco industry, shown in Table 5.8.

The first group contains the words of the trade: the product and its components, words for the act of using it (*smoke, smoking, smoker*), and company names. The second group shows the vocabulary of selling the product, including brand names and marketing strategies (*blend, flavor, lights, taste*) as well as business terms like *advertising, market, retail*. The third group comes from the industry's attempt to confront the health effects of smoking. The last group

Table 5.8 *Words more frequent in tobacco documents (adapted from Kretzschmar, Darwin, Brown, Rubin, and Biber 2004: 42–43)*

Industry Words					
Word	50 s	60 s	70 s	80 s	90 s
CARTON		neg	pos		pos
CIGARETTE(S)	pos	pos			neg
FILTER	neg	pos			neg
MENTHOL	neg	neg		pos	
MORRIS	pos		neg		pos
PACK		neg	pos	neg	pos
PHILIP	pos		neg		pos
PRODUCT(S)	neg	neg	neg	pos	pos
REYNOLDS		neg	neg	pos	
RJR	neg	neg	neg	neg	pos
SMOKE	pos	pos		neg	
SMOKER(S)		neg			
SMOKING				neg	neg
TOBACCO		pos		neg	
Marketing Words					
Rank Word	50 s	60 s	70 s	80 s	90 s
ADVERTISING			neg		
BLEND			pos		neg
BRAND(S)		neg	neg		
CAMEL	pos	neg	neg	neg	pos
FLAVOR					
KOOL					
LIGHTS	neg	neg	neg	pos	neg
MARKET		neg	neg	pos	pos
MARLBORO	neg	neg	neg	pos	pos
MEDIA					
PROMOTION	neg	neg	neg	neg	pos
RETAIL	neg	neg		neg	pos
SALEM			neg	pos	
SALES	neg				pos
SHARE	neg	neg	neg		pos
TASTE		pos	neg	pos	
WINSTON		neg	neg		pos
Health Words					
Word	50 s	60 s	70 s	80 s	90 s
CANCER	neg	pos	pos	neg	neg
EXPOSURE	neg	neg	pos	neg	pos
HEALTH	neg	pos		neg	
LUNG	neg	pos		neg	
NICOTINE	neg	neg	pos	neg	
TAR	neg			pos	neg

Table 5.8 (*cont.*)

Research/Marketing Words					
Word	50 s	60 s	70 s	80 s	90 s
ANALYSIS	neg	neg			pos
DATA	neg	neg			
LEVELS	neg				
LOW	neg	neg			pos
PROJECT		neg	pos	pos	neg
REPORT		pos			neg
RESEARCH	neg	pos	neg		neg
RESULTS					
SAMPLE(S)	neg			pos	
STUDY(IES)	neg		neg		
TEST	neg	neg	neg	pos	neg
TESTING	neg			pos	
Unclassified Words					
CURRENT			neg	pos	

consists of words with applications to research, both market research and product research, and thus represents a combination of the marketing and health concerns in the industry. Only one word from the top fifty, *current*, cannot fairly be classified into just one of the groups.

In addition to the words themselves, Table 5.8 also indicates whether each word is statistically significantly correlated, positively or negatively, with any decade, as indicated by a comparison of rate of occurrence of the word in the "reference" corpus as a whole with the rate of occurrence in each decade. That is, for instance, the frequency of the word *carton* in a given decade was compared to the frequency of the word overall in the corpus; *carton* was significantly less frequent in the 1960s than in the corpus overall, but significantly more frequent in the 1970s and 1990s than in the corpus overall. Of the 22,000 word types in the "reference" corpus, 1538 were significantly correlated with at least one decade. Table 5.8 in effect shows a history within industry documents of the words most associated with it. For example, *RJR* is negatively associated with the first four decades of the period, and positively associated with the 1990s: this follows from the change in how the R. J. Reynolds company was known after its merger with Nabisco to form *RJR Nabisco*. The other words in the industry set change their rate of use over time, not always predictably. It is interesting to note that *cigarette(s)* changes from a highly used term in the 1950s to a term used at a significantly lower rate in the 1990s, while the words *carton*, *pack*, and *product* are used at significantly higher rates in the 1990s; this may indicate less focus in the industry on what the product is, and more emphasis on its packaging for sale. The health set shows perhaps the most telling trend. All of the words were negatively associated with the 1950s, before the health issue became big news. In the 1960s and 1970s the health terms are used at significantly higher rates in industry documents, first having to do with cancer, and somewhat later with nicotine. In the 1980s the industry used words in this set at significantly lower rates, except for *tar*, which was associated with the marketing of low-tar cigarettes during that period. The same is true for the 1990s, except for *exposure*, which at that time was a word commonly used in discussion of what has come to be called *secondhand smoke*. The marketing set shows what the industry was talking about instead of health in the 1980s and 1990s. In the first three decades of the document set, only the occasional brand or market strategy is positively associated with any decade (*camel, taste, blend*). But in the 1980s and 1990s a large number of marketing terms come to be used at significantly higher rates. The research/marketing words tend to bear out these trends; they are used at significantly lower rates in the 1950s, before either the expansion of health research or marketing efforts, but different words from this set rise to notable rates of use in the following decades.

These findings confirm the utility of statistical processing in several ways. First, statistical comparison of the "reference" corpus to a balanced, general corpus of American English for the same general time period revealed a list of content words that have clear associations with the tobacco industry. Forty-nine of the fifty words with the highest likelihood of difference between the corpora had such associations, so the statistical process showed great "precision" (i.e., it found just the words of interest). Second, words from this list could readily be sorted into semantic sets with clear association to known aspects of the tobacco industry and its history. The statistical results, therefore, went right along both with the general expectation for the existence of semantic sets in corpus linguistics, and with more specific expectations about the discourse of the tobacco industry. Finally, statistical processing showed patterns of variability in word frequency across the decades which corresponded to significant historical changes in the behavior of the tobacco industry. Not only was the process of sampling both manageable and predicable in itself, the statistical processing that it enabled was also highly effective when its results are compared to what we know about the tobacco industry from its narrative history.

These results also confirm for us something that we already knew, that time is an important variable for study of the linguistics of speech. Time was clearly an important variable in Johnson's survey research study, discussed at the end of the previous chapter, although differences in the scale of the surveys in that chapter complicated interpretation of the effects of time. For the TDs, in which the time variable was built into the sample, statistical analysis showed temporal differences more clearly and demonstrated that the study of the dimension of text can contribute to our knowledge of speech in time. Textual sampling is effective across time periods, as observation of content word frequencies by decade in conjunction with the history of the tobacco industry has shown. As it happens, regarding the comparison of coordinators above, in a comparison of the American written 1960s Brown corpus with the 1990s Frown corpus, both *and* and *or* occur statistically significantly less often in the 1990s than they did in the 1960s. It is not just the industry connection that makes text sampling across the decades work: the differential frequency of words, including their association in semantic prosodies, across time as well as across text types and across geographical and social variables, is a basic property in the linguistics of speech.

Conclusions

The evidence of corpus linguistics has brought us much closer to a model for the linguistics of speech. First and foremost, it has demonstrated the existence of a textual dimension for the model which parallels and interacts with the geographical and social dimension highlighted by survey research. The variants of linguistic features, whether distributions of sounds or words or grammar, can vary independently in text types as well as in geographical and social space. And yet the behavior of feature variants is similar in each dimension. Time is an important factor. At any given time, we always see much more variety in language behavior than might have been predicted by a structural approach in which speakers are assumed to share some unitary fixed system. Proximity matters, whether of words in texts or of speakers on the land or in social settings. Feature variants tend to cluster, measurably, whether words in texts or words in geographical or social space. There are no natural boundaries for text types, just as there are no natural boundaries for dialects or languages: language behavior in both dimensions occurs along continua of relative frequencies of use for particular features as we choose to extract them from the stream of speech. And yet in both dimensions we can observe patterned behavior, even if it is not always regular according to traditional "realities" for units of analysis. To adapt the words of John Sinclair, complete freedom of choice for a feature variant is rare, and so is complete determination. We need to use effective sampling and inferential statistics to help us make decisions about relationships between feature variants in both dimensions and at all levels of analysis. Finally, the same logic of analysis can be applied both to the textual dimension and to the spatial dimension, including both attributive and blind discovery methods.

Is Firthian linguistics, and more recently NeoFirthian linguistics, the same as the linguistics of speech? It is certainly closer to speech than the North American approaches that stay close to the linguistics of linguistic structure. Several primary Firthian tenets do fit with aspects of the linguistics of speech. The idea of "renewal of connection" recognizes the essential fact that instances of language behavior are not merely typical as examples of linguistic structure, but are each valuable in themselves as particular instantiations of possibilities along the continuum of language behavior. They need to be recoverable so that the analyst can go back and find what was different about them, not just what fit a pattern. At the same time, the idea of "(relatively) recurrent situations of use" recognizes the essential fact that language behavior is not merely one off on each occasion of use, but instead corresponds to patterns of use, not absolutely but relatively. Finally, the idea that the analyst should have freedom in identification of units of analysis, whether of sounds or lexicon or text types, recognizes the essential fact that our categorization of aspects of language behavior is always contingent. We can respect traditional "realities," so long as we are not so dominated by them that we fail to observe other opportunities for relative patterns of language behavior that fit the situations of use under analysis.

Still, to the extent that (Neo)Firthian linguistics is polysystemic, it continues to align what we can observe about language behavior with particular situations of use. It is still about the creation of structures, though now multiple structures instead of the single underlying structure of North American structuralism and generativism. To some extent, such unitization of language behavior is unavoidable. The analyst should always make clear decisions about what is the same and what is different, as Saussure pointed out in his discussion of the recognition of "identities" from the stream of speech. This is as much true for text types as it is for speech sounds or words. In the Firthian view, the "structure" or "system" for some relatively recurrent situation of use consists of the specific array of units and their frequencies (sounds, words, grammar) that correspond to the situation. Thus, the claim is sometimes made that "each text has its own grammar," in the sense that the analyst can describe the array of variants and their frequencies observed for a particular text, or for a recurrent situation of use (when "text" is taken to mean 'text type'). This attributive claim is true as far as it goes, but it does not go far enough. The linguistics of speech should be able to observe and describe regularities of language behavior that go beyond the measurable characteristics of any text or text type – and then come back again from such meta-analysis to text types and texts. In other words, the linguistics of speech must be able to cope with the problem of scale, with the problem of how to make generalizations about language behavior in the local terms of particular text types and also in global terms that combine text types. There are indeed regularities that go beyond the limits of recurrent situations of use. The linguistics of speech should also be able to account for more than linguistic production, which has been the focus of Neo(Firthian) linguistics, in order to address the other side of Saussure's speech circuit, linguistic perception. We must, for example, be able to explain how a speaker's typical experience with language, at the rate of something like 35 million words per year, can allow us as individual speakers to understand and apply the patterns that we as analysts can extract from aggregated language behavior in the linguistic corpora we study. These are the subjects of the next two chapters.

6   Speech as a complex system

The advances in procedures for effective statistical inference and valid sampling during the twentieth century discussed in the previous chapters depend on the "normal distribution," also called the "Gaussian distribution." The Empirical Rule permits us to decide what experimental results might be significant for us, provided that they come from normally distributed data. The Central Limit Theorem permits effective estimation from samples, since the results of repeated experiments on the same population yield normally distributed results. However, the bell curve became the twentieth-century model for what was "normal" in a wider sense for the social sciences (if not for the physical and natural sciences), so that many social situations, such as assessment of human intelligence (as by the educational psychologists against whom Labov wrote, described in Chapter 1), or assessment of socioeconomic status, or performance evaluation in educational settings, have tended automatically to be evaluated with respect to it. However, as we shall see, not all distributions are normal in the social sciences, as they are not in the physical and natural sciences. Distributions such as Zipf's Law for the relationship between rank and frequency for words in texts, or Pareto's Law for salaries in economics, do not conform to the bell curve. Benoit Mandelbrot has written, regarding the acceptance of these "other" distributions, that (1977: 273):

Even the less bold among physicists would find it hard to imagine the fierceness of the opposition that the very same procedure and outcome experienced in the social sciences. The procedure was unforgivable because its outcome flew in the face of the Gaussian dogma, which has long ruled uncontested among professional statisticians and hence among social scientists.

Indeed, in his 1982 revision of this passage, Mandelbrot strengthened his position (403–404):

The most diverse attempts continue to be made, to discredit in advance all evidence based on the use of doubly logarithmic graphs ... Unfortunately, a straight doubly logarithmic graph indicates a distribution that flies in the face of the Gaussian dogma, which long ruled uncontested. The failure of applied statisticians and social scientists to heed Zipf helps account for the striking backwardness of their fields.

174

Strong words, the voice of someone who is not merely sympathetic to the work of Zipf and Pareto but who has experienced a reaction from the entrenched position. Mandelbrot's point is not to undermine the usefulness of Gaussian statistics, which as a mathematician he fully embraces under appropriate conditions, but rather to complain about inappropriate extension of their use to situations where the facts do not warrant it. Social scientists had found an excellent tool in Gaussian statistics, and in Mandelbrot's view – to apply the old saw – if what they had was a hammer, everything looked like a nail.

The last quarter of the twentieth century brought the development of new approaches to just such situations. Mandelbrot was in the forefront of this movement with his advocacy of "fractals" (1982: 1):

I claim that many patterns of Nature are so irregular and fragmented, that, compared to [standard geometry] Nature exhibits not simply a higher degree but an altogether different level of complexity ... The existence of these patterns challenges us to study those forms that [standard geometry] leaves aside as being "formless," to investigate the morphology of the "amorphous." ... Responding to this challenge, I conceived and developed a new geometry of nature and implemented its use in a number of diverse fields. It describes many of the irregular and fragmented patterns around us, and leads to full-fledged theories, by identifying a family of shapes I call *fractals*. The most useful fractals involve *chance* and both their regularities and their irregularities are statistical. Also, the shapes described here tend to be *scaling*, implying that the degree of their irregularity and/or fragmentation is identical at all scales. The concept of *fractal* (Hausdorf) *dimension* plays a central role in this work.

Mandelbrot's books caught the public imagination of the time, since graphic representations of complex repeating mathematical phenomena like "monkey trees" and "Koch islands" are visually attractive, and also fascinating because they diverge from popular expectations based on standard Euclidean geometry. The key word here, however, is "complexity." Mandelbrot's claim was not limited to geometry; he asserted that such complexity was a property of Nature. He illustrated its behavior in "diverse fields" in discussion of measurement of the length of coastlines, Brownian motion, galaxy clusters, river discharges, economics, and Zipf's Law, among other examples. His achievement was to show the connection between many natural phenomena and abstract mathematical problems involving continuous nondifferentiable functions (1982: 4; or, "curves without tangents," problems that cannot be solved with Euclidean geometry or Newtonian calculus). As Freeman Dyson has written, modern mathematics can be characterized by "discovery of mathematical structures that did not fit the patterns of Euclid and Newton" and so might be regarded as "pathological." Mandelbrot, he continued, showed that "the same pathological structures that the mathematicians invented to break loose from nineteenth-century naturalism turn out to be inherent in familiar objects all around us" (quoted in Mandelbrot 1982: 3–4; originally from Dyson 1978). The basic properties of fractals – chance operation, scaling with self-similarity, and dimensionality – were shown by Mandelbrot to characterize objects of study in the physical, natural, and social sciences.

At the same time that Mandelbrot was writing, the Nobel-Prize-winning chemist Ilya Prigogine published *Self-Organization in Non-equilibrium Systems* (Nicolis and Prigogine 1977), which came at this same problem of complexity from the viewpoint of the physical sciences.[1] In 1984, the Santa Fe Institute was established by scientists from the Los Alamos National Laboratory and physicist Murray Gell-Mann, another Nobel laureate, just for the purpose of investigating complexity science and complex systems, "emphasizing multi-disciplinary collaboration in pursuit of understanding the common themes that arise in natural, artificial, and social systems" (www.santafe.edu). In 1999 the journal *Science* offered a special section on complex systems called "Beyond Reductionism" (Gallagher and Appenzeller 1999), an "initial scan" of related work which contained articles on ecology, physics, chemistry, biological systems, the human nervous system, animal aggregation, landform patterns, climate, and the economy. As Gallagher and Appenzeller note, complexity science addresses the question of how the different fields of science relate to one another, within a predominate approach of reductionism (1999: 79):

> Questions in physical chemistry can be understood in terms of atomic physics, cell biology in terms of how biomolecules work, and organisms in terms of how their component cell systems interact. We have the best reasons for taking this reductionist approach – it works. It has been the key to gaining useful information since the dawn of Western science and is deeply embedded in our culture as scientists and beyond.

Gallagher and Appenzeller go on to point out, however, that "shortfalls in reductionism are increasingly apparent," and suggest that "perhaps there is something to be gained from supplementing the predominately reductionist approach with an integrative agenda" – complex systems. Momentum in various sciences thus built throughout the last quarter of the century to incorporate non-linear models alongside the normal Gaussian and Newtonian ones, and to consider evidence in a wider scope than "the specialization of sub-sub-disciplines" might otherwise allow (1999: 79).

---

[1] I am indebted to Joseph Kuhl for raising for me the relevance of complex, natural systems to language. This chapter does not develop the notion of Kuhl (2003) that speech between individuals can be either closer to equilibrium or further from equilibrium, and that in the latter case speakers attempt to reach "concord," a state that requires less energy to maintain than the default condition far from equilibrium. This discussion of complex systems, on the other hand, considers speech data in the aggregate, rather than at the level of the idiolect.

Complex systems

This is not the place for an extensive treatment of the theory of complex systems, yet just as the basic ideas in statistics and sampling were briefly presented in previous chapters, it is important to introduce and clarify basic terms. An initial distinction, from physics, describes the difference between a system at equilibrium and a non-equilibrium system. Stuart Kauffman (1995: 10–20; Kauffman has been affiliated with the Santa Fe Institute) describes equilibrium systems as closed; they do not exchange matter or energy outside the system, and the components they have are balanced. Equilibrium systems are thus static. However, according to the second law of thermodynamics, systems at equilibrium tend towards entropy, or disorder, within the system. The property "order" is not the same as equilibrium. In Kauffman's example, following Ludwig Boltzmann, when a quantity of gas molecules enters a tank, the molecules do not stay ordered in a group at the point of entry; they tend to occupy the whole tank. Their state in the tank may appear to be well ordered, but actually it is not. The gas molecules keep moving around in the tank (gas molecules are high-energy objects), and according to the "ergodic theory" they move randomly through all of the statistically possible states of arrangement. Order, according to Kauffman, might be defined as the small number of possible states with all the molecules in the corner of the tank at the point of entry, or all in a single layer at the top; we might also consider that the molecules could form themselves into a regular matrix, equidistant from each other, the opposite of clustering in a corner or at the top. While those states will in theory occur from time to time, their number is vanishingly small in comparison to all of the possible random states approximating CSR (Complete Spatial Randomness; see Chapter 4) in which the molecules appear, more or less, to fill the tank. Thus, in a high-energy equilibrium system like the one with gas molecules in a tank, while ordered states do still occur from time to time, order appears to vanish beneath the random movement of the gas molecules. It would take "work," the use of energy, to maintain the system in one of the ordered states – which in turn suggests that the system would then no longer be at equilibrium, if energy were added to the system to maintain an ordered state. To consider another aspect of equilibrium from another of Kauffman's examples, order may be present in an equilibrium system at low energy: if a small ball is dropped inside the edge of a large bowl, the ball will roll around randomly for a while before, its kinetic energy dissipated, it comes to rest eventually at the bottom (1995: 20). No further energy is required for it to maintain its spatial order (i.e., a ball at the bottom of a bowl, as opposed to occupying random positions along the side of the bowl) – it has become a static, low-energy system. Systems, then, need not be well-ordered per se. Just because we call some set of objects under particular conditions a "system," the property of order is not a given. Further, equilibrium is not the same thing as order, and for order to be maintained in a system at equilibrium requires that the system's energy level be low.

Non-equilibrium systems by definition are open, and exchange energy and matter in a dynamic fashion. They very often show order. Kauffman's initial example is the small whirlpool that forms when the bathtub drains: this ordered structure can be maintained as long as the drain remains open and water keeps being added to the tub (1995: 20). The order in such a non-equilibrium system is sustained by persistent dissipation of matter and energy, and thus the whirlpool can be called a "dissipative structure" of the kind first described by Prigogine (for which he won the 1977 Nobel Prize in chemistry). No stirring is required to start the whirlpool, no single and simple cause, and still a whirlpool does not spin one way yesterday and the other way after today's bath: it exemplifies the principle of self-organization which accounts for order in non-equilibrium systems. As Kauffman points out, free-living systems are also dissipative structures far from equilibrium, composed of cells which "hum along as complex chemical systems that persistently metabolize food molecules to maintain their internal structure and to reproduce" (1995: 21). And as Kauffman colorfully observes, for cells "equilibrium corresponds to death" (1995: 21). Cells and the free-living systems composed of them are complex systems, and along with other kinds of complex systems they can display emergent order.

Complex systems, also known as complex adaptive systems, share a number of characteristics besides being open, dynamic, and not at equilibrium. First, they all contain a large number of interactive components, whether the components are molecules or cells or, as Arthur (1999) suggests, "economic agents [like] banks, consumers, firms, or investors" (1999: 107). Arthur emphasizes interactivity within complex systems (1999: 107):

Common to all studies on complexity are systems with multiple elements adapting or reacting to the pattern these elements create … Elements and the patterns they respond to vary from one context to another. But the elements adapt to the world – the aggregate pattern – they co-create. Time enters naturally here via the processes of adjustment and change: As the elements react, the aggregate changes; as the aggregate changes, elements react anew. Barring the reaching of some asymptotic state or equilibrium, complex systems are systems in process that constantly evolve and unfold over time.

Emergent order, as Mandelbrot said of fractal regularities, comes from the operation of chance within the components and their interactions. "Chance" here refers not to merely erratic behavior but to the formal idea of randomness discussed in Chapter 4. As we have seen, clustering and regular distribution can be measured and distinguished from CSR for language behavior in geographical/social and in textual space. Random operations in complex systems lead to the emergence of non-random distributions, such as clusters or regular patterns, without immediately apparent cause.

Gaussian statistics are linear by nature, so that observed effects are always proportional to their causes. The "general linear model," for instance, includes the t-test, linear regression, ANOVA, and MANOVA, all very common univariate and multivariate statistics. By way of illustration, linear regression involves the determination of the difference of observed results from the mean, which on a graphical plot should yield a straight line that best fits the series of observed experimental values. Complex systems, on the other hand, have distributions that are exponential, or logarithmic; unlike "normal" distributions, the distribution of events within complex systems is non-linear. Mandelbrot's "straight doubly logarithmic graph" (cited above) refers to the fact that a straight line on a logarithmic graph of exponents corresponds to a hyperbolic curve of actual values from observations, not a Gaussian straight line for actual values. Goldenfeld and Kadanoff suggest the practical consequences of this difference (1999: 88):

Improbable (very bad) events are much more likely with the exponential form than with the Gaussian form ... Estimates, particularly Gaussian estimates, formed by short time series will give an entirely incorrect picture of large-scale fluctuations ... Complex systems form structures, and these structures vary widely in size and duration. Their probability distributions are rarely normal, so that exceptional events are not that rare.

This means that, while the emergence of order is common for complex systems, the particular structures that emerge are inherently not predictable.

Finally, complex systems have the property of scaling, or nesting. The properties of the system may be observed at different levels of analysis, not just overall. In Mandelbrot's example, maps made of coastlines (which are fractal, or complex, phenomena) scale robustly (1982: 34):

Although maps drawn at different scales differ in their specific details, they have the same generic features. In a rough approximation, the small and large details of coastlines are geometrically identical except for scale.

What is the same about maps at different scales is the curve or shape of the coast, not any particular distance but the proportion of distances. As another example, one might think of the historical demographic pattern for European markets (see, e.g., Russell 1972: 29–37, in which Zipf's work is cited). Village markets deal in a limited variety of chiefly local goods. Towns are spaced within a day's return travel of numerous villages, and the town markets deal in more specialized goods for the larger area in addition to local goods. Cities are spaced at a still greater distance from numerous towns, and markets there deal in still more specialized goods, now for the entire region, besides local and area goods. This pattern has been somewhat obscured in modern times by improved modes of transportation and the rise of modern retailers like Walmart, but still the general pattern of local, area, and regional marketing continues. The "shape" of activity in markets (e.g., the kinds of economic agents cited above from Arthur (1999), or the effects of supply and demand on transactions) is similar at each level of scale, even though the particular agents and transactions are different at each level. Further, the pattern of exchange overall, say for a country, including transactions in villages and towns and cities together, may also be observed to have the same "shape" of market activity, but the pattern of transactions in the aggregate will not match the pattern at any of the lower levels of analysis, just as the particular transactions conducted are not the same. Scaling is thus evident in the complex network of transactions, based on very large numbers of people interacting in markets, out of which a non-linear distribution of markets emerges (many villages with few transactions, few cities with many transactions), not according to any specific plan or cause but as something that just happens, a result of chance operation in the complex system.

State cycles and simulations

While complex systems have much in common with chaos theory and chaotic systems, they can be differentiated on the basis of their sensitivity to initial conditions in the kind of order that emerges. Chaos theory famously depends upon the "butterfly effect" (the phrase comes from the title of Lorenz 1972, "Predictability: Does the Flap of a Butterfly's Wings in Brazil Set Off a Tornado in Texas?"). Chaotic systems, not to be confused with the popular sense of *chaos* as 'disorder,' are characterized by intermittency, or cyclic behavior. They are said to be deterministic, since small changes in initial conditions lead to significantly different future behavior. Such determinism can be seen in examples of fractals presented by Mandelbrot (see esp. 1982: 193–204), and perhaps the best illustrations of the butterfly effect come from the study of climate (see Rind 1999). Complex systems, on the other hand, are non-deterministic. Kauffman (1995: 80–92) has demonstrated the difference by means of computer simulations of a Boolean network of 1000 lightbulbs, each of which is switched on or off according to how it is interconnected with other bulbs at a given moment.[2] Each moment corresponds to a "state" of the network, a particular pattern of lit bulbs. Given a network of N bulbs with K random interconnections per bulb, and given Boolean rules to control whether the bulb is on or off (i.e., a set of

---

[2] Goldenfeld and Kadanoff (1999) suggest that experimental, computational, and theoretical modes of investigation can all be valuable for understanding complex systems. They stress that the analyst must "use the right level of description to catch the phenomena of interest. Don't model bulldozers with quarks" (1999: 88). Kauffman's computer simulation is presented here along with some theoretical discussion, but experimental evidence takes pride of place in this volume.

conditions corresponding to the possible status of the interconnected bulbs), larger or smaller groups of bulbs will over time settle into a state cycle (or "attractor"), on/off patterns of bulbs that repeat over time. For a large network of bulbs, an ordered condition consists of settling into a relatively small number of stable state cycles (that is, attractors insensitive to small changes), while a chaotic condition consists of occupying a large number of state cycles. For a network of 1000 lightbulbs, to cycle through every possible on/off pattern ($=2^{1000}$ states) would take an impossibly long time, as would any significant fraction of the total. If the state cycles were sensitive to any change, so that they broke out of their state cycles if it happened that one or two bulbs were flipped from on to off or from off to on by means other than the established Boolean rules, then an extremely long period of cycling through huge numbers of possible states would occur – a chaotic system. Thus, sensitivity to initial conditions, to small stimuli that change cycles of repetitive patterning, determines the chaotic condition of a system. On the other hand, the ordered condition of a non-chaotic complex system is not sensitive to changes in a bulb or two and thus can be called stable (or "homeostatic"), not determined by the butterfly effect that creates the initial condition for the formation of new and different long-term sequences of state cycles.

Kauffman's computer simulations allow him to make generalizations about the conditions under which ordered or chaotic conditions occur in networks. He reports in summary (1995: 80–81):

Two features of the way networks are constructed can control whether they are in an ordered regime, a chaotic regime, or a phase transition between these, "on the edge of chaos." One feature is simply how many "inputs" control any lightbulb. If each bulb is controlled by only one or two other lightbulbs, if the network is "sparsely connected," then the system exhibits stunning order. If each bulb is controlled by many other lightbulbs, then the network is chaotic. So "tuning" the connectivity of a network tunes whether one finds order or chaos. The second feature that controls the emergence of order or chaos is simple biases in the control rules themselves. Some control rules, the AND and OR Boolean functions ... tend to create orderly dynamics. Other control rules create chaos.

If lightbulbs are connected only to one other bulb ($K=1$), very short state cycles occur and the network "freezes up." If the lightbulbs are all interconnected ($K=N$), groups of bulbs form numerous state cycles smaller than the total number of possible states, which are sensitive to small stimuli: chaos. According to Kauffman, most Boolean networks of this kind are still chaotic as the value of K retreats from N towards $K=1$. However, when $K=2$, and only then, the network of 1000 bulbs achieves an ordered condition and cycles through only 32 states (approximately the square root of the number of bulbs). In Kauffman's colorful description, "the spontaneous dynamics drive the system into an infinitesimal corner of its state space and hold it there, quivering for an eternity. Order for free" (1995: 83). Thus order emerges from random interactions in the network according to the conditions obtaining in the network.

In Kauffman's simulations, it is also possible to achieve an ordered condition for networks with more interconnections than $K = 2$ by manipulating the Boolean control rules. If the rules switch all of the bulbs either on or off, the system will "freeze up" immediately as either all on or all off, no matter what its initial state, similar to the situation for $K = 1$ with randomly assigned rules in which half the rules turn bulbs on and half turn them off. Kauffman suggests that it is possible to bias the control rules away from random (half switching bulbs on and half switching bulbs off), closer but not all the way to completely determinate (all on or all off), and find the critical point at "the edge of chaos" where the network changes from a frozen or from a chaotic condition to an ordered condition. Under either of these conditions, whether at $K = 2$ or with control bias at the critical point at the edge of chaos, the behavior of the complex system becomes non-determined and available for the spontaneous emergence of order.

As Arthur has noted for social systems (1999: 107):

Unlike ions in a spin glass, which always react in a simple way to their local magnetic field, economic elements (human agents) react with strategy and foresight by considering outcomes that might result as a consequence of behavior they might undertake. This adds a layer of complication to economics that is not experienced in the natural sciences.

When Kauffman's simulations are compared to actual situations in the natural sciences, it must be the case, given the natural order that we observe, that by nature some complex systems can possess a particular level of interconnection, or by nature can possess control bias near the critical point that allows for emergent order. In human systems, however, Arthur's "layer of complication" corresponds to potential changes in control bias as human agents change their reaction to conditions. Still, whether in the physical and natural sciences where reactive adaptation may be simple, or in the social sciences where reactive adaptation may be more complicated, order is still the result of the interaction of the density of interconnection of many elements and the control bias that exists in the system. The word "spontaneous" may not be the best term for the order that emerges, if it implies that the order is sudden and unexpected; "self-organization" is a better way to describe order that responds in this way to very particular conditions for random interactions.

Linguists and complexity

This short description of the terms and concepts for complex systems may have been tough going for linguists unaccustomed to the language of mathematics or physics. Still, as we shall see, the linguistics of speech must be a complex system, because the evidence from survey research and from corpus linguistics shows all the characteristics of complex systems. This is not the first time that chaos theory and complex systems have been suggested as models for language. Edgar Schneider has speculated about chaos theory as a possible model for dialect variation and change, and referred to Lightfoot's observation that "in linguistics the butterfly effect corresponds to a 'constant, chaotic flux in the linguistic environment' which in the long run, at some point, causes 'a new parameter setting'" (1997: 26). Ronald Butters has written about chance as a cause for variation and change (2001). Relying largely on Keller (1994) for his model of chance operation, Butters concluded that "particular causes were not demonstrable for many effects observed in language varieties, but that was not a bad result because there need be no other explanation than chance/chaos" (2001: 210). Valuable as they are, these are clearly high-level comparisons of language to general features of complex systems, not detailed expositions that align experimental data (Keller 1994: 100–104 describes a simulation; see also Kretzschmar 1992b) with specific findings in complexity science. Kuhl (2003) does make a serious effort to align complexity science with particular data, but not for populations. Kuhl treats particular speaker interactions and, as he put it, "the idiolect as autonomous adaptive organism" (2003: 78). The linguistics of speech as discussed here encompasses interactions in groups of speakers, although it will be important to consider how individuals respond to the language behavior of populations (Chapter 7).

To my knowledge, Joan Bybee has conducted the most extensive work intended to make use of complexity science in linguistics (2001, 2007; see also Bybee and Hopper 2001, an edited collection of articles). For her (2001: 3), "the basic idea behind emergence as it will be applicable here [viz., to linguistics, especially phonology] is that certain simple properties of a substantive nature, when applied repeatedly, create structure." Bybee cites Lindblom, MacNeilage, and Studdert-Kennedy (1984) as "the first to apply the notion of emergent structure in linguistics, and further cites Hopper (1987) and Keller (1994) in support of the idea that for "emergence in complex systems, substance and form are related via the *process* by which the structure is created" (2001: 4). This emphasis on repetition and process is recapitulated in many of Bybee's articles (reprinted in Bybee 2007), especially those concerned with sound change and grammaticization. She makes use of a distinction between high-frequency words as a class from low-frequency words in her discussion of sound change, and links the idea of repetition to cognition (2007: 8):

What are the cognitive responses to repetition? There are multiple responses and their effects can change according to the extent of repetition. The chapters of this volume represent my investigations into these effects over the last thirty years, from the first recognition of the potential explanatory power of frequency effects through a continuing effort to understand them and their interaction with processing factors, as well as phonetics, semantics, and grammar.

Study of frequency effects led Bybee away from generative linguistics, notably in her influential 2001 monograph which replaces generative tenets with a "usage based model for phonology and morphology" (2001: 19). Still, even in Bybee (2001) the linguistics of linguistic structure remains the target (2001: 18):

This book is a linguist's book: it applies the established methods and data of linguists to the understanding of language as an emergent system resulting from the general cognitive capacities of humans interacting with language substance over many instances of language use.

Bybee attempts to map "the established methods and data of linguists" onto complexity science, such that linguistic structure is taken to be the order that emerges from the complex system. While the effort is laudable and suggestive in its alignment of linguistics with a contemporary scientific movement, Bybee has not fully addressed the characteristics of complex systems even as briefly described above, issues like non-determinism and non-linearity. Bybee has thus not established that the necessary conditions for emergent order are satisfied by language use. It would be difficult to understand how she could have done so and still retained her priority for established modes of linguistic structure, which prejudge the outcomes of chance operation on instances of language use. Bybee has done well to extract parts of her ideas from complex systems, notably repetition and process, but her theoretical work has not fully engaged complexity science. Her "understanding of language as an emergent system" so far remains an understanding by analogy, not by identity.

Speech as a complex system

In this volume about the linguistics of speech, we are not limited to the established methods and data of the linguistics of language structure, and we can attempt to see all of the characteristics of complex systems in the survey and corpus evidence presented in earlier chapters. In order for speech to be a complex system, we should be able to observe the following conditions:
(a) speech is open and dynamic, thus not at equilibrium;
(b) speech includes a very large number of interactive components/agents;
(c) speech shows emergent order;
(d) the distribution of units in speech is non-linear;
(e) speech has the property of scaling.
Further, we should be able to show that speech is not inherently a chaotic system, so that we can distinguish it as a complex system with emergent order. Finally, we need to show that speech demonstrates the characteristics for emergent order developed in Kauffman's simulation experiments, sensitivity to the density of interconnection of components and sensitivity to "control bias." Consideration of these issues will occupy the remainder of this chapter.

The idea that speech is open and dynamic can be found in Saussure. His principle that dialects and languages have no natural boundaries anticipates the later finding for complex systems that their boundaries are difficult to determine. Where does one economic system clearly separate itself from another system? Where does one ecological system separate itself from another one? For studies both of the economy and of ecology, the size of the system to be analyzed often rises to global magnitude, as in discussion of the "world economy" and globalization, or of Mother Earth and global warming. Nobody has yet proposed, to my knowledge, that speech constitutes a global system (unless in the search for linguistic universals, which is certainly motivated by other purposes). Yet, the clear implication of the old demonstration of the European speech continuum – riding a bicycle across the continent to discover that all neighboring locations understand each other, when speakers at the beginning and end of the ride do not (see Chambers and Trudgill 1998: Chapter 1 for a more empirical description of linguistic continuum in Europe) – must be, should anyone choose to draw it, that the ride could continue still further across the globe. Descriptions of English as a world language already have to cope with the question of what counts as English, as it is used by L1 and L2 speakers globally (see, e.g., Crystal 2003). As for experimental evidence, Saussure relied on the early dialectologists, and one of the central findings from more modern, sampled survey evidence in Chapter 3 is that lines and boundaries fail to capture the facts of language variation, even within a large regional survey, much less a national, international, or global one. Variation in speech, whether in the lexicon or in pronunciation, occurs on a continuum in the frequency of realization of feature variants across geographical and social space. It also occurs on a continuum of possible realizations of feature variants. Moreover, the frequency of feature variants alone or in combination is continuously variable in the textual dimension, across text types. Closed, categorical sets are simply not characteristic of speech, which always exists as an open continuum.

The fact that speech is dynamic has never been a matter of dispute. Change was a central idea for Saussure, who attributed geographical differentiation in speech behavior to differential change over time, saying that "Geographical diversity has to be translated into temporal diversity." Indeed, as we have seen, evident language change has been the driving motivation for many linguists, from the NeoGrammarians to Labov to Bybee. New conversations and writings among members of the speaking population occur continuously at unimaginable rates. In these spoken and written transactions, new feature variants emerge, and other established ones decline over time. New speakers continuously enter and continuously leave any speaking population, at minimum through birth and death but also commonly through movement across geographical and social space, and this exchange of speakers can only stimulate additional change in speech. To paraphrase Kauffman, for speech, equilibrium corresponds to death.

So-called dead languages, like Latin, are not as dead as defunct biological organisms, since new speakers may learn them and even occasionally invent new words or phrases, say for objects that did not exist when Latin was a living language. The case is similar for Native American languages whose original speakers have died out, when their descendants try to recover their ancestral languages, as for example with the help of the University of California (see Chapter 1). Under such circumstances, the language might be said to be at low-energy equilibrium. On the other hand, high energy is the normal state for speech in L1 populations of speakers, as speech in all known populations of L1 speakers changes continuously. Thus, speech does meet the initial conditions for a non-equilibrium system. As we shall see, however, characterization and measurement of change in the linguistics of speech must be different from the way that the linguistics of linguistic structure handles change (Chapter 8).

For speech to be a complex system, it must have a very large number of interactive components/agents. This condition appears to be more complicated for social systems than for physical or natural systems. As Arthur said, ions react in a simple way to magnetic fields, while human agents may have more freedom to decide how they react (cited above). However, in chemistry, catalytic agents may be required before a potential reaction takes place, and organic molecules may offer multiple potential binding sites, so interaction between components is not always so simple as it is for ions (see Kauffman 1995: 58–66, 142–144). When climate is modeled as a complex or chaotic system, atmospheric processes and the ocean do not have simple interactions (see Rind 1999: 105). For complex systems in the social sciences, the problem of human agents may indeed introduce uncertainty, but in this respect social systems are not essentially different from complex systems in the natural sciences where reactions are also uncertain. As we shall see, human agency becomes relevant to complex systems for the issue of control bias, not for the more basic condition of interactivity among components. The economic system is based on transactions; the speech system is also based on a kind of transaction, spoken or written conversations. Thus it is not the people themselves, as consumers or as speakers, who are components in the system, but instead the systems are composed, respectively, of the units of value exchanged in economic transactions, and of the units of speech exchanged in conversations. Consumers and speakers are agents whose activity makes the system work, like catalysts for a chemical reaction, and for that reason the characteristics of the speakers must be considered in any model for the linguistics of speech (see Chapter 7). However, the components of the complex system of speech consist not of speakers, but of speech sounds, words, and other concrete entities extracted from the stream of speech.

Experimental evidence from both survey research and from corpus studies indicates that the number of components available to interact is very much larger than previously anticipated. Survey questions about everyday words for weather events might yield over 200 different types of response, words and short phrases, as for *cloudburst* in Chapter 3. Even when the list was pared down to remove superficial morphological differences like articles and plurals while retaining phrasal entries, and to remove entries that have some difficulty of interpretation, 80% of the response types remained. An even wider range of variation was observed for the stressed vowel in *fog* in Chapter 3, which occupied a large proportion of the available impressionistic IPA positions for height and frontness, and which also varied by length. The extent of variation in these counts is high for items in the survey (for purposes of illustration in Chapter 3) but not unusual. Modern acoustical phonetic measurement only adds to the variability observable for speech sounds through traditional transcription, because it does not constrain the categories for measurement as greatly as does the IPA symbol set. Similarly, the evidence of corpus linguistics indicates that words tend strongly to be deployed in the company of particular other words, whether as collocations or through semantic preference. This finding suggests that multi-word units should be the types for analysis rather than individual words, which greatly multiplies the number of components and the complexity of their potential interactions. Indeed, multi-word units account for a large proportion of the lexical variability in *cloudburst* – but not all, since forty-nine different noun heads were employed in the list. Similarly, it was not just differences in unitary vowels that accounted for the great range of variability in the vowel of *fog*; diphthongization, vowel combinations, accounted for a large proportion of the different realizations. Therefore, both survey research and corpus research demonstrate that combinations of words may be reasonable units to extract from the stream of speech for analysis, not just single words. Similarly, survey research shows that combinations of speech sounds may be reasonable units to extract instead of single vowels.

To turn from evidence to theory, the theoretical number of possible combinations for N words, or for N vowels, is N^2 for diphthongs or for sets of two words, and N^3 for triphthongs or for sets of three words. The number of entries for headwords in the dictionary therefore grossly underestimates the possible units in the lexicon. If we consider just the 100,000 words in a typical desk-size dictionary, we theoretically increase the number of available components from 100,000 single words to ten billion two-word combinations – multiplied by 100,000 again to count three-word combinations, an unimaginable number. For pronunciation, if we consider the height (20) and front/back (20) steps on the IPA vowel list in use for the LAMSAS project, and then consider that each step might be modified by a shift sign for raising/lowering or fronting/backing, we see that vowel space for the survey includes 60×60, or 3600 possible positions for single vowels. The number of possible positions for diphthongs is thus 3600×3600, or 12,960,000; the

number of possible positions for triphthongs is 46,656,000,000. These calcu-
lations are too low, of course, because they neglect relative length, degree of
realization (strong/weak), and other factors that affect vowels – and acoustical
phonetic processing yields continuous, theoretically infinite variation for each
formant. The dictionary as a mode of presentation for information about
speech greatly idealizes the facts of language in use for the lexicon, just as
modern notions of phonology and phonetics (including the inventory of units
available in the IPA) greatly idealize and simplify the representation of speech
sounds. Experimental evidence shows that speech does include a very large
number of components: if not the theoretically possible number of components,
the evidence contains a number of components several orders of magnitude
greater than the existing idealized language "realities" might suggest. The
massive numbers arise because the components are in fact demonstrated in
the evidence to be highly interactive. Once again, the conditions for speech
to be a complex system have been satisfied in experimental evidence, not just
in theory.

Experimental evidence does indicate that emergent order can be observed
in speech, even if such order does not consist of the structures that the linguistics
of linguistic structure has traditionally described. Feature variants in survey
research very often possess non-random extralinguistic correlates. Most variants have statistically significant associations with independent variables such
as location, type, sex, age, race, community type, education, and occupation,
and the same variant often has significant associations with several independent
variables at the same time (Chapter 4). Variants of linguistic features are thus
correlated in complex ways with different geographical and social factors.
Moreover, feature variants were very often spatially autocorrelated, significantly clustered by location at least 75% of the time, as opposed to being either
randomly distributed or evenly distributed over the survey area. This result
suggests that speech is a local phenomenon, that geographical and social
proximity for interaction is a powerful factor in the emergence of order. The
patterns of coherence in the distribution of feature variants noted in Chapters 3
and 4 correspond to what are called attractors in complexity science. Moreover,
the evidence from corpus linguistics shows that word frequencies can vary
significantly according to text types as well as in geographical and social space.
Word and feature frequencies are sensitive to differences in Biber's registers as
well as text types, and they can also be shown to change significantly at different
time periods. We can observe patterned behavior in corpora, emergent order,
even if it does not necessarily occur according to traditional "realities" of
popularly accepted text types for units of analysis. John Sinclair's notion that
complete freedom of choice for a feature variant is rare, and so also complete
determination, turns out to be an apt description for the order that emerges in
speech as a complex system.

Dimensionality

As we move to a more extended discussion of aspects of complex systems that are also important elements in Mandelbrot's fractals, non-linearity and scaling, we must give some initial consideration to the notion of dimensionality. The subject of dimensions does not usually arise in description of complex systems, and yet it is present. For example, Kauffman's discussion of DNA and the emergence of living systems (1995: 36–38) requires that he describe the molecule both as a double helix, a two-dimensional object with width in the bond between strands as well as length, and for purposes of replication as a pair of strands or sequences of amino acids, one-dimensional objects with length, even though the molecule actually exists in three dimensions. The dimensional transformation turns out to be crucial in the process of replication. For speech, experimental evidence has revealed two important dimensions, speech in a geographical/social dimension and speech in a textual dimension. The dimensions clearly must interact: every conversation naturally occurs in both dimensions. Every conversation is located in the geographical and social space of its speakers (or author and audience), and every conversation also belongs to some text type along the continuum of possible texts. Ideally, descriptions of speech should always discuss the characteristics of both dimensions. In practice, however, analysts often discuss the variables of one dimension without explicitly addressing those of the other. Mandelbrot offers the term "effective dimension" to address this problem (1982: 17):

Effective dimension concerns the relation between mathematical sets and material objects. Strictly speaking, physical objects such as a veil, a thread, or a tiny ball should all be represented by three-dimensional shapes. However, physicists prefer to think of a veil, a thread, or a ball – if they are fine enough – as being "in effect" of dimensions 2, 1, and 0, respectively. For example, to describe a thread, the theories relating to sets of dimension 1 or 3 must be modified by corrective terms. And the better geometrical model is determined after the fact, as involving the smaller corrections. If luck holds, this model continues to be helpful even when corrections are omitted. In other words, effective dimension inevitably has a subjective basis. It is a matter of approximation and therefore of degree of resolution.

Thus in practice a thread might well be described as a one-dimensional object, as if it were a geometrical line and not actually a real object in three dimensions. But if it is so described, the result is an approximation, an estimate that more or less reflects reality but leaves room for error. Statistical estimation, as from sampling, is accounted for in formulas by changing a term: if n is applied for population statistics, $(n-1)$ is applied for estimations. For description of multidimensional systems like speech, to describe only the geographical/social dimension without also describing the textual dimension, or vice versa, is likewise an estimation, but it is not so easy just to replace a term to account for it.[3] In what follows, the dimensionality of the data will not be completely described, but the distributions illustrated are so robust that there is little chance that we will be misled – no need for Mandelbrot's luck in this case. However, the issue of effective dimension has important consequences for the linguistics of speech in other ways, and it will be raised again in Chapter 7.

Zipf and non-linear distributions in speech

Once we get past the idealization of units of analysis, single words and speech sounds in dictionary lists and in phonological systems, and we see the massive number of components in the speech system, we can also observe that in experimental evidence the components always possess a non-linear distribution.[4] This distribution was introduced to the field of linguistics by George Zipf. "Zipf's Law," so-called, says that if one counts the frequency of words in any large text and then puts the frequencies in descending order, there is an inverse relationship between each frequency and its rank in the order, roughly $P = 1/r$, where P is the frequency and r is the rank. This formula yields a logarithmic plot of frequency and rank with the slope of -1 (Figure 6.1). If one multiplies the frequency times the rank, the result is a number that remains (roughly) constant for every word in the text. Manning and Schütze (1999: 23–29) offer a concise account of Zipf's Law, using the text of Mark Twain's novel *Tom Sawyer* for illustration. Zipf's basic insight has led to developments in information sciences, such as the idea that frequently occurring words carry little information (like English function words) while infrequently occurring words tend to be rich in information (like all the Latinate nouns of scientific vocabulary). Zipf's Law does not apply just to single texts, but to any sufficiently large collection of texts: its current entry in Wikipedia (s.v. but NB: en.wikipedia.org entries are editable and therefore likely to be ephemeral) attempts to illustrate it from word frequencies in the Brown Corpus, not from a single text (see also the use of the Brown Corpus in relation to Zipf in Manning and Schütze 1999: 25–27).

Mandelbrot, in his first published article, showed that the word frequency/rank relationship is not quite so simple as Zipf suggested (1951). He provided an improved formula that offered a better fit of the frequency/rank relationship to the facts of the words in any text while it confirmed the basic distributional pattern: $P - F(r + V)^{-1/D}$, where F and V are constants and D is a fractal dimension derived from the logarithms of the words and

---

[3] While otherwise motivated, Labov's notion of style, in which the sociolinguist observes linguistic variables in casual, interview, reading, and word-list styles (each of which may be considered a text type), begins to address this problem.

[4] This section is based on Kretzschmar and Tamasi (2003) "Distributional Foundations for a Theory of Language Change," *World Englishes* 22: 377–401. With the kind permission of Blackwell Publishing, Oxford.

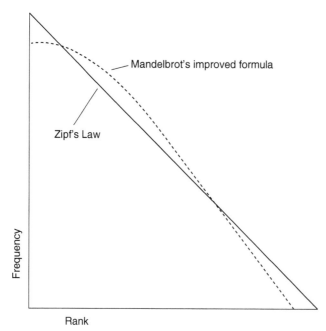

Figure 6.1 Plot (logarithmic) of Zipf's Law in comparison to Mandelbrot's improvement
(Source: Adapted from Mandelbrot 1968: 269)

their ranks.[5] As shown in Figure 6.1, Mandelbrot's improved formula yields a curve on the logarithmic plot, in which the top-ranked words have a lower

[5] A central article in English to offer proofs related to this formula is Mandelbrot (1961). Formal mathematical proofs are beyond the scope of this volume; for more detailed treatment of many relevant mathematical issues, see Baayen (2001) and Manning and Schütze (1999). Mandelbrot (1977: 240) explains that the F term is determined by the independent parameters D and V, of which D is most important. For a summary of Mandelbrot's argument, see Mandelbrot (1982: 344–347); see also Rapoport (1982). It is true that one can build a mathematical model employing Zipf's Law by using random assignment of letters and nonsense sequences of letters (Li 1992), which might suggest that the distribution has nothing to do with language and is merely a property of the ranking procedure. Mandelbrot himself pointed out that such random modeling is not a good fit for language because "many short sequences of letters never occur and many long sequences are fairly common" (1982: 346). Günther et al. (1996) argued that letter sequences are not independent (parallel to the implication of Mandelbrot's reservation), which Li's hyperbolic mathematical model assumed, and thus the appearance of the distributional pattern must in some way be a property of the subject matter being counted, and not just an artifact of the counting and ranking method. Finally, it has been suggested that the hyperbolic curve of Zipf's Law might just be an artifact of charting frequencies of frequencies. That is, it has been suggested that, given a normal distribution, reordering the points on the curve by frequency will automatically yield the Zipfian curve. This is clearly not the case, however, because normal distributions are symmetrical. Given a repeated experiment with many observations at the same value, such as the number of

slope than expected in Zipf's Law, and the lower-ranked words also deviate but now with a steeper slope. This second slope depends on what Mandelbrot (1968: 269) calls "the 'wealth of vocabulary' of the subject," and thus the values of the parameters in the formula may differ by subject, but the formula itself is robust across different subjects and languages (Mandelbrot 1982: 344). Exponential functions like the ones of Zipf's Law are "hyperbolic," in that they can theoretically have infinitely large or infinitely small frequencies. However, in real life, we know that there are real upper and lower limits for frequencies expressed as integers, whether of words or other countable objects. Thus we should refer to real distributions of speech as asymptotic distributions, which are, according to Mandelbrot, "defined and finite, and one of the limits is positive" (1982: 343; thus my use of the term "A-curve" in Chapter 3). Also, given Mandelbrot's improved formula, rank/frequency plots deviate from the perfect hyperbolic curve associated with Zipf's original law. Good examples of the characteristic "bump" on non-logarithmic plots of speech data following Mandelbrot's formula occur in Figures 3.19 through 3.23, and the deviation in the logarithmic plot appears in Figure 6.1. Asymptotic (or asymptotically hyperbolic) distributions as found in speech are thus a subset related to hyperbolic functions. Finally, it is worth quoting Mandelbrot's assessment (1982: 403) of Zipf (1949):

> It is one of those books … in which flashes of genius, projected in many directions, are nearly overwhelmed by a gangue of wild notions and extravagance. On the one hand, it deals with the shape of sexual organs and justifies the Anschluss of Austria into Germany because it improved the fit of a mathematical formula. On the other hand, it is filled with figures and tables that hammer away ceaselessly at the empirical law that, in social science statistics, the best combination of mathematical convenience and empirical fit is often given by a scaling probability distribution.

The important thing here is the distributional message, not Zipf the messenger.

Zipf's analysis, called "frequency of frequencies," may sound arcane, but it is really a simple way to represent the distribution of linguistic types and tokens. For example, say that in a given hypothetical text there are fifteen word types (Figure 6.2); one of them has twenty tokens, one of them has eight tokens, one of them has four tokens, two of them have three tokens, three of them have two tokens, and the remaining seven types have one token each. We could make two different kinds of graph out of this data (Figure 6.2). If we plot the frequency of the tokens for each type, as we usually do, we will have one type with a value of twenty, one type with a value of eight, and so forth. But we can also plot the types against the tokens, that is, we can make a data point on the graph for each

---

"heads" in a hundred coin tosses, reordering a normally distributed graph of values as a frequency of frequencies graph will in effect fold the left half of the curve onto the right half. Since each data point of the half-curve will be doubled, its slope will be proportionately less steep. The operation of reordering by frequencies will not result in a hyperbolic curve, but in a double-curving shape approximating one side of a normal distribution, only less steep.

Word A	20 times	Frequency "1"	7 words
Word B	8 times	Frequency "2"	3 words
Word C	4 times	Frequency "3"	2 words
Word D,E	3 times each	Frequency "4"	1 word
Word F,G,H	2 times each	Frequency "8"	1 word
Word I,J,K,L,M,N,O	1 time each	Frequency "20"	1 word

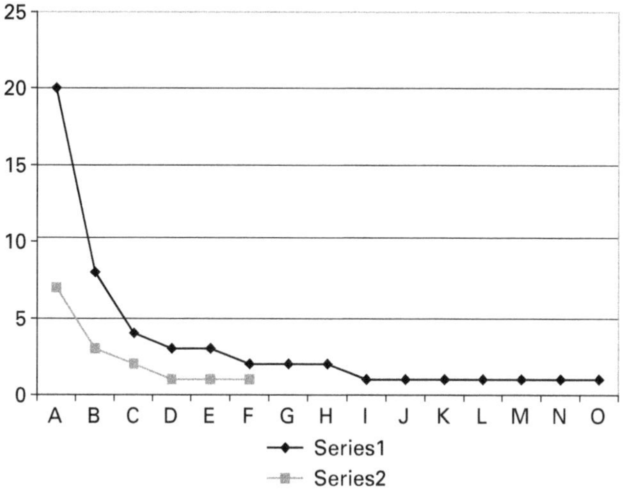

Figure 6.2 Illustration of frequency of frequencies

token frequency. Thus, there are seven single occurrences, so frequency "1" has a value of seven; there are three double occurrences, so frequency "2" has a value of 3; there are two words that occur three times, so frequency "3" has a value of two. The other data points (twenty, eight, and four occurrences, respectively) each have a value of one. It is clear that the two curves plotted from this data have the same basic shape, but the "frequency of frequencies" curve has fewer data points, and the numbers are smaller than the usual type/ token curve. The effect of this representation of the data, then, is to reduce the statistical variance found in the original type/token curve, while retaining its basic shape.[6]

Linguists have recently treated some issues related to Zipf's ideas, notably Krug (1998, 2001) and Kortmann (1997), besides those noted above such as Bybee. Pustet (2004) is a review article with particularly good coverage of Zipf's notion that more frequent items tend to be shorter, which is referenced in

---

[6] Günther *et al.* (1996) says in summary, "we have found that ranking at its best is a way of reducing random fluctuations and narrowing broad probability distributions in order to get meaningful quantitative measurements in systems which are evolving, nonstationary, and exist in one realization only" (p. 408).

arguments by Bybee and others about grammaticization. The non-linear distribution of Zipf's Law, however, has not attracted much attention in contemporary linguistics. In Pustet's overall judgment, "Zipf's work in linguistics has never been appreciated by practitioners of the discipline as much as it might deserve to be appreciated" (2004: 3). As opposed to the introduction and description of Zipf's Law early in Manning and Schütze's textbook on Natural Language Processing (1999), Jurafsky and Martin's NLP textbook (2000) does not mention the Zipfian distribution until a passing reference on page 603, the only mention of Zipf in the volume (it must be said that Manning and Schütze mention Zipf on only two occasions after the initial description, both in passing). Mandelbrot's general opinion of such an evaluation has already been cited at the beginning of this chapter. Zipf's Law has been much more attractive as a rallying point beyond linguistics, where its distribution is generally recognized as a "power law." Both Mandelbrot and more recently Günther, Levitin, Schapiro, and Wagner have observed that the asymptotic hyperbolic distribution is present in many other aspects of the natural and social world. Mandelbrot worked particularly in the field of economics (1982: 334–340, 347–348). Günther *et al.* (1996) refers to the presence of the distribution in physics, biology, demography, and the social sciences (pp. 395–396), and discusses particularly its application to the species populations in ecosystems and to evolutionary biology.[7] As Manning and Schütze have observed (1999: 26; see also the comments on "Gaussian" statistics in Mandelbrot 1982: 247, 423, and elsewhere), the asymptotic hyperbolic distribution appears to be one of the standard distributional patterns of the world around us which can stand beside the Gaussian "normal" distribution upon which so much of modern statistics is based. The online bibliography of works on Zipf's Law maintained by Wentian Li (www.nslij-genetics.org/wli/zipf) offers no fewer than 563 entries at this writing; among those for the last three years with complete listings (2003–2005, about 30 entries per year), about half are concerned with language in some way, while the others discuss fields from animal behavior to chromosomes/genes to urban studies, besides those fields already mentioned above. Of the articles related to language, many are about website popularity and other topics related to information science, not to formal linguistics. Mandelbrot mused that "it had originally been hoped that Zipf's law would contribute in the field of linguistics but my explanation shows this law is linguistically very shallow" (1982: 346), i.e., that it applies broadly to different languages and subjects. For the linguistics of linguistic structure, Zipf's Law has

---

[7] (1996: 397–400). William Labov has recently written about the relationship between language and evolutionary biology. Labov (2001) begins by drawing the parallel between Darwin and language, and then denies that the mechanism of natural selection accounts for linguistic change in what he calls "the Darwinian Paradox." See below for comments on Mufwene (2001), currently the best thorough application of the evolutionary model to speech and language.

remained chiefly a curiosity, akin perhaps to the odd finding of Hudson (1994) that one-third of word tokens across many texts and corpora are nouns.

For the linguistics of speech, on the other hand, the distribution represented by Zipf's Law extends to experimental data from survey research as well as to words in texts, and thus it stands as a primary characteristic of speech as a complex system. The A-curve described in Chapter 3 as a general property of lexical and pronunciation evidence from the Atlas is the same curve that Zipf described for texts. When the frequencies of the variants for lexical items like *cloudburst, thunderstorm*, and *mantel*, and for the vowels in words like *fog, fifth, first*, and *night*, are set in descending order, the curve which describes the frequency of each response type is an excellent fit for the Zipf/Mandelbrot distribution. This experimental finding thus constitutes an essential expansion of Zipf's Law, not just another analogical application of it. Speech as a complex system can be characterized by the non-linear distribution of the A-curve in both of its dimensions, in geographical/social space as well as in texts.

Zipf's Law is derived from the frequency of frequencies of words. The raw data constituted by the frequency of words or of sounds in the Figures presented in Chapter 3 does not itself fit the Zipf/Mandelbrot model, but it can easily and transparently be converted to frequency of frequencies. The frequency of frequencies table for *mantel* is shown in Figure 6.3 as the "Series 1" line, and also plotted there is the raw frequency of words as the "Series 2" line.

It is clear that the frequency of frequencies plot substantially reduces the variance in the data: the plot showing only Series 1 illustrates the asymptotic hyperbolic distribution for the frequency of frequencies for *mantel*, but the curve of the Series 1 plot nearly vanishes when it is compared to the size of the frequency of words line in Series 2 in the chart that displays both Series 1 and Series 2. This difference in the scope of the variance accounts for the difficulty of fitting a mathematical function to the frequency of words data, which is more highly variable. The distribution of phonetic segments in the data often (though not always) fits the Lerch distribution, which is a generalized model of the Zipf type (see Zörnig and Altmann 1995).[8] This finding accords with the smaller scale of the variance in the phonetic data, which has fewer possible data points than the lexical data because of the limited set of possibilities inherent in the vectors of the phonetic symbols. Further research will be required to fit a mathematical model to the raw word and sound frequency data.[9] At this point, though, it is fair to say that the asymptotic hyperbolic distribution does

---

[8] I am grateful to Jee-Hee Han and Maria Salustio, working under the direction of Dan Hall in the Statistics Department of the University of Georgia, for their detailed analysis of the fit of several different mathematical models for our linguistic data.

[9] My thanks to Harald Baayen for pointing out several directions for detailed curve fitting (which is sensitive to sample size), such as Evert (2004) and the models in Baayen (2001), and for other comments on issues in this section.

Count	Frequency
16	1
6	2
2	5
2	7
1	11
1	29
1	58
1	62
1	160
1	183
1	513
1	622

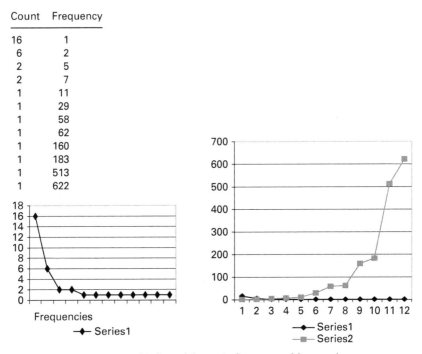

Figure 6.3 *mantel* (adjusted data set), frequency of frequencies

characterize our linguistic survey data in both its raw form as word and sound frequencies, and in its derived presentation as frequency of frequencies.

As a final illustration of the appearance of the A-curve distribution, we can return to the textual dimension and consider, not the frequency of words in a text, but the distribution of documents which appear to fit a text type. "Prediction" can, for this example, serve as a recognizable discourse type. People generally know when a prediction is being made, as opposed to alternative discourse types such as "historical account" or "statement of current fact." "Prediction" overlaps with other imaginable discourse types such as "offer" and "threat," which illustrates the need for care in the selection of speech characteristics belonging to any conceivable discourse type. While the full list of such characteristics might be extensive, some words surely belong to a small set that defines the semantic preference for predictions. The presence of these words – *expectation, forecast, prognosis/prognostication*, and the word *prediction* itself – can serve to help identify documents as possible members of the "prediction" type. Among the 500 documents of the Brown Corpus, only sixty-eight documents contained any uses of these words. Of these sixty-eight documents, fifty-two documents contained only one use; seven documents each contained two uses; six documents each

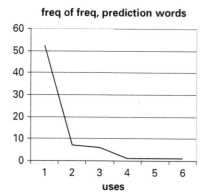

Figure 6.4 Frequency of frequencies, "prediction" words

contained three uses; and one document contained four, one document contained five, and one document contained six uses. The distribution of these frequencies should come as no surprise (Figure 6.4).

Excluding the fifty-two documents with only one use of a "prediction" word, inspection of the remaining documents shows that two of the three documents with the most uses of "prediction" words were methodological documents about making predictions (in science), and the other was an editorial piece about predictions made by others. Eleven of the remaining thirteen documents contained actual predictions (whether the entire document constituted a "prediction," or only part of the document), and the other two documents contained predictions that had already come to pass. The A-curve, then, describes not just the distribution of words in texts and of feature variants in survey research, but also documents of a discourse type found within a broad corpus. The A-curve describes the distribution of a great many aspects of speech, in both dimensions, as a robust general property of speech.

This thorough-going non-linear distribution is just what we should expect in a complex system. Günther *et al.* (1996) concludes that "the appearance of Zipf's Law is not caused by pure accident, but can be understood on a level which considers the interplay between laws in complex systems, which, unlike physical laws, may be evolving" (p. 410). Rapoport (1982: 26–27) suggests that "many social phenomena may well be describable in terms of stochastic processes … a typology of stochastic processes may provide a methodologically fruitful classification of social processes. The approach carries promise for constructing 'unified' theories of social phenomena, unified not in the sense of similarity of content but rather in the sense of a structural similarity of underlying stochasticall[y] formulated dynamics." No case will be made here for any more general impact of the "power law" in the social sciences than what we see in the language data. It is, however, worth emphasizing once more that the analysis here is based on actual findings in survey and textual data, and not merely on the abstract mathematical possibilities of the hyperbolic function. Thus, the asymptotic distribution of feature variants that we have observed in both survey data and textual data is not an accident of counting. It is a distribution that others have regularly observed in the language of written texts and in other phenomena in the world around us, especially as a characteristic of complex systems. We can expect that it will be present in speech, not occasionally but consistently, and in consequence we can expect that speech will behave as a complex system.

Scaling

The final characteristic required for speech to be a complex system is the property of scaling. Mandelbrot provided a formal definition of scaling (1982: 343): "a random variable X is *scaling under the transformation* $T(X)$ if the distributions of X and $T(X)$ are identical except for scale." For present purposes, this means that, if speech data is scaling, then the A-curve distribution should be present at different levels of scale in the experimental data. We have already had some indication that this is true from the phonetic data presented in Chapter 3, where different aspects of vowel pronunciation displayed an A-curve distribution. Table 6.1 shows the list of variants for the LAMSAS *chest of drawers* item. The top list shows the variants gathered from 1162 people from the Middle and South Atlantic States interviewed mainly in the 1930s and 1940s, followed by the list of variants elicited by Ellen Johnson when she conducted a smaller survey with the same methods in the early 1990s. The list at the bottom comes from Allison Burkette's survey of 60 college students ten years later.[10] When the lists are charted, each has the same shape of curve, the A-curve. Johnson's data shows not only that the curve is durable over time (not just a product of the old days), but that it is scalable from the large area of the entire LAMSAS region to the smaller area of about thirty communities that she studied. Burkette's survey shows that a survey conducted with a different method, picture elicitation, and on a different population, students instead of largely middle-aged rural speakers, again shows the same distribution. Moreover, the separate tally of terms elicited from each of the five pictures (not reproduced here, see Burkette 2001) also shows the same distribution, though with fewer different terms. Burkette (2001) carefully documented that all of

---

[10] The Burkette data was acquired by showing the students six different pictures of case furniture. The list in the figure was assembled by combining the figures from five picture elicitations, excluding the picture that most students recognized as a "table." If that picture had been included, the number of responses for "table" would have increased by twenty-three, and two more words with single responses would have joined the list, with differences of one or a few responses for some other terms: the overall distribution would have been the same. Still, since one picture was clearly identified as different from the others, it seemed best to exclude it here.

Table 6.1 *chest of drawers* data from three studies (after Burkette 2001: 140–142)

LAMSAS		LAMSAS	
Responses	Occurrences	Responses	Occurrences
bureau	1104	case of drawers	3
dresser	382	dresser drawers	3
chest of drawers	227	stand of drawers	2
chest	44	set of drawers	2
sideboard	34	blanket chest	1
washstand	30	cabinet	1
highboy	27	checkrobes	1
chiffonier	22	chest upon a chest	1
trunk	22	clothes stand	1
drawers	19	clothespress	1
bureau drawers	19	chifforobe drawers	1
commode	17	cupboard	1
dressing table	9	bookcases	1
box	8	cabinet table	1
stand	7	kast	1
lowboy	5	vanity dresser	1
chest on chest	4	wardrobe	1
vanity	4	wash hands stand	1
desk	3		

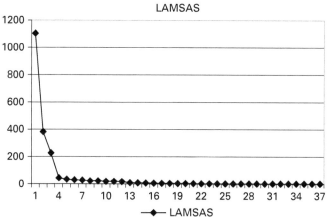

Johnson data		Johnson data	
Responses	Occurrences	Responses	Occurrences
dresser	18	bachelor's chest	1
chest of drawers	17	chest on chest	1
bureau	5	dressing table	1
chest	5	linen press	1
wash stand	2	press	1

Table 6.1 (*cont.*)

Johnson data		Johnson data	
Responses	Occurrences	Responses	Occurrences
highboy	2	vanity dresser	1
dresser drawers	1		

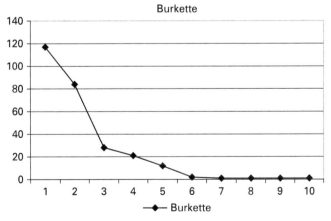

Burkette data		Burkette data	
Responses	Occurrences	Responses	Occurrences
dresser	117	highboy	2
chest of drawers	84	buffet	1
drawers	28	chester drawers	1
chest	21	china cabinet	1
cabinet	12	dresser drawer	1
bureau	11	highboard	1
night stand	5	hutch	1
desk	4	secretary	1
dressing table	3	vanity	1
table	3	vanity table	1
armoire	2		

the infrequent forms for *chest of drawers*, all of the oncers, had historical roots, which she illustrated from colonial American woodworking books, so we can think of the low-frequency variants as a kind of historical storehouse for furniture language. The main point here, however, is that the same non-linear distribution of terms, though not necessarily the same terms, can be found in each survey at every level of scale – a fine illustration of scaling with similarity.[11]

The same sort of scaling behavior can be observed by subsampling in the LAMSAS survey. Table 6.2 shows the tally for all speakers for a single state, New York. Table 6.3 shows the tally for all speakers in the Deep South region of South Carolina, Georgia, and Northern Florida. Finally, Table 6.4 shows the tally for all women speakers in the entire survey area. Each subsample shows the same non-linear distribution, though again there are differences in the order of the frequencies for particular terms, and not every term is on every list. The lists are uncorrected for superficial differences, but as we have seen, the distribution in not affected by removing minor morphological differences and anomalous responses. The A-curve distribution, in every case, scales perfectly from subsample to subsample. Indeed, the scaling property cuts across different variables: not only do regions of different size possess the same A-curve distribution, but subsampling the same data by social criteria (here, by sex) also yields the A-curve. This sort of subsampling could also be carried out on textual data to the same effect, say to measure the words in the text types and individual texts of the Brown Corpus, but the non-linear distribution is so well known in the textual dimension that no illustration is provided here.

Scaling also occurs in pronunciation evidence from the LAMSAS survey. It would be possible to repeat the subsampling procedure of Figures 6.2, 6.3, and 6.4, to yield the same kind of results. Instead, however, Table 6.5 presents a final, different illustration of scaling. The word *Baltimore* includes three vowel segments, each of which may also have diphthongal or triphthongal elements, and five consonantal segments. Scaling appears in the distribution of feature variants for every single one of these segments, and in every aspect in which the vowel segments are presented. The A-curve for the consonantal segments tends to be attenuated, because the IPA offers fewer resources to indicate variation in consonants than for vowels. /b, m/ offer the fewest options, espe-cially /m/; more variation can be indicated for /l, t, r/, however, and the

---

[11] The same sort of distribution appears in other surveys, such as in the tallies presented for every item in the *Linguistic Atlas of the Gulf States* (Pederson 1990), and in the smaller survey of farming terms in southwest Georgia carried out by Hoover (2001). Hoover found the same sort of change of frequencies from earlier Linguistic Atlas of the Gulf States (LAGS) data that Johnson and Burkette showed in their real-time historical studies for LAMSAS, and produced A-curve graphs in illustration. Hans Goebl reports (p.c.) that this is also the expected distributional pattern for items from his French and Italian surveys.

Table 6.2 bureau, *New York*

bureau	159	chifforobe	3	chamber	1
dresser	63	commodes	3	chambers	1
chests of drawers	37	drawers	3	chiffoniers	1
bureaus	16	glass	3	dry goods box	1
commode	12	highboy	3	large drawer	1
dressers	9	chest	2	little stand	1
washstand	8	a bureaus	1	lowboy	1
stand	7	a drawers	1	pot	1
chiffonier	6	a peer glass	1	sideboard	1
looking glass	5	big drawers	1	slop jar	1
mirror	5	black ash	1	wash hand stands	1
highboys	4	bureau drawer	1		

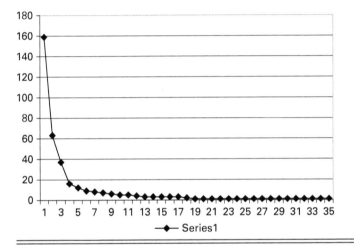

A-curves for these segments are clearly evident.[12] The vowel nuclei (1a, 2a, 3a) all show A-curve distributions in every aspect in which they are ranked by frequency – height and frontness and length. Where diphthongs are present (1b, 2b) and where triphthongs are present (3c), the A-curve distribution occurs yet again. The word *Baltimore* is a good example here because it has a number of segments for which variation can be indicated within the limitations of the IPA symbol set, and variation does indeed occur. As mentioned earlier,

---

[12] Postvocalic -r, as in the Atlas data for *Baltimore*, shows especially rich variation. Kretzschmar and Johnson (1993) analyzed postvocalic -r with both a binary categorization and a four-category approach, and got different statistically significant results from the same data because of the difference in categorization.

Table 6.3 bureau, *South Carolina/Georgia/Florida*

bureau	165	clothes chest	2	dresser is	1
dresser	89	commode	2	glass on it	1
chest of drawers	83	dresser drawers	2	glasses	1
bureaus	48	highboys	2	heavy	1
dressers	27	homemade chest	2	high table	1
chest	25	lowboy	2	in and out	1
mirror	23	a glass attached	1	large mirror	1
washstand	18	a glass on top	1	liquer	1
sideboard	17	basin	1	lowboys	1
trunk	13	big boxes	1	made chests	1
bureau drawers	11	blanket chest	1	made ones	1
chiffonier	11	bookcases	1	make them ourselves	1
drawers	11	bought ones	1	mirror attached	1
chifforobe	9	box trunk	1	mirrors	1
dressing table	9	box-like	1	moveable sideboard	1
glass	9	cabinet	1	night table	1
highboy	8	cabinet table	1	pitcher	1
bureau drawer	6	camphor chest	1	plain	1
sideboards	6	cedar chests	1	safety drawer	1
trunks	6	checkrobes	1	set of drawers	1
looking glass	5	chest of drawer	1	sets of drawers	1
box	4	chest upon a chest	1	slanting	1
cedar chest	4	chests	1	sugar chest	1
chest on a chest	4	chests of drawers	1	table	1
vanity	4	chiffoniers	1	tables	1
desk	3	chifforobe drawers	1	taller	1
drawer	3	clothespress	1	trunk chest	1
washstands	3	cupboard	1	vanity dresser	1
bedroom	2	deep drawers	1	white night stand	1
big mirror	2	dresser drawer	1	with a mirror	1
boxes	2	dresser dresser	1	with drawers	1

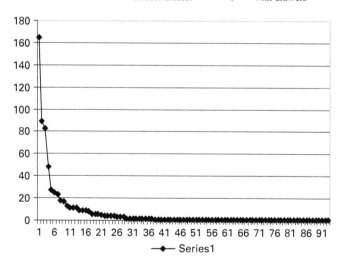

Table 6.4 bureau, *women speakers*

bureau	330	highboys	3	deep drawers	1
dresser	115	looking glass	3	desk	1
chest of drawers	109	lowboy	3	dresser drawers	1
bureaus	16	bedroom	2	large drawer	1
mirror	13	bureau drawer	2	large mirror	1
washstands	11	safe	2	little stand	1
dressers	10	stand of drawers	2	lowboys	1
chest	9	a bureaus	1	made chests	1
chiffonier	8	a drawers	1	mirror attached	1
dressing table	7	a glass on top	1	mirrors	1
highboy	7	a peer glass	1	night table	1
sideboard	7	blanket chest	1	set of drawers	1
bureau drawers	5	box	1	sugar chest	1
chifforobe	5	camphor chest	1	taller	1
glass	4	checkrobes	1	trunk	1
vanity	4	chest upon a chest	1	trunk chest	1
cedar chest	3	chests of drawers	1	vanity dresser	1
chest on a chest	3	chiffoniers	1	white night stand	1
commode	3	chifforobe drawers	1		

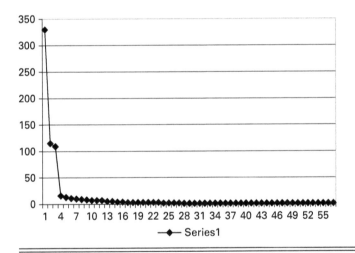

acoustical phonetic measurement may offer a better means to measure variation because it is not restricted to the IPA symbol set. Still, even using IPA, and even for words with fewer segments, we can expect to see that the non-linear distribution of feature variants scales to every level of phonetic analysis. The scaling property is very robust for both words and pronunciation, and therefore again the experimental evidence shows that experimental data has the characteristics required for speech to be a complex system.

Table 6.5 *LAMSAS pronunciation of*
Baltimore *(1034 responses)*

consonant 1	
b	1019
bb	1
b̥	13
p̬	1
vowel 1a	
raising/lowering	
ɒ̂	261
ɒ	38
ɔ̂	29
ɔ	322
ɒ˙	377
ɒ̠	5
ɒ̠̂	2
front/back	
ɒˏ	32
ɒ	267
ɵ	27
ɔ	700
ɔˏ	1
ɒ̠ˏ	2
ɒ̠	5
lengthening	
ɒ̠	5
ɒ̠:	2
ɔ	226
ɵ	482
ɔ:	20
ɒ̠	127
ɒ̠˙	172
other	
ɒ̠	7
ɵ̵	7
ɒ̆	1
ɒ̯	1
ɔ̯̠	1
ɵ	7
ɵ̵	2
vowel 1b	
{ə}	63
{ə̯}	2
ə̆	1
ə	1
{ɚ}	1
{ɔ̂}	4
{ɵ}	23

Table 6.5 (*cont.*)

{ɔˊ}	8
ɔ	81
ɔˆ	15
ɔˎ	1
ɔˊ	5
ɔ̆ˊ	1
o	15
oˊ	3
ŏ	1
oˆˎ	1
oˊ	2
ɒˆˎ	1
{ɒˆ}	3
ɒ̄ˆ	1
{ɒˆˎ}	2
ɒ	1
ɒˆ	1
0	797
cons. 2	
l	110
ļ	7
ɾl	1
{ɫ}	38
{ɫ̥}	1
ɫ	853
ɫ̷	2
ɫ̥	20
0	2
cons. 3	
t	297
tˋ	2
ˑt	424
ˍt	10
{d}	2
d	9
ʻd̥	2
{ˌt}	253
ʼt	2
ˋt	11
{ʼt}	1
{ˋt}	4
{t}	10
{ʔ}	1
{ɾ}	1
ɾ	3
0	2

Table 6.5 (*cont.*)

vowel 2a	
raising/lowering	
ə̂	22
ə	491
ɪ̂	3
ɨ̂	55
ɨ̆	335
ɨˑ	80
0	6
front/back	
ə	513
ɪˑ	3
ɨˤ	59
ɨ	451
ɨˑ	2
0	6
lengthening	
ə	513
ɪ	3
ɨ	511
ɨˑ	1
0	6
other	
ə̃	13
ɨ̃	10
ɚˑ	7
vowel 2b	
NO DIPHTHONGS	
cons. 4	
m	1032
m̥m	2
vowel 3a	
raising/lowering	
ô	55
o	533
oˇ	104
ɵ	10
ɵˇ	1
ə	100
ɔ̂	92
ɔ	129
ɔˇ	2
0	8
front/back	
ə	100
ɔˤ	6
ɔ	217
ɵˤ	1

Table 6.5 (*cont.*)

ɵ	6
ɵˏ	4
oˋ	155
o	537
0	8
lengthening	
ə	100
ɔ	171
ɔ·	40
ɔː	12
ɵ	7
ɵ·	4
o	359
o·	332
oː	1
0	8
other	
ʔ	1
ɵ̃	1
ŏ	4
õ	1
o̞	41
ɵ	1
vowel 3b	
0 (w/3a)	197
0	8
{ə}	98
ə	554
ɚ·	3
ə̣	47
ə̂	1
{ə̰	1
{ə}	12
{ə̂}	2
ə̃	9
ɚ̃	1
ə̃ˏ	1
ɚ·	4
ɚˏ	1
ə̂ˏ	1
{ə}	1
əˏ	1
ə̌	1
ə̂ˏ	1
{ə̃}	1
{ʊ}	50
ʊˋ	16
{ʊˋ}	7

Table 6.5 (*cont.*)

ŭ	1
ʋ	2
ʊ	1
{ʊ}	1
{ʊ˙}	1
{ʊ˙ʻ}	1
{o}	1
vowel 3c	
ɚ˙˙	1
{ə}	7
{ə˙}	1
ə	1
ə˙	1
ə	13
ə̃	2
ə̰	2
consonant 5	
r	36
ɾ	16
ɾɾ	1
r̪	1
{r}	2
{r̪ɹ}	4
{ɹ}	1
ɹ}	1
ɚ˙	497
·	53
·{}	12
{ɚ}	11
ɚ˙˙	4
0	395

Speech and chaos

Now that every required characteristic of complex systems has been shown to be present in speech data, in both the geographical social and textual dimensions, it remains to show that speech is not inherently chaotic. Experimental evidence for this question is slim, but it is possible to offer several arguments that speech is not in fact chaotic. First, Mandelbrot has noted (1982: 344) that, for social sciences like economics with "an awfully mixed bag" of data:

the distribution of the data is the joint effect of a fixed underlying "true distribution," and of a highly variable "filter." ... [A-curve distributions] are very "robust" in that respect, meaning that a wide variety of filters leave their asymptotic behavior unchanged. On the other hand, practically all other distributions are highly *non*robust. Therefore an hyperbolic true distribution *can* be observed with consistency: different sets of distorted data suggest the same distribution with the same D. But the same treatment applied to most other distributions leads to "chaotic" incompatible results. In other words, the practical alternative to the asymptotically hyperbolic distribution is not any other distribution but chaos.

It is not certain that Mandelbrot meant to invoke the intermittent, long-state-cycle chaos of chaos theory, but clearly he is talking about the homeostatic quality of the A-curve as opposed to other distributions. Since we have seen that the A-curve distribution for speech data behaves just as robustly as Mandelbrot describes for other social science data – we can understand his "filter" to refer to arbitrary categories, like text types or other units extracted from the speech continuum – we are entitled to say that speech data is not chaotic on those grounds.

It may seem difficult to consider the problem of sensitivity to initial conditions for speech data, since languages appear to have long and continuous histories. However, another approach would consider that local populations of speakers are often subject to serious disruptions, and that such events are just the kind of stimulus that, in a chaotic system, should provoke the system to break out of its current pattern and take a new course. If this in fact happened, we should have noticed before now that catastrophic events like the Great Chicago Fire, or the Great Fire of London, or the San Francisco Earthquake, changed the direction of speech, that local speakers would lose whatever local speech characteristics there might be and eventually develop new ones. On the contrary, the history of English and the histories of other languages are not punctuated with accounts of such changes. We may be used to thinking of linguistic change in English over the sweep of centuries, but local conditions on the ground do not necessarily provide the long-term demographic stability that one might expect to accompany such a long-term view of change. The fact that we continue to think of speech as a homeostatic system, in spite of the continuous occurrence of local catastrophes that should stimulate chaotic changes in patterns, is evidence that speech is not in fact chaotic.

Another situation in which speech might show characteristics of chaos theory is in the development of local speech habits in newly settled, or newly resettled places. The best information on this process comes from the nineteenth-century settlement of New Zealand.[13] The Mobile Disc Recording Unit of Radio New Zealand made recordings, in the late 1940s, of over 250 native New Zealanders born between 1851 and 1898 (Gordon 1998: 66). This period corresponds to the most active stage in the English settlement of New Zealand, which grew from 2000 non-Maori residents in 1840 to half a million by the 1880s (1998: 62). According to research by Elizabeth Gordon and Peter Trudgill, the first generation of native-born New Zealanders showed what they call

---

[13] For a fuller description of the mechanics of new dialect formation see Kretzschmar (2002b). For a contrasting model, see Schneider (2003, 2007).

"embryonic variants" of features that would later become characteristic of New Zealand English (Gordon and Trudgill 1999), and Gordon suggests that some of the features of later New Zealand English were present with some frequency for first-generation speakers, having been carried there from England (Gordon 1998: 79–80). Overall, recordings of New Zealanders born in the 1870s and 1880s, which we might think of as late in the first generation or early in the second generation of native New Zealanders, can be recognized as "sounding like old New Zealanders" (Gordon 1998: 79). If speech were a chaotic system, development of the beginnings of New Zealand English should not have occurred so quickly. According to Kauffman's simulations, a system in chaos is characterized by long state cycles in which it is difficult to perceive order. For speech in New Zealand, then, it should have taken a long time to work through possibilities for a new dialect pattern before it became possible to notice the repeating patterns that constituted order. The New Zealand situation, on the other hand, showed nascent New Zealand speech patterns, emergent order, already by the second generation of settlers. Again there is reason to think that speech is a complex, not a chaotic system.

Speech and evolution

Discussion of chaotic systems has necessarily involved discussion of change over time. While that subject will be treated in some detail in Chapter 8, it will be valuable now to consider a prominent model for change in living systems, evolution. William Labov opened the second volume of his *Principles of Linguistic Change* (2001) with a chapter called "The Darwinian Paradox," in which he cites Darwin's comments on parallels between linguistic and biological evolution. Labov, however, concluded that (2001: 9–10):

the general consensus of 20th-century linguists gives no support to [the parallel], and finds no evidence for natural selection or progress in linguistic evolution … But it is not merely the absence of evidence for evolutionary adaptation that runs counter to Darwin's argument for natural selection. The almost universal view of linguists is the reverse: that the major agent of linguistic change – sound change – is actually maladaptive, in that it leads to the loss of the information that the original forms were designed to carry.

Language change, in his view, is a "destructive force" because it tended to break down the system of language.

Roger Lass had also rejected any direct parallel between linguistic and biological evolution, on more general grounds (1990: 79):

One of the less rewarding of our common interdisciplinary pursuits is lifting theoretical concepts from subjects not our own, and using them in contexts very distant from those they were intended for. Such borrowings often turn from theoretical claims into sloppy metaphors, leading to varieties of "vulgar X-ism", the result of overenthusiastic appropriation with insufficient sense of the subtlety or precise applicability of the originals ... Linguistics, being less unique than linguists often think, is no exception: Praguian and neo-Praguian functionalism may be a kind of vulgar Darwinism, extending notions of "adaptation" or "selective pressure" to the inappropriate domain of language systems.

Still, Lass ventured to suggest that the notion "exaptation" from evolutionary biology could profitably be carried over into linguistics. Exaptation in evolutionary biology refers to the fact that there are quantities of "junk" or "surplus" DNA in the genetic code, and that such DNA may serve as a "locus of change" if later again expressed, so that "a typical exaptation is the redeployment for a new purpose of one of yesterday's adaptations" (1990: 80–81). Lass then suggests the parallel, that we can look at languages not "as systems where (almost) *tout se tient*" but rather as "bundles of historical accidents, not perfect and predictable machines" (1990: 81). In other words, Lass would allow that languages contain "junk," redundant features that can later be repurposed in a kind of linguistic change different from the adaptive change that Labov considered to be destructive. From the point of view of the linguistics of linguistic structure the biological analogy makes sense, that some low-frequency elements in effect get readopted as exaptations after they drop away from the core system and hang around for a while as "junk." The idea makes less sense from the point of view of the linguistics of speech. If there is no system, just the A-curve distribution, then "exaptation" does not have meaning because nothing gets dropped from the main system later to be readopted for another purpose; in speech nothing loses function, just changes frequency. It is all the more important to note this difference in perspective because of the property of "scaling," which makes it possible for the same feature variant to be prominent at one scale and not at another, so that the all-or-nothing, single-scale perspective of Lass's exaptation is relevant to just one scale, the largest out of many possible scales for analysis. The idea of exaptation attempts to find a place for low-frequency phenomena in the linguistics of linguistic structure,[14] which requires no special explanation in the linguistics of speech.

Salikoko Mufwene has written extensively about the potential relationship of the evolutionary model of change to language, particularly in Mufwene (2001),

---

[14] Lass's comments will remind the careful reader of those quoted from Kurath and McDavid (1961: 3) in Chapter 2: "all natural languages are historical products developed in the give-and-take between individuals and social groups of a speech community and between speech communities. In this complicated historical process, so different from the creation, once and for all, of an artificial code, features taken from other social and regional dialects are not always adapted to the native system, and innovations in the native system may as yet not be established with consistency, so that elements of an older system survive as relics." Kurath and McDavid did not call these elements "junk," but instead just considered them to be inconsistencies peripheral to the regularities of system.

The Ecology of Language Evolution, with more recent adjustments to the basic argument presented there in Mufwene (2006, 2008). His detailed treatment certainly avoids the criticism, as from Lass, of "overenthusiastic appropriation with insufficient sense of the subtlety or precise applicability of the originals." Mufwene (2001) asserted that languages are "Complex Adaptive Systems"; Mufwene (2008) says that idiolects are complex adaptive systems, and that communal languages have that status by extension. Mufwene does not develop the statement about complex systems in detail, as Bybee has not really developed the idea. Complex adaptive systems remain underspecified, as an underlying factor in Mufwene's overriding bio-evolutionary metaphor for language. Mufwene (2001) developed the ideas of competition, selection, and restructuring from biological evolution from the starting point that language is like a Lamarckian bacterial species, parasitic on its host population. There are many points of agreement with the discussion so far in this volume. Mufwene emphasizes the role of individual speakers and questions traditional notions of linguistic systems. He predicts pools of variant features, and those are documented here in non-linear distributions. Mufwene writes that "Norms emerge out of communicative habits of individual speakers. What the habits share, including patterns of variation, form the community's norms" (2001: 112). Further, he talks about "[individuals] setting their respective features in competition and having to accommodate one another by dropping some features, or accepting new ones" (p. 151), and claims that "Differences between two varieties may lie in the weights accorded to the competing variants and/or to their conditioning factors" (p. 151). In Mufwene (2008: 250–251) he concludes that:

In the end, it all boils down to a speaker being driven by some ecological pressures to integrate only particular features as dominant in his/her idiolect. Thus, while idiolects of a particular language variety are similar, the subsets of units and principles that prevail in them as dominant vary from one another, reflecting the individual personalities of their speakers/signers and their particular interaction histories. For the student of language evolution, what matters is whether the total population of features in competition and/or their distributional patterns within the community of speakers/signers change. This is really what evolution in a communal language amounts to.

The distribution of features in experimental data documents the widespread "competition" of features that Mufwene, because he focuses on syntax, can only suggest in a few examples.[15] The idea of speech as a complex system promotes "ecology," because it incorporates the idea that feature variants are predominantly clustered so that language comes to be a local phenomenon, and includes the notion that any feature is likely to be significantly correlated with

---

[15] Indeed, Mufwene had to conduct an "informal survey" of nineteen colleagues in his academic department in order to document the extent of variation in judgments of example sentences (2008: 231).

different geographical and social factors, even simultaneously. Mufwene later invokes the analogy of highway traffic to develop the idea that language change occurs as the result of many individual acts. He speaks of an "invisible hand" (following Keller 1994, ultimately from economist Adam Smith) that creates order (2008: 144):

The focus on individual speakers, like on individual drivers on a highway, makes it possible to account for population contact and the various ways in which they coexist, depending on whether or not their individual members interact with, and influence, each other's behavior. Interaction and all it entails among the interactants is where the action that brings about change lies. That is where the "invisible hand" operates. One way or another, individual actions of drivers in traffic and speakers in a language community cumulate to produce what is later identified as evolution, i.e., the long-term changes that are observable in the behavior or characteristics of a species or, more generally, a population.

Clearly, although Mufwene does not say so and Adam Smith could have had no such notion, the "invisible hand" here must refer to emergent order in a complex system.

At the same time, one is perhaps entitled to ask what evolutionary "selection" might mean in the context of the A-curve distributional pattern. There is no particular linguistic reason to privilege the most common variants as having been "selected" and therefore have status as being "systematic" or "phonemic," and to relegate less-common variants to "noise" in the system. All of the variants on the A-curve are actually just as relevant for inclusion in the system. The notion of language-internal selection, then, cannot operate within the A-curve because nothing is really chosen or preferred; even loss is rare, according to Burkette's evidence of low-frequency variants preserving historical forms. But we do know that different features are in fact associated by frequency with different ecologies. We may also ask what "restructuring" might mean in the context of the A-curve pattern. It is highly likely that any feature variant, whether common or rare, will at some subsequent time change in frequency, and that new social and regional associations with variants will form. What is truly stable and systematic about this situation is the curve itself, not any perceived system of arrangement of variants. Mufwene says that "restructuring amounts to a reorganization of the mechanical system of a language and/or the pragmatic principles regulating its use" (2001: 12), but his frank use here of the traditional term "mechanical system" is out of character with the rest of his argument. Better is his subsequent definition, that "any change in the structural system of a language involves restructuring, including loss of some units or rules, addition of new ones, and certainly modifications ... by the addition of conditions to the application of a rule" (2001: 13). Indeed, in Mufwene (2008) he assigns restructuring to language acquisition by individuals (pp. 247–248). It is certainly better to prefer a complex adaptive system which is attuned to both syntagmatic and paradigmatic change, than to retreat to the traditional, merely mechanical notion of system.

Finally, the particular analogy of language to a "parasitic species" constitutes a creative way to try to bridge the gap between speech as a complex system and traditional ideas of language structure. No analogy is required to show that speech is a complex system, since that has been demonstrated here from experimental evidence. Mufwene's final comment that "a language is more like a bacterial, Lamarckian species than like an organism" (2001: 207) begins to recognize that fact. An organism may be thought to be a mechanical system, in the flesh. But a bacterial species is essentially multiple, arising out of a population of individuals in which one may observe many differences in particular characteristics. As Mufwene points out, a "species" is itself an abstraction, a generalization made from comparison of the characteristics of individuals. While Mufwene sometimes blurs this distinction, as when he claims "life" for a species in order to be able to talk about the topic of language endangerment, his argument crucially depends, I believe, on the distinction between a living organism and an abstract species. He avoids thinking of language as a system *in rebus* (2006: 245):

> As the universe of our experience and knowledge is continuous, the boundaries of both species and languages are naturally fuzzy and operationally arbitrary, imposed by particular ideologies or other practical or theoretical considerations, especially within the same genetic family. It must be difficult to draw the boundary between adjacent vernacular varieties of Italian and French or between those of Dutch and German, a problem aggravated by the arbitrariness of political boundaries.

Unlike Bybee and other linguists for whom complex systems are only an analogy for language, Mufwene begins to cross over into a model that makes use of the dynamics of complex systems.

Kauffman offers extended discussion of the possible relationship between self-organization in complex systems and evolutionary selection in biology (1995: 149–243). He argues that selection cannot replace self-organization as the means to create order. Some parts of that argument ("fitness landscapes") will be covered in the following chapter, but for now it is enough to cite his conclusion (1995: 188), the "tantalizing possibility":

> that self-organization is a prerequisite for evolvability, that it generates the kinds of structures that can benefit from natural selection. It generates structures that can evolve gradually, that are robust, for there is an inevitable relationship among spontaneous order, robustness, redundancy, gradualism, and correlated landscapes. Systems with redundancy have the property that many mutations cause no or only slight modifications in behavior. Redundancy yields gradualism. But another name for redundancy is robustness. Robust properties are the ones that are insensitive to many detailed alterations … Robustness is precisely what allows such systems to be molded by gradual accumulation

of variations. Thus another name for redundancy is structural stability – a folded protein, an assembled virus, a Boolean network in the ordered regime. The stable structures and behaviors are the ones that can be molded.

Self-organization in a complex system, then, allows ordered structures to emerge that, in turn, may be modified by some sort of selection. This passage picks up many of the key terms from the foregoing discussion of complex systems – robustness, insensitivity to initial stimuli, stability (or homeostasis), and scaling (in the folded protein) – and brings the discussion back to the Boolean networks that Kauffman uses for simulations. The addition of the notion of selection and the possibility of co-evolution, however, changes the behavior of Kauffman's simulations, so that the most probable number of interconnections between components that may result in emergent order is no longer $K=2$, as described earlier in this chapter, but now $K=10$ (1995: 228–230). The density of interconnections in Kauffman's network simulations now approximates the size of social networks (e.g., Milroy 1980, Milroy 1992) and communities of practice (e.g., Eckert 2000, Childs 2005) commonly studied by sociolinguists. The network simulations now parallel the basic findings of study of networks and language: that local networks or communities of practice with appropriately dense interactions among small groups of speakers do develop and maintain "ordered" feature variants that characterize them. This is true among groups of speakers in Belfast neighborhoods, and also among Michigan high-school students and North Carolina church ladies and porch sitters. These patterns differ from those of the wider population in which the small groups are located, because the possibility for the emergence of order arises from interactions among small groups of speakers. Thus, the dynamics of complex systems are responsible for the continuum we observe in language behavior, from small group to small group, and also for the coherence that we observe in the distribution of features in speech.

The problem of "control bias" remains, which amounts for speech to the selection of particular features by speakers. As Arthur suggested, human agents can "react with strategy and foresight by considering outcomes that might result as a consequence of behavior they might undertake" (1999: 107). This is as much true in speech as it is in economics, and is treated in the next chapter.

The fact that speech is a complex system tells us a great deal, and not just about language behavior. First of all, the linguistics of speech can take advantage of work in many other scientific fields that also work with complex systems, from biological systems and chemistry to economics, from climate and ecology to the human nervous system, even to physics. Recognition of speech as a complex system tells us what to expect from it, and suggests methods for approaching problems of interest, whether in theory or application. When we study speech, we can expect to find order instead of chaos, but we cannot expect to find simple causes for complex patterns. We can expect to observe what amounts to an unlimited series of Russian dolls in speech, in which the dolls have the same shape at different scales, but may each be painted with different motifs and colors. The property of scaling tells us, regarding both the dolls and speech, to look for the same patterns composed of different elements at different scales of observation, pattern within pattern, as closely as we might ever like to observe them. We know that we will need good counting and sorting methods in order to cope with frequency effects of feature variants among populations of speakers, and that we cannot rely exclusively on Gaussian statistics, since the non-linear A-curve distributional pattern appears at every turn. Above all, we need not, like Saussure, abandon speech as a pathway for linguistics because it is simply intractable for analysis, because when we recognize speech as a complex system, we have a way forward to study it right alongside the many scientific fields that have to work in the same direction. The linguistics of speech can be its own science, but need not remain as isolated from other sciences as Saussure thought for linguistics of linguistic structure.

7 Speech perception

Dennis Preston has been the central figure in recent decades for the renewal of interest in what he has called "perceptual dialectology" (1989, 1999). While much work in the area has concerned itself with whether people can perceive dialect boundaries asserted by linguists (see Chapter 3, and below), the stakes for "perceptual dialectology" are actually larger than that (Kretzschmar 1999: xvii):

The general view would have it that the linguistics of speech should be concerned with what people actually say. Speech production surely has had the majority of the attention in empirical linguistics, whether under quantitative or qualitative analysis. However, there is not only room for study of the reception of speech, but the necessity that we study it. Constraints upon what we say are not only determined by accident of birth but are also to some degree a matter of choice. We choose our words according to how we perceive them, or how we believe that others will perceive them. Every conversation is to some extent an exercise in such psychological brinksmanship. And in order more fully to understand the words that people actually produce, we therefore need to understand how people perceive those words. Empirical linguistics here meets psychology, whether the social psychology of groups or the individual psychologies of the participants in a conversation, in that what people actually say is bound up with how people perceive and understand their choices in what to say.

This chapter confronts the frontier between speech and psychology, and between speech and physiology as it is manifested in neuroscience.

Saussure wrote during a great age in the development of psychology. Both Max Wertheimer, who with others developed gestalt psychology, and Sigmund Freud were active in the opening decades of the twentieth century. They were both promoters of cognitive approaches, as opposed to the more physical and mechanical ideas of the nineteenth century. Saussure was in sympathy with these new approaches. For example, Saussure cites the work of Paul Broca, who "discovered that the faculty of speech is localized in the third frontal convolution of the left hemisphere of the brain," only in order to argue from the evidence of aphasia that there was more to speech than brain function ((1916)1986: 10–11):

All this leads us to believe that, over and above the functioning of the various organs, there exists a more general faculty governing signs, which may be regarded as the linguistic faculty *par excellence*.

Saussure did not deny the importance of physiology any more than Freud, who himself conducted research on neurophysiology including cerebral palsy, besides his more famous work on psychoanalysis. Saussure included both physiology and psychology in his "speech circuit" ((1916)1986: 12):

Let us suppose that a given concept triggers in the brain a corresponding sound pattern. This is an entirely *psychological* phenomenon, followed in turn by a *physiological* process: the brain transmits to the organs of phonation an impulse corresponding to the pattern. Then sound waves are sent from *A*'s mouth to *B*'s ear: a purely *physical* process. Next, the circuit continues in *B* in the opposite order: from ear to brain, the physiological transmission of the sound pattern; in the brain, the psychological association of this pattern with the corresponding concept.

So far in this volume, we have been concerned with speech production, with the part of the speech circuit that Saussure calls a physical process. Speech from the viewpoint of the individual speaker has not yet played its role alongside aggregated data, which has turned out to compose a complex system. As even Saussure knew, however, physiology and psychology in the speech circuit, even though they belong to individual speakers, require discussion because they provide the foundation in individuals for what we observe in the aggregate.

The field of neuroscience is the contemporary counterpart of Saussure's physiology. Broca and Wernicke in the nineteenth century were followed by study of many aspects of aphasiology in the twentieth century. Such study was primarily based on patients with brain damage and consequent speech impairment. Neuroscience has recently enjoyed greatly expanded possibilities owing to the invention of non-invasive means to study brain function, notably PET and fMRI scanning and the use of EEG. These methods can be used to study normal subjects, instead of having to predict normal function primarily from patients with impaired abilities. Description of basic findings about brain function are beyond the scope of this book, except to say that Saussure's "impulse," whether from brain to "organs of phonation" or "from ear to brain," is actually not a single process but a massively interconnected one, a neural network. According to the prevailing connectionist model (e.g., Pulvermüller 2003), neurons develop billions of connections in a massively parallel network, in which no action or perception could be considered to have a single or simple "impulse." Bybee's proposal that phonological information is stored on the basis of words (2001) must be understood in neuroscience not as the brain having some single particular location to store a word, but rather as the brain having a collection of interconnected neuronal pathways whose activation is related to a word. In hearing, for instance, Saussure's seemingly unitary "impulse" corresponds to thousands of neural fibers (specialized hair cells) in the inner ear that vibrate in response to specific frequencies, and in turn activate neurons that fire repeatedly and transmit signals to the brain. Thus the brain is sent patterns in response to a speech sound, changing every moment, that might be compared to the pixels on a visual monitor (or to Kauffman's network of lightbulbs), some turned off and some turned on at any given moment in response to the stimulus of physical sound waves (see further below). The emergent order of the network constitutes what we consider to be a unitary speech sound. As suggested in the opening sections of many previous chapters, new technology offers new possibilities for the study of questions that Saussure recognized, but was not in any position to answer.

Prototypes and schemas

Contemporary cognitive linguistics, according to Evans and Green (2006: 3):

emerged in the early 1970s out of dissatisfaction with formal approaches to language. Cognitive linguistics is also firmly rooted in the emergence of modern cognitive science in the 1960s and 1970s, particularly in work relating to human categorization, and in earlier traditions such as Gestalt psychology.

Again, this is not the place for extensive treatment of the field, except to comment on the problem of perception as it relates to speech. As Evans and Green point out, "perceptual mechanisms … provide structure that is not necessarily apparent in the raw perceptual [i.e., sensory] input. In other words, what we perceive is not necessarily the same as what we experience directly" (2006: 65). Gestalt principles are important because they "allow unconscious perceptual mechanisms to construct wholes or 'gestalts' out of incomplete perceptual input" (p. 65). Evans and Green offer a list of principles that, while illustrated from visual stimuli, can also apply to speech (2006: 65–67):

figure-ground segregation:	a "figure," an entity with dominant shape, stands out against an undifferentiated background
proximity:	things close to each other are seen as belonging to a group
similarity:	things that share characteristics are seen as belonging to a group
closure:	incomplete entities are often seen as completed
continuity:	things are seen as continuous, even if interrupted
smallness:	smaller entities tend to be identified before larger entities

These principles can be seen to supply a description for the human thought process (or intuition), which makes sense for us out of objective sensory information by helping to provide categories and boundaries for it. As we have seen, categorization and boundaries are a serious problem in speech, which is characterized by continua in both dimensions of speech and at all levels of scale. Experimental evidence presented in earlier chapters highlighted the importance of proximity, which encourages the cognitive creation of groups, even when possible patterns lack closure or coherence (i.e., incomplete or interrupted distributions in geographical, social, or textual space). The A-curve consistently presents a "dominant" feature variant or textual collocation to stand out against the background of other possibilities. Our individual experience with speech as it occurs in use demands a perceptual mechanism with characteristics just like those listed by Evans and Green, in order to help us to fill inevitable gaps and discontinuities in that experience.

As a discipline, cognitive anthropology provides a bridge between neuroscience and cognitive processes as they occur in individuals, and the occurrence of similar processes in populations. D'Andrade locates the genesis of cognitive models of anthropology with Chomsky, in opposition to the positivism of the behaviorists (1995: 8–11). The ethnographic agenda of anthropology changed at this period, and "the shift from the study of institutional behavior – 'natural systems' – to the ethnographic study of 'idea systems' or 'symbolic systems' appears to have been a very general trend" (D'Andrade 1995: 12). During the 1960s and 1970s, anthropologists developed the feature model and folk taxonomies which, like Saussure's notion of linguistic value (see Chapter 2), explored relationships between the terms in use by a population. While such study began with semantic matrices not dissimilar from those discussed by Saussure, the interest of anthropologists again changed (D'Andrade 1995: 91):

The goal of definition *per se* drops out of the later work, and the new emphasis is on finding which, out of the many features that potentially apply to a set of items, are the most salient and frequently used. The basic task was no longer to find out how particular items are defined, but rather to discover the most general categories people use to understand their world.

Modes of categorization replaced objective structures as the direction of analysis.

The work of Eleanor Rosch in the 1970s, important both to cognitive linguistics and to cognitive anthropology, further developed principles of categorization with reference to gestalt theory to create the theory of prototypes. In order to investigate prototypical "basic level objects," Rosch and others surveyed numerous people in order to get their ratings of different particular things in order to assess which one might be most prototypical. In an illustration of this process for the category "birds," D'Andrade (1995: 119; emphasis original) concludes that:

In general, the birds that are considered most prototypic are the *passerines* [such as robins and bluejays] ... These birds are closely related to each other and similar in shape and behavior. It is as if people *averaged* across the properties of all kinds of birds that they knew and developed a representation of a generalized profile of a bird.

Actually, there are two claims here, two kinds of "average." First, any individual person "averages" characteristics of different birds in order to create a personal cognitive prototype for "birds" which is not necessarily identical with the characteristics of any particular bird, but instead a gestalt or "configurational whole" of the "bird" prototype. However, the implicit claim is also that research-ers can determine something about how individuals think by calculating the mean ratings of possibly prototypical birds from a survey of how many people rated birds. Thus, in the survey conducted, not every individual may consider that passerines are the most prototypical bird (some people may think of eagles, some of chickens), but collectively the passerines are the most popular choice for a more general cultural prototype for "birds." Individual cognitive behavior in this way is taken to contribute to collective cognitive behavior. The idea of a prototype in speech would be the "perfect speaker," a speaker who used each of the feature variants associated with some language or variety. This is not the same thing as a "representative speaker" from the linguistics of linguistic structure, who is identified as one speaker from the group of speakers assumed to share a linguistic system. In contrast, a speaker "prototype" would be constructed from the different possible variants in use among some set of actual speakers, and no actual speaker might use exactly the set of variants of the prototype. Any actual speaker would be only relatively prototypical, just as any actual bird would be only relatively prototypical. A prototype is an abstraction from individual or collective experience, in which different possible feature variants that may not belong to any single actual individual are combined to construct a configurational whole.[1]

Schema theory has largely superseded prototypes for both kinds of claims, individual and collective. According to George Mandler (cited in D'Andrade 1995: 122):

> Schemas are built up in the course of interaction with the environment. The schema that is developed as a result of prior experience with a particular kind of event is not a carbon copy of that event; schemas are abstract representations of environmental regularities. We comprehend events in terms of the schemas they activate.
>
> Schemas are also processing mechanisms; they are active in selecting evidence, in parsing the data provided by our environment, and in providing appropriate general or specific hypotheses. Most, if not all, of the activation processes occur automatically and without awareness on the part of the perceiver-comprehender.

Schema theory is not about objects with particular, established characteristics (of which an individual is a concrete example, and a prototype is an abstract example), but about abstract specifications for what might be relevant in what comes to be recognized as a category of experience. Mandler's "event" includes

---

[1] If the argument of Mufwene (2001) were adjusted to the terms of this chapter, it would seem to locate the cognitive basis of language as prototypes in which particular characteristics can be selected, whether by averaging characteristics or by frequency, as belonging to a fixed cognitive object. Mufwene has subsequently assigned selection and restructuring to language acquisition by individuals (2008), so that cognitive prototypes would appear to be individual rather than cultural. Mufwene's use of terms like "selection" and "restructuring" would seem to create objects, not the more flexible arrays described below for schemas.

the notion of activity, but can also refer to things; in D'Andrade's example, the *writing* schema includes within it sub-schemas for *pens*, *paper*, *English*, and *authors* (1995: 124). Individuals develop their own cognitive schemas, but cultural schemas also exist, and can be described and measured by survey research, as D'Andrade does for the *germ* schema (1995: 126–130). Cultural schemas "average" the ratings of individuals in the same way that a cultural prototype can be constructed from a survey of individual ratings, except that now specifications, or slots, for relevant characteristics within a schema are the target for analysis, and not fixed characteristics themselves.

Schemas, however, are not the same as social institutions. D'Andrade concludes that (1995: 132):

These ethnographic examples of schemas – the *germs*, *romance*, the *American family*, and the *real self* – are culturally shared mental constructs. These schemas as cognitive objects should be clearly distinguished from the *institutionalized behavior* to which they are related. The institution of the *American family*, for example, with its social roles and their behavioral norms, is not the same as the ideas or schemas that people use to represent, understand, and evaluate the behavior of family life.

Schemas are different from institutions in two ways. For every individual, a schema is a cognitive array of possible characteristics, and individual schemas contribute to a collective schema in the same way that individual prototypes contribute to a collective one; cultural schemas represent the mean ratings of many individuals about the relevant aspects of some category of experience. Institutions, on the other hand, are behavioral entities, not mental constructs. Cultural institutions are also concrete, not just the average of what people do as cultural prototypes and schemas represent the average of what people think. For speech, the difference between schemas and institutions describes the difference between judgments about kinds of speech (in geographical/social and textual space) on the one hand, and "Standard" English (or other language) on the other. Standard English is a cultural institution, a concrete object with particular, known characteristics. As an institution, Standard English is not a prototype for language in use. The characteristics selected for Standard English are not the "average" of the feature variants in use by different speakers, and often they are not even the most popular variants. As an institution, Standard English is also not comparable as an entity to kinds of speech based on cultural schemas. Under these terms, Lippi-Green's characterization of Standard English as a "myth" (1997) should be qualified. Standard English is very real as a cultural institution, but it is a "myth" to consider it to be just another language variety on a par with other language varieties developed as either individual or cultural schemas. We will return to this issue in the next chapter.

Mandler's notion of schemas as a processing mechanism refers more specifically to cognition by individuals. Schemas are not composed of a particular set of characteristics to be recognized (an object), but instead of an array of slots for characteristics out of which a pattern is generated, and so schemas must include a process for deciding what to construct. One description of such a process is the serial symbolic processing model (D'Andrade 1995: 136–138), in which a set of logical rules is applied in sequence to information available from the outside world in order to select a pattern. A refinement of this model is the parallel distributed processing network, also called the connectionist network, or neural net (D'Andrade 1995: 138–141; as in the connectionist model described above), which allows parallel operation by a larger set of logical rules. The logical rules are the same Boolean operators used by Kauffman in his simulations based on networks of lightbulbs (Chapter 6) – this is not a coincidence. Given a very large network of neurons that either fire or not, depending upon external stimuli of different kinds, binary Boolean logic is appropriate to model "decisions" in the brain which arise from the on/off firing patterns of neurons. Kauffman's simulations also apply binary Boolean logic, because the chemical and biological reactions he is trying to model are similarly binary, either happening or not happening given their state (or pattern) of activation, as the system cycles through its possibilities. The comparison yields similar results: as D'Andrade reports (1995: 139–140), serial processing can be "'brittle' – if the input is altered very slightly or the task is changed somewhat, the whole program is likely to crash" (or as Kauffman might say, likely to enter a chaotic state cycle), while parallel processing appears to be much more flexible given mixed or incomplete input or a disturbance to the system (or as Kauffman might say, it can achieve homeostatic order). As we shall see, just as the idea of prototypes is still useful in some situations besides the more flexible idea of schemas, the idea of serial processing is still useful in some situations besides the more flexible idea of parallel processing.

D'Andrade suggests two key implications of this individual cognitive processing mode for the study of culture. First (1995: 144):

that anthropologists and other social scientists sometimes ascribe *rules* to the actor when it is only the actor's *behavior* that is being described. In many cases in which behavior is described as following rules, there may in fact be no *rules* inside the actor – only networks of certain kinds … the only thing *in* the actor may be a network of differentially interconnected elements.

The role of an individual in culture looks different, if the individual's cognitive recognition and decision process obeys the logical operation of networks instead of, as Saussure wrote, having concepts trigger reactions. For speech, D'Andrade's second implication "involves the relation between the structures in the mind and the structures that are in the external world" (1995: 146). The earlier view, D'Andrade reports, saw culture as "purely *mental* phenomena" so that external structures were "more or less a *reflection* of these mental cultural structures." However, connectionist networks suggest that "many of the structures that develop in the mind will be to some extent a *reflection* of the structures in the external physical world" (p. 146). Thus contemporary cognitive anthropology bridges the chasm between individual cognition and the culture of populations, and does so in terms sympathetic to the foregoing discussion of complex systems in the previous chapter. Moreover, the connectionist cognitive model demands attention to structures in the physical world that correspond, for language, to those so far described for the linguistics of speech.

Contemporary neural-network analysis is both a way to model connectionist brain function, and a model that can be exported and applied to other kinds of data including speech evidence (e.g., Kretzschmar 2006b, 2008b; Thill, Kretzschmar, Casas, and Yao 2008). However, even initial applications of neural-network analysis to speech evidence clearly do not produce any single "right" answers to questions about speech patterns. These applications yield multiple possible patterns, and any particular group of data points that the neural-network process selects as a pattern may not be readily interpretable according to the perceptions and received knowledge of the analyst. As Kretzschmar (2006b, 2008b) argues in detail, controlled experiments with repeated application of neural-network analysis begin to show validatable results only from types of patterns that recur in the applications, not from any individual patterns selected. The real problem with neural-network analysis of speech data is thus not the algorithm but valid interpretation of the results. Indeed, this is a problem predicted by the connectionist model and complex systems, because the results are emergent patterns, not patterns determined by some single or simple cause. Thus we should expect that there will be no one "right" answer or pattern, but instead an array of possible patterns given the evidence, patterns of self-organization. To look for mutual synergies between neuroscience research and the linguistics of speech is a promising avenue for future research.

Spatial perception

One aspect of the bridge between individuals and populations offered by cognitive anthropology can be clarified by cultural geography. Peter Gould and Rodney White have described "spatial perception" by considering the images that people have of their local environments in connection with the construction of national images (1986). Their initial comments on "perception of the environment" accord well with contemporary cognitive anthropology, but also add to it. Gould and White say that (1986: 12):

cities are not always pleasant places to live in, and the information that goes into building a mental image of a particular area may reflect much more than just the knowledge of landmarks and routes … people's information about a particular area in one of the USA's cities may vary considerably, and the mental images they build up may reflect not only their surroundings but many other aspects of themselves and their lives.

This suggests that the physical space of a city neighborhood is accompanied for its residents by schemas that carry social and psychological elements. Gould and White illustrate this point with the very different maps drawn of the same neighborhood by three of its residents, who each include a different selection of elements, shown at sizes that do not necessarily match their true geographical proportions. Clearly each resident has different content that fills the slots in the cultural schema for their *neighborhood*, one filling slots with educational opportunities and the other two filling them with perceived threats (each weighted through significant size on the maps), all of which are possible entries in the array of places, people, and activities that constitute a *neighborhood*. Gould and White thus emphasize the potential for individuality of schemas, when cognitive anthropologists often focus on "the most general categories people use to understand their world" and derive their content by "averaging" individual ratings. Gould and White suggest that such averaging is possible in spatial perception, as in a survey of Birmingham residents who on average preferred "things at a human scale" to skyscrapers, and thus caused city planners to construct a local map that featured people-centered organizing landmarks (e.g., stores or meeting places) other than just monumental structures (1986: 12–13). Still, the granularity of mental images of locations stands out as a consistent finding for Gould and White, as against any unexamined assumption that average ratings are likely to be shared ratings. Speech evidence, too, will suggest below that it is important not just to suppress individual perceptions in favor of averages.

As the geographical scale moves from local to national, Gould and White show the prevalence of "local domes" on the national landscape. In order to measure spatial perception, they asked numerous people at each of several locations to rank their preferences for a set of places, and then compared what the individuals said. Statistical comparison of the ratings was used to make "smooth" maps of the whole country which indicated preferred and dispreferred regions. This smoothing function, similar to the "kernel method" and in contrast to the "nearest neighbors method" presented for density-estimation maps of speech data in Chapter 4, reduces the granularity of the responses that Gould and White had earlier demonstrated. The result, from studies in both Britain and in North America, shows that (1986: 51–52):

any mental map … from a particular place is a rather subtle convolution of (1) a shared national viewpoint and (2) a dome of local desirability, representing feelings people have for the familiar and comfortable surroundings of their home area.

No map from the respondents from a local area matched the national map, because all such local maps had "local domes" of preference, and yet aside from these local domes the local-area maps were not dissimilar from the national map composed of all the aggregated responses. Thus it is possible and useful to talk about national preferences, at the same time that "local domes" consistently appear in the data, and at the same time that we know that individual spatial perceptions are likely to be very different from each other. Again, this finding is clearly relevant for speech, as individual, local, and larger perceptions of speech are discussed below.

The grounds on which such preference judgments are made are similarly complex. Gould and White say that "social space and physical space are so tightly linked that most people simply do not distinguish between the two" (1986: 16–17). Further to the same point (1986: 73):

> people seem to evaluate an area on four scales [i.e., physical environment such as climate and landform, politics, economic opportunities, and social and cultural aspects; 1986: 66], but collapse these into one to avoid the difficulty of dealing with conflicting images and information. We also have evidence that distances in perception space and physical space are positively related. Thus, most people tend to see the most distant states as being least like their own home state.

The four scales may be seen to be related to schemas with sets of sub-schemas, all of which might be seen to overlap and interconnect in different ways as they are processed in parallel, leading to the composition of an overall preference that may not be capable of rational deconstruction in individual cases. Gould and White argue that "there need be no direct correlation between preferences and accuracy of location, nor between imageability and the task of locating a place exactly" (1986: 82). Respondents often show "appalling expressions of geographical ignorance" (p. 82), so that preference maps are routinely created on the basis of absent and defective information about the places rated. But that does not stop people from rating them. People's interest in places (or their emotional involvement with them) "falls off roughly with the square root of the distance" (1986: 23): people care about their locale, but care sharply less about places the further they are away. This makes geo-graphical proximity a non-linear function (see Chapter 6). Gould and White further propose that the information that people have about places is another non-linear function, this time of a location's population divided by its distance from the respondent. In the particular case for data from Illinois, they report that (1986: 93):

$$I = 0.24 \left(P^{0.87}/D^{0.40} \right)$$

where I = information, P = population, and D = distance

Stated in words instead of a formula, the information that the Illinois respondents have about any other place is a product of non-linear factors for the population size of the other place and distance from Illinois of the other place, multiplied by a constant. The effects of distance and population strongly influence the information that people have about places, which in turn is subject to evaluation according to numerous interconnected schemas and sub-schemas. Given the exponential effect of proximity, what people really know is their local surroundings, and they do not agree on their mental images even of local neighborhoods. The study of spatial perception, then, does not disagree with connectionist cognitive science, but it does suggest caution about the development and status of proposed cultural schemas in relation to individuals and local groups within any overall population. The evidence of spatial perception indicates that national, local, and individual perceptions are just not homologous; perceptions at each level are not all the same, just at different sizes. At levels beyond the local, relative similarity of perceptions may arise from the *lack* of information that people have about other places, rather than from any actual shared perceptions. Thus an overall "average" is likely to fail to capture actual similarities and differences in aggregated evidence of perceptions. Yet again, this finding evidently will relate to speech data, as demonstrated below in the work of perceptual dialectology.

Contemporary advances in the cognitive sciences, in psychology, linguistics, anthropology, and geography, all contribute to a richer picture of the speech circuit than Saussure was able to supply. Key findings suggest that the brain itself is much like a complex system, and that it may demonstrate self-organizing behavior in much the same way that other complex systems show emergent order. Contemporary cognitive models emphasize the constructive mental activity of individuals, as they assemble gestalts or configurational wholes out of incomplete or conflicting input, whether as prototypes or in schemas as relational patterns for potential characteristics. The connectionist model not only includes dynamic interaction of large numbers of components to produce emergent order, but appears to be robust when the process is confronted by small changes or disruptions in stimuli. Scaling is an important part of schema theory and spatial perception. Cognitive anthropology and the study of spatial perception show that these cognitive principles can be applied not just to individuals but to populations, as long as due consideration is given to analytical methods that respect scaling properties and distributional facts of the evidence. All of these things bear on the linguistics of speech, and the task for the rest of this chapter is to show how evidence from speech perception and speech production parallels these findings from contemporary cognitive science.

Evidence from perceptual dialectology

In order to consider the effects of perception with regard to speech, let us turn to perceptual maps of American English. Given the advances in contemporary cognitive science, we should be interested to observe possible operation of prototypes or schemas, and to consider analytical methods and scaling properties.

As already mentioned, Dennis Preston has led the recent movement for American perceptual dialectology (1989, 1999). He has produced a separate treatment of the South, which is generally regarded as the most "marked" of American dialect areas, potentially a prototypical area (1997; Gould and White 1986: 54–63 refers to the "Southern Trough" of low ratings in the American national mental image). Two maps from Preston (1997) illustrate one of his methods for getting at people's perceptions of language varieties, and also tell us something about the perceptions themselves. Figure 7.1 contrasts the perceptions of a Chicago speaker with those of someone from South Carolina, from Preston's Draw-A-Map task. Both speakers drew a Southern region but not the same one (e.g., the Chicagoan includes Tennessee and Virginia and cuts off South Florida, while the Carolinian does none of these), and clearly the maps show the results of contrasting evaluations of the areas (i.e., "Worst English" vs. "Damn Yankees"). Such perceptual differences clearly show individual orientation, and at the same time show that different schemas have been invoked in order to draw lines: *War between the States* by the Carolinian, and several intersecting schemas by the Chicagoan including *ethnicity, social class, regionalism*, and *quality* with respect to speech. Preston's evidence confirms for speech what Gould and White (1986) discussed for spatial perception generally, that individuals may have very different impressions of the same space, and that their geographical views are not likely to be separated from their social views.

Figure 7.2 shows results from four maps in Preston (1997), each a generalization from a set of maps from some Michigan respondents. No matter what we consider "perceptual consensus" to be, we cannot find it here. If we consider consensus to consist of all of the area indicated in their drawings by at least one respondent (the largest ellipse), the area appears to be too large to satisfy most people familiar with American English: Cleveland or Iowa in the South? On the other hand, if we consider consensus to consist of the areas that every respondent mentioned we are also out of luck – there is no 100% region. The ellipse at the 96% level of agreement shows only a tiny area, somewhere near the sister cities of Phenix City (AL) and Columbus (GA) in the central part of the Deep South. We are left with the question of how much agreement is enough. The ellipse for the 91% agreement level does include a core area from near Charleston across parts of the old plantation region, but many Americans would still consider this area too small for the South; it excludes, for example, most of the area of the old Confederacy. The two ellipses for the 50% agreement level are better in some ways, but the fact remains that only half of the respondents participated in it – and the Indiana neighbors of the Michigan speakers did not quite agree with them at their own 50% level; the Indiana

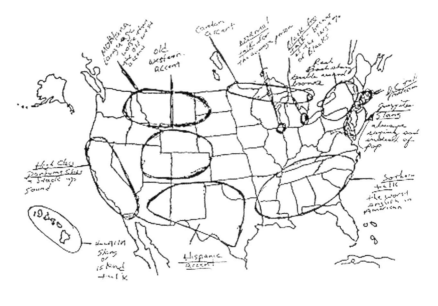

Figure 7.1 Two examples of Preston's Draw-A-Map perceptual maps (Preston 1997: Figures 10, 12)
(Source: The South: The Touchstone, by Dennis Preston. In C. Bernstein, T. Nunnally, and R. Sabino, eds, *Language Variety in the South Revisited* (Tuscaloosa: University of Alabama Press), 311–351. With the kind permission of the University of Alabama Press, Tuscaloosa)

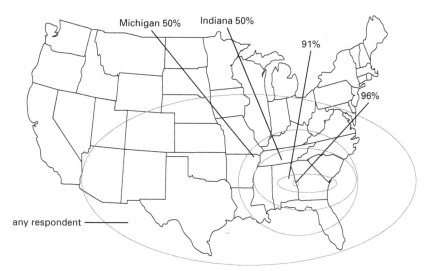

Figure 7.2 Location of the Southern Dialect (adapted from Preston 1997: Figures 3–6)

speakers' 50% level includes substantially less territory. It is also the case that "50% agreement level" does not indicate that half of the respondents (whether from the Michigan or Indiana set) would draw exactly the 50% ellipse in Figure 7.2. Indeed, the method used to make Preston's maps says otherwise: if 50% of the respondents included at least the area indicated, many respondents must actually have drawn a different area (thus the use here of ellipses in the figure redrawn for this volume, which clearly indicate a "smoothed" generalization that ignores precise boundaries). Preston's research clearly tells us that, even though just about all of his respondents named the South as a dialect region in some way, respondents could not agree where it was even in gross terms, not to mention detailed boundaries. Preston's findings again are consistent with those of Gould and White (1986). When means or averages are applied to ratings by individuals, the result does not describe a shared mental image but instead a picture that few individuals and no localities actually possess. If the South is a prototype, it is one in name only. On the other hand, since Preston's respondents readily drew areas on the map, it appears highly likely that *speech type* is a schema that the respondents were willing to apply, in connection with *American South, War between the States, ethnicity, social class, regionalism, quality*, and no doubt many other schemas that might be related to speech, or might not be clearly separate from it.

Susan Tamasi replicated Preston's Draw-A-Map method with some Georgia respondents (Tamasi 2000, 2003), who also could not agree on dialect areas

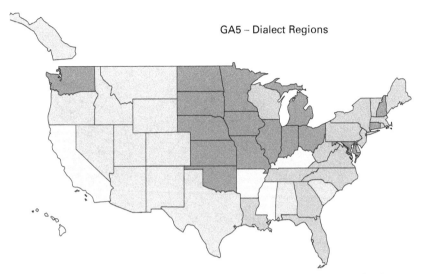

Figure 7.3 Tamasis map of one respondent's cognitive classification of perceptual dialects (Tamasi 2003: 195)
(Source: Cognitive Patterns of Linguistic Perceptions, by Susan Tamasi. Dissertation, University of Georgia. With the kind permission of Susan Tamasi)

except in probabilistic terms. She subsequently developed new methods based on the pile-sorting task used in cognitive anthropology to study the cognitive bases of perceptual assessments (2003). Figure 7.3 is a transformation in grayscale of Tamasi's map, originally in color. The mottled Southern region indicates that this Georgia respondent does not have a coherent map of Southern speech. The different shades of gray represent the different categories into which the respondent classified the different Southern states. Some of Tamasi's respondents did classify a number of the Southern states together, but others also created discontinuous classifications of the Southern states.[2] The fact that they could do so suggests that the Draw-A-Map method may "smooth"

---

[2] Gould and White report, based on a comparative study of Texas and Georgia respondents, that "Georgians are not only more parochial than Texans, but also less capable of discriminating between other states far away from them" (1986: 66). To the extent that Gould and White's Georgians are comparable to Tamasi's, the local orientation of Georgia respondents might be considered to be responsible for more detailed discrimination of neighboring states and more erratic discrimination of distant states, both of which might give the appearance of an incoherent mental image. However, sorted piles containing discontinuous states also occurred among Tamasi's parallel New Jersey sample, so regional incoherence in mental maps does not just belong to "parochial" Georgians.

the data into coherent regions that are not necessarily consistent with respondents' cognitive patterns. Thus Tamasi has found an experimental method to demonstrate what Gould and White (1986) could show only by qualitative comparison of individuals. Tamasi's research shows us that we should understand Preston's regional generalizations, and by extension the national generalizations of Gould and White (1986), as smoothed interpretive abstractions from the evidence, rather than as evidence of cognitive regularities. Construction of such regional or national maps necessarily suppresses individual or local variation in the interest of getting at the big picture. However, we need not, and given Tamasi's findings we should not, just assume that we all possess coherent mental maps of dialect areas. Even if we did have coherent mental maps, Preston's and Tamasi's evidence together agrees that we do not share consensus about the number or location of areas on our mental maps. Perceptual coherence is an issue, not a given, just as the coherence of geographical distributions of speech production data is an issue. Perceptual research has made mapping mental images of the South as complex and interesting as research on speech production.

Further information about the coherence of Tamasi's pile-sort data comes from her use of hierarchical agglomerative cluster analysis (Figure 7.4, based on data from New Jersey respondents). This process calculates the relative likelihood that states will be combined in the same pile: values at the top, close to 1, show high likelihood of having been put in the same pile, while values at the bottom, close to 0, show little likelihood for combination; states are ordered at the top of the table according to how they fall into groups. When (like Tamasi) we choose to observe the plot near the quartile points, .25, .50, and .75, the greatest likelihood of association in the pile-sort task (at the .75 level) belongs to pairs of adjoining states, eight pairs of states and one triplet (ME/NH/VT). All of these groups are states relatively distant from the New Jersey respondents; New Jersey itself has not yet joined a cluster. At the .50 level (not the same as the 50% level of agreement in the Preston experiment, but still a moderate degree of likelihood), no fewer than twelve groups of states are associated. This number nearly matches the average number of piles created by Tamasi's New Jersey respondents, thirteen. According to the "chunking" documented by cognitive anthropologists to facilitate memory (D'Andrade 1995: 44–45), and the extension of the chunking phenomenon in folk taxonomies (D'Andrade 1995: 92–95), we should expect people to retain a smaller number of simultaneous categories, typically five but sometimes up to seven. We may suspect, then, that the average number of piles and the number of categories at both the highest level of association and at the moderate level of association are actually driven by a lack of information (as discussed by Gould and White), and not by definite ideas about spatial similarity of speech. As Tamasi said, "I do not believe the Dakotas clustered together with the strongest similarity because of a common

```
New Jersey cluster analysis
JOHNSON'S HIERARCHICAL CLUSTERING

Level  C R M M N V N N D M P O T F N S V K L A G A M T W H A K N M I I I O M M W C N A N C U S N O W I M W
       T I A E H T J Y E D A K X L C C A Y A L A R S N V I K S E O L N A H I N I A V Z M O T D D R A D T Y
------
0.9000 . . . . . . . . . . . . . . . . . . . . . . . . . . . . . . . . . . . . . . . . . . XXX . . . . .
0.8667 . . . . XXX . . . . . . . . . . . . . . . . . . . . . . . . . . . . . . . . . . . . . XXX . . . . .
0.8333 . . . . XXX . . XXX . . . . XXX . . . XXX . . . . . . . . . . . XXX . . . . . . . . . XXX XXX . . .
0.7889 . . . XXXXX . . XXX . . . . XXX . . . XXX . . . . . . . . . . . XXX . . . . . . . . . XXX XXX . . .
0.7333 . . . XXXXX . . XXX . . . . XXX . . . XXX XXX . . . . . . . . . XXX . . . XXX . . . . . XXX XXX . . .
0.7083 . . XXXXXXX . . XXX . . . . XXX . . . XXX XXX . . . . . . . . . XXX . . . XXX . . . . . XXX XXX . . .
0.7000 . . XXXXXXX . . XXX . . . . XXX . . . XXX XXX . . . . . . . . . XXXXX . . XXX . . . . . XXX XXX . . .
0.6741 . . XXXXXXX . . XXX . . . . XXX . . . XXXXXXX . . . . . . . . . XXXXX . . XXX . . . . . XXX XXX . . .
0.6444 . . XXXXXXX . . XXX . . . . XXX . . . XXXXXXX . . . . . . . . . XXXXX . XXXXX . . . . . . XXX XXX . . .
0.6333 . . XXXXXXX . . XXX . . . . XXX . . . XXXXXXX . . . . . . . . . XXXXX . XXXXX . . XXX . . XXX XXX . . .
0.6222 . . XXXXXXX . . XXX . . . . XXXXX . . XXXXXXX . . . . . . . . . XXXXX . XXXXX . . XXX . . XXX XXX . . .
0.6000 . . XXXXXXXX . . XXX . . . . XXXXX . . XXXXXXX XXX . . . . . XXXXX . XXXXX . . XXX XXX XXX XXX . XXX
0.5933 . XXXXXXXXX . . XXX . . . . XXXXX . . XXXXXXX XXX . . . . . XXXXX . XXXXX . . XXX XXX XXX XXX . XXX
0.5867 . XXXXXXXXX . . XXX . . . . XXXXX . . XXXXXXX XXX . . . . . XXXXX . XXXXX . . XXX XXX XXX XXX . XXX
0.5815 . XXXXXXXXX . . XXX . . . . XXXXX . XXXXXXXX XXX . . . . . XXXXX . XXXXX . . XXX XXX XXX XXX . XXX
0.5667 . XXXXXXXXX . . XXXXX . . . XXXXX . XXXXXXXX XXX . . . . . XXXXX . XXXXX . . XXX XXX XXX XXX . XXX
0.5401 . XXXXXXXXX . . XXXXX . . . XXXXX XXXXXXXXXX XXX . . . . . XXXXX . XXXXX . . XXX XXX XXX XXX . XXX
0.5333 . XXXXXXXXX . . XXXXX . . . XXXXX XXXXXXXXXX XXX . . . . . XXXXX . XXXXX . XXXXX XXX XXX XXX . XXX
0.5000 XXXXXXXXXX . . XXXXX . . . XXXXX XXXXXXXXXX XXX . . . . . XXXXX . XXXXX . XXXXX XXX XXX XXX . XXX
0.4778 XXXXXXXXXX . . XXXXX . . . XXXXX XXXXXXXXXX XXX . . . . . XXXXX . XXXXX . XXXXX XXX XXX XXX XXXXX
0.4683 XXXXXXXXXX . . XXXXX . . . XXXXX XXXXXXXXXXXX XXX . . . . . XXXXX . XXXXX . XXXXX XXX XXX XXX XXXXX
0.4667 XXXXXXXXXX XXX XXXXX . . . XXXXX XXXXXXXXXXXX . . . . . XXXXX . XXXXX . XXXXX XXX XXX XXX XXXXX
0.4389 XXXXXXXXXX XXX XXXXX . . . XXXXX XXXXXXXXXXXX . . . . . XXXXX . XXXXX . XXXXXXX XXX XXXXXXX
0.4351 XXXXXXXXXX XXX XXXXX . . . XXXXXXXXXXXXXXXX . . . . . XXXXX . XXXXX . XXXXXXX XXX XXXXXXX
0.4333 XXXXXXXXXX XXX XXXXX . . . XXXXXXXXXXXXXXXX . . XXX . XXXXX . XXXXX . XXXXXXX XXX XXXXXXX
0.4200 XXXXXXXXXX XXX XXXXX . . . XXXXXXXXXXXXXXXX . . XXX . XXXXX . XXXXX . XXXXXXX XXX XXXXXXX
0.4000 XXXXXXXXXX XXX XXXXX XXX . XXXXXXXXXXXXXXXX . . XXX . XXXXXXX . XXXXX . XXXXXXX XXX XXXXXXX
0.3776 XXXXXXXXXX XXX XXXXX XXX . XXXXXXXXXXXXXXXX . . XXX . XXXXXXX . XXXXXXX . XXXXXXX XXXXXXXXX
0.3560 XXXXXXXXXX XXX XXXXX XXX . XXXXXXXXXXXXXXXX . . XXX XXXXXXXXX . XXXXXXX . XXXXXXX XXXXXXXXX
0.3111 XXXXXXXXXX XXX XXXXX XXX . XXXXXXXXXXXXXXXX . . XXX XXXXXXXXXX XXXXXXX . XXXXXXX XXXXXXXXX
0.2803 XXXXXXXXXX XXX XXXXX XXX . XXXXXXXXXXXXXXXX . . XXX XXXXXXXXXX XXXXXXX XXXXXXX XXXXXXXXX
0.2756 XXXXXXXXXX XXX XXXXXXXXX XXX . XXXXXXXXXXXXXXXX . . XXX XXXXXXXXXX XXXXXXX XXXXXXX XXXXXXXXX
0.2683 XXXXXXXXXX XXXXXXXXXX XXX XXXXXXXXXXXXXXXXX . . XXX XXXXXXXXXX XXXXXXX XXXXXXXXXXXXXXXXX
0.2665 XXXXXXXXXX XXXXXXXXXX XXX XXXXXXXXXXXXXXXXX . . XXXXXXXXXXXXX XXXXXXXXXXXXXXXXXXXXX
0.2314 XXXXXXXXXX XXXXXXXXXX XXXXXXXXXXXXXXXXXXXX . . XXXXXXXXXXXXX XXXXXXXXXXXXXXXXXXXXX
0.1845 XXXXXXXXXX XXXXXXXXXX XXXXXXXXXXXXXXXXXXXX . . XXXXXXXXXXXXX XXXXXXXXXXXXXXXXXXXXX
0.1140 XXXXXXXXXX XXXXXXXXXX XXXXXXXXXXXXXXXXXXXX . XXXXXXXXXXXXX XXXXXXXXXXXXXXXXXXXXX
0.0643 XXXXXXXXXX XXXXXXXXXXXXXXXXXXXXXXXXXXXXXXX . XXXXXXXXXXXXX XXXXXXXXXXXXXXXXXXXXX
0.0575 XXXXXXXXXX XXXXXXXXXXXXXXXXXXXXXXXXXXXXXXX XXXXXXXXXXXXX XXXXXXXXXXXXXXXXXXXXX
0.0332 XXXXXXXXXX XXXXXXXXXXXXXXXXXXXXXXXXXXXXXXXXXXXXXXXXXXXXXXX XXXXXXXXXXXXXXXXXXXXX
0.0085 XXXXXXXXXXXXXXXXXXXXXXXXXXXXXXXXXXXXXXXXXXXXXXXXXXXXXXXXXXXXXXXXXXXXXXXXXXXXXXXXXX
```

Figure 7.4 Cluster analysis of New Jersey data (Tamasi 2003: 64)
(Source: Cognitive Patterns of Linguistic Perceptions, by Susan Tamasi. Dissertation, University of Georgia. With the kind permission of Susan Tamasi)

perception about the speech there, but instead clustered due to a lack of knowledge about this area among respondents" (2003: 84) – a comment that echoes one made by Gould and White about the Dakotas (1986: 83). The location of states near to each other on the map made up for lack of knowledge about their speech, and in two cases the North/South descriptors applied to Dakota and Carolina may have influenced the sorting. Among the gestalt principles, proximity, similarity, and closure seem to have been invoked. The number of groups that one might expect in a folk taxonomy, five or so, finally appears at the .25 level, in groupings that might be labeled New England, MidAtlantic (including, finally, New Jersey itself), Southern, Midwestern, and Western states. But the components of the groups associate only weakly at this level, poor evidence that the respondents were confident that people spoke the same in these groups of states. The cluster table was quite similar for Tamasi's Georgia respondents at the quartile points, though with some differences in groupings, and the average number of piles was also thirteen. Tamasi's pile-sort task shows that, for both Georgia and New Jersey respondents, spatial perceptions of speech are most likely motivated as much by non-speech information, or lack of information, as they are by speech, and that perceptions of speech fail to aggregate at other than a low likelihood of association either among the separate parallel samples of respondents or overall. This finding further supports the idea that, while people may have a cultural *speech type* schema, the extent to which individuals share or average the characteristics that fill out the schema, in order to create prototypes as instantiations of the schema, is sharply limited.

Kretzschmar (2003) argues that scholars, too, draw maps of the South and other dialect areas on perceptual grounds, even when they make it appear that they are mapping production data. There is no reason that scholars should not themselves activate the *speech type* schema and its interconnections. Inspection of even the article titles in Preston (1999) shows that, in the history of perceptual dialectology beginning with the origins of such study in Holland and Japan, most studies assume that there are such things as dialect boundaries and areas, and the authors expect perceptual studies to confirm or to disconfirm production studies. The problem with this approach consists of authors understanding the *speech type* schema as a shared mental image or prototype, rather than as a pattern in which they themselves fill in characteristics out of their individual experience. Evidence from speech production suggests that, while it may well be appropriate to posit the existence of attributive dialects or blind dialects on the terms described in Chapter 2, those dialects will not have "natural" boundaries but instead the arbitrary boundaries of the area of attribution or of the area of a survey in which blind dialects are sought – the boundaries arbitrarily applied by the individual analyst. For authors to expect their research subjects to confirm the real existence of such dialect areas and boundaries on the basis of the subject's perceptions is like the snake chasing its own tail. The only way that the research subjects could be right is if they agreed with the researcher's personal perception or attribution of areas. Again as argued in Chapter 3, researchers often use selective production evidence in order to make the claim that dialect areas that they perceive to be present are actually there; this is a deductive process valid only if dialect areas are assumed to be real and present, which goes back to the activation of the researcher's own personal *speech type* schema.

Perceptual information about speech, however, remains valuable even if matching speech production patterns with perception patterns is not the point of collecting it, a point made by Wales (2006). Contemporary cognitive science, in D'Andrade's formulation already cited, suggests that "many of the structures that develop in the mind will be to some extent a *reflection* of the structures in the external physical world." Thus we still need to know about perceptions of speech, at least in order to consider how they might be a reflection of distributions of speech data as it is actually produced. We must be aware, however, that lack of information (especially about speech beyond one's local area) and our perceptual habit for making configurational wholes on the basis of incomplete and interrupted information, will constrain the perceptions that speakers report.

Perceptions of scaling

As a first approach to how the external world may be reflected in speech perception, we can return to Mandelbrot, scaling, and dimensionality. In a passage that will remind readers of Kauffman's gas-in-a-tank illustration from Chapter 6, Mandelbrot reported a thought experiment described by Jean Perrin, Nobel laureate for his work on Brownian motion, on what happens to the apparent density of a gas at different scales of measurement: for all volumes above, say, 1/1000th of a cubic centimeter, the mean density of the gas does not appear to vary, but as the volumes get smaller and smaller, the movement of the gas molecules causes fluctuations in the measurement, eventually to the point that most of the time the density of the gas vanishes, whereas at a few measurements the density is infinite, depending upon whether the volume measured contains a gas molecule or not (Mandelbrot 1982: 6–9). This passage introduces the notion that, even though we may measure with great accuracy, our results may still vary because they are affected by the scale of the experiment.

In another apt illustration, Mandelbrot considered the effective dimensions of a ball of thread (1982: 17–18; see Chapter 6). Given a ball 10 centimeters in diameter, of thread 1 millimeter thick:

To an observer placed far away, the ball appears as a zero-dimensional figure: a point ... As seen from a distance of 10 cm resolution, the ball of thread is a three-dimensional figure. At 10 mm, it is a mess of one-dimensional threads. At 0.1 mm, each thread becomes a column and the whole becomes a three-dimensional figure again. At 0.01 mm, each column dissolves into fibers, and the ball again becomes one-dimensional, and so on, with the dimension crossing over repeatedly from one value to another. An analogous sequence of dimensions and crossovers is encountered in a sheet of paper.

The notion that a numerical result should depend on the relation of object to observer is in the spirit of physics in this century and is even an exemplary illustration of it.

This illustration, too, suggests that our measurements may be accurate, but still may vary because of point of view. These passages are not about Labov's famous "observer's paradox" in which the act of observation interferes with the speech we are trying to observe. They are also not about Heisenberg's even-more-famous uncertainty principle to the same effect in physics. Both Labov and Heisenberg were commenting on the observer's actual interference with the subject of the observation, leading to faulty or inaccurate observations.

Mandelbrot's point is about relativism, about the fact that the same event or object necessarily looks different, even though unchanged by the observer, when inspected from different scales or points of view. Before Einstein and the twentieth century, essentially the same point was made in literary fashion by Swift in *Gulliver's Travels*, when Gulliver had a giant's point of view among the Lillipiutians (their arrows felt like pinpricks), and a tiny creature's perspective among the Brobdignagians (their small blemishes seemed like gruesome deformities). Because of the properties of scaling and of the non-linear distribution of feature variants in speech, the problem of relativism must dominate our perception of speech.

Barbara and Ronald Horvath have demonstrated the idea of what they call "scale dependency" in speech by pointing out that variation in speech looks different depending on how the observer groups the data (2003). They carried out a study of /l/ vocalization, in which they conducted short interviews with 312 speakers spread across nine localities in Australia and New Zealand, each of whom was supposed to have responded to 84 different cues for possible /l/ vocalization (see Horvath and Horvath 2001). Unlike Atlas survey research that recorded all of the different variants elicited, the Horvath experiment coded /l/ vocalization as either present or absent for each type of cue. This means that we cannot observe the A-curve effect from their presentation, because they have reduced the possible realizations to just two.[3] For the Horvaths, frequency refers to the rate of occurrence of a variant in a type/token experiment, while for the Atlas frequency refers to the number of times a realization occurred among the many respondents. In our Atlas data for the word *Asheville* (Table 7.1), we see that a choice to make just a binary division between presence or absence of /l/ vocalization would actually obscure a great deal of variation in both vowel quality and potential diphthongization, and in the quality of the final consonant; following the distributional pattern illustrated in Chapter 6, each segment involved in /l/ vocalization has an A-curve distribution. To the extent that Australian speakers are generally like the Atlas speakers, the Horvath experiment thus focuses on examination of contexts for /l/ vocalization at the expense of reporting the phonetic detail. This is a choice with consequences for their results, but their main point of scale dependency shows through clearly in any case, and their analysis is not in any essential conflict with the A-curve distributional pattern.

Table 7.2 shows the different rates of /l/ vocalization when the data is reported at nine different localities, when the same data is regrouped into four regions, when it is again regrouped into two nations, and finally when it is regrouped into one supranational group. If we want to ask whether /l/

---

[3] The Horvaths were interested in constraint hierarchies and a continuum of "universality," not in recording all of the feature variants realized by their speakers.

Table 7.1 *LAMSAS pronunciation of*
Asheville *(594 responses; this place name*
was not elicited from all LAMSAS speakers)

vowel 1a	
raising/lowering	
æˆ	48
æ	501
æˇ	40
aˆ	2
a	2
aˇ	1
front/back	
æˋ	1
æ	568
æˀ	20
aˆ	2
aˀ	3
lengthening	
a	3
a·	2
æ	509
æ·	80
vowel 1b	
{e}	1
{ɛ}	48
ɛ	6
{ɨˇ}	43
{ɪ}	43
{ə}	109
{əˋ}	1
{əˆ}	2
{əˆˋ}	26
0	315
cons. 1	
ʃ	594
cons. 2	
f	3
v	527
γ̥	7
w	10
{w}	2
{ꞵ}	4
{ꞵ‿v}	1
{ʊ}	1
ꞵ	5
ꞵ̶	2
ʔv	1
ʊ	29
ʋ̥	2

Table 7.1 (*cont.*)

vowel 2a	
raising/lowering	
ɪ̂	22
ɪ	232
ɪ̌	2
ɯ	2
ɨ̂	2
ɨ	75
ɨ̌	3
ɤ	6
ə	21
0	229
front/back	
ɤ	6
ɯ	2
ə	21
ɪ	239
ɪ̓	17
ɨ	66
ɨˤ	12
ɨ̓	2
0	229
lengthening	
ɤ	6
ɯ	2
ə	21
ɪ	233
ɪˑ	23
ɨ	80
0	229
other	
ə̃	17
ɨ̌	14
vowel 2b	
ɤ	1
ɯ	1
{ə}	233
0 (w/2a)	130
0 (w/out 2a)	229
cons. 3	
l	95
ˌl	3
{l}	1
{ɬ}	6
ɬ	484
ɬ-	2
0	3

Table 7.2 *Rates of /l/ vocalization (adapted from Table 2, Horvath and Horvath 2003: 147)*

Geographical scale	Rate of /l/ vocalization
Supranational	
Australasian	33%
National	
Australia	15%
New Zealand	58%
Regional	
SE Queensland	3%
SE Australia	11%
S Australia	28%
New Zealand	58%
Local	
Brisbane	3%
Melbourne	9%
Sydney	15%
Hobart	10%
Mt. Gambier	28%
Adelaide	26%
Auckland	57%
Wellington	58%
Christchurch	60%

vocalization occurs in Australasian English, the answer is yes, at the rate of 33%. However, we may find it remarkable to see that no single country, region, or locality in Australasia exhibits a 33% rate of /l/ vocalization. To move further down the scale, we can observe that Australian English has a 15% rate of /l/ vocalization, but that none of the three Australian regions shows just that rate, and that only one Australian locality, Sydney, shows the national rate. It appears that generalizations at the level of country and region also do not reproduce localities very well. Indeed, when the Horvaths discuss the "individual scale," how many of the speakers in any locality shared the same rate of /l/ vocalization, we hear not only that they did not find uniformity, but that the individual scale "is the scale of greatest variability" (2003: 162). So, even the percentage of /l/ vocalization created for each locality is a generalization, a generalization that almost certainly would fit at most a few of the speakers from each place – and might match none of them. As we have seen in the Atlas data, not only is there no guarantee that all the residents in a group at any scale will share a single feature variant, there is the certainty that an A-curve distribution of variants will exist within the data from the group for any and every feature. The Horvath data shows that it is important to accept scaling as a property of speech even with binary coding of a feature variant, when the non-linear distribution of variants is not reported.

The speech production evidence from the Horvath experiment and also from Atlas survey research parallels the Gould and White data on spatial perception, where individuals are not bound to share local perceptions, and local aggregated mental images do not match aggregated national images. The Horvaths find that locality, or "place," emerges as a central factor in their analyses (2003: 166):

place consistently made the most important contribution to the variability of /l/ vocalization for all three [statistical] supranational analyses. In addition, our scale analysis showed that the national border between Australia and New Zealand is the locus of the variability [within their linguistic analysis]

As the Horvaths also point out, "the concept of place, as geographers understand it, is first and foremost a social category" (2003: 166), which echoes the suggestion of Gould and White that social circumstances are inseparable from spatial perception. Social intercourse itself is a common factor that may underlie the reflection of speech data in the spatial perception of speech. The rocks and trees and buildings of a place have some influence on the speech there but, just as for the map of Birmingham that emphasized "things at a human scale," reference to a "place" or "locality" can be a proxy term for reference to the people who interact in a place by means of speech. We have reason, therefore, to think that the Gould and White description of spatial perception, to the extent that it is based on factors also in play for the spatial perception of speech, may reflect the scaling that the Horvaths recorded in speech production for /l/ vocalization.

The circumstances for speech production thus create what appears to be an impossible perceptual burden for individual speakers. No individual can know how all of the speakers in Australasia vocalize /l/, or how all of the speakers in a country vocalize /l/, or even how all of the speakers in a locality vocalize /l/. We should not, therefore, expect that either speakers or analysts will be able to apply generalizations at higher levels of scale to lower levels of scale (called the "ecological fallacy" by the Horvaths (2003: 162)). Even at the local level of scale, individual speakers are confronted with a great many interconnected patterns of use in the feature variants produced by different people on different occasions, corresponding both to social characteristics and to text types in the textual dimension. We cannot, therefore, expect any single individual to have access to or to represent the aggregate behavior of a locality (called the "individual fallacy" by the Horvaths (2003: 162)). By extension, no locality's speech will fairly represent the behavior of a region or nation, as we have seen in aggregated spatial perceptions in Gould and White.

The scaling properties of speech data invoke Mandelbrot's relativism. Any individual speaker's view of the speech of the population is like Perrin's thought experiment about gas molecules: at such a tiny level of scale, what individuals may observe is inherently unpredictable except in probabilistic terms. Speech production for individuals behaves just opposite from the assumption of homogeneity in the linguistics of linguistic structure: speech is not composed of homologous parts of a homogeneous whole. Individual speech perception, then, never has regular and consistent input from speech production. The problem of Mandelbrot's ball of thread appears to confound the perceptual situation for individuals even further, especially for the individual scholars who are trying to characterize speech across populations. As the scale of observation changes, the dimensionality of the speech production input changes, so that different aspects of the dimensionality of speech – geographical and social factors, text types – sometimes become more perceptually relevant at different scales, and sometimes become less relevant. And as Mandelbrot points out, the direction of change in relevance is not consistent with change in scale, because the effective dimensions of perception may shift back and forth as the scale of observation decreases, and may also shift back and forth as the scale of observation increases. In consequence, the point of view from the linguistics of speech may appear just to be chaotic.

The best that individuals can do, in the end, is to perceive and react to speech production near them, either physically or socially nearby. The central importance of proximity is one of the principle findings of Gould and White about spatial perception, which reflects a principle distributional finding from speech survey data. If what people really know is their local surroundings, in both physical and social space, speech production around them is available for perception in the same way as other aspects of their environment. The prevalent geographical and social clustering of feature variants demonstrated in Chapter 4 provides structure in the external environment that can be reflected in speech perception, especially as it is distributed according to the A-curve.

Perceptions of the non-linear distribution of speech

The best possibility for creation of coherence from external information in speech perception is the non-linear, A-curve distribution of feature variants. As we have seen in Chapter 6, the A-curve distribution is present at every level of scale in both dimensions of speech, so that the distribution itself provides the regularity and predictability that individuals can use for speech perception. Günther, Levitin, Schapiro, and Wagner believe that ranking, as a cognitive process, "gives animals and humans the ability to structure their perceptions, of course at the risk of observational artifacts" (1996: 409–410). The perception of ranked frequencies in speech according to the A-curve, at whatever scale in any dimension, allows speakers to identify a feature variant at or near the top of the A-curve for some category as "right" for that category. Analysts of survey data make long lists of feature variants and careful tabulations to document their

A-curves, as illustrated in the preceding chapters. However, the same A-curve distribution exists not just globally or regionally, but also for the local variants that individuals experience in their own geographical and social neighborhoods, and in the situations of use with which they become familiar. The nature of the A-curve does not require that individuals retain detailed frequency lists, only that speakers recognize, whether consciously or unconsciously, the one variant that is massively more frequent than any other in its category. In so doing, the individual speaker can identify the variant with the cognitive category as a "normal" characteristic of it. Individuals may remember that other variants are "possible" for the category, but need not necessarily keep track of their frequencies. For example, individuals can perceive that, even though lots of people pronounce *pin/pen* the same sometimes, the people who do it most often are American Southerners. Alternatively, individuals can perceive that American Southerners sometimes pronounce *pin/pen* differently but most often they pronounce them the same, so that the merged pronunciation becomes a "normal" Southern feature. In the former case, the focus is on how often different kinds of people might merge *pin/pen*, external to any schema, and the thought leads to the *American Southern* schema, the collection of possible characteristics for that cognitive category, because *pin/pen* merger has Southerners at the top of the distribution of its possible users. In the latter case the focus is on Southern speech behavior, within the *American Southern* schema, and evaluation of the position of a specific feature variant among the possible variants.

What Günther *et al.* refer to as an "observational artifact" is the idea that, having identified *pin/pen* merger with Southerners in either of these cases, there must be such a thing as "Southern speech," an object with particular characteristics. The creation of an observational artifact thus corresponds to the creation of a configurational whole, in which incomplete, interrupted, or lacking information can be perceived as a gestalt and made into an object, or artifact. By extension, an observational artifact can be considered to be a prototype, an object with particular characteristics which is constructed from possible properties but which may not exist in an actual exemplar. Thus, the use of the ranking process creates an artifact which would not otherwise exist, whether the object is considered to exist *in rebus* or just as a prototype, as opposed to the recognition of an object which does actually exist *in rebus*. Both the use of ranking as a perceptual process and the creation of observational artifacts are important for speech perception.

While ranking as a perceptual strategy for the variants of one feature appears simple, application of the process in a realistic setting is another matter. Speakers must simultaneously perceive the rank of feature variants for a host of possible categories. Cognitive schemas can provide the framework that allows for such perceptions to occur in a structured way. Kauffman offers a good way to visualize the problem in an illustration for evolutionary genetics, the adaptation landscape (1995: 149–189). In the evolutionary genetics illustration, the "landscape" is composed of a great many peaks and valleys corresponding to genetic combinations, and the activity of the system works to select the best genetic combination and thus to improve the species.[4] If we adapt Kauffman's illustration to create a model for the problem of speech perception, the "landscape" would be composed of peaks representing top-ranked variants and valleys representing lower-ranking variants for speech features. The adaptation landscape as adapted here for speech is a hypothetical model, not yet an experimentally demonstrated process.[5] Still, it is worth imagining as an idea of how speech production and perception can work together in a new version of Saussure's speech circuit.

Let us begin the perceptual model with the point of view of an individual as receiver of speech, say in a conversation. Every individual possesses an array of cognitive schemas, each with layers of sub-schemas, some of them more or less aligned with cultural schemas, that is, relatively the same as those of other speakers in a population, and some with more individual and personal characteristics. Every individual also possesses experience with speech, in the form of mostly unconscious awareness of non-linear distribution of variants for any speech feature among the speakers in geographical and social proximity, and in different text types.[6] The immediate task of the individual as receiver at the start of a speech transaction is to identify the transaction as likely belonging to some particular schema. In this case, the adaptation landscape is composed of feature peaks that show the top-ranked variants and A-curves for the possible elements of different schemas. Cognitive processing matches speech input from the conversation to peaks on the landscape. Another task for the individual is to consider the adaptation landscape within the schema after it has been identified, which is again composed of peaks and valleys, now corresponding to the top-ranked variants and A-curves for the elements within the schema. As the

---

[4] The evolutionary theme is developed for brain physiology in Edelman (1987), called *Neural Darwinism*, a prominent argument for the connectionist processing model.

[5] Experimental demonstrations may take different avenues to test the model. A recent example of work that indirectly speaks to the model is McMurray (2007), which addresses the theory that specialized cognitive mechanisms must be available to facilitate children's rapid and accelerating vocabulary acquisition. McMurray argues that "acceleration in vocabulary growth could arise from occurrence statistics alone. The vocabulary explosion is a by-product of parallel learning and variation in the time to learn words … The ease-of-acquisition distribution provides a framework for integrating linguistic, psychological, and statistical factors in word learning. These mundane structural features of the organism-environment complex, not specialized learning processes, determine the form of growth" (2007: 631).

[6] According to the currently accepted idea in neuroscience, some trace of the relative frequencies of different events may be encoded in the brain through the enhancement of neural pathways that occurs with repeated behaviors. For this illustration, we need to posit for the biological neural network no more than the difference between a trace of high-frequency use as opposed to a singular memory of use of some speech variant.

cognitive process matches the words of the conversation to their ranks among the possible variants, recognition of the highest-ranking words for the elements would be a sign of "normal" use of the schema. The benefit of such use of rankings, then, is to identify the most likely cognitive schema for the situation, and to evaluate whether the speech variants received are "normal" (the most frequent ones) or whether some question remains about their use. These tasks are not strictly sequential: the parallel processing model suggests that multiple tasks can be processed simultaneously, which here means the simultaneous evaluation of different possibilities for schemas and for different possibilities within schemas.

The perceptual advantage of using rankings is clear: the load for cognitive processing is reduced greatly, because ranking greatly reduces the variation in the raw speech input (see Chapter 6). The number of ranks for variants is far smaller than the number of possible realizations for any feature. Cognitive processing is enhanced to an even greater degree by expectation as "normal" of the top-ranked variants on the peaks (i.e., the distinction for neural pathways between high-frequency repeated input vs. possible input). Of course conversations are composed of a great many speech features, and so the continuing layered use of rankings creates a more and more secure impression of the meaning of the exchange, as the selection of a schema is confirmed or adapted by the processing of additional entities from the stream of speech, and as rankings within the schema indicate whether the schema is being applied "normally" or somehow creatively. The key facts for cognitive processing, however, remain the stable and regular existence of an A-curve distribution for the variants of all speech features at all scales of reference, from which rankings may be processed, and the stable and regular existence of cognitive schemas whose slots for characteristics are not determined (as for prototypes) but instead are available for use with A-curve rankings.

Kauffman, in his evolutionary genetics simulation, allows for co-evolutionary processes. In the adaptation landscape as converted for speech, co-evolution corresponds to the idea, natural enough, that more than one schema might be identified as relevant to a conversation, or that more than one option for the status of a schema might be maintained, so that different possibilities for meaning are kept open. It also opens the way for "weighting." Cultural schemas are in part constituted by learned, attributive patterns, not just personal experience with the local environment, and such learned patterns might be thought to weight patterns from experience and so to affect the identification of input. This sort of behavior amounts to what Arthur referred to as reactions by human agents "with strategy and foresight" (1999: 107), as opposed to automatic, mechanical identification. In the terms of Kauffman's lightbulb simulations discussed in Chapter 6, the possibility for parallel processing of multiple lines of thought adjusts the "control bias," and thereby creates a more complex reactive adaptation of speech to circumstance. Indeed, according to Kauffman's simulations, adjustment of "control bias" is an important contributor to the emergence of order in complex systems, and co-evolutionary processes are also crucial to the development of increasing order in evolutionary genetics. The co-evolutionary maintenance of multiple lines of thought corresponds to parallel distributed processing networks according to the connectionist model.

In order to make a speech circuit, the procedure of matching words or other speech features with rankings that identify schemas and indicate status within schemas can also be applied by individuals as transmitters of speech. The speech circuit remains a circuit, with cognitive processing required at each end. The difference between Saussure and contemporary cognitive science is just the replacement of Saussure's unitary "impulse" with scaling, layered schemas, and a complex identification process that can deal with the parallel complexities of neural function and non-linear distributions of feature variants at different levels of scale. When we consider the whole speech circuit, it is easy to see why conversations may fail to exchange the meaning that their participants wish to share. When transmitters and receivers of speech are both engaged in such a complex pattern-matching exercise, a great deal can go wrong. Participants may not share the same rankings of feature variants or slots in schemas, because their experience may have yielded different A-curves. The degree to which the participants share schemas may be limited, either because they do not maintain the same array of schemas given their individual experiences, or because their individual schemas are only incompletely identified with cultural schemas. Participants may not evaluate potential schemas for the conversation in the same way. Each of these possibilities for error can be increased or reduced by the proximity – geographical/social and textual – of the participants, because speakers can be expected to know and to cope with their local ecology much better than they know remote environments.

To return to the beginning of this chapter and neural function, this perceptual model is consonant with Edelman's model for physiological brain development (1987). He describes his theory of neuronal group selection in a nutshell (1987: 317):

the organism receives stimuli from its environment or econiche as polymorphous sets. As a result of action, stimuli select among various dynamic nervous system states and arrangements that have already been established prior to the receipt of these stimuli, leading to enhancement of some states and suppression of others. Such stimulus sets constitute information, in the instructionist sense, only *after* selection, response, and memory have occurred; and information processing, in the larger and more specific sense of the term, occurs only *after* social transmission has emerged as an evolutionary development.

Edelman's stimulus sets can be interpreted as schemas, according to the way that cognitive anthropologists describe them. The perceptual model just supplies ranking as a means by which selection can occur. The idea that such sets become information only after an initial matching process has occurred corresponds to the difference between schemas as potential states and subsequent matching and identification of words or other entities that create an actual arrangement. Edelman's description of neural processing similarly resonates with the perceptual model (1987: 319):

The constitution of a procedure or of a representation of categories in a spatiotemporal order occurs by mapping and reentry among parallel channels. While the *minimal* neuronal structure capable of carrying this out is a classification couple, in general, such couples do not act in isolation. Instead, they are embedded in large collections of parallel mapped channels, including reentry to and from nonmapped regions as well as to motor output systems. The collection of such components forms the smallest unit capable of a rich categorical response, called a global mapping. The emergence of global mappings as a result of action provides a critical part of the answer to the psychological question inasmuch as they provide the substrate for perceptual categorization.

Parallel processing and global mappings that may amount to what cognitive anthropologists call configurational wholes correspond well to the last matching step of the perceptual model. Edelman, of course, was not talking just about speech but more generally about physiological brain function. His global mappings may refer to things like physically "kicking the football" (which of course also has cultural associations), not just to evaluation of conversations. Still, Edelman's proposals not only do not contradict the perceptual model, they amplify ideas from cognitive anthropology and make the perceptual model more plausible as an analog to neuroscientific function. It is enough here to note the resonance, and as mentioned earlier, to suggest that neuroscience and the linguistics of speech may well produce synergies in future research.

Perception and complex systems

Complex systems yield emergent order as the result of random interactions, given particular conditions for control bias. The perceptual model, on the other hand, relies on schemas which are mental constructs, whether merely individual or to some degree culturally shared. These two parts of the linguistics of speech are not in conflict with each other. The application of schemas by individuals does not make the interactions of speech features non-random. As we have seen, individuals are all different and their language behavior is inherently unpredictable. The adaptation landscape of A-curve peaks and valleys of feature variants is what it is, the product of random interactions as influenced, but not determined, by the control bias of proximate speakers. However, to repeat what Evans and Green said of perception, "what we perceive is not necessarily the same as what we experience directly" (2006: 65). When we conceive regularities in the speech around us, we lack complete information and so we need a perceptual mechanism to fill in gaps and discontinuities in order to make a configurational whole. It is not true to say that we make speech patterns out of nothing – as we have seen, there is emergent order in speech features as they are used in populations, and we do make use of the order that we can perceive from our local ecologies. To repeat D'Andrade's statement about the significance of the connectionist model, "many of the structures that develop in the mind will be to some extent a *reflection* of the structures in the external physical world" (1995: 146). We do not just perceive the emergent order that exists and reify it, but rather we make use of our perception of emergent order when we create our own patterns on the basis of it. The key point is that it requires a definite cognitive act in order to conceive speech patterns, and in turn to use those patterns either for reception or transmission of speech.

The best analog for the adaptive landscape perceptual model in the linguistic literature is Le Page and Tabouret-Keller's *Acts of Identity* (1985). Individual speakers, they assert, use particular features according to their perceptions of the association of different features with different regional and social ecologies. Le Page claims that "groups or communities and the linguistic attributes of such groups have no existential locus other than in the minds of individuals, and that groups or communities inhere only in the way individuals behave towards each other" (1985: 4–5). Tabouret-Keller would go even further, to claim that "linguistic items are not just attributes of groups or communities, they are themselves the means by which individuals both identify themselves and identify with others" (p. 5). Both of these statements accord with the perceptual model. Speaker groups and speech communities exist within the realm of speech perception as schemas, in the repeated processing of speech input as part of the cognitive adaptive landscape, not in any external structure of speech production such as natural boundaries. Linguistic items, as top-ranked variants, are exactly the means in the perceptual model by which individuals recognize and enact the schemas of language behavior. Le Page and Tabouret-Keller reject the linear continuum that is frequently applied to their creole subject matter, in favor of a multidimensional model that can recognize "complex social rules for switching between and mixing items from two (or more) codes in a shared repertoire" (1985: 180) – this even when the (Gaussian) multidimensional statistics they applied did not produce clear results from their data, a puzzling result then, perhaps less so now that we are aware of the A-curve and non-linear distribution of speech variants. They refer to the interactional process as "projection, focussing, diffusion" (1985: 181–182):

We see speech acts as acts of projection: the speaker is projecting his inner universe, implicitly with the invitation to others to share it ... The feedback that he receives from those with whom he talks may reinforce him, or may cause him to modify his projections, both in their form and in their content. To the extent that he is reinforced, his behaviour in that particular context may become more regular, more focussed; to the extent that he modifies his behaviour to accommodate to others it may for a time become more variable, more diffuse, but in time the behaviour of the group – that is, he and those with whom he is trying to identify – will become more focussed.

Focusing does not mean the creation of systems as objects,[7] but rather is part of a process that Le Page and Tabouret-Keller compare colorfully to water in motion (1985: 232):

> It helps if we view the history of man as a history of more or less continual migration in response to ecological pressures, so that cultural and ethnic "focussing" and "re-focussing" have taken place from time to time rather as eddies and whirlpools form as features of flowing water, affected by geography and the nature of contact between different streams.

It is fortuitous, though probably not mere coincidence since great minds think alike, that Le Page and Tabouret-Keller's eddies and whirlpools anticipate Kauffman's use of the whirlpool as exemplary of a complex system. While Le Page and Tabouret-Keller were most likely not influenced by the rapid development of complexity science as they researched and wrote, their conclusions reflect the scientific tenor of their time.

An interesting corollary of recognition of the cognitive act required to conceive speech patterns is that, from the point of view of the linguistics of speech, each linguistic system developed according to the linguistics of linguistic structure must be what Günther et al. called an "observational artifact." Observation of feature distributions in speech production is a useful and necessary activity, but to attribute object status to any distributions thus observed corresponds to the creation of an artifact which would not otherwise exist, as opposed to the recognition of an object that has some actual existence

---

[7] Mufwene (2001) frequently cites from Le Page and Tabouret-Keller their notion of "focussing" as part of his argument for evolutionary selection and restructuring. From the point of view of the linguistics of speech, nothing can be selected in speech production data, because all feature distributions in aggregated data, local and regional and global, exist outside of the perceptual capacity of individual speakers. Production data is also subject to scaling effects that make it impossible to generalize up and down the scale of the data owing to the ecological and individual fallacies, as in the Horvath experiment. There is no particular reason in the linguistics of speech to privilege the most common variants as having been "selected" and therefore to be "systematic" or "phonemic," and to relegate less-common variants to be "noise" in the system. But there are indeed perceptual reasons to associate top variants with regional and social ecologies implicated in schemas. From the point of view of the linguistics of speech, as for Le Page and Tabouret-Keller, the idea of focusing can lead us to define a speech community, not as a group of people who share a linguistic system (as in the linguistics of linguistic structure), and not as a distributional pattern of occurrence in speech production (as implied by prototypes), but as a group of people who share perceptions about what feature variants belong to their local speech. Even then, no object results, just the continual process of focusing and re-focusing in the continual interaction of speakers.

outside of perception. Professional linguists are thus engaged in the same activity as non-linguists, when they use necessarily incomplete and discontinuous evidence from speech to describe syntactic and structural patterns. Linguistic systems thus proposed are no less real and no less potentially valuable when described in this way, but their existence must derive essentially from the operation of cognitive processes on the A-curve distributions of speech production data. This is not a criticism of the linguistics of linguistic structure, but the view from the linguistics of speech offers perspective, developed further in the next chapter, that may be of value for structuralist and rationalist linguistics.

As a conclusion to the discussion of speech perception, it is worth introducing one further idea from Günther *et al.* (1996). Besides the idea that the ranking process offers perceptual advantages, they also suggest that "a Zipf structure may evolve because basic mechanisms of observation favor exactly such a structure in an evolving complex system" (1996: 410). That is, they suggest that the presence of the non-linear distribution in aspects of the external world may arise *because* of the perceptual advantage in cognitive processing. The identification of one feature over another improves the operation of the process, and subsequent iterations in a repeating process of perception and enaction (as in the speech circuit) tip the balance even more in favor of identification of one feature as "normal," thus generating the Zipfian distribution. Miller and Page refer to this process as "positive feedback" (2007: 51). Le Page and Tabouret-Keller suggest that "focussing" may intensify over time, as a result of what we can recognize as control bias from the psychology of interaction. Günther *et al.* have suggested something still more fundamental, a basis for regular existence of the A-curve. They have thus offered an unanticipated new role for the speech circuit, and an elegant potential explanation for the genesis of a key aspect of self-organization in complex systems like speech.

8   Speech models and applications

At the turn of the last century Saussure made the choice that he had to make when he elected to focus on the linguistics of linguistic structure over the linguistics of speech. He had no effective means to cope with the problems presented by speech, and the study of language per se deserved its own place in academia rather than just serving as ancilla to so many other worthy social disciplines. Times have changed. The study of language still deserves its own place among the academic disciplines, but we now have the means to work effectively with speech. We can record it, we can manage great volumes of it on computers, and we can process what we record and manage with modern statistics to assess its dynamics. In the preceding chapters, it is clear that we get results when we do study speech on its own terms. We have no reason to abandon the linguistics of linguistic structure, but we now have every reason to establish the linguistics of speech, not just because we now can but because we ought to, at least in order to clarify the relationship of linguistic structure to its empirical base, a relationship that all agree it must have. Saussure said as much ((1916)1986: 19):

speech ... is necessary in order that a language may be established. Historically, speech always takes precedence. How would we ever come to associate an idea with a verbal sound pattern, if we did not first of all grasp this association in an act of speech? Furthermore, it is by listening to others that we learn our native language. A language accumulates in our brain only as the result of countless experiences. Finally, it is speech which causes a language to evolve. The impressions received from listening to others modify our own linguistic habits.

Experience with speech builds our cognitive capacities, and our language behavior then continues to develop and change in a highly interactive speech environment. We need to understand speech production and speech perception as well as we can if we are to make the most of our study of linguistic structure. When we do study the linguistics of speech, we achieve definite findings that can help us to determine the relationship of speech to the linguistics of linguistic structure, to reconsider developments in historical linguistics, and to address the sort of problems between linguists and the public described in the first chapter.

Towards a formal model of speech

Speech is a complex system. This simple statement conveys a great deal of information, especially in contrast to notions of language considered as linguistic structure:

(a) speech is open and dynamic, as opposed to a static structure;
(b) speech includes a very large number of interactive components/agents, as opposed to a hierarchical arrangement of types;
(c) speech shows emergent order, as opposed to rule-bound relations;
(d) the distribution of units in speech is non-linear, as opposed to an assumption of random use or normal distribution;
(e) speech has the property of scaling, as opposed to homogenous unity.

Beyond the general properties of complex systems, speech has its own characteristic conditions:

(a) it exists as a continuum, as opposed to occurring in naturally bounded units;
(b) proximity of its components and agents constrains its operation, as opposed to context-free operation;
(c) while its distributional pattern is constant, scaling makes it impossible to predict higher levels from lower ones (and vice versa), as opposed to an assumption of homologous parts;
(d) individual language behavior is inherently unpredictable, as opposed to an assumption of representative speakers;
(e) coherence is always an issue for both speech production and speech perception, as opposed to a given.[1]

All of these properties and conditions may at first appear to be too diverse to manage within a model, but they come down to just two elements, speech production and speech perception as required for interactions in the speech circuit. Both production and perception can each be described as a set of relations in formulaic terms. The value of moving in this way towards a formal model lies in the need to specify relations more exactly than what is normal for a more discursive treatment alone. Refinement of the model, say with weighting of its elements or addition of unforeseen elements, should certainly occur in future to the extent that the model succeeds in descriptions of linguistic behavior. Even without refinement, the model begins to account for speech as a

---

[1] As William Labov has asked (1994: 605), "It is perfectly true that I can arrange with someone to meet me at a time and place quite distant from the time and place of speaking, and that no other animal can do this. Why, then does the system so often fail, and we spend much of our time waiting for someone who never comes?" System failure of this kind, lack of coherence, comes to many people as a surprise, not just to linguists interested in linguistic structure. In the linguistics of speech, one might ask instead, as I did in a review of Labov (1994) (Kretzschmar 1996b), "When language is so various, and there are so many things that can interfere with effective communication, isn't it a wonder that we so often do meet as agreed?"

complex system in the same way that econometric models and climate models attempt to account for the evidence in those disciplines.

As a first step towards a formal conceptual model,[2] we can state that:

$$S = S_{pcpt} \times S_{prod}$$

In other words, speech is the result of the application of speech perception to speech production. Clearly, however, this does not just happen once. Speech is a process, not an object, and it might best be imagined, given the operation of complex systems, as a massively parallel sequence of interactions in which features and feature variants, the raw materials of speech as extracted from the stream of speech ("concrete entities" in Saussure's term), are deployed and received by human agents. The state of speech production influences perception, and perception influences following production (as control bias), so that it will be useful to consider that speech moves from state to state of perception and production, and that in the operation of the complex system this process results in self-organization and emergent order. At any moment, "speech" might best be characterized as the state of production and perception, which is the product of interactions at that time.

Speech production, separated for the moment from cognition and perception, is constituted by unimaginably large quantities of language in use, by a massive number of human agents. Speech production consists of conversations and things written by people as talkers and writers. Its units are arbitrarily carved from the stream of speech by analysts, whether speech sounds (or features taken to compose them), or words (or morphemes taken to compose them), or collocates, or phrases and larger collections of words. Thus, a first approach to speech production, S_{prod}, should consider actual speech as collected from at least one human agent (up to any number of human agents), in the form of the variants for at least one speech feature (up to any number of speech features):

$$S_{prod} = \Sigma(\text{speakers}_{1...\infty}) \times \Sigma(\text{features}_{1...\infty})$$

Experimental evidence has also shown that speech has at least two relevant dimensions, the geographical/social dimension (gs, for the human agents) and the textual dimension (tt, for the text types). No experiment can control for all of the possible categories of social and textual variation, since, like concrete entities from the stream of speech, any categories carved for them

---

[2] Formal mathematical proofs are beyond the scope of this volume. As discussed in Chapter 6, there is an extensive mathematical literature about Zipf's Law and related frequency phenomena, as for example in the bibliography on Wentian Li's website (www.nslij-genetics.org/wli/zipf; see also an earlier site, http://linkage.rockefeller.edu/wli/zipf/index_ru.html). Baayen (2001) is an excellent reference in this area.

will necessarily be arbitrary because both social variation and textual variation also occur on continua. Thus both *gs* and *tt*, again like features from the stream of speech, can best be represented as a set of at least one and up to any number of variables, $\Sigma(\text{variables}_{1...\infty})$. We can apply the range of variables for the geographical/social dimension to the human agents, and the range of variables for the textual dimension to the features, as divisors of the sum of speakers and features, respectively. The last element to add to the production model is some indication of proximity (*P*), how close together the language behavior under study occurred. This is a more abstract consideration than concrete entities extracted from speech, or categories created from the social and textual continua, and yet relative proximity, clustering behavior, appears all the time as a result in the experimental evidence as it is related to geographical/social variables and feature variants in texts. Moreover, in cultural geography, the effects of proximity are exponential, again non-linear, such that states change with the square root of the distance. The best way to include proximity is to show it as P^x, where *P* is a measure of distance and *X* is fractional (near .5), in relation to the *gs* variables (since different *gs* variables will have a different measure of distance) and in relation to the features under study (since the production of feature variants is known to vary by textual proximity). We can add these features to a formal production model:

$$S_{prod} = \frac{\Sigma(\text{speakers}_{1...\infty})}{\Sigma(gs \text{ variables}_{1...\infty} \times P^x)} \times \frac{\Sigma(\text{features}_{1...\infty}) \times P^x}{\Sigma(tt \text{ variables}_{1...\infty})}$$

Not every experiment controls for both *gs* and *tt*, and it is still possible to achieve reasonable results, with some luck, given Mandelbrot's notion of effective dimensions. Still, clearly, the better the analyst can control multiple variables related to both *gs* and *tt*, the better the experiment is likely to reflect the behavior of the features under study. The base form of the model for production thus remains valid, even without consideration of social and textual variation, but it is not very likely to give a good approximation of experimental evidence unless seen as from a great distance, as a ball of thread may look like a dimensionless point as seen from a great distance (to recall Mandelbrot's ball of thread illustration about relativism). The addition of the exponential proximity term leads to Zipfian non-linear distributions in the results. Experimental evidence shows that whatever concrete entities are taken to constitute units of analysis, they will be distributed according to the A-curve, as a relation of rank and frequency. Mandelbrot's formula for the curve, $P = F(r + V)^{-1/D}$, where *D* is near 1 (Chapter 6), describes such experimental results, and thus is not itself a factor in the formal model, but a consequence of interactions based on the factors present. The scaling property of experimental results comes from the summation of speakers and geographical/social variables, and the summation of features and text types, because the model applies to any level of scale selected by the analyst. Finally, it should be obvious that, even though one can talk about speech production on the basis of a single feature, consideration of a larger number of features will flesh out the picture obtained by the experiment. The formal production model can be applied to any population of speakers, with the proviso that, owing to the ecological and individual fallacies, the results of the experiment cannot be used to predict higher levels from lower ones (and vice versa).

Speech perception, separated for the moment from speech production, is constituted by the cognitive and perceptual factors that people use to process speech. The current connectionist model used both by neuroscientists and cognitive anthropologists appears from the perceptual model of the preceding chapter to be a good match for speech perception. The notion of schemas from cognitive anthropology in particular appears to be a good match for speech perception, because it does not specify fixed characteristics, as prototype theory does, but instead relational slots with different possible characteristics that might occupy them. The first cognitive processing step for speech perception by individuals corresponds to matching speech input with available schemas, in which elements of the current conversation (S_{input}) are processed for their intersection with the set of top-ranked elements (E_{top}) within the set of available cognitive schemas (C_{all}):

$$S_{pcpt} = S_{input} \cap (E_{top} \cap C_{all})$$

The second processing step corresponds to parallel processing in order to evaluate the relationship of all of the elements (E_{all}) from selected possible schemas ($C_{A, B, C}$) against the elements of S_{prod}:

$$S_{pcpt} = S_{input} \cap (E_{top} \cap C_{all}) \rightarrow \begin{array}{l} \cap (E_{all} \cap C_A) \\ S_{input} \cap (E_{all} \cap C_B) \\ \cap (E_{all} \cap C_C) \\ \cap \ldots \end{array}$$

Gould and White have provided a useful caveat from spatial perception that must be applied to the model. Their own data, and the most likely interpretation of Tamasi's evidence, suggest that proximity again plays a role in the information available to people to aid cognitive processing. Gould and White suggest that information (I) is a function of population (N) and proximity (P) as modified by a constant (K), which we can recast here, to keep variable names straight, as

$I = K \times \underline{N}^y$ where N = population and Y is fractional (near 1)

$\qquad P^x$ where P = a measure of distance and X is fractional (near .5)

Since proximity again has an exponential relationship to information, as does population, the result will be non-linear.[3] Moreover, the experimental data shows that people supplement incomplete information with other kinds of social information, or even accidents of state names, in order to create configurational wholes. An additional term must be added to the formula to account for such supplemental information, which we can call by another name, bias (B), to yield ($I + B$). The information that people have about places, as supplemented by social and other opinions, must be added to the perception formula to yield the following:

$$S_{pcpt} = \frac{S_{input} \cap (E_{top} \cap C_{all})}{(I + B)} \to \frac{S_{input} \cap (E_{all} \cap C_A)}{(I + B)} \quad \begin{array}{l} \cap (E_{all} \cap C_A) \\ S_{input} \cap (E_{all} \cap C_B) \\ \cap (E_{all} \cap C_C) \\ \cap \ldots \end{array}$$

This formula applies to speech perception by any individual; it remains non-linear, because of I.

All that remains to create a model that combines speech production with speech perception, to represent speech in the aggregate (S), is to indicate that the perceptual process can be aggregated for populations of more than one speaker, and that S_{input} now equals S_{prod}, which specifies the range of speakers in the population under study. In the aggregated model, the schemas should correspond to cultural schemas, not to schemas particular to any individual. The first processing step in the perceptual model can be collapsed with the second, because aggregated production is compared to at least one cultural schema (and up to any number of cultural schemas), and the selection of cultural schemas to process will not necessarily depend upon the top-ranked elements in the schemas.

$$S = S_{prod} \begin{array}{l} \cap (E_{all} \cap C_A) \\ \cap (E_{all} \cap C_B) \\ \cap (E_{all} \cap C_C) \\ \cap \ldots \end{array} \Big/ (I + B)$$

This formulation can qualify as a first approach to a complete formal model for speech, since it incorporates relationships between all of the aspects of both

---

[3] Trudgill's "gravity model" (1974b) suggests that the diffusion of linguistic features may leap from city to city and then spread out through the countryside in between. The approach also identifies population and distance as relevant factors, but it rates population density much more highly than distance. A recent paper by Nerbonne and Heeringa (2007) finds that the gravity model does not apply to data in the Netherlands, where distance still dominates.

speech production and speech perception. This model is not an equation that can be solved once and for all, both because several aspects of it are either infinite (possible features, possible variables) or potentially so large as to approach the infinite in practical, experimental situations (speakers), and because it is non-linear in multiple ways in the relationships created both for speech production and speech perception. At the same time, it remains possible to make reasonable approximations according to the model, through the use of estimates from sampling, especially for carefully selected and defined subsets of speakers and text types. Limited solutions that neglect parts of the model may also be worthwhile, though Mandelbrot's notion of effective dimensions suggests that such partial solutions may be misleading in unpredictable ways.

A less formal model

These relationships can be expressed more discursively under a set of four headings.

(I) Continua and complexity Language behavior exists in continua wherever we try to observe it, whether in the extraction of arbitrary units from the continuous stream of speech, or across geographical and social space, or across texts. There are no natural boundaries in any dimension. At the same time, massive numbers of speech components (however delimited for description) and human agents in a complex system interact to generate order on every level, regularities that we can use to characterize language behavior. Thus when we come to observe speech, the task is not to justify or to find evidence that matches any pre-existing ideas of structure, but instead to see what order emerges from the complex system in speech production, as mediated by speech perception.

(II) Non-linear distribution A regular pattern emerges in the distribution of components of speech production at every level, in every dimension, provided only that we apply categorizations and measurement tools in enough detail to observe it: the A-curve. We can thus expect, in every experiment on speech, that the results will follow this consistent pattern, and that we can use the A-curve as the basis for evaluation of the results of the experiment. The consistent presence of the A-curve, as Mandelbrot has complained, also means that Gaussian statistics will not always be a good match for analysis of speech evidence. That is, when the consistent distribution of speech variants is skewed in Gaussian terms (although perfectly regular as an A-curve), then statistics that are sensitive to the Gaussian normal distribution may not provide a good test of significance for all of the data. For example, in the discussion of join-count analysis (discriminant analysis) in Chapter 4 that demonstrated the prevalence of geographical clustering in speech data, it was not possible to test feature variants that occurred too often or too infrequently (i.e., most of the variant types, on the A-curve). Their skewness from the Gaussian normal distribution caused the statistic to group infrequent occurrence with non-occurrence, as if low frequency variants had not occurred at all, and to treat frequent variants as if they were categorical and not variable. Join-count analysis succeeded in demonstrating clustered behavior in Chapter 4, which as we have seen contributed greatly to the conclusion that speech is a complex system, but it did so at the cost of effectively disregarding some of the evidence. Gaussian statistics must be used with care on speech evidence, and with an awareness of the regular A-curve distribution. For example, while Gaussian statistics are likely to be misleading within a single distribution, they may well be used to assess the status of feature variants in a comparison between two distributions, each with its own A-curve. Such comparisons may associate the language behavior of two different populations of speakers (whole to whole), or at different scales within the same populations (whole to part, part to part), depending on the needs of the analysis. Whenever Gaussian statistics are applied to single populations, skewness can be expected and requires interpretation. Infrequent variants are important to speech, not something just to be thrown away by the analyst.

(III) Proximity, scaling, and the logic of aggregation The importance of proximity for speech cannot be overestimated. Language behavior begins with individuals, as they interact with others in conversations, but at the same time the language behavior of individuals is inherently unpredictable because of the myriad potential choices that each individual can make, consciously or unconsciously, on the basis of personal experience with speech production and of personal perceptual information and bias. The observation of speech, therefore, should begin with aggregation of speech data from local groups of speakers, proximate in one or more aspects of the geographical or social dimension. The further apart speakers are, whether in geographical or social space, the less likely their speech production will be correlated, and the more likely that non-speech information will substitute for missing speech experience as speakers attempt to find meaning. The property of scaling becomes increasingly important as the level of scale, and thus the average distance between speakers, increases. The dynamics of proximity and scale, both in speech production and perception, combine to demand a particular logic of aggregation: it is impossible to predict higher levels of speech production from lower ones (and vice versa). We should not, according to this logic, expect to apply generalizations at higher levels of scale to lower levels of scale (the ecological fallacy in Horvath and Horvath 2003), and we should not expect any individual fairly to represent the behavior of a locality, or any locality fairly to represent the behavior of a region (the individual fallacy in Horvath and Horvath 2003). A parallel situation exists for speech in the textual dimension, where feature variants are highly likely to be used in proximity to each other; moreover, different scales of analysis in the textual dimension are also subject to the ecological and individual fallacies. As for the geographical and social dimension, the relationship between individual textual data and local aggregations of textual data will always be probabilistic, as will the relationship between textual data from different levels of scale in analysis.

(IV) <u>Coherence in production and perception</u> Coherence is a property to be expected in both speech production and speech perception, but a given in neither. The operation of interactions in complex systems allows order to emerge in speech production, such as geographical and social clustering of speech variants, and co-occurrence of variants within short spans in texts. But such order only emerges. It is not itself demanded in every case. As for speech perception, the regular presence of the A-curve at every level in every dimension gives top-ranked variants a perceptual advantage, so that top-ranked variants can be considered "normal" while other variants can be evaluated in other ways.

Sets of possible characteristics arranged in cognitive schemas, in combination with identification of "normal" top-ranked variants for each characteristic, give rise to the conception of observational artifacts, the idea that speech production occurs in prototypic patterns (and not as it actually does, in continuous variation). That is, while only a minority of the tokens for any feature, and only a tiny fraction of the actually occurring variant types for any feature, are accounted for by the top-ranked variants, the top-ranked variants tend to be perceived and reified by receivers of speech as constituting the system for a schema or category. Thus the existence of actual coherence in speech production may not be perceived, while language users, linguists included, may conceive coherence that is an artifact of the mechanics of perception, coherence that does not actually exist in speech production. Analysts should be aware of the difference between such observational artifacts and the observed facts of speech production.

These principles fit together nicely to form a discursive model. As long as we take Mandelbrot's relativism seriously, so that we do not make generalizations about speech that reach beyond our evidence and point of view, we can use the model to guide observations of speech at all levels and in any dimension. If we wish to limit the number of variables in an analysis, then we should look first to proximity and a sense of place. Horvath and Horvath (2003) found that locality, or place, is a notion that represents complex combinations of social factors among groups of people; in this they recapitulate a basic finding of Gould and

White (1986). The Horvaths also found that locality emerges as the primary factor for managing study of speech. Locality, then, is an idea that we can use to approximate speech behavior without having to pile variable upon variable in our experiments. The fact that place can stand in for an array of social variables explains the common feeling, both in popular thought and historically in the thinking of linguists, that speech varies by locality in dialects.

Relationship with the linguistics of linguistic structure

In Saussure's *Course*, linguistic value, the aspect of language that we can only describe through analysis of structure, is the heart of the matter. The linguistics of linguistic structure still consists essentially of the description of linguistic values which are established in the collectivity of language among its speakers, as a result of the relational fit of each linguistic feature within the system of the language. Its basic principles, then, are just the opposite of those for the linguistics of speech:

(a) linguistic structure is a static structure, as opposed to being open and dynamic;
(b) linguistic structure consists of a hierarchical arrangement of types, as opposed to a very large number of interactive components/agents;
(c) linguistic structure exhibits rule-bound relations, as opposed to emergent order;
(d) linguistic structure has homogenous unity, as opposed to the property of scaling.

One more principle from the linguistics of speech has no counterpart here, non-linear distribution, because there is no place for variation by frequency among feature variants in a fixed system of types. Linguistic structure, then, is the yin for the yang of speech; they are complementary. They are not two ways of doing the same thing, one of which must be wrong. All of the experimental evidence from speech just confirms Saussure's idea that speech and linguistic structure are two possible ways of doing linguistics.

The linguistics of linguistic structure begins with idealization in order to avoid the complex interactions of speech, and yet it must still have some empirical connection with speech. From the point of view of the linguistics of speech, linguistic structure begins with speech perception, not speech production. The idea that there is a fixed objective language hierarchy, a linguistic system, originates as an observational artifact. The perceptual model can account for the universal belief of language users in the real existence of language and dialects, even though experimental evidence from speech has never identified such unities. Speakers apply ranking to perceived distributions of feature variants, in combination with the association of non-speech information, in order to create configurational wholes. Still, linguistic structures do find instantiation in the speech of populations. Language behavior is never homogenous, and individuals are always unpredictable, but aggregated speech data always has an A-curve distribution with top-ranked variants of speech features. From the point of view of the linguistics of speech, the components of a linguistic structure for some particular population of speakers are first and foremost the top-ranked variants that together can be constructed by the linguist into a cognitive prototype. While the perceptual model uses schemas, not proto-types, to account for cognitive processing of speech, prototypes with selected characteristics match the requirement for a fixed objective hierarchy in the linguistics of linguistic structure. Even though the non-linear distribution of tokens is not something that the linguistics of linguistic structure takes into account, it is the non-linear distribution that enables linguists both to conceive the existence of a linguistic structure, and to find it instantiated through rankings of feature variants for a given population of speakers. Linguistic structure is thus, in Saussure's terms, "a social phenomenon," something "social in its essence and independent of the individual." Saussure follows Durkheim (according to Firth's comments, cited in Chapter 5) to "regard the structures formulated by linguistics or sociology as *in rebus*." Both of these formulations can be seen, from the point of view of the linguistics of speech, to derive from perception of non-linear feature distributions with attendant idealization and reification.

Contemporary sociolinguistics addresses the evident problem of establishing linguistic structures from populations: different groups of speakers, whether distinct according to geographical/social criteria or just at different levels of scale, have different language behavior and thus different structures. Labov's notion of parallel grammars begins to address this fact, and recent movements like the study of communities of practice have expanded the number of potential grammars from just those of the style/class model to a much larger possible number. Still, linguistic structure can only be defined for the language behavior of one population at a time, because it derives from perception of non-linear feature distributions available from a particular population of language users. If we invoke the model of speech production, we see that there must be literally an infinite number of possible structures – because the number of possible group-ings of speakers along the geographical/social continuum is infinite. The real problem is no longer the existence of multiple structures, but how to relate the linguistic structures described for different population groups, either as part to whole or between different parts of the whole. The individual and ecological fallacies indicate that we cannot generalize from individuals or small popula-tions to larger populations, and vice versa. From the point of view of the linguistics of speech, such relations can only ever be probabilistic. If the formal model for speech is applied to two populations, otherwise using the same array of variables in the model, then comparison of the results will show that some feature variants will be higher on their A-curves, and some lower. The analyst can quantify the difference between feature variants for the comparison, which would be a normal and desirable activity within the linguistics of speech. However, for the linguistics of linguistic structure, the differences necessarily create categorically different structures that, because of the ecological and individual fallacies, are inherently not comparable except to note the different linguistic values that emerge from the structural differences.

The same problem has been addressed by the NeoFirthians for the textual dimension. Recurrent situations of use certainly show different distributions of variants, especially when new units like collocations and colligations, and the effects of proximity as in semantic preference, are taken into account. Labov's parallel grammars have had a salutary influence in America on more monolithic thinking about language, and text-centered, polysystemic accounts of language have had the same influence to an even greater extent in England. The notion that "every text has its own grammar" is true, for text types, in the same way that the language behavior of different groups can be thought to yield parallel grammars, and for particular texts in the same way that the language behavior of individuals is inherently unpredictable. Biber's demonstration of the continuum of texts, in contrast just to application of traditional text types, moves towards the linguistics of speech. However, even if we accept that language is polysystemic, we are still left with the problem of how to relate the structures described for different groups of texts, either as part to whole or between different parts of the whole. The individual and ecological fallacies still prevent us from generalizing from individuals to small groups to larger groups, and vice versa. From the point of view of the linguistics of speech, such relations must be probabilistic for comparison of texts as well as for comparison of the language behavior of populations.

Finally, there is the question of the structure of Standard English and its relation to other possible structures. In the terms of the cognitive anthropologists, Standard English is an institutional construct, not an ethnographic one (D'Andrade 1995: 132):

[ethnographic] schemas as cognitive objects should be clearly distinguished from the institutionalized behavior to which they are related. The institution of the *American family*, for example, with its social roles and their behavioral norms, is not the same as the ideas or schemas that people use to represent, understand, and evaluate the behavior of family life.

Just like the idea of the *American family*, which is not somehow an average of actual behavior in actual family life in America, the idea of Standard English is of a different order from the linguistic structures that we can conceive from language behavior, as prototypes instantiated in the top-ranked variants in particular populations. Because Standard English is institutionalized, it promotes variants as if they were top-ranked, even though they may not in fact be top-ranked across large populations. The variants promoted institutionally in Standard English are often presumed to be those of some preferred population of speakers, but in fact experimental speech evidence shows that highly educated speakers (the group typically assumed to embody Standard English) vary substantially in their language behavior, whether between countries (British vs. American Standard), or between regions, or between localities. The relationship between Standard English and any individual speaker, or any group of speakers, will remain probabilistic from the point of view of the linguistics of speech. Again, for the linguistics of linguistic structure, the differences necessarily create categorically different structures that, because of the ecological and individual fallacies, are inherently not comparable except to note the different linguistic values that emerge from the structural differences. Linguistic value extracted from the structure of Standard English would be relevant just for the institutionalized construct, since no population has been identified for it.

Observations from the point of view of the linguistics of speech offer a new perspective from Saussure's on the linguistics of linguistic structure, because we now can find regularities in speech of which Saussure was unaware. Speech is still infinitely varied across its continua, and yet its consistent non-linear distribution of components and scaling properties can begin to explain puzzling aspects of the relationship between linguistic structure and the language behavior of populations. In the end, the only way to acquire a set of variants in order to study the linguistic values in a structure is to identify a single population of speakers (from as few as one, to as many as all) in the geographical/social dimension, and to specify a single set of types in the textual dimension (from as few as one, to as many as all). While the non-linear distribution of speech and our cognitive process enable us to conceive linguistic structure, the lack of distributional equivalence between levels of scale blocks extended application of generative and structural generalizations that would otherwise appear to be very plausible. The Saussurean (following Durkheim) idea of linguistic structure is not undercut by the linguistics of speech, so long as the population for which a linguistic structure is defined is clearly identified. On the contrary, now that the status of feature variants can be clearly established in the linguistics of speech, as top-ranked or lower-ranked variants, those who prefer to study linguistic structure can make more informed decisions about which feature variants to include in the structural hierarchies they conceive.

Speech and time

Language change and historical linguistics are important questions that the linguistics of speech must be able to address. This is even more the case because the formal model of speech presented here describes states in a process, not one solution for all time. In the linguistics of speech, we should begin any historical consideration with the idea that, at any moment in time, it is possible to make generalizations at any level of scale, from small groups to supranational groups, and that our generalizations will very likely be different at each level of scale, and the ecological fallacy and the individual fallacy about generalizations will again apply.[4] For any group, at any level of scale, we should be interested in relative similarity of linguistic behavior, not categorical behavior. Further, for any group at any level of scale, we should expect that one or a few variants for any given linguistic feature will be very common on the A-curve, and that there will be a wide range of other variants in less-frequent use.

The main problem for historical linguists in the linguistics of speech is the same as it has ever been, the paucity of the evidence. Since we know that the A-curve applies to texts as well as to survey research evidence, historical linguists can try to assemble bodies of well-localized textual evidence so that A-curves for the variants of features of interest can be plotted. If all we have are a few scraps of text or inscriptions as evidence for a feature of interest, then we may have only single occurrences for every variant, and few variants at that. But even in such a difficult case, we can make historical arguments that follow the logic of non-linear distribution and scale, and avoid arguments that mistake the paucity of evidence for monolithic proof. That is, we can estimate the likelihood that our variant of interest is at some particular point on the A-curve, whether that point is at the top, in the middle, or on the tail of the curve at the time of the analysis. In effect, this estimate would create a situation for a Bayesian stat-istical analysis, in which we must consider the quality of our estimate of the status of the variant, and not just accept that we know the truth from the observed status of the variant.[5] Our knowledge of the A-curve supplies input probabilities for such decisions. Even though we may well not have enough data for a formal statistical analysis of many historical linguistic questions, indeed most such questions at any great depth of time, we may still use our knowledge of the existence of the A-curve to guide the logic of the analysis.

What marks a change in complex systems is called a "phase transition." Kauffman has illustrated the principle by means of a "random graph," in which there is an array of nodes called buttons (such as the lightbulb network), only now instead of the bulbs being either turned on or off, each button can be connected to another button by a thread (1995: 55–58). Given an experiment in which two buttons are randomly chosen and connected with a thread, then two more chosen and connected, and so on, at first isolated buttons are connected, and then sometimes an already connected button will get a second thread. As Kauffman describes it (1995: 56):

[4] This section is based on Kretzschmar and Tamasi (2003) "Distributional Foundations for a Theory of Language Change," *World Englishes* 22: 377–401. With the kind permission of Blackwell Publishing, Oxford.
[5] Hinneburg *et al.* (2007) is a valuable article about the use of bootstrap and Bayesian methods on small samples in historical linguistics. It does not address the A-curve.

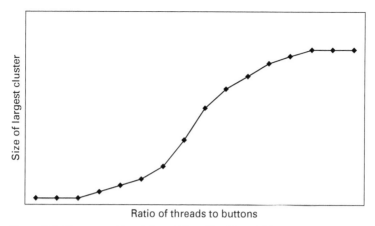

Figure 8.1 Phase transition (adapted from Kauffman 1995: 57)

When there are very few threads compared with the number of buttons, most buttons will be unconnected ... but as the ration of threads to buttons increases, small clusters form. As the ratio of threads to buttons continues to increase, the size of these clusters of buttons tends to grow ... As the ratio of threads to buttons passes the 0.5 mark, all of a sudden most of the clusters have become cross-connected into one giant structure ... As the ratio of threads to buttons continues to increase past the halfway mark, more and more of the remaining isolated buttons and small clusters become cross-connected into the giant component. So the giant component grows larger, but its rate of growth slows as the number of remaining isolated buttons and isolated small components decreases.

Kauffman's simulation models density of contact, the basic mechanics of the spread of a feature variant in speech through a population by random interaction of speakers. The progress of the change follows the form of an "S-curve" phase transition, as illustrated in Figure 8.1.

The sequential connection of threads constitutes a control strategy, like turning the lightbulbs on and off in Kauffman's network simulation described in Chapter 6. With human agents as nodes, no doubt the control bias of "foresight and strategy" must alter the behavior of the network somewhat, and a Bayesian probability should be applied to favor connections between proximate nodes over random connection. Still, contact density is a good match for the operation of change in the complex system of speech, and the same S-curve has already been described for the progress of linguistic change (notably in Kroch 1989, Labov 1994: 65–67).

The A-curve distribution is in no way at odds with the S-curve. The two curves are different expressions of the same basic distributional facts. As we have seen, the A-curve plots frequency for its Y axis, and the different variants for a given speech feature as the X axis (or, in a frequency of frequencies plot, the X axis shows the different relative frequencies in the data). Thus, any particular linguistic variant will have an identifiable location on the curve while the curve plots the counts of all the variants in the set. The S-curve, on the other hand, takes frequency as the Y axis just like the A-curve, but it plots the frequency of only a single variant instead of all the variants, and its X axis measures the time variable (in Figure 8.1, the ratio of threads to buttons increases with time). The S-curve describes the successive frequencies of a single variant at different moments in time. Figure 8.2 shows two different A-curves that correspond to different moments in time for the same variant, and

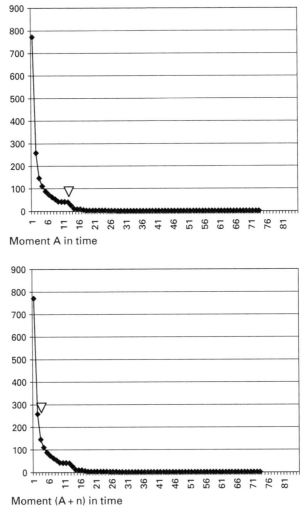

Figure 8.2 A-curves at different moments in time (hypothetical)

locates the position of the variant on each curve. Of course other variants have also changed their frequency on the graph, and some new variants may have joined it and some old ones departed; these changes are not indicated. We can rely, however, on the fact that the A-curve will still be present at both moments in time, since the non-linear distribution regularly occurs. If we then draw A-curve charts that correspond to different times on a given S-curve chart, as in Figure 8.3, we can see that the characteristically sudden positive movement of variants on the S-curve is mirrored by the shape of the A-curve.

When change occurs at a constant rate over time, and a particular variant "climbs" the A-curve by moving up in frequency rank, the distributional patterns of both the A-curve and the S-curve predict that there is a larger relative change in the middle of the curves. Rankings in the tail of the A-curve tend to be ties at the frequency of a single occurrence, but as a variant moves from one rank to the next in the middle of the curve, each step in rank describes an increasingly large number of occurrences. The S-curve refers not to raw data, but to proportional completion of a change. This means that the small number of occurrences when a variant begins to become more frequent will be expressed as a slowly growing proportion, and the larger number of occurrences in the middle of the curve as a rapidly growing proportion. Even though a large number of occurrences charac-terizes the first rank of the frequency distribution, continuing to increase the frequency of a first-rank variant will appear as a slow increase in proportion in the S-curve. For instance, a change from 95% to 97% frequency may include a large number of occurrences, but only a small proportional increase. The A-curve and the S-curve are thus complementary descriptions of the distributional facts of variant linguistic forms at different moments in time.

Linguistic change in the linguistics of speech is very different from the traditional mechanical model of linguistic change. The linguistics of linguistic structure generalizes on the linguistic situation at any moment in time to select a single variant as representative of the linguistic feature for that moment. A change is said to have occurred when a different variant is selected for a subsequent time. From the point of view of the linguistics of speech, we see that practitioners of the structural model may in the best case select the most frequent variant to represent a feature at a given moment, or they may sometimes select a less-frequent variant. The variants selected for successive moments in time determine whether a change is said to have occurred, and control the direction of change. For example, Kretzschmar (1996a) reviewed in detail Labov's evidence for vowel raising in New York City (Labov 1994: Chapter 4), and showed that Labov did not always select the most frequent variant from the evidence for his account of change. Of course Labov was not thinking of the A-curve when he selected variants, and his selection of variants does respect what variants were in use at the relevant times in New York City. Still, the fact that he did not always select the most frequent variant must call into question

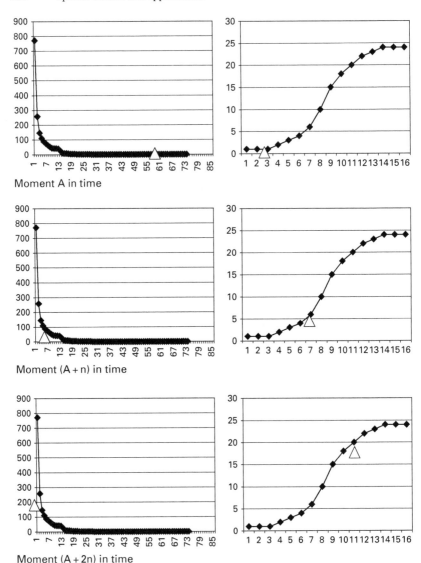

Figure 8.3 A-curves at different moments in time, with associated S-curves (hypothetical)

what the structural notion of "change" may mean in his analysis. The evidence for sound change even in New York is fragmentary for the period before the invention of the IPA. The quality and quantity of the evidence is much worse for deeper historical periods, when historical linguists must interpret spelling differences for what they may have to say about pronunciation, an uncertain and speculative process. Uncertainly about spelling, including doubt about its trans-mission when texts were copied, also makes it difficult to extract word-level information of value for the study of inflectional, lexical, and grammatical change. Because of these problems, and the overriding problem of uncertain and erratic preservation of historical evidence in any form, historical linguists have to make a special effort to estimate the relative frequency of the variants that they select to represent the features of the language at each moment in time. Once we know about the A-curve, the effect of frequency should be a part of any qualitative assertions about the status of features and whether a change has occurred. Those who prefer to think about linguistic structure can no longer afford to neglect what we know about the non-linear distribution of feature variants.

The linguistics of speech offers very different answers for the famous five central questions of Weinreich, Labov, and Herzog (1968). The actuation problem, how a change starts, is much less of a problem in the linguistics of speech. Since experimental evidence shows that any linguistic feature exists in many variants at any time, there will always be a pool of variants, each of which may either increase or decrease in frequency. The addition of variants to the pool, linguistic innovation, may occur at any time, and the model easily allows for innovation of variants at low frequencies. Why exactly some variants should increase and others decrease can be attributed to the operation of speech as a complex system, and there is less urgency to explain a situation in which many variants coexist than there is in the structural model that focuses on a single variant at a time. The button-and-thread simulation shows that random connections, left to themselves in a sufficiently interactive network, can form clusters that lead to an S-curve phase transition, subject to control bias. Thus random interactivity is a sufficient cause for change to occur, and indeed the one real certainty about speech and language is that changes are always occurring. Proximity, the degree of interactivity in the network, and the possibility of control bias through perception are the varia-bles that are most likely to condition whether the variants of a feature become more or less frequent.

The transition problem, how a change can become instantiated, is readily accommodated in the linguistics of speech because all of the variants for a feature might be said to be continually changing in frequency, and thus always in a state of transition. At the same time, since variants are always embedded in a set of possible variants of differing frequencies, there is no real transition from one variant form to another, of the kind assumed within a closed system of the sort envisioned by Weinreich, Labov, and Herzog. Thus, the old question about whether linguistic change is sudden or gradual also has its answer, at least within the linguistics of speech. The constraints and embedding problems, how changes might be affected by the rest of the system, are similarly less troubling because multiple variants for a feature exist at any time, and thus speakers must already be accommodating the different competing variants in their speech; again, there is no longer a question of a single variant replacing another in a system, but instead a continual state of multiple variants. Finally, the question of evaluation of variants by speakers, how language users perceive a change, appears in a new light. Now, instead of the problem of how speakers evaluate the incoming and outgoing single variants as a change occurs, we have the situation where speakers always have to evaluate multiple coexisting variants. The experimental evidence shows that multiple variants are simultaneously correlated in complex ways with different geographical and social factors, and with different text types in the textual dimension. Indeed, instead of a problem to be resolved, the availability of multiple variants serves parallel cognitive processing by providing the possibilities for content to fill slots in a large number of cognitive schemas.

Stockwell and Minkova (1988, and elsewhere) have characterized the history of English as a series of mergers and splits (as opposed to chain shifts, as notably presented in Labov 1994), and this issue, too, is addressed by the A-curve in the speech model. Whether vowels are said to be merged, or split, in a phonemic system is separate from the matter of the frequency distribution of phonetic segments. The existence of phonemes is a cognitive and perceptual problem. As already suggested, for any linguistic change, speakers always have to evaluate multiple coexisting variants and not just the incoming and out-going single variants as a change occurs. The notion of merger and split requires that speakers comparatively evaluate the multiple coexisting variants in the frequency distributions of phonetic segments for many different words, in order to make generalizations of distinctiveness, that members of some class of words sound the same and members of another class of words sound different. The speech model tells us that such comparative evaluation may not be easy for speakers, since every word in every word class will have its own frequency distribution of phonetic realizations. Speakers have cognitive reason to maintain and to use both high-frequency and low-frequency variants in schemas, another complication for generalizations about distinctiveness. In the historical record, especially the written historical record where different spellings are our only evidence of pronunciation, these problems are that much worse, even in those (unusual) cases where evidence is plentiful. For the purpose of functional communication, whether synchronic interaction or over an expanse of time, we can be grateful that we have syntax, collocation, and other cues besides comparative evaluation of speech sounds or spellings in order to disambiguate words.

Unlike the structural notion of sudden and mechanical change, the idea of mergers and splits easily admits a relativistic interpretation which accommodates the reality of frequency distributions and can help to account, for example, for a Middle English scribe's decision to spell words one way and not another – and also to account for the common case that the same Middle English scribe can spell the same word in more than one way in the same document. Labov's idea of "near merger" (1994: Part C) begins to consider this relativism, although it never gets to the central consequence of the speech model that there will always be a pool of linguistic variants at different frequencies for speakers to evaluate. To the extent that mergers and splits admit relative frequency as a factor in speakers' comparative evaluation of sounds in word classes, they can be an effective heuristic for addressing the perceptual and psychological generalizations that we know that speakers make.

There is no particular reason in the linguistics of speech to privilege the most common variants as "systematic" or "phonemic," or to relegate less-common variants to the marking of social or personal identity. All of the variants on the A-curve are actually just as relevant for inclusion in the system, and even the higher-frequency variants can bear social or regional associations. It is highly likely that any variant, whether common or rare, will at some subsequent time change in frequency, and that some new variant will rise to the top of the curve for a feature, and that new social and regional associations with variants will form. What is truly stable and systematic about language behavior is the A-curve itself, not any perceived system for arrangement of variants. In order to plot historical change in the linguistics of speech, the A-curve is the pivotal structure on which change can be observed and measured.

Speech and public policy

Observations from the point of view of the linguistics of speech offer a new perspective on linguistic structure and language change that addresses traditional puzzles in those areas. However, the new perspective from speech cannot fix those problems, which still require solutions from within the linguistics of linguistic structure. Similarly, new perspectives from the linguistics of speech cannot by themselves fix the problems regarding language and public policy noted in Chapter 1, such as the swirl of public and academic reactions to the Ebonics debate. Speech perspectives, however, do address the contradictions of those public and academic debates, the evident mess that we have gotten ourselves into.

First of all, correctness and rightness are not merely a matter of public opinion, ill-formed ideas that can be replaced with better ones. They respond to two different aspects of speech perception. The notion of rightness derives from cognitive perception shared by all language users that creates local language schemas, configurational wholes, out of a combination of speech and social information from the speakers near them. The notion of correctness derives from the institutional nature of Standard English, big S. Correctness, then, can indeed be measured as conformity to the relatively small set of rules sanctioned as part of institutional behavior, but not evaluated on the same terms as any other linguistic structure derived from the language behavior of a population. Standard English (just as for the "standard" forms of other languages) has no population on whose language behavior it is continuously based, and its set of rules is thus not governed by the mechanics of perception and production for speech in populations. One need only consider fixed Standard English spelling, as against continuing change of pronunciation habits among various populations of English speakers, to find evidence of its institutional status, and thus resistance to change in the same way that change occurs in populations of speakers. For the same reason, Standard English is mostly restricted to writing, because its institutional set of rules is largely removed from the continuing interactions among speakers in conversations that characterize speech in populations. Lippi-Green (1997) may well label such institutional language as "ideology" since it does not derive directly from language behavior, from interactions in the complex system of speech. Instead, the rules of Standard English are sanctioned partly by tradition and partly by self-appointed guardians of linguistic propriety, who attempt to influence the institutional tradition of Standard English with their own ideas.

Rightness, on the other hand, is cut off from correctness because it does indeed respond to the mechanics of perception and production in the continuing interactions of the complex system. For that reason, rightness has no unity in itself; speech can be *right* for a great many, indeed for a literally infinite number of groups of speakers defined by circumstances and levels of scale. The features of Standard English have no fixed relationship with rightness in general, but only with the language behavior of groups taken one at a time, so that the aggregated speech of a particular group can be recognized as categorically different from Standard English, or compared in probabilistic terms to the set of rules of the institutional structure. Any such comparison will necessarily be limited: because the institutional rule set for Standard English has always been quite small in comparison to the wide range of possible features and their variants, it has always left room for a great deal of social information to be applied to it, to complete it as a configurational whole, and thus to be sanctioned along with the rule set as institutional language behavior. Standard English, then, is a myth as some linguists have asserted, in the sense that it is a structure without a population of speakers, but it is very real as an institutional construct, one composed of more than just language features. By its nature, along with its rule set it incorporates the social, even moral beliefs of the society that accepts it and passes it down as an institution. On the other hand, while there are myriad groups of speakers whose language behavior can be aggregated and perceived as *right* for the group, the idea of the real existence of entities like "Southern English" is largely mythic, since such constructs amount to observational artifacts composed of top-ranked variants and also, as for Standard English, of a great deal of social and other non-speech information.

Both the correctness of Standard English and the rightness perceived for groups of speakers are dominated by Mandelbrot's relativism. For speech, the analyst's point of view has overwhelming importance that arises from the unpredictability of the language behavior of each individual, and from our inability to make fair generalizations either from higher levels of scale to lower ones, or from lower levels of scale to higher ones, according to the individual and ecological fallacies. Speech is not a homogenous whole, and it does not have homologous parts. At the same time, since our cognitive faculties operate in parallel on schemas, language users construct configurational wholes all the time, even though their perception of speech production evidence is necessarily incomplete. What we don't really know about speech becomes compounded with what we don't really know about society and geography, and the amalgam of information, disinformation, and lack of information produces the sort of incoherent cognitive models that Tamasi has described. Under such circumstances, it is no wonder that we do not all share the same ideas about speech, at either smaller or larger scales. We might agree, most of us, that there is such a thing as "Southern English," and yet disagree wildly about where it is, what features might compose it, and what opinions we might have about it.

It is no wonder that North American professional linguists interested in structure have attempted, as in the Ebonics affair, to assert their own more systematic understanding as a replacement for individual and collective public incoherence about correctness and rightness in language. And yet, as indicated earlier in this chapter, the linguistics of linguistic structure might best be applied to single solutions for the speech model, to the speech of particular groups and particular texts. Linguistic structure is as much subject to scaling problems in analysis, to Mandelbrot's relativism, as are the perceptions of the public. Even if what the linguistics of linguistic structure had to offer was not limited in these ways, it could never be a replacement for popular notions. Correctness and rightness have their origins in perceptual patterns that cannot just be dismissed. Indeed, the basic idea of the linguistics of linguistic structure, that there are well-bounded languages whose structure yields linguistic value, itself originates from the same mode of cognitive processing. To the extent that institutional Standard English sometimes influences or even becomes the prototype for their linguistic structures, professional linguists may be guilty of blurring the division that does exist between institutional language and speech patterns derived from the flow of interactions in human populations. On the other hand, linguists can usefully bring their systematic attention to the question of rightness, by examining the speech of a particular population in order to show how it differs from the institutional standard by comparison of their respective prototypic structures. Whether it is appropriate, however, for the *right* language to be used to teach the institutional standard, the question that motivated the Oakland School Board, is not a linguistic but a political question.

The viewpoint of the linguistics of speech suggests that social and political factors do not intrude on speech – they were always there as part of the perceptual process and in turn as part of the speech circuit. The success of the Afrocentrists in the Ebonics affair came about because they promoted the sociopolitical ideas that are built right in for both the correctness and rightness of language. Popular notions of language already include social and political ideas (whether well-founded or biased in different ways) that serve to make up for incomplete and discontinuous information from experience with speech, and no approach to public policy regarding language can afford to neglect that fact. Attempts to take the social mores and politics out of language policy are doomed to fail, because members of the public will put them right back in, as happened in both Internet jokes and Senate hearings about Ebonics. The existence of general consensus about language among the public – even while speakers hold and enact contradictory ideas about Standard English and the speech of particular groups – should tell us that correctness and rightness respond to important constituents of our linguistic environment. As students of language, whether interested in speech or structure, we will do well to respect what the public knows and to work with it as best we can. Interactions between professional linguists and the public are bound to be less a matter of public reception of science, and more a matter of those with special, systematic knowledge of speech and language trying to shape the political and social debate in which language is already by necessity embroiled.

Current events are rife with examples of conflict between belief systems, including the conflict between science (considered as a set of beliefs about observation of things and events in the natural world and use of the observations to control our environment) and religion (any of many alternate sets of beliefs about the status and control of things and events), or between different religions. Attempts by scientists like Richard Dawkins (as in Dawkins 2006) to use the methods of science to attack religion, as when he analyzes the "roots of religion" with Darwinian principles (2006: 161–208), or the "roots of morality" with Darwinian principles (2006: 209–234), can influence nobody except those who already accept science's set of beliefs and reject those of religion. Dawkins would be preaching to the choir, if science had one. Alternatively, attempts by conservative religious groups in America to have "creationism" or "intelligent design" inserted into school science curricula, on grounds that they offer theories on a par with Darwinism, were similarly preaching to their choirs and were thus doomed to failure – and have been outlawed in America by the courts.

Science and religion are not mutually exclusive beliefs for all of their adherents. Many scientists are religious, and many religious people also believe in science; such people have found ways to accommodate their two belief systems.[6] For others, however, the sets of beliefs are indeed mutually exclusive, and it is literally the case that no accommodation is possible between such polarized beliefs. The public reception of science is less automatic than some linguists have believed.

We are luckier than that with speech and language. Correctness, the ideology of Standard English, is something in which people believe, even to the extent that they associate correctness with morality and citizenship. It is unlikely that linguists would ever be able to substitute for correctness another set of beliefs ("authentic understanding"), whether beliefs about some linguistic structure or about speech. But most people also believe implicitly in the rightness of language for particular groups of people, as a result of our perception of speech around us, and most linguists can also value the rightness of language in use for the population that uses it, both those interested in structure (for instance those in the endangered languages movement) and those interested in speech. Unlike the debate between science and religion, for public discussions of speech and language we can begin with the common ground of rightness. Any sense of rightness, however, as we have seen, will not be based exclusively on linguistic information but will be incomplete and compounded with other sorts of information. Thus we must also begin with negotiation, in order to make sure that linguists and members of the public are discussing the speech of the same groups of people, and that we understand how much our sense of rightness depends on speech and how much it depends on social information or bare assumptions. We can then proceed to consider how the right language might relate to correctness, essentially a political question, since it comes down in the end to the issue of how particular groups of people are served by cultural institutions, and how institutions might better be managed to serve the people.

We also know that some more extreme members of the public will place their exclusive belief in correctness, just as some linguists will restrain their belief just to their own authentic understanding. They will try to polarize questions of speech and language, just as some scientists and true believers in religion have tried to polarize debate, as when Dawkins has attacked religion with science, and

---

[6] Part of Dawkins' (2006) argument, that God is the reification of an abstract idea, recapitulates the problem that Firth saw in Saussure (following Durkheim) that *langue* was actually the reification of an abstract idea. Both Firth and Dawkins propose that real-world problems result from such reification. The perceptual model of the linguistics of speech, however, suggests why it is plausible for linguists interested in structure to construct a prototype out of the distributional facts of language production, and thus reification is not the problem here that Dawkins and Firth thought it to be. This book stands with the pluralists who can accommodate more than one set of beliefs.

creationists have attacked science curricula in schools with faith-based alternative theories. Others will try to insert their own political views into discussions of language behavior, as the Afrocentrists did in the Ebonics affair, so that the politics come to overwhelm discussion of speech and language. These are all things to resist, because they inevitably carry us away from our common ground. Discussions of speech and public policy are best carried out in local communities by involving the speakers themselves, because they possess the common ground, the *right* knowledge of local speech, that can make their negotiations both realistic and effective. Discussions of speech and public policy for larger populations can at best only provide frameworks under which the disparate language behavior of particular local groups can be accommodated. We can agree, for instance, that we are committed to an institutional Standard English in national policy, without demanding that all groups of speakers must address it in the same way, and without preventing local groups from addressing their local situations in what they consider to be the most effective manner (as happened, for instance, when California restricted bilingual education; see Wiley 2004, Fillmore 2004). There is irony in the fact that the views of the relatively small numbers of people with exclusive beliefs may be best suited to the creation of arguments for national speech and language policy (such as language academies, or promotion of national standardized tests, or the English Only movement in America) because such extreme views are already remote from the common ground of local speakers. There is further irony in that less-extreme and less-exclusive voters often respond to such arguments, as occurred in California as part of the backdrop to the Ebonics affair (see Wiley 2004), even when the broad public policies that result do not recognize or enhance the voters' local situations. The viewpoint from the linguistics of speech suggests that we resist such global practices, in favor of local negotiation about the appropriate relation of rightness and correctness in local speech and language that, when applied in many localities, will actually serve the majority of speakers.

If the Oakland School Board could have retained its focus on local issues of language and speech and acted just in the local schools, the rest of us would not have heard of Ebonics and Oakland students would have been better served. Of course the board members did not have that choice: they were public servants, their actions were a matter of public record, and they were subject to state policies in California. At the same time that linguists and members of the public need to discuss local speech and language issues, they also need to join the wider debate. The public interest demands that, on issues of speech and language, we do not abandon the debate to extreme and exclusive points of view, but instead that we assert local interests. As messy as it was, the Oakland Ebonics affair points the best way forward for speech and public policy – assertion of the importance of solving speech and language problems locally by means of local knowledge. In future, as other local boards inevitably have to deal with local speech and language issues, we can hope that the equally inevitable social and political discussions will better promote doing the *right* thing for local speakers.

A last thought

Dostoyevsky wrote in *Notes from the Underground* that "Man has such a predilection for systems and abstract deductions that he is willing to distort the truth intentionally, he is ready to deny the evidence of his senses in order to justify his logic." This is just the sort of complaint that linguists have sometimes made against their colleagues. The problem of relativism in how we experience speech makes it possible, indeed commonplace, for each of us to wonder how someone could ever have arrived at their formulation for how language works. Still, Dostoyevsky notwithstanding, we do have reason from our perception of the interactions of speech, incomplete and imperfect as our perceptions may be, to accept the existence of patterns. The linguistics of speech addresses how we take the evidence of our senses and construct systematic descriptions of it. The essential findings in the linguistics of speech might be cast as a metaphor adapted from the language of Le Page and Tabouret-Keller (1985: 232), that the patterns we perceive in speech are emergent eddies and whirlpools that continually form, reform, and dissolve in the flow of interactions in speech; none of these eddies consume the entirety of the flow, and all of them are contingent upon local conditions in the flow; different observers, no two the same, will attend to different eddies, and no observer can see or record, much less constrain, them all.

The principles of the linguistics of speech are not a replacement for the principles of the linguistics of linguistic structure, whether as practiced in North America, or in England, or in other places. The study of linguistic structure has undoubted value, particularly for the study of what Saussure called "linguistic value," which can be identified and studied in no other way. At the same time, the regularities that we can observe in language behavior also have value. Indeed, the special value of the linguistics of speech is to suggest how to connect language in use with structures to be made from it, and thereby to help us to improve any systems and abstract deductions we wish to make.

The best way forward will recognize both of Saussure's two paths, which diverge as surely as Robert Frost's two roads in his New England yellow wood. The linguist, as Frost observes in a poetic phrase that echoes Saussure's opinion, cannot travel both and be one traveler. Saussure lacked the means to follow both of the paths that he described, but we can no longer afford just to ignore one of the roads before us, now that we have effective tools for recording, management, and quantitative analysis of speech data. We must choose the path with better claim for the task at hand.

References

Aarts, Jan. 1991. Intuition-based and Observation-based Grammars. In K. Aijmer and B. Altenberg, eds, *English Corpus Linguistics* (London: Longman), 144–62.

Agha, Asif. 2007. *Language and Social Relations*. Cambridge: Cambridge University Press.

Andor, József. 2004. The Master and His Performance: An Interview with Noam Chomsky. *Intercultural Pragmatics* 1: 93–112.

Antieau, Lamont. 2006. A Distributional Analysis of Rural Colorado English. Diss., University of Georgia.

Arthur, W. Brian. 1999. Complexity and the Economy. *Science* 284.5411 (April 2): 107–109.

Baayen, Harald. 2001. *Word Frequency Distributions*. Text, Speech and Language Technology 18. Dordrecht: Kluwer.

Bailey, Richard W. 1991. *Images of English: A Cultural History of English*. Ann Arbor: University of Michigan Press.

1996. *Nineteenth-Century English*. Ann Arbor: University of Michigan Press.

Baugh, John. 2000. *Beyond Ebonics: Linguistic Pride and Racial Prejudice*. New York: Oxford University Press.

2005. Conveniently Black: Self-Delusion and the Racial Exploitation of African America. *Du Bois Review* 2: 113–26.

Biber, Douglas. 1988. *Variation across Speech and Writing*. Cambridge: Cambridge University Press.

1989. A Typology of English Texts. *Linguistics* 27: 3–43.

1993. Representativeness in Corpus Design. *Literary and Linguistic Computing* 8: 243–57.

Biber, Douglas, Susan Conrad, and Randi Reppen. 1998. *Corpus Linguistics*. Cambridge: Cambridge University Press.

Bloor, Thomas, and Meriel Bloor. 2004. *The Functional Analysis of English*. 2nd ed. London: Arnold.

Burkette, Allison. 2001. The Story of Chester Drawers. *American Speech* 76: 139–57.

Butters, Ronald. 2001. Chance as Cause of Language Variation and Change. *Journal of English Linguistics* 29: 201–213.

Bybee, Joan. 2001. *Phonology and Language Use*. Cambridge: Cambridge University Press.

2007. *Frequency of Use and the Organization of Language*. Oxford: Oxford University Press.

Bybee, Joan, and Paul Hopper, eds. 2001. *Frequency and the Emergence of Linguistic Structure*. Amsterdam: John Benjamins.

Chambers, J. K. 2003. *Sociolinguistic Theory*. 2nd ed. Oxford: Blackwell.

Chambers, J. K., and Peter Trudgill. 1998. *Dialectology*. 2nd ed. Oxford: Blackwell.

Childs, Rebecca. 2005. Investigating the Local Construction of Identity: Sociophonetic Variation in Smoky Mountain African American Women's Speech. Diss., University of Georgia.

Chomsky, Noam. 1957. *Syntactic Structures*. The Hague: Mouton.

1959. Review of B. F. Skinner, *Verbal Behavior, Language* 35: 26–58.

1961. On the Notion "Rule of Grammar." In Roman Jakobson, ed., *Structure of Language and Its Mathematical Aspects*, Proceedings of Symposia in Applied Mathematics 12 (Providence: American Mathematical Society), 6–24.

1965. *Aspects of the Theory of Syntax*. Cambridge: MIT Press.

1995. *The Minimalist Program*. Cambridge: MIT Press.

Cowie, A. P. 1998. *Phraseology: Theory, Analysis, and Applications*. Oxford: Oxford University Press.

Crystal, David. 2003. *English as a Global Language*. 2nd ed. Cambridge: Cambridge University Press.

2007. *The Fight for English: How Language Pundits Ate, Shot, and Left*. Oxford: Oxford University Press.

D'Andrade, Roy. 1995. *The Development of Cognitive Anthropology*. Cambridge: Cambridge University Press.

Davis, Lawrence M. 1990. *Statistics in Dialectology*. Tuscaloosa: University of Alabama Press.

Dawkins, Richard. 2006. *The God Delusion*. New York: Houghton Mifflin.

Dinneen, Francis J. 1967. *An Introduction to General Linguistics*. Washington: Georgetown University Press.

Duranti, Alessandro. 1997. *Linguistic Anthropology*. Cambridge: Cambridge University Press.

2001. *Linguistic Anthropology: A Reader*. Oxford: Blackwell.

2004. *A Companion to Linguistic Anthropology: A Reader*. Oxford: Blackwell.

Dyson, Freeman. 1978. Characterizing Irregularity. *Science* 200.4342 (May 12): 677–78.

Eckert, Penelope. 1990. The Whole Woman: Sex and Gender Differences in Variation. *Language Variation and Change* 1: 245–67.

2000. *Linguistic Variation as Social Practice*. Oxford: Blackwell.

Eckert, Penelope, and Sally McConnell-Ginet. 2003. *Language and Gender*. Cambridge: Cambridge University Press.

Eco, Umberto. 1998. *Serendipities: Language and Lunacy*. Trans. by W. Weaver. San Diego: Harcourt Brace.

Edelman, Gerald. 1987. *Neural Darwinism: The Theory of Neuronal Group Selection*. New York: Basic Books.

Evans, Vyvyan, and Melanie Green. 2006. *Cognitive Linguistics: An Introduction*. London: Lawrence Erlbaum.

Evert, Stefan. 2004. A Simple LNRE Model for Random Character Sequences. In C. Purnelle, C. Fairon, and A. Dister, eds, *Proceedings of the 7èmes Journées Internationales d'Analyse Statistique des Données Textuelles* (Louvain-la-Neuve, Belgium), 411–22.

Fillmore, Lily Wong. 2004. Language in Education. In Edward Finegan and John Rickford, eds, *Language in the USA: Themes for the Twenty-first Century* (Cambridge: Cambridge University Press), 339–60.

Firth, J. R. 1935. The Technique of Semantics. *Transactions of the Philological Society*, 36–72. Reprinted in Firth 1957: 7–33.

1957. *Papers in Linguistics 1934–1951*. London: Oxford University Press.

Francis, W. Nelson. 1983. *Dialectology: An Introduction*. London: Longman.

Francis, W. Nelson, and Henry Kucera. 1999. *Brown Corpus Manual*. Rev. ed., 1979. In ICAME 1999.

Fromkin, Victoria, *et al*. 2007. *An Introduction to Language*. 8th ed. Florence, KY: Wordsworth.

Frost, Robert. 1916. *Mountain Interval*. New York: Henry Holt.

Gallagher, Richard, and Tim Appenzeller. 1999. Beyond Reductionism: Complex Systems, Introduction. *Science* 284.5411 (April 2): 79–109.

Gilliéron, Jules. 1902–10. *Atlas linguistique de France*. Paris: Champion.

Gilliéron, Jules, and J. Mongin. 1905. *Scier dans la Gaule romance*. Paris: Champion.

Goebl, Hans. 1982. *Dialektometrie*. Vienna: Austrian Academy of Science.

1990. Methodische und Wissenschaftgeschichtliche Bemerkungen zum Diskussionskomplex "Unita Ladina." *Ladinia* 14: 219–57.

2003. Graziadio Isaia Ascoli, Carlo Battisti e il ladino. In A. Trampus and U. Kindl, eds, *I Linguaggi e la Storia* (Bologna: Soc. ed. il Mulino), 273–98.

Goldenfeld, Nigel, and Leo Kadanoff. 1999. Simple Lessons from Complexity. *Science* 284.5411 (April 2): 87–89.

Gordon, Elizabeth. 1998. The Origins of New Zealand Speech. *English World-Wide* 19: 61–85.

Gordon, Elizabeth, and Peter Trudgill. 1999. Embryonic Variants in New Zealand English. *English World-Wide* 20: 111–24.

Gould, Peter, and Rodney White. 1986. *Mental Maps*. 2nd ed. London: Routledge.

Graddol, David, Dick Leith, and Joan Swann. 1996. *English: History, Diversity, and Change*. London: The Open University, Routledge.

Günther, R., L. Levitin, B. Schapiro, and P. Wagner. 1996. Zipf's Law and the Effect of Ranking on Probability Distributions. *International Journal of Theoretical Physics* 35: 395–417.

Halliday, M. A. K. 1985. *An Introduction to Functional Grammar*. London: Arnold.

1991. Corpus Studies and Probabilistic Grammar. In K. Aijmer and B. Altenberg, eds, *English Corpus Linguistics* (London: Longman), 30–43.

Halliday, M. A. K., and R. Hasan. 1976. *Cohesion in English*. London: Longman.

1989. *Language, Context and Text: Aspects of Language in a Social-Semiotic Perspective*. Oxford: Oxford University Press.

Halliday, M. A. K., and C. Matthiessen. 2004. *An Introduction to Functional Grammar*. 3rd ed. London: Arnold.

Hamilton-Brehm, Anne Marie. 2003. A Foundational Study of El Paso English. Diss., University of Georgia.

Harris, Roy. 1987. *Reading Saussure: A Critical Commentary on the Cours De Linguistique Generale*. LaSalle, IL: Open Court.

2002. *Saussure and his Interpreters*. New York: New York University Press.

Harris, Roy, and Talbot Taylor. 1989. *Landmarks In Linguistic Thought: Volume I: The Western Tradition From Socrates To Saussure*. London: Routledge.

Hedderson, John. 1987. *SPSS X Made Simple*. Belmont, CA: Wadsworth.

Heeringa, W., and J. Nerbonne. 2001. Dialect Areas and Dialect Continua. *Language Variation and Change* 13: 375–400.

Hinneberg, Alexander, Heikki Mannila, Samuli Kaislaniemi, Terttu Nevalainen, and Helena Raumolin-Brunberg. 2007. How to Handle Small Samples: Bootstrap and Bayesian Methods in the Analysis of Linguistic Change. *Literary and Linguistic Computing* 22: 137–50.

Hoey, Michael. 2005. *Lexical Priming: A New Theory of Words and Language*. London: Routledge.

Honey, John. 1989. *Does Accent Matter?* London: Faber and Faber.

Hoover, Sandra. 2001. Lexical Variation and Change in Farming Words: 1970–2001. MA thesis, University of Georgia.

Hopper, Paul. 1987. Emergent Grammar. *Berkeley Linguistics Society* 13: 139–57.

Horvath, B., and R. Horvath. 2001. A Multilocality Study of a Sound Change in Progress: The Case of /l/ Vocalization in New Zealand and Australian English. *Language Variation and Change* 13: 37–58.

    2003. A Closer Look at the Constraint Hierarchy: Order, Contrast, and Geographical Scale. *Language Variation and Change* 15: 143–70.

Hudson, Richard. 1994. About 37% of Word Tokens are Nouns. *Language* 70: 331–39.

ICAME. 1999. *ICAME Corpus Collection on CD-ROM*. Version 2. Bergen: International Computer Archive of Modern and Medieval English, Avdeling for kultur, språk og informasjonsteknologi (Aksis).

Jauss, Hans Robert. 1977. *Alterität und Modernität der mittelalterlichen Literatur*. Munich: Wilhelm Fink.

    1979. The Alterity and Modernity of Medieval Literature. *New Literary History* 10: 181–229.

    1982. *Toward an Aesthetic of Reception*. Trans. by Timothy Bahti. Minneapolis: University of Minnesota Press.

Johnson, Ellen. 1996. *Lexical Change and Variation in the Southeastern United States 1930–1990*. Tuscaloosa: University of Alabama Press.

Jolles, André. 1930/1972. *Einfache Formen*. Tübingen: Max Niemeyer. Translated into French by Antoine Buguet as *Formes simples* (Paris: Seuil, 1972).

Jurafsky, Daniel, and James Martin. 2000. *Speech and Language Processing: An Introduction to Natural Language Processing, Computational Linguistics, and Speech Recognition*. Upper Saddle River, NJ: Prentice Hall.

Kauffman, Stuart. 1995. *At Home in the Universe: The Search for the Laws of Self-Organization and Complexity*. New York: Oxford University Press.

Keller, Rudi. 1994. *On Language Change: The Invisible Hand in Language*. Trans. by B. Neerlich. London: Routledge.

Kennedy, Graeme. 1998. *An Introduction to Corpus Linguistics*. London: Longman.

Kerswill, Paul. 1996. Milton Keynes and Dialect Levelling in South-eastern British English. In D. Graddol, J. Swann, and D. Leith, eds, *English: History, Diversity and Change* (London: Routledge), 292–300.

Kerswill, Paul, and Ann Williams. 2000. Creating a New Town Koine: Children and Language Change in Milton Keynes. *Language in Society* 29: 65–115.

Keyser, Samuel K. 1963. Review of Kurath and McDavid 1961. *Language* 39: 303–16.
Knoop, Ulrich, Wolfgang Putschke, and Herbert Ernst Wiegand. 1982. Die Marburger Schule: Entstehung und frühe Entwicklung der Dialektgeographie. In Werner Besch *et al.*, eds, *Dialektologie. Ein Handbuch zur deutschen und allgemeinen Dialektforschung*, Vol. 1 (Berlin: de Gruyter), 38–92.
Kortmann, Bernd. 1997. *Adverbial Subordination*. Berlin: Mouton de Gruyter.
Kretzschmar, William A., Jr. 1992a. Dialects: Traditions in Culture and Innovations in Analysis. In *Papers from the Fifteenth Annual Meeting of the Atlantic Provinces Linguistic Association*, edited by W. J. Davey and Bernard LeVert (Sydney, NS: UCCB, SSHRC), 38–63.
    1992b. Isoglosses and Predictive Modeling. *American Speech* 67: 227–49. [Reprinted in M. Linn, ed., *Handbook of Dialects and Language Variation* (Orlando: Academic Press, 1999), 151–72.]
    1992c. Caxton's Sense of History. *JEGP* 91: 510–28.
    1995. Dialectology and Sociolinguistics: Same Coin, Different Currency. *Language Sciences* 17: 271–82.
    1996a. Quantitative Areal Analysis of Dialect Features. *Language Variation and Change* 8: 13–39.
    1996b. Review of William Labov, *Principles of Linguistic Change*, Vol. 1. *American Speech* 71: 198–205.
    ed. 1998a. Ebonics. Special issue, *Journal of English Linguistics* 26.2.
    1998b. Analytical Procedure and Three Technical Types of Dialect. In M. Montgomery and T. Nunnally, eds, *From the Gulf States and Beyond: The Legacy of Lee Pederson and LAGS* (Tuscaloosa: University of Alabama Press), 167–85.
    1999. Preface. In Dennis Preston, ed., *Handbook of Perceptual Dialectology*, Vol. 1 (Amsterdam: John Benjamins), xvii–xviii.
    2002a. Dialectology and the History of the English Language. In Donka Minkova and Robert Stockwell, eds, *Studies in the History of English: A Millennial Perspective* (Berlin: Mouton de Gruyter), 79–108.
    2002b. American English: Melting Pot or Mixing Bowl? In K. Lenz and R. Möhlig, eds, *Of Dyuersitie & Chaunge of Langage: Essays presented to Manfred Görlach* (Heidelberg: C. Winter), 224–39.
    2003. Mapping Southern English. *American Speech* 78: 130–49.
    2005. Review of William Labov, *Principles of Linguistic Change*, Vol. 2. *American Speech* 80: 321–30.
    2006a. Review of Geoffrey Sampson, *Empirical Linguistics*. *Journal of English Linguistics* 34: 161–65.
    2006b. Art and Science in Computational Dialectology. *Literary and Linguistic Computing* 21: 399–410.
    2008a. Public and Academic Understandings about Language: The Intellectual History of Ebonics. *English World-Wide* 29: 70–95.
    2008b. The Beholder's Eye: Using Self-Organizing Maps to Understand American Dialects. In Anne Curzan and Michael Adams, eds, *Contours of English* (Ann Arbor: University of Michigan Press).
Kretzschmar, William A., Jr., J. Anderson, J. Beal, K. Corrigan, L. Opas-Hänninen, and B. Plichta. 2006. Collaboration on Corpora for Regional and Social Analysis. *Journal of English Linguistics* 34: 172–205.

Kretzschmar, William A., Jr., and Rodolpho Celis. 1998. Modeling Language Variation. In Alan Thomas, ed., *Proceedings of the Ninth International Conference on Methods in Dialectology* (Bangor: Dept. of Linguistics, University of North Wales), 14–21.

Kretzschmar, William A., Jr., Clayton Darwin, Cati Brown, Donald Rubin, and Douglas Biber. 2004. Looking for the Smoking Gun: Principled Sampling in Creating the Tobacco Industry Document Corpus. *Journal of English Linguistics* 32: 31–47.

Kretzschmar, William A, Jr., and Ellen Johnson. 1993. Using Linguistic Atlas Databases for Phonetic Analysis. Paper presented at ACH/ALLC, Washington.

Kretzschmar, William A., Jr., and Sonja Lanehart. 2005. Introduction to the Atlanta Survey. Paper presented at ADS/LSA, Oakland.

Kretzschmar, William A., Jr., Sonja Lanehart, Betsy Barry, Iyabo Osiapem, and MiRan Kim. 2004. Atlanta in Black and White: A New Random Sample of Urban Speech. Paper presented at NWAVE 2004, Ann Arbor.

Kretzschmar, William A., Jr., Virginia G. McDavid, Theodore K. Lerud, and Ellen Johnson. 1993. *Handbook of the Linguistic Atlas of the Middle and South Atlantic States*. Chicago: University of Chicago Press.

Kretzschmar, William A., Jr., and Charles Meyer. 1997. Statistical Measurement Within and Across Corpora. Paper presented at ICAME, Chester.

Kretzschmar, William A., Jr., Charles Meyer, and Dominique Ingegneri. 1999. Uses of Inferential Statistics in Corpus Studies. In Magnus Ljung, ed., *Corpus-based Studies in English* (Amsterdam: Rodopi), 167–77.

Kretzschmar, William A., Jr., and Edgar Schneider. 1996. *Introduction to Quantitative Analysis of Linguistic Survey Data: An Atlas by the Numbers*. Thousand Oaks, CA: Sage Publications.

Kretzschmar, William A., Jr., and Susan Tamasi. 2003. Distributional Foundations for a Theory of Language Change. *World Englishes* 22: 377–401.

Kroch, Anthony. 1989. Reflexes of Grammar in Patterns of Language Change. *Language Variation and Change* 1: 199–244.

Krug, Manfred. 1998. String Frequency: A Motivating Factor in Coalescence, Language Processing, and Linguistic Change. *Journal of English Linguistics* 26: 286–320.

2001. Frequency, Iconicity, Categorization: Evidence from Emerging Modals. In Bybee and Hopper 2001, 309–335.

Kuhl, Joseph. 2003. The Idiolect, Chaos and Language Custom Far from Equilibrium: Conversations in Morocco. Diss., University of Georgia.

Kurath, Hans. 1939. *Handbook of the Linguistic Geography of New England*. Providence: Brown University, for ACLS. [2nd ed., rev., New York: AMS Press, 1973.]

1939–43. *Linguistic Atlas of New England*. 3 vols. in 6. Providence: Brown University, for ACLS.

1949. *A Word Geography of the Eastern United States*. Ann Arbor: University of Michigan Press.

1972. *Studies in Area Linguistics*. Bloomington: Indiana University Press.

Kurath, Hans, and Raven I. McDavid, Jr. 1961. *The Pronunciation of English in the Atlantic States*. Ann Arbor: University of Michigan Press. [Rpt. 1982, Tuscaloosa: University of Alabama Press.]

Labov, William. 1963. The Social Motivation of a Sound Change. *Word* 19: 273–307.

1972. The Logic of Nonstandard English. In *Language in the Inner City* (Philadelphia: University of Pennsylvania Press), 201–40.

1981. Resolving the Neogrammarian Controversy. *Language* 57: 267–309.

1991. The Three Dialects of English. In P. Eckert, ed., *New Ways of Analyzing Sound Change* (Orlando: Academic Press), 1–44.

1994. *Principles of Linguistic Change: Internal Factors.* Language in Society, 20. Oxford: Basil Blackwell.

2001. *Principles of Linguistic Change: Socal Factors.* Language in Society, 29. Oxford: Basil Blackwell.

Labov, William, Charles Boberg, and Sherry Ash. 2006. *Atlas of North American English: Phonetics, Phonology and Sound Change.* Berlin: Mouton de Gruyter.

Lass, Roger. 1990. How to Do Things with Junk: Exaptation in Language Evolution. *Journal of Linguistics* 26: 79–102.

Lee, Jay, and William A. Kretzschmar, Jr. 1993. Spatial Analysis of Linguistic Data with GIS Functions. *International Journal of Geographical Information Systems* 7: 541–60.

Le Page, Robert, and Andree Tabouret-Keller. 1985. *Acts of Identity.* Cambridge: Cambridge University Press.

Li, W. 1992. Random Texts Exhibit Zipf's-Law-like Word Frequency Distributions. *IEEE Transactions on Information Theory* 38: 1842–45.

Light, Deanna, and William A. Kretzschmar, Jr. 1996. Mapping with Numbers. *Journal of English Linguistics* 24: 343–57.

Lindblom, Björn, Peter MacNeilage, and Michael Studdert-Kennedy. 1984. Self-Organizing Processes and the Explanation of Phonological Universals. In Brian Butterworth, Bernard Comrie, and Östen Dahl, eds, *Explanations for Language Universals* (New York: Mouton), 181–203.

Lippi-Green, Rosina. 1997. *English with an Accent; Language, Ideology, and Discrimination in the United States.* London: Routledge.

Lorenz, Edward. 1972. Predictability: Does the Flap of a Butterfly's Wings in Brazil Set Off a Tornado in Texas? Paper delivered at the American Association for the Advancement of Science, Washington.

Malinowski, Bronislaw. 1923. The Problem of Meaning in Primitive Languages. In Ogden and Richards 1923, 296–336.

Mandelbrot, Benoit. 1951. Adaptation d'un message à la ligne de transmission. I & II. *Comptes Rendus* (Paris) 232: 1638–1640, 2003–2005.

1961. On the Theory of Word Frequencies and on Related Markovian Models of Discourse. In Roman Jakobson, ed., *Structure of Language and Its Mathematical Aspects*, Proceedings of Symposia in Applied Mathematics 12 (Providence: American Mathematical Society), 190–219.

1968. Information Theory and Psycholinguistics. In R. C. Oldfield and J. C. Marshall, eds, *Language: Selected Readings* (Harmondsworth: Penguin), 263–75.

1977. *Fractals: Form, Chance, and Dimension.* San Francisco: Freeman.

1982. *The Fractal Geometry of Nature.* San Francisco: Freeman.

Manly, John, and Edith Rickert. 1940. *The Text of the Canterbury Tales.* 8 vols. Chicago: University of Chicago Press.

Manning, C., and H. Schütze. 1999. *Foundations of Statistical Natural Language Processing.* Boston: MIT Press.

McDavid, Raven I., Jr., and Virginia McDavid. 1951. The Relationship of American Negroes to the Speech of Whites. *American Speech* 26: 3–17. Reprinted in

W. Kretzschmar *et al.*, eds, *Dialects in Culture: Essays in General Dialectology by Raven I. McDavid, Jr.* (University, AL: University of Alabama Press, 1979), 43–51.

McMurray, Bob. 2007. Defusing the Childhood Vocabulary Explosion. *Science* 317.5838 (August 3): 361.

Mehl, Matthias, Simine Vazire, Nairan Ramirez-Esparza, Richard Slatcher, and James Pennebaker. 2007. Are Women Really More Talkative than Men? *Science* 317.5834 (July 6): 82.

Meyer, Charles. 1996. Coordinate Structures in the British and American Components of the International Corpus of English. *World Englishes* 15: 29–41.

Millar, Sharon. 1997. British Educational Policy, Sociolinguistics, and Accent. *Journal of English Linguistics* 25: 107–121.

Miller, John, and Scott Page. 2007. *Complex Adaptive Systems: An Introduction to Computational Models of Social Life.* Princeton: Princeton University Press.

Milroy, James. 1992. *Linguistic Variation and Change.* Oxford: Blackwell.

Milroy, James, and Lesley Milroy. 1999. *Authority in Language: Investigating Standard English.* 3rd ed. London: Routledge.

Milroy, Lesley. 1980. *Language and Social Networks.* Oxford: Blackwell.

Mitzka, Walther. 1943. *Deutsche Mundarten.* Heidelberg: Carl Winter.

Moore, Samuel, and Albert Marckwardt. 1951. *Historical Outlines of English Sounds and Inflections.* Ann Arbor: George Wahr.

Moore, Samuel, Sanford Meech, and Harold Whitehall. 1935. Middle English Dialect Characteristics and Dialect Boundaires. *(University of Michigan) Essays and Studies in English and Comparative Literature* 13: 1–60.

Mufwene, Salikoko. 2001. *The Ecology of Language Evolution.* Cambridge: Cambridge University Press.

2006. Language Evolution: The Population Genetics Way. *Marges linguistiques* 11: 243–60.

2008. *Language Evolution: Contact, Competition, and Change.* London: Continuum Press.

Nerbonne, J., and W. Heeringa. 2001. Computational Comparison and Classification of Dialects. *Dialectologia et Geolinguistica* 9: 69–83.

2007. Geographic Distributions of Linguistic Variation Reflect Dynamics of Differentiation. In Sam Featherston and Wolfgang Sternefeld, eds, *Roots: Linguistics in Search of its Evidential Base.* Berlin: Mouton De Gruyter, 267–298.

Newmeyer, Frederick J. 1996. *Generative Linguistics: A Historical Perspective.* London: Routledge.

Nicolis, G., and I. Prigogine. 1977. *Self-Organization in Non-equilibrium Systems.* New York: Wiley.

Oakes, Michael P. 1998. *Statistics for Corpus Linguistics.* Edinburgh: Edinburgh University Press.

Ogden, C. K., and I. A. Richards. 1923. *The Meaning of Meaning.* London: Routledge and Kegan Paul.

Orton, Harold, *et al.* 1962–71. *Survey of English Dialects.* Intro. and 4 vols. in 3 pts. Leeds: Arnold.

Orton, Harold, Stewart Sanderson, and John Widdowson. 1978. *The Linguistic Atlas of England.* London: Croom Helm.

Paltridge, Brian. 2002. Thesis and Dissertation Writing: An Examination of Published Advice and Actual Practice. *English for Specific Purposes* 21: 125–43.

Pederson, Lee. 1990. *Linguistic Atlas of the Gulf States: Volume 3: Technical Index.* Athens: University of Georgia Press.

Poplack, Shana. 1993. Variation Theory and Language Contact: Concepts, Methods and Data. In Dennis Preston, ed., *American Dialect Research* (Amsterdam: John Benjamins), 251–86.

Preston, Dennis. 1989. *Perceptual Dialectology.* Dordrecht: Foris.

  1997. The South: The Touchstone. In C. Bernstein, T. Nunnally, and R. Sabino, eds, *Language Variety in the South Revisited* (Tuscaloosa: University of Alabama Press), 311–51.

  1999. *Handbook of Perceptual Dialectology.* Amsterdam: John Benjamins.

Pulvermüller, Friedemann. 2003. *The Neuroscience of Language: On Brain Circuits of Words and Serial Order.* Cambridge: Cambridge University Press.

Pustet, Regina. 2004. Zipf and his Heirs. *Language Sciences* 26: 1–25.

Pyles, Thomas. 1952. *Words and Ways of American English.* New York: Random House.

Quirk, Randolph, Sidney Greenbaum, Geoffry Leech, and Jan Svartvik. 1985. *A Comprehensive Grammar of the English Language.* London: Addison Wesley.

Rapoport, Anatol. 1982. Zipf's Law Revisited. In H. Guiter, ed., *Studies on Zipf's Law* (Bochum: Brockmeyer), 1–28.

Renouf, Antoinette, and John Sinclair. 1991. Collocational Frameworks in English. In K. Aijmer and B. Altenberg, eds, *English Corpus Linguistics* (London: Longman), 128–43.

Rickford, John R., and Russell J. Rickford. 2000. *Spoken Soul: The Story of Black English.* New York: Wiley.

Rind, D. 1999. Complexity and Climate. *Science* 284.5411 (April 2): 105–107.

Robins, R. H. 1979. *A Short History of Linguistics.* 2nd ed. London: Longman.

Russell, J. C. 1972. Population in Europe 500–1500. In Carlo Cipolla, ed., *The Fontana Economic History of Europe: The Middle Ages* (London: Collins/Fontana), 25–70.

Sampson, Geoffrey. 2002. *Empirical Linguistics.* London: Continuum.

Sanders, Carol, ed. 2004. *The Cambridge Companion to Saussure.* Cambridge: Cambridge University Press.

Saussure, Ferdinand de. 1916. *Cours de linguistique générale.* Ed. by C. Bally, A. Sechehaye, and A. Reidlinger. Paris: Payot.

  (1916)1986. *Course in General Linguistics.* Trans by Roy Harris. LaSalle, IL: Open Court.

Sayers, Dorothy. 1926. *Clouds of Witness.* London: Dial.

  1935. *Gaudy Night.* London: Harper and Row.

Schneider, Edgar. 1997. Chaos Theory as a Model for Dialect Variability and Change? In A. Thomas, ed., *Issues and Methods in Dialectology* (Bangor: University of North Wales), 122–36.

  2003. The Dynamics of New Englishes: From Identity Construction to Dialect Birth. *Language* 79: 233–81.

  2007. *Postcolonial English: Varieties around the World.* Cambridge: Cambridge University Press.

Scott, Jerrie. 1998. The Serious Side of Ebonics Humor. In Kretzschmar 1998a, 137–55.

Sinclair, John. 1991. *Corpus, Concordance, Collocation.* Oxford: Oxford University Press.
2004. *Trust the Text.* London: Routledge.
Stockwell, Robert, and Donka Minkova. 1988. The English Vowel Shift: Problems of Coherence and Explanation. In D. Kastovsky and G. Bauer, eds, *Luick Revisited: Papers Read at the Luick Symposium at Schloss Lichtenstein* (Tübingen: Gunter Narr), 355–94.
Stubbs, Michael. 1996. *Text and Corpus Analysis.* Oxford: Blackwell.
2001. *Words and Phrases.* Oxford: Blackwell.
Swales, John. 1990. *Genre Analysis: English in Academic and Research Settings.* Cambridge: Cambridge University Press.
2004. *Research Genres: Explorations and Applications.* Cambridge: Cambridge University Press.
Tamasi, Susan. 2000. Linguistic Perceptions of Southern Folk. Paper presented at ADS, Chicago.
2003. Cognitive Patterns of Linguistic Perceptions. Diss., University of Georgia.
Tannen, Deborah. 1990. *You Just Don't Understand: Women and Men in Conversation.* New York: Morrow.
Thill, J. C., W. A. Kretzschmar, Jr., I. Casas, and X. Yao. 2008. Detecting Geographic Associations in English Dialect Features in North America within a Visual Data Mining Environment Integrating Self-Organising Maps. In P. Agarwal and A. Skupin, eds, *Self-Organising Maps: Applications in GI Science* (London: Wiley), 67–86.
Trudgill, Peter. 1972. Sex, Covert Prestige, and Linguistic Change in the Urban British English of Norwich. *Language in Society* 1: 179–95.
1974a. *The Social Differentiation of English in Norwich.* Cambridge: Cambridge University Press.
1974b. Linguistic Change and Diffusion: Description and Explanation in Sociolinguistic Dialect Geography. *Language in Society* 2: 215–46.
1984. *On Dialect.* New York: New York University Press.
Truss, Lynne. 2004. *Eats, Shoots & Leaves: The Zero Tolerance Approach to Punctuation.* London: Gotham.
Upton, Clive. 2006. Modern Regional English in the British Isles. In Lynda Mugglestone, ed., *The Oxford History of English* (Oxford: Oxford University Press), 305–333.
Upton, Clive, and John Widdowson. 2006. *An Atlas of English Dialects.* London: Routledge.
Wales, Katie. 2006. Dialects in Mental Contact: A Critique of Perceptual Dialectology. In H. Grabes and W. Viereck, eds, *The Wider Scope of English* (Frankfurt: Lang), 57–66.
Webster, Noah. 1828. *An American Dictionary of the English Language.* New York: S. Converse.
Weinreich, Uriel. 1954. Is Structural Dialectology Possible? *Word* 10: 388–400. [Reprinted in Harold Allen and Michael Linn, eds, *Dialect and Language Variation* (Orlando: Academic Press, 1986), 20–34.]
Weinreich, Uriel, William Labov, and Marvin Herzog. 1968. Empirical Foundations for a Theory of Language Change. In Winifred Lehmann and Jakob Malkiel, eds, *Directions for Historical Linguistics* (Austin: University of Texas Press), 95–188.
Wenker, Georg, and Ferdinand Wrede. 1895. *Der Sprachatlas des deutschen Reichs.* Marburg: Elwert.

Widdowson, H. G. 1978. *Teaching Language as Communication*. Oxford: Oxford University Press.

Wikle, Thomas, and Guy Bailey. 1993. Methods of Sampling and Mapping Distributions for a Survey of Oklahoma Dialects (SOD). Paper presented at Language Variety in the South II, Auburn.

Wiley, Terrence. 2004. Language Planning, Language Policy, and the English Only Movement. In Edward Finegan and John Rickford, eds, *Language in the USA: Themes for the Twenty-first Century* (Cambridge: Cambridge University Press), 319–38.

Wolfram, Walt. 1998. Language Ideology and Dialect. In Kretzschmar 1998a, 108–121.

Woods, Anthony, Paul Fletcher, and Arthur Hughes. 1986. *Statistics in Language Studies*. Cambridge: Cambridge University Press.

Zipf, George. 1949. *Human Behavior and the Principle of Least Effort*. Cambridge, MA: Addison Wesley.

Zörnig, Peter, and Gabriel Altmann. 1995. Unified Representation of Zipf Distributions. *Computational Statistics and Data Analysis* 19: 461–73.

Index

tobacco documents (TDs) 166–71
tokens 84, 87
top-ranked variants, *see* frequency
Trudgill, Peter 20, 61, 72, 185, 210, 256
Truss, Lynne 17
Turner, Lorenzo 109
types
    linguistic 73, 84, 86, 94
    speakers 66, 110
    see also classification
typology 21

undergo 154, 155, 165
Upton, Clive 70, 72

variance (statistics) 105, 193, 195
variants, *see* features
Varro 35
vernacular 22

Wales, Katie 235
Webster, Noah 15, 38
weighting 245
Weinreich, Uriel 59, 269
Wenker, Georg 51, 55, 59
Wernicke, Carl 219
Wertheimer, Max 218
White, Rodney, *see* Peter Gould

Whitehall, Harold 69
Whorf, Benjamin 148
Widdowson, H. G. 158
Widdowson, John 69
Wikipedia 65
Wikle, Thomas 144
Wiley, Terrence 276
Williams, Ann 61
Wolfram, Walt 26, 27
Woods, Anthony 104, 163
words 53–54
    content vs. function 155
Wright, Laura xi
writing 65, 272
Wyld, H. C. 16

Y'all 1
Yao, X. 225
yet 166

"zero" particle 140
Zimmerman, Matt xi
Zipf, George 192
Zipf's Law 174, 175, 190–98, 253
    bibliography 194
    in linguistics literature 193–95
    in fields other than linguistics 194
Zörnig, Peter 195

CPSIA information can be obtained
at www.ICGtesting.com
Printed in the USA
LVHW010134010820
662091LV00010B/627